READINGS
in **Information
Technology Project
Management**

READINGS
in Information Technology Project Management

Gary L. Richardson, Ph.D., P.M.P.

University of Houston

Charles W. Butler, Ph.D.

Colorado State University

THOMSON

COURSE TECHNOLOGY ™

Australia • Canada • Mexico • Singapore • Spain • United Kingdom • United States

THOMSON

COURSE TECHNOLOGY

Readings in Information Technology Project Management is published by Course Technology.

Gary L. Richardson, Ph.D., P.M.P. and Charles W. Butler, Ph D

Acquisitions Editor:
Maureen Martin

Senior Marketing Manager:
Karen Seitz

Text Designer and Compositor:
Cadmus Professional Communications

Senior Product Managers:
Eunice Yeates, Tricia Coia

Senior Manufacturing Coordinator:
Justin Palmeiro

Cover Designer:
Laura Rickenbach

Developmental Editors:
Lynne Raughley, Betsey Henkels

Editorial Assistant:
Allison Murphy

Production Editors:
Daphne Barbas, Elena Montillo

Copy Editor:
Harry Johnson

Proofreader:
Christine Clark

Indexer:
Alexandra Nickerson

Disclaimer
Some of the product names and company names used in this book have been used for identification purposes only and may be trademarks or registered trademarks of their respective manufacturers and sellers.

Each of the readings presented in this text is included with the express approval of the author or copyright holder. The original source reference is shown with each reading. In some cases a serial reading was edited and adapted to a single view with approval of the author. The editors are grateful to these authors for their willingness to share royalty-free their work in this format.

A significant portion of the text is dedicated to foundation work authored by the Project Management Institute (PMI) as contained in their document A Guide to the Project Management Body of Knowledge *(PMBOK® Guide)*, 3rd Edition (2004, Project Management Institute, all rights reserved). Material from this source is used with the permission of the Project Management Institute, Inc. Four Campus Boulevard, Newtown Square, PA 19073-2399, USA. Phone: (610) 356-4600, fax (610) 356-4647. Project Management Institute (PMI) is the world's leading project management association with over 160,000 members worldwide. For further information contact PMI Headquarters at (610) 356-4600 or visit the Web site at *www.pmi.org*.

PMI, PMP, and PMBOK are registered trademarks of the Project Management Institute, Inc.

Course Technology reserves the right to revise this publication and make changes from time to time in its content without notice.

ISBN 0-619-21750-2

We dedicate this effort especially to our spouses, Shawn and Teri, who provided a positive environment while their spouses were off doing a lot of late night work that could have been spent with them. The Richardson/ Butler family web continues to grow into one after working and playing together for some thirty-five years.

Our thanks also go to our graduate students who helped in so many ways along the evolution of this project. Kevin Fulk at the University of Houston was invaluable as was Scott M. Sievers at Colorado State University.

We hope that our extended families will someday see this work and think kind things about us, even though they won't understand why in the world we did this.

To our IT industry comrades, we hope this collection of material will add positive insights to your understanding of this dynamic area.

—GLR
—CWB

BRIEF CONTENTS

DETAILED CONTENTS

PREFACE

This text is non-conventional in at least two ways. First, it was designed to be in a *Reader's Digest* format—short readings dealing with the broad topic of information technology (IT) project management. The readings will not overwhelm you with numbers and research results. They are written by people we consider to be working experts in their fields of expertise, so their views are relevant and contemporary. With content from these contributors, the readings present the working vocabulary and a breadth of real-life experiences regarding the major topics of information technology project management. Collectively, the topics provide good exposure to this dynamic business area, and the text offers reference information on how to delve deeper into the various subject areas.

A second unique aspect of this text's approach is that the authors have spent considerable time combing the Web to identify and provide in this text a working directory of sources on IT project management. In the credits pages beginning on page 468, the original source is indicated for each reading so that the reader can check into that source for more details if desired. The authors encourage readers to use the URLs listed in the credits pages to further research these topics. When doing so, readers should note, however, that URLs frequently change. In addition, some of the readings in this text are available on Web sites that require free membership. In these cases, the host site is used to point readers in the right direction. When an executable URL is available, the authors included it in the credits pages. The footnotes listed in many readings are further sources of information for readers who want to delve more deeply into a particular topic. Please note, however, that the footnotes in some original readings are not always accurate; in some cases, superscripts were missing for references and/or references were missing for superscripts. To avoid confusion for these readings, the reference numbers have been deleted.

One of the primary design goals of the text was to produce a collection of topical articles that are readable and technically worthwhile. We included, as far as possible, authors who work professionally in the information technology project management arena, rather than academic researchers. We chose this path based on our belief that this subject is still more experientially than theoretically based. The contemporary basic core theory and some of the emerging theories are covered, but this is surrounded with practical articles on the topic as well. Over the past ten years, a great deal of knowledge has been published regarding how to execute an IT project successfully, but it needs to be recognized that these theories have still not become heavily engrained in the operational management fabric of the typical project.

Readings in Part I describe four basic issues surrounding the project environment: IT in the enterprise, project management concepts, the historical project track record, and the goal of aligning IT initiatives with business goals. We view these topics as the context for actual projects, and we therefore feel that these topics should be covered before jumping into a basic discussion about the mechanics of project management.

Throughout the text we give great umbrage to the Project Management Institute and their published Body of Knowledge (called the *PMBOK® Guide*). Both of these sources are internationally recognized, and it would be short-sighted to ignore their contributions to this field. In concert with this, the certification label Project Management Professional (PMP) continues to gain recognition in all industry segments, and we believe that criteria for project manager selection will be based increasingly on some form of professional certification. As a result of these beliefs, the PMI conceptual project model structure was selected for focus. Other management methodologies would be generally compatible with this view, but we use the PMI vocabulary extensively.

Part II of the text focuses on an overview of the *PMBOK® Guide* with its rigorous process orientation and nine knowledge areas. The readings presented in this part of the text are basically organized by knowledge area and provide insight into why dealing with these areas is important to project success. It is recognized that there are several existing textbooks that discuss these topics at the mechanical level, but the goal here is to add some breadth and general understanding to these areas beyond the mechanics. In a few cases the readings and notes selected have been taken from academic teaching libraries. These latter items are academic in nature, but clearly describe an application area in the real world as well.

Part III contains a series of topics that are judged to be contemporary, meaning that the underlying theories and mechanics of use are not yet well defined. However, each of these topics represents strategic subject areas that will mature over the next few years and become part of the main body of knowledge. Some mature organizations are dealing with these topics today, but the majority of organizations are just now evaluating how to move forward with them. Material in this part of the text is more theoretical in nature than that found in the previous two parts.

The idea of having multiple authors' views on a single topic area has both good and bad attributes. On the positive side, the reader gets a more balanced view of the subject. On the negative side, there is less continuity in the material and writing style than in a text written by a single author. Nevertheless, from an educational viewpoint we believe there is value in being exposed to more than one view. That need for diversity seems especially important for this subject of IT project management. To ensure that the key ideas are obvious and to provide appropriate subject continuity, each part begins with a brief topic overview.

Many of the readings selected here are Internet-based and most of these are relatively new (this could be considered a third aspect of the text's unique approach). We recognize that the Internet is not the typical source for collecting knowledge material, but in the case of project management we feel that some of the real-world thinkers are publishing their opinions on the net, and the topic area tends to evolve quicker than print media can keep up with. To aid the reader in finding good professional source Web sites, Appendix A provides a general listing of topics with Web references. However, search engines can also uncover a wealth of project-related material if one is willing to browse long enough. Given this open-sourcing strategy, you might ask what have we added in this text? Basically, we have spent thousands of hours searching the Internet and other published sources to compile what we believe to be valid expert opinions on selected topics and readable material. The readings cover the broad scope of the topic area from introductory basics to conflicting views. This compilation saves the reader many hours of searching and ending up with voluminous results that are hard to evaluate. This compiled and condensed introduction to the topic area prepares you to deal with the variety of materials that will surface in the future and helps you to search deeper into a particular area of specialization. In addition, after this exposure you will have a good understanding of the key topics and a working vocabulary. The editors have over fifty years of combined industry experience in this area and we are comfortable with the content selected for presentation.

The reading audience for this material is anticipated to include readers from various professional and academic backgrounds. A majority of readers will probably use this material as a supplement to a standard project management textbook. Selected readings are slanted towards the information technology arena; however, we believe that the principles discussed are similar across all project types, especially technology-related projects. It should be pointed out that the *PMBOK® Guide* is designed as a general-purpose project management model, and all of the material in Part II fits that model. Readers who feel that they have the basic theory already and are now studying for the PMP certification exam will also find the text useful, because the material offers something beyond memorization of vocabulary. We know of no other source that offers this breadth of material for these purposes. In addition, this compilation makes it easy for you to access supplementary material, which is important and extends somewhat the views defined in the *PMBOK® Guide*.

It is important to recognize that memorizing *PMBOK® Guide* vocabulary, knowledge processes, and example quizzes will not turn a poor project manager into a good one. Many factors are involved in producing a good project manager, and the topics in this text help tie together concepts that could be considered more basic. In this regard the articles presented bring life to the more abstract *PMBOK® Guide* principles. Experienced project managers who want to compare their practical experience with others and understand the *PMBOK® Guide* theoretical view of projects will also find this text useful. For most readers, using this material in addition to a good PMP prep text (such as Rita Mulcahy's PMP Exam Prep) will suffice with some reasonable probability for passing the PMP.

The topic outline structure of the text is derived with the notion that the *PMBOK® Guide* material would be at the core. That structure became the basic organization for Part II and it is the keystone material. The process view and the nine knowledge areas described in this section represent the primary topic categories. The goal for Part II is to explain the *PMBOK® Guide* key points and why that particular knowledge area topic is an important one for the project manager. After Part II was defined, the remaining question was what should be done to make the total package more complete. Stopping at a set of *PMBOK® Guide* supplementary readings was not good enough in our view. So, Part I was laid out as a series of topics that were felt to be fundamental prerequisite material before diving into the core project management world. Some readers might be able to skip this introductory section, but it does constitute a good background review to make sure you have the right conceptual perspective of a project in the organizational context. Each topic area in Part I is somewhat independent, but collectively they form a reasonable context for viewing project processes.

Lastly, Part III is organized as Project Management Contemporary Topics. Each of these subject areas has been recognized as legitimate topics by the industry, but in each case there is either no widespread use of the concept or an incomplete quality to the recognized theory surrounding it. For example, the project management office (PMO) term has recently crept into the *PMBOK® Guide* (2004) vocabulary as well as into many other industry sources. However, in many organizations this term is not widely standardized or project management offices do not exist. Nevertheless, the concept is important and sound, plus it is vital to the success of the IT function in the modern organization. For that reason it is a worthy topic. In similar fashion, we believe that the list of topics in Part III represents a valuable supplement to the basic *PMBOK® Guide* material. These new topics are collectively part of the knowledge set that the modern project manager needs to understand.

In performing the research to compile this text, the authors learned a tremendous amount about IT project management. We hope as readers that you will learn a great deal from reading the book. This is truly a dynamic knowledge area, and all professionals involved in this activity will need to continue tracking innovations as they become visible. The project management profession is a difficult one, and it will be necessary to stay armed with every trick and tool you can find if you are to survive.

Gary Richardson
Charles Butler

Introduction to Project Management Concepts

PART ONE Contents

Part Overview

The goal of Part One is to highlight certain basic characteristics that shape the subject of project management. Readings presented in Part One are chosen to position the topic of project management within the larger sphere of the business organization. We first focus on the role of IT in the firm. Information technology applications continue to proliferate in the contemporary organization, and that role often is not well understood by the internal management and employees.

Readings in Part I, Chapter 1 focus on the IT organization and its basic role set for the enterprise. Views related to the human interaction with this technology are also reviewed here.

Part I, Chapter 2 focuses on a conceptual framework within which the project management activity resides, and offers a working definition for some key terms.

Part I, Chapter 3 describes factors that are associated with success and failure of project initiatives. Once the project is defined and execution is initiated, a reasonably high probability for failure still exists regarding schedule, budget, or desired functionality. It is important to have a general understanding of these issues as one starts to read about project activities.

The final subject area in Part I, Chapter 4 is a broad overview describing the need for aligning project activity with business goals. Creation

---

of positive business value out of project activities requires that activity be strongly aligned with the higher-level business-planning processes. The desired result of the alignment process is to create an optimum portfolio of projects to support long-term organizational needs. Failure to align projects properly will cause even the best-managed projects to yield little or no value to the enterprise. The phrase "garbage in-garbage out" describes a poorly derived project portfolio.

Building on the foundation established by Part I, which is somewhat conceptual and introductory, Part II has a more "how to" theme. Part II, Exploring the *PMBOK® Guide*, is based on the Project Management Institute's (PMI) internationally recognized model called the *PMBOK® Guide*.

Role of IT in the Firm

Chapter 1 Contents

Chapter Overview

There is no single information technology (IT) organizational structure that can be used alone as a model for this discussion. Different organizations handle the functions of IT differently. Some have fragmented and decentralized groups with multiple titles indicating that they are IT, while others might have large aggregations of IT professionals in a centralized support organization. Regardless of the physical groupings of these functions, there is a common set of related organizational needs that should be properly delegated to the appropriate groups.

Many look at the IT organization as a combination of a code development, code support, and user help desk operation. The truth is, these are the more visible pieces of the organizational activity, but there are many other aspects to having a viable IT function. The list below summarizes some of the major IT management process activities necessary to achieve success:

1. Balance technology with organizational needs.
2. Promote efficient and effective communication systems.
3. Support the enterprise infrastructure of hardware, software, and telecommunications.
4. Define technology roles and responsibilities in the enterprise.
5. Maintain appropriate electronic security.
6. Assist in engineering automated processes.
7. Manage technology change.
8. Select and implement technology-related tools (for example, coding languages, hardware, database software, and network tools).
9. Recruit and maintain adequate technical resource skills.
10. Manage the allocation of scarce technical resources.
11. Define and collect operational metrics to support IT decision making.

Most professionals who work in the IT functional area would say that this list constitutes a significant, if not overwhelming, task. To provide a better understanding of why this might be true, one must have a historical view of the function. First, IT is one of the newest disciplines in the enterprise with its roots in the latter 1950s for most organizations. This function has simply not had sufficient time to mature to the state of other areas such as accounting, finance, or legal. A second important factor is the continual exploding nature of information technology. One does not have to be very old to have seen more than one major technology shift occur. In a few short years, we have witnessed the emergence of minicomputers, personal computers, mobile computers, Internet technology, and whatever the most current technology is labeled. Because of the rapid advance of tools and capabilities, it has been hard to settle on a singular management path and mature that into repeatable forms. In addition, one of the latest trends is for the non-IT community to become very proficient at using a set of tools that look like things that only professional IT staff could manipulate a few short years ago. That increased literacy level has placed even more pressure on the IT organization to do things differently.

Many references are made in various articles presented here indicating that IT as a profession has not been very successful in the outsiders' views. IT projects have high failure rates, and the IT professional has been labeled "geek" (some would say that this is a compliment to intelligence, while others would argue that point). Thus, we enter the debate about IT and its value in the organization. Is it a needed function? Should it be outsourced? Can we do away with it and simply let the new generation of users do their own thing? All of these are interesting questions for sure! Our biased view is that IT holds the keys to an organization's productive future. Done poorly, it can lead to failure of the business. Done well, it can make for a competitive advantage. Our global vision for this set of material is to highlight the components for success as viewed by experts in the field.

If IT is so valuable, then what keeps it from being universally recognized as an important function in the business? Note that we did not say that IT was the most important function. We said that it is necessary to manage it well to achieve competitive advantage. Let's use the metaphor of IT as a business lever. It allows you to pick up more weight than you could without it. You still need the operational businessperson and a visionary to push the lever. To work effectively, IT needs to be a partner with the business. When the partnership is handled well, the business defines the *What* and IT supplies the technical *How.* This means that the business segment should drive issues related to cost, schedule, and function. From this scoping structure it is then up to IT to deliver those expectations (assuming that they have been properly derived in partnership). This latter step is the place where the linkage to project management enters the scene. We envision the project management model as the most productive way to structure human beings around a defined problem.

Problem Domain

IT projects tend to draw from one of seven problem domains. These are:
1. **New systems development:** This is the classic process of creating a new system from the ground up. Much of the existing project

management literature surrounds this model, however it is important to point out that it typically consumes much less than half of the total IT budget—maybe as little as 10% in stable, low-technology organizations. The other areas listed in the following are also fruitful targets for project management methodologies.

2. **Legacy systems:** Keeping an existing system running is much like keeping a car running. There are daily chores that are repetitive and others that are not. Although this area often is not treated like a project environment, it should be. One way of doing this is to package work tasks (for example, enhancements, upgrades, and bug fixes) and execute them in project fashion. This approach would place more control around a process that tends to be operated too loosely.

3. **Data:** IT organizations today are awash in data. Much of the work in proper data management is repetitive and falls under the category of daily work tasks; however various non-recurring initiatives also arise. For example, moving to new versions of hardware and software fit the project environment well.

4. **Infrastructure:** The infrastructure is constituted by the collection of development and production hardware, software, and telecommunications required by the enterprise. One could view this as the plumbing upon which the overall information environment operates. It is not uncommon for this area of the IT function to constitute one-third or more of the operational budget. The underlying architecture for this area is constantly changing, and for this reason the recurring change management process is vital to success. However, the work activities that lead from one technology state to the next fit the project management model quite well and should be incorporated into that model more rigorously than typically is the case.

5. **Operations:** This functional group is charged with keeping the installed set of hardware, software, and telecommunications working as installed. Their internal use of the project model is likely least of all areas, but they are a vital partner to assist other project initiatives from other areas that will eventually find their way into the operational sphere. For this reason, these skill groups need to be aware of the formal project management process and participate in that process.

6. **Human resources (HR):** This is an area in many organizations that is ignored from a formal management view. We believe that the human element of the organization is the most vital component driving success. In the case of IT professionals, the challenge of staying technically competent requires planning, resource commitment, and management support. Upgrading the IT skill base can be viewed as a macro project for both the IT organization and the user community. These activities compete for the same resources as do the other areas, and for that reason they are part of what we will call the IT project portfolio management base.

7. **Technology management:** Last, but certainly not least, is the process of managing the evolution of technology in the organization. Deciding when it is time to invest in emerging technologies such as the Internet, Customer Relationship Management, storage networks,

new hardware, or the myriad other technology opportunities that surface each year is a vital IT management process. This assessment process needs to be managed and controlled just like other areas. The key process is to allocate resources for this type of activity and work toward finding productive new uses of identified items. These search processes should be viewed as a project with identifiable goals and quick willingness to bail out when it is obvious the technology is not ready or suitable.

So, IT is shown to be a very intensive project environment from a conceptual view. For stakeholders to view IT more positively, it is necessary to execute IT tasks more predictably. It is no longer feasible for IT to deal in foggy "black art." The function must move upward into a more engineered profession. That is the main goal of the principles that are presented here.

Readings

The two readings for this section are presented by Paul Glen of C2 Consulting. Mr. Glen first takes a look at the future role of the IT organization in "Competing Visions of Corporate IT's Future." He then discusses effective manager style in "What Kind of Manager Are You, Anyway?"

From this introduction, we are led to conclude that the IT organization of the future is likely to be as chaotic and dynamic as the past phases have been. There are many change drivers impacting IT organizations today. Management is pressing hard to cut IT expenses, yet they want improved and expanded services. Working with tools such as Microsoft Excel and Access, users are attempting to take over activities that previously were handled by IT professionals using industrial-strength software. Third-party vendors continue to bring an improved suite of utilities and tools that promise a decrease in the need for building (coding) new systems. And to top off all of this, new IT professional technologies are bringing exciting new capabilities to play. All of these factors are out of synchronization at the time of this writing, and we should expect dissenting forces for the foreseeable future. A strong management focus is going to be needed to wade through this organizational minefield.

Competing Visions of Corporate IT's Future

PAUL GLEN

www.c2-consulting.com. Reprinted here with the permission of the author.

Paul Glen is the author of the award-winning book "Leading Geeks: How to Manage and Lead People Who Deliver Technology" (Jossey Bass Pfeiffer, 2003) and Principal of C2 Consulting. C2 Consulting helps IT management solve people problems. Paul Glen regularly speaks for corporations and national associations across North America. For more information go to www.c2-consulting.com. He can be reached at info@c2-consulting.com.

Speaking at and attending the recent *Forbes Magazine* CIO Forum meeting, I had the opportunity to explore the emerging trends in the strategies and concerns of the CIOs of corporate America. At the end of the year, it's always tempting to write a year-in-review or a year-to-come prediction article, declaring the movement of the herd, giving shape to the attitudes and ideas of the populace.

But the ideas and concerns being discussed there led me to believe that there are really two distinct camps of CIOs. It seemed that there's a bifurcation, a split among CIOs as to where the IT organization and the CIO's job is heading.

First, what the camps agree on: After almost 30 years, the CIO role is getting some respect. The corporate CIO is more and more being viewed as a business executive rather than as a technical lead. Other C level executives (CEO, CFO, etc.) are beginning to understand how pervasive IT has become and how much more so it is likely to be in the future. And as such, they are now looking at CIOs as partners in strategy and operations and not just as internal service providers.

This newfound prominence will bring both opportunities and challenges to the IT department of the future. Technical groups will no longer be able to just accept passively the requirements of users as guidelines for action. They will have to be more proactive in seeking out and implementing ways to improve the bottom line competitiveness of the entire company. And they will be under constant pressure to reduce their own costs while improving the productivity of the whole enterprise.

But how the IT organization achieves that goal seems the subject of some debate. One view seemed to hold that the role of the IT organization of the future is that of a brokerage of computing resources and people. The employees within an IT group would be responsible for negotiating and monitoring outsourcing contracts without performing any technical tasks. Ralph Szygenda, CIO of General Motors, said that even with their multi-billion dollar annual budget for IT, there was no longer a single employee writing code. Think of this as extreme outsourcing.

Advocates for this view focused mostly on cost reduction, flexibility, and rapid cycle time for definition and deployment of new systems. The conversations around this view did suggest that the IT organization would be part of strategy discussions within the enterprise, but never mentioned how outsourced technology could become a competitive weapon.

More common though, was the view that the IT organizations will carry the dual roles as both broker and partial implementer. Most agreed that for some functions, outsourcing, especially to India and China, would continue to grow as a way of reducing costs for support and operations. For other functions, such as application development to support process or product innovation, would likely stay in house or be done in partnership with local service providers.

But regardless of which view prevails, most agreed that being a CIO today is still a very difficult job that few possess the skill mix to perform. It will continue to be the job that *Forbes Magazine* recently called "America's worst C-Title job."

What Kind of Manager Are You, Anyway?

PAUL GLEN

of C2 Consulting

It's often said that there are two types of managers: those who manage things and those who manage people. And a great divide of misunderstanding lies between them, rarely to be crossed or reconciled.

The managers of things are those who see the world through the lens of stuff. They focus their attention on production, processes, projects, materials, milestones, methods, deliverables, and details. They share an orientation with engineers who tend to focus on the what and how of life more than on the who.

On the other hand, the managers of people see things though the lens of relationships. Where managers of things see matter, managers of people see humans who happen to be working with matter. They focus their attention on culture, politics, leadership, teamwork, and organizational designs.

In this conception, the people orientation is usually represented by senior executives, and everyone below them falls into the category of managers of things. The divide is often cited as one of the key reasons for difficulty with business/IT alignment. CIOs and CEOs talk past each other; they view the same world through different lenses, and each is unable to understand the other's perspective.

So which kind of manager are you? Be honest. You might pay attention to both perspectives, but most people have a primary and secondary orientation. We seem to come prewired with a bias toward one or the other.

If you honestly can't answer this question, you may fall into a third category. Over the past decade, we in IT have created jobs that call for an orientation distinct from either things or people. I call the people who naturally fit into these jobs the managers of abstractions.

Managers of abstractions see things through the lens of theory. Where most of us see projects and people, they see examples of theories almost as expressions of pure Platonic forms. (The Greek philosopher Plato believed that physical things drew their characteristics from abstract categories or forms in which they participated. So, for example, a horse was a physical thing that participated in the form of horseness and expressed the features of the form.) These managers are most comfortable with the world of the conceptual, with ideas disassociated from specifics.

They have titles like "director of project management," "chief security officer," "czar of quality" or "overlord of strategy." Where most managers are focused on ends, these managers are responsible for particular features of the means to those ends. Their jobs are to oversee the adjectives and adverbs, rather than the nouns and verbs of IT. While most managers are responsible for delivering products and services, abstraction managers work to ensure that other managers deliver efficiently, effectively, securely, consistently, and appropriately.

Abstraction managers have hard jobs. They're responsible for developing and interpreting theory and applying policy to projects. They are always in danger of being viewed and—perhaps more dangerously, of viewing themselves—as a priesthood, as mediators between the temporal and spiritual realms. Their relationships with both the managers of people and the managers of things are frequently strained. Without the power to produce, they're frequently viewed as having only the power to obstruct on ideological grounds. That's why many project management offices are viewed as the process police and not considered the midwives of progress and productivity.

Can you find yourself now in this tripartite taxonomy of managerial orientation? Is your natural interest in people, things, or theory? There is no right or wrong answer, but there may be better or worse assignments for individuals of each perspective.

As IT has become pervasive in business organizations, it has become increasingly important that technical managers appreciate the different outlooks. Working effectively with stakeholders of IT at all levels requires the following skills:

- Knowledge of your own natural perspective.
- Awareness of other managers' perspectives.
- The flexibility to view reality through all three lenses.
- The wisdom to reconcile the issues and options that differ between them.

If you develop the ability to recognize and reconcile all three perspectives, everyone will know exactly what kind of manager you are—a good one.

Project Management Concepts

Chapter 2 Contents

Chapter Overview

The purpose of this chapter is to briefly explore the following key concepts regarding the topic of IT Project Management:

1. What is the definition of IT Project Management?
2. Is there value in the apparent overhead introduced by formal project management?
3. What are some of the key management components in the project life cycle? What is the contemporary view of this topic?
4. What are some project myths?
5. What are some of the changes occurring in this field today?

Kerzner, in his well-received text, offers a good starting place for the definition of a project. He describes the following characteristics of a project:

1. Contains a series of activities and tasks
2. Contains a specific objective and specifications
3. Has a defined start and completion date
4. Has established funding limits
5. Consumes resources (human and non-human)
6. Typically cuts across organizational functional lines [Kerzner]

So, project management would represent the activities necessary to accomplish the goals established for the project. We could cut out a lot of words by simply saying, "Get it done!"

Types of Projects

Various research efforts are underway from PMI and others to categorize projects. Table 1 shows the list of categories and subcategories being reviewed at the time of this writing.

It is important to note that projects within these different categories and often within the subcategories have the following characteristics:

- Typically exhibit or require very different life cycle models
- Require different planning and control methods, systems, and tools
- Use different terminologies [Archibald]
- Demand different knowledge, skills, and experience of the project managers and project team members
- Place differing emphases on the detailed aspects of planning, scheduling, cost estimating, reporting, controlling, executing, and closing

TABLE 1   **Proposed Project Categories and Subcategories**

Project Categories: Each having similar life cycle phases and a unique project management process	Examples
1. Aerospace/Defense Projects	
1.1 Defense systems	New weapon system; major system upgrade
1.2 Space	
1.3 Military operations	Satellite development/launch; space station mod
	Task force invasion
2. Business and Organization Change Projects	
2.1 Acquisition/Merger	Acquire and integrate competing company
2.2 Management process improvement	Major improvement in project management
2.3 New business venture	Form and launch new company
2.4 Organization restructuring	Consolidate divisions and downsize company
2.5 Legal proceeding	Major litigation case
3. Communication Systems Projects	
3.1 Network communications systems	Microwave communications network
3.2 Switching communications systems	Third-generation wireless communications system
4. Event Projects	
4.1 International events	2004 Summer Olympics; 2006 World Cup Match
4.2 National events	2005 U.S. Super Bowl; 2004 Political Conventions
5. Facilities Projects	
5.1 Facility decommissioning	Closure of nuclear power station
5.2 Facility demolition	Demolition of high-rise building
5.3 Facility maintenance and modification	Process plant maintenance turnaround
5.4 Facility design/procurement/construction	Conversion of plant for new products/markets
Civil	Flood control dam; highway interchange
Energy	New gas-fired power generation plant; pipeline
Environmental	Chemical waste cleanup
High rise	Forty-story office building
Industrial	New manufacturing plant
Commercial	New shopping center; office building
Residential	New housing subdivision
Ships	New tanker, container, or passenger ship

TABLE 1   **Proposed Project Categories and Subcategories—continued**

Project Categories: Each having similar life cycle phases and a unique project management process	Examples
6. Information Systems (Software) Projects	New project management information system (Information system hardware is considered to be in the product development category.)
7. International Development Projects 7.1 Agriculture/rural development 7.2 Education 7.3 Health 7.4 Nutrition 7.5 Population 7.6 Small-scale enterprise 7.7 Infrastructure: energy (oil, gas, coal, and power generation and distribution), industrial, telecommunications, transportation, urbanization, and water supply, sewage, and irrigation	People- and process-intensive projects in developing countries funded by The World Bank, regional development banks, U.S. AID, UNIDO, other UN and government agencies; and Capital/civil works-intensive projects—often somewhat different from Category 5. Facility Projects as they might include, as part of the project, creating an organizational entity to operate and maintain the facility, and lending agencies impose their project life cycle and reporting requirements
8. Media and Entertainment Projects 8.1 Motion picture 8.2 TV segment 8.3 Live play or music event	New motion picture (film or digital) New TV episode New opera premiere
9. Product and Service Development Projects 9.1 Information technology hardware 9.2 Industrial product/process 9.3 Consumer product/process 9.4 Pharmaceutical product/process 9.5 Service (financial, other)	New desktop computer New earth-moving machine New automobile, new food product New cholesterol-lowering drug New life insurance/annuity offering
10. Research and Development Projects 10.1 Environmental 10.2 Industrial 10.3 Economic development 10.4 Medical 10.5 Scientific	Measure changes in the ozone layer Study how to reduce pollutant emission Determine best crop for subSahara Africa Test new treatment for breast cancer Determine the possibility of life on Mars
11. Other Categories?	

Project Management Issues

When we observe the organizational reaction to formal project management activities such as those outlined, it is common to find disagreements regarding the role and magnitude of this activity. Typically, one major point of resistance to instituting formal project management is that it adds nonproductive time and overhead cost to the project, thus, it is viewed as making an already poor process worse. It is important to realize that most of the items that will be discussed do represent extra steps for the traditional IT project environment. The knowledge topics cover areas such as planning, requirements definition, change control, risk assessment, quality, communication, HR-related activities, and a host of others that some might say would be better done "on the fly," meaning do it, but don't write it down. Culturally, the typical IT personality type hates written procedures and IT professionals are often not good at verbal communication (especially with external nontechnical stakeholders). For the topic of project management to be embraced in the proper frame of mind, one must recognize that much of the basis for project failure is mismatched expectations caused by poor planning and communication.

Maybe it is still not obvious why planning, control, and communication can increase the success of a project. Two fairly obvious ways to increase success are to discontinue an unsuitable project and to keep the scope of a project focused on higher priority needs. Less obvious is the synergistic value of a repeatable process. The Center for Business Practices performed a survey to document management's value perceptions of project management. [CBR, 2003] Twenty performance areas were reviewed in the survey, and those organizations with a formal project management approach graded a 21% improvement in those metrics over the unstructured organizations. The return on investment for project management was estimated at 27.9%, and 97% of senior executives stated that it added value to their organization. Positive responses were also found for budget, schedule, quality, productivity, and goal alignment. Other studies undertaken by the Software Engineering Institute and William Ibbs have documented similar results. In these latter studies, the basic approach was broader and encompassed organizational maturity, within which project management is a subset.

Mark Mullaly of Interthink Consulting offers some insights into the need for a formal definition for project management. [Mullaly] At the core of this definition are three attributes that the project manager needs:

1. Responsibility for the project
2. Accountability for the results
3. Authority to execute and achieve results

The history of IT has been a "blow and go"-type organization—get it done! Much of this occurred during times in which technology was rapidly changing and other business functions did not really understand their role. Installing the new technology was the predominant need, so the decisionmakers were willing to let budgets and schedules slide. The fact is, IT organizations have done a reasonable technical management job over the past 40 or so years in their quest to install system-related hardware, software, and networks. The management problem during this period was that the project targets were not always correctly chosen, and resulting outcomes for cost, schedule, and functionality were not met. That does not say that the project teams were not working hard, but generally the underlying management processes were not sufficiently rigorous to execute project goals as promised. When IT was not a significant part of the organizational budget or business process, such failures were overlooked and thought to be unavoidable. What has changed over the past few years is that the IT budget grew to where it is now often 50% of the capital budget and a significant part of the tactical operating budget. IT-automated systems are also now very much embedded in the operational fabric of firms, so failures to achieve project goals are significant. Poorly managed large systems efforts have the potential to bankrupt a company. Beyond this, all organizations today appear to be very focused on overall cost control; that brings us back full circle to the role of project management. Simply stated, we believe that the project team format is the most effective means for organizations to accomplish desired changes and to control the associated expenditures. To accomplish this, a project must be properly selected, be approved by management before significant resources are allocated, and have planned start and completion dates, a managed execution, and a defined output. That set of activities is in essence project management and briefly explains why this skill area is one of the hottest professional growth segments.

Readings

The first reading in this chapter "The Value of Project Management in IT Organizations," summarizes the results of a survey conducted by the Research Center for Business Practices. The results of this survey are insightful regarding the perceptions of project management by external, non-IT functions, and regarding some characteristics observed by organizations that have gone through the process of formalizing project management.

The second reading is titled "Project Management in an Information Technology (IT) World." This white paper provides a summarized broad view of the topic and sets the stage for various discussions later in the text. Neville Turbit provides another high-level view of project terms and concepts in his white paper on "Vision, Business Problem, Outcome, Objectives and all that stuff. . . ." The topics outlined here are fundamental to the project vocabulary and should be reviewed by all readers.

Barry Flicker's reading approaches this topic from the standpoint of five myths that cause projects to break down and what you can do to mitigate these myths. These ideas are good philosophies for us to begin our search for a project management solution. This reading reminds us of the old Groucho Marx joke about, "Doctor, doctor my arm hurts." The doctor responds with, "When does it hurt?" Groucho says, "When I do this." The doctor's punchline response is then, "Don't do that!" Our advice on the myths then would be, "Don't do that."

The final reading in this chapter is an interview with Jim Highsmith, who is one of the founding members of the Agile (system development) methodology. The Agile school believes that speed of development is the key theme for success, and all extraneous overhead should be avoided. This raises the question of how much project management is worth in their view. Mr. Highsmith talks about "The Face of Project Management" today and what is needed as a new focus. In some circles, the Agile approach to development is changing the organizational culture of system development and obviously has a worthy goal. However, recognize that the traditional school would argue it is not industrial strength, and therefore is only for toy projects. Regardless of what you believe is the best way to build a system, the Agile approach is interesting in its focus on time improvement, and it is necessary to keep one's mind open to this sort of thing if we are to make progress in this discipline.

References

Archibald, Richard. "Project Management: State of the Art." A paper presented to the Project Management Symposium on PM: Project Manager Role Evolution, Rome, Italy, 2004.

Ibbs, William. "Searching for the $$$ Value of Project Management." Presented to the PMI Houston 2003 Conference, Houston, Texas, November 7, 2003.

Mullaly, Mark E. *Project Management: A New Definition*, July 23, 2003. Originally published at *www.gantthead.com*.

Kerzner, Harold. *Project Management*, 8th Ed. John Wiley & Sons, Inc., 2003.

Software Engineering Institute (SEI), Reference *www.sei.cmu.edu*.

The Value of Project Management in IT Organizations

RESEARCH CENTER FOR BUSINESS PRACTICES

Implementing project management adds significant value to IT organizations. This conclusion is the result of a survey of senior-level project management practitioners by the Center for Business Practices, the research arm of the consulting and training organization, Project Management Solutions, Inc. Over 97% of senior-level project management professionals stated that implementing project management added value to their IT organizations. Overall return on investment is 27.9%. All size organizations in all industries reported improvement.

What should organizations expect when implementing project management initiatives? The implementation of project management initiatives showed, on average, more than 21% improvement in the 20 project management metrics surveyed. The greatest improvements were shown in schedule estimating (38.6%), customer satisfaction (37.6%), and alignment to strategic business goals (37.0%). Positive improvement was shown in all areas surveyed. Those organizations that do not implement project management will be at a competitive disadvantage to those who do.

The CBP surveyed senior practitioners with knowledge of their organizations' IT project management practices and their organizations' business results. The results showed improvements to the organization because of the implementation of project management initiatives. Results of the survey show that improvements were shown in 20 IT measures, including time to market (21.7%), customer satisfaction (37.6%), alignment to strategic business goals (37.0%), time and budget to date (32.5%), quality (31.9%), labor hours performance (25.6%), schedule performance (32.1%), cost performance (23.8%), defect rate (12.9%), component size (3.9%), defect per peer review (11.9%), staff productivity (22.8%), response time (23.0%), average time to repair defect (11.8%), schedule estimating (38.6%), cost/hours estimating (32.8%), defect rate estimating (12.9%), component size estimating (5.1%), and quality estimating (7.6%).

The survey respondents also agreed that project management adds value to IT organizations. To the question, how valuable is project management to your IT organizations, respondents answered: very valuable (30.3%), valuable (37.2%), moderately valuable (30.3%), of little value (2.3%), not valuable (0%).

The survey sample was segmented according to the number of employees in the IT organization, including small businesses with under 100 employees, midsize organizations with 100-999 employees, and large companies with 1,000 employees or more. The study sample was also segmented according to several industries.

The Value of Project Management in IT Organizations survey goes a long way in validating the considerable gains an IT organization can make by planning and instituting formal project management practices.

Observations and conclusions drawn from the study include the following:

- The responses to the survey were almost all significantly positive, for all measures, for all industries, for all size organizations—project management definitely adds value to organizations.
- Those measures that received the most responses revealed significant gains—schedule estimating, customer satisfaction, alignment to strategic business goals, cost/hours estimating, time and budget to date, and quality.
- Some organizations showed enormous gains in specific measures (these huge gains skew the mean; in many cases, the median provides better insight than the mean).
- A large percentage of respondents (41.9%) represented Fortune 1000 organizations, although all size organizations were represented.
- Many companies do not collect the kinds of metrics used in this survey, metrics that show the value of a process or program or project to an organization.

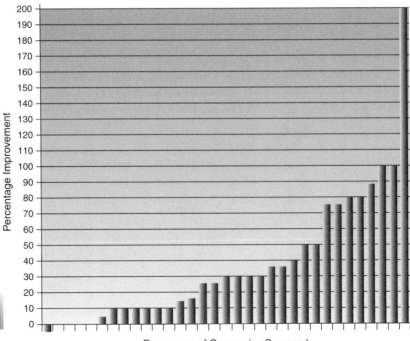

Mean	Median	Std. Dev.	N
38.3%	30.0%	42.6%	33

What is the improvement in **Schedule Estimating** due to the implementation of project management in your IT organization ?

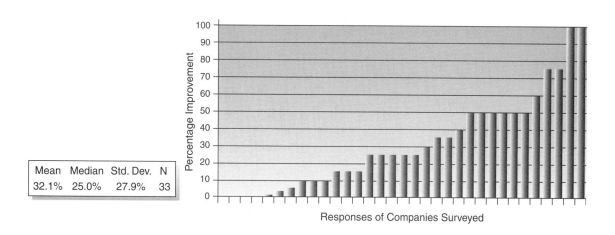

Mean	Median	Std. Dev.	N
32.1%	25.0%	27.9%	33

What is the improvement in **Schedule Performance** due to the implementation of project management in your organization?

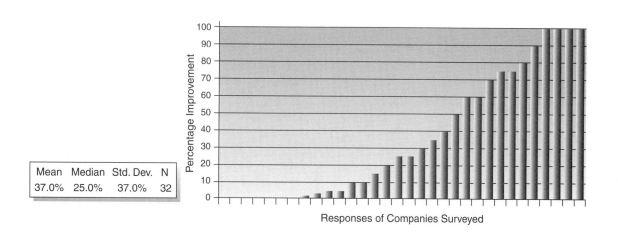

Mean	Median	Std. Dev.	N
37.0%	25.0%	37.0%	32

What is the improvement in **Alignment to Strategic Business Goals** due to the implementation of project management in your IT organization?

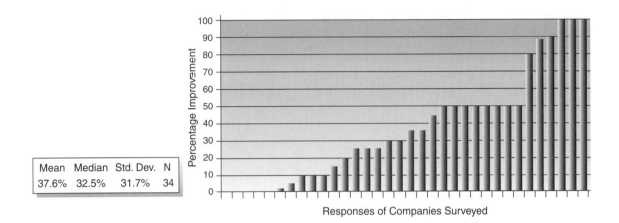

Mean	Median	Std. Dev.	N
37.6%	32.5%	31.7%	34

What is the improvement in **Customer Satisfaction** due to the implementation of project management in your IT organization?

Project Management in an Information Technology (IT) World

Comprehensive Consulting Solutions, Inc., Published: March 2001, Reference *www.comp-soln.com/whitepapers*

Preface

The playwright George Bernard Shaw once said, "The road to Hell is paved with good intentions, not with bad ones. All men mean well." This white paper will give you insight into successful project management—project management as differentiated from a collection of "well-meaning" activities.

Reading Overview

Project management doesn't qualify as one of the world's oldest professions, but it has been with us for several decades. The Information Technology (IT) industry was among the early adopters of this new way of doing things. However, while the IT industry started early, it lagged far behind other industries that were already implementing complex and sophisticated methods of managing their projects. Initially, and for many years to come, IT projects were managed as exercises in controlling budget and the time spent by personnel in completing their tasks.

Fortunately, IT has grown-up over the intervening years. Today, most large IT organizations are dealing with tens and sometimes hundreds of simultaneous projects. Obviously, the management techniques needed to effectively deal with such volumes of work must not only allow for accurate cost and time accounting, but also render fundamental management decisions easier to make, allow for the tracking of multiple critical paths within a given project, and facilitate the effective and efficient use of an organization's limited resources across multiple projects. That is quite a tall order to fill!

Project Evolution

While the ways that projects are being used within organizations change, the practice of project management itself has evolved. The key skills of a Project Manager have changed in recent years in that projects themselves have become much more complex. Matrixing, the management of multiple concurrent projects, has become the norm. One of the most fundamental and often misunderstood concepts of effective project management today is that of a reversal of traditional methods of management. Project Managers now assign tasks to resources, rather than assigning resources to tasks. While this may appear to be the same thing it really is not. Projects are under more and more management scrutiny and are generally cost sensitive. Maximizing efficiency often means having people working part-time on multiple projects. That introduces a new set of issues and a new layer of complexity.

A successful Project Manager also understands that there must be a correlation between business issues and technology. The simplest approach to solving a problem is often not the best one today. Not only must the current business criteria be taken into account, but future growth and expansion, shifts in technology and customer needs, and the ever-increasing globalization of business must be addressed by today's solution to a problem.

Project Management Basics

How does all of this affect the basic tenets of project management? The fundamental tasks and issues of project management remain largely the same. Various forms of analysis such as PERT, CPM, GANNT, and WBS are used during project planning and throughout the life of the project. Understanding the value and purpose of each tool, and then having the expertise to implement a solution using those tools also remains unchanged. So what, then, is different?

One Major Change

Because organizations are now faced with large numbers of complex projects, one tenet of project management has changed—that of assigning tasks to human resources. The availability of skilled people to work on a project is often limited, and is very often the most limiting factor in project performance. With multiple concurrent projects vying for these valuable resources, the Project Manager must strategically organize the use of whatever resources they have at their disposal. This often includes the use of Consultants. Managing external resources adds another dimension of complexity to a project.

As an example, if two concurrent projects require a database specialist with migration skills, and only one is available, the Project Manager needs to be able to organize the structure of his or her projects so that the database specialist is available to work on each project. This may require performing some tasks of one or both projects out of the initially planned sequence, which may require that other tasks be shifted as well. Unfortunately, this is often not limited to two projects as it is in this example, but in reality may involve tens of projects. In addition, in a large organization, the Project Manager may also have to coordinate his or her use of these limited resources with other Project Managers who also have multiple concurrent projects.

A Successful Project Plan Will Contain the Following:

- *Problem Definition*—a detailed definition of the problems and/or business needs which the project is meant to address.
- *Project Deliverables*—specific deliverables that provide specific features and functionality in order to satisfy a specific business need.

- *Impact Analysis*—the implementation of a new system or method of doing business can have many consequences—not all intended. It is important to identify and quantify the impact of these changes, which is used to determine the true cost of the project.
- *Value Proposition*—this answers the question "why are we spending all of this time and effort on the project?"
- *Project Tasks*—a detailed definition of the tasks that must be performed during the project to reach the final goals of the deliverables.
- *Infrastructure Analysis/Estimate*—an analysis of the technological resources/infrastructure and an estimate of the level of effort and cost to satisfy the requirements for the project. It is important to identify gaps in current levels compared to the required levels.
- *Human Resources Estimate*—an estimate of the human resources needed, detailed by function and time required per project task for each function.
- *Time Estimate/Time To Completion Estimate*—an estimate of the total time required for each phase of the project and an estimate of the total time to completion for the project.
- *Cost Estimate/Total Cost of Ownership*—an estimate of total cost of the project and total cost of ownership to the business. A follow-on step is to perform a cost-benefit analysis to ensure that the project makes both business and fiscal sense.
- *Project Budget*—an auditable budget detailing expenses for all phases of the project. The larger the project the more difficult this task becomes.
- *Risk Assessment & Mitigation Plan*—an assessment of the project risk and ways of mitigating those risks. This step is a critical but often overlooked step.
- *Review Methods*—a definition of the ways in which the project and its progress will be reviewed. This is an area where Independent Verification and Validation (IV&V) can play an important role.
- *Communication & Reporting Methods*—a definition of the ways in which the status of the project will be reported, to whom, and at what frequency. Often the lack of progress and/or status reports in a project is an indication of severe problems. A well-defined communication plan can act as an early warning system.

The project will have a *Sponsor* who has the authority and desire to make sure that all necessary resources needed for the project are made available, a *Project Board and/or Steering Committee* who review and help to oversee the project and its progress, and a *Vision Holder* who envisions the ultimate goal.

The Project Manager will be responsible for defining and managing the project. This includes management of technological/infrastructure resources, human resources, project budget, project tasks, and the myriad pieces that make up the whole of the project. In addition, the Project Manager will make decisions about what project tasks may be performed in parallel, ensure that prerequisite tasks are finished on schedule so that dependent tasks may begin, etc. The Project Manager's ultimate goal is to complete the project on time and within budget. *The Project Manager needs to be held accountable for the progress and ultimate success of the project.*

Who Defines the Project?

Is it the Business Analyst or the Project Manager? This is a bone of contention in many organizations.

Traditionally, the Business Analyst investigates the problems and/or business needs and requirements to discover the availability of a solution, what the best solution may be when multiple solutions are available, and reports in detail on this solution, its impact on the business departmentally and as a whole, the advisability of instituting the solution, and what its value proposition is. After these things are accomplished, the Project Manager then defines the project using these basic reports as a starting platform. Is this the best way of doing things?

While utilizing the same talent to define and even to manage the project might provide a certain level of continuity, it usually introduces more problems than it solves. There are a few exceptional individuals that are capable of consecutively performing business analysis, project definition, and project management, but in general, the skills and personality traits needed to perform these diverse tasks do not reside in a single person.

While a good Project Manager needs to have many of the same skills of analysis as a good Business Analyst, in order to determine the validity of a proposed solution and to assess change during a project, their personality traits are usually quite different, and the Project Manager will usually not possess the same level of investigative skill as the Business Analyst. Conversely, the Business Analyst will usually not possess the same level of management skill as the Project Manager.

Lack of Qualified Project Managers

Most IT organizations have run into the same problem: there is a great lack of qualified project management personnel available today. Those that are highly experienced and qualified are among the most expensive talent on the market today, as well as the hardest to attain.

Many organizations are answering this growing need by both utilizing the services of professional Project Management Consultants, and training Project Managers in-house, usually with the help of an outside agency specializing in project management and its related disciplines.

Selecting a Project Manager

A qualified, experienced Project Manager can often mean the difference between success and failure in a project. The more complex, visible, and/or critical the project, and the more concurrent projects the Project Manager must handle, the more vital it becomes that he or she be properly qualified.

The Project Manager should also be willing and able to manage vendor relationships. If vendors are required to make the project a success, then the Project Manager should have input to the contract terms and conditions, and should have control over issues such as payment disbursement.

Business Evolution—Management-by-Projects

As companies strive to compete more effectively and economically in today's increasingly global marketplace, a major change is taking place.

Business practices are being redefined to enable these companies to increase their productivity, the quality of their products, and the overall satisfaction of their customer base. All organizational tiers of these companies are being re-evaluated and redefined. The new thrust is to meet new business objectives and goals on every level of the company.

The result is that more and more companies are becoming project oriented. Their business is defined as projects and they are planning, budgeting, and measuring their business success and failures via the success and failures of the incremental projects that define their business.

This may be a radical departure from the traditional ways of doing business, but many organizations are finding that it works, and it works economically, thus enabling the company to maintain an even greater competitive edge. Don't be fooled into thinking that Management-by-Projects is just a clever rearrangement of an old phrase—it isn't. The philosophies behind the concepts are different.

As a comparison: Project Management is project-wide, a profession unto itself, and is defined as the management of a project or projects. Management-by-Projects is business or enterprise wide, an environment, and is defined as the control, integration, prioritization, and inter-communication of multiple projects across the enterprise.

Problems Still Occur

Of course all of the old nemeses of successful projects are still with us, such as scope creep, dependence on deliverables from outside organizations over which the Project Manager has no control, etc. Multiplying the number of projects also multiplies the number of problems the Project Manager is faced with. Is there a solution to this? Not really. Only careful planning, reassessment of projects throughout their life cycle, and the ability to accommodate change can help to avoid disaster.

And yes, projects fail. Few experienced Project Managers have navigated their career without a failed project. Projects fail for many reasons, but seldom without signs. The Project Manager can address some issues, but some are outside their sphere of influence and control. Lessons learned now help prevent future failures.

Summary

We hope that this provides more insight into the value of professional project management. Successful projects do not just happen; they are carefully planned and managed. Failure to recognize and properly address this can lead to costly project failures. That is both bad for an organization and bad for careers. Most importantly, it is almost always avoidable.

Let Us Show You How to Succeed!

Call today to discuss a proposed, ongoing, or delayed project. See how we can help you achieve your project's goals. Our experience and proven abilities will ensure the best possible outcome for you and your company. We provide the ***confidence*** that you want and deliver the results that you need.

Vision, Business Problem, Outcome, Objectives, and all that stuff...

NEVILLE TURBIT

Project Perfect Pty Ltd, Project Management Software, Consulting and White Papers, Reference *www.projectperfect.com.au*

Neville Turbit has had over 15 years experience as an IT consultant and almost an equal time working in Business. He is the principal of Project Perfect. Project Perfect is a project management software consulting and training organization based in Sydney, Australia.

Establishing the Project Context

In this white paper, we will define a number of terms that typically cause confusion when a project is being set up. I have seen many project charters or project definitions that misused the terms, ignored the definitions, or had no idea why they were being defined. The terms we will look at are:

- Vision
- Business Problem
- Outcome
- Stakeholder
- Constraint
- Risk
- Assumption
- Objective
- Critical Success Factor

Solution Oriented

It is always tempting to dive in and solve the problem before you understand it. Most IT people are solution oriented. In other words, the first response to hearing about a problem is to develop a solution. If the solution comes to mind before the problem is fully articulated, so much the better!

That is not to say being solution oriented is a bad thing. It is a good thing provided we have the patience to fully understand the problem. The following example takes you through the steps you should put in place before starting a project.

Example

For the example, we will use a customer tracking system.

Vision

The vision is a ten thousand-foot view of what the new situation will bring. It is not necessarily active in terms of an outcome. It focuses more on how the project will contribute to the bigger picture of where the organization is going. Think of "Vision" as being the alignment with corporate objectives.

Answer the question:

- The direction of the company is ... (What specific part of that direction is relevant to the project?)

Example:

The company is focusing on providing better customer service. To meet this need we plan to invest in various programs that contribute to this goal.

Business Problem

This is sometimes hard to define. In fact often, different people see the problem in different ways. Unless the problem is clearly defined, articulated, documented, and understood, there is not much chance of delivering a successful project.

Answer these three questions:

- The business problem is ... (What is the adverse situation?)
- Which affects ... (Who are the stakeholders?)
- The impact of which is ... (What is the impact of the problem?)

Example:

The business problem is that we cannot track contact with each customer, *which affects* our staff—particularly in Sales and Dispatch. *The impact of which is* that we do not know of problems with orders until it is too late to do anything to resolve the problems.

Outcome

By fixing the business problem, something will change in the organization. This is the "Outcome." It is not the nuts and bolts of what we deliver. The "Outcome" is the change in the way the business operates. It is at a lower level than the "Vision" in that it contributes to achieving the "Vision."

Answer this question:

- A successful solution will cause ... (What change in the organization?)
- This will result in ... (How will the organization benefit?)

Example:

A successful solution will cause all parties to be aware of who has spoken to each customer, what was said, and be able to reduce the incidence of no communication on a specific topic, or duplication of communication on a topic. *This will result in* better communication with customers, and hence a better relationship resulting in increased sales.

Stakeholders

By identifying who has an interest in the project, and why, we can more clearly see how they will be involved, and what we need to tell them.

Obviously when it comes to preparing a communication plan more information will be required.

Answer the following questions:

- The stakeholders are ... (Who are the stakeholders?)
- Their interest is ... (Why are they stakeholders?)
- They need to know/tell ... (As a consequence of the "why", what do we need to tell them?)

Example:

Stakeholder	Interest	Need to know
Sponsor	Final owner Responsible for the budget	Progress to date Expenditure What is being developed and when it will be available
Customers	They will benefit from better communication They know what they want to hear about and how they want to be told	Progress to date How it will work How it will benefit them Provide input on design

Constraints

Constraints are the things that restrict our creativity in the project. They stop us from doing whatever we like. Constraints are facts of life with which we must live. They are documented to keep us focused on finding solutions that can be developed or implemented. We do not want to waste time looking at options that will never see the light of day.

Answer the question:

- The project must take into account the following constraints ... (What can I not change?)

Example:

The project must take into account the following constraints:

- Development will be in Delphi on an Oracle database.
- Only one business user will be available from the sales area during June.

Risks

Risks are a double-edged sword. Firstly we need to understand what might cause us to fail, but in doing so, it provides the opportunity to do something about those situations and lessen our chance of failure. It is important to understand risks early in the project because if they are too high, the project might be better not started.

Answer the question:

- What might go wrong, and what will be the effect?

Example:
The people responsible for entering the data will not see the benefit and this will cause the system to be unreliable and not used.

Assumptions

Projects always have a high degree of uncertainty. In order to make any progress, we need to assume things. The reason to document them is two-fold. Firstly it allows people to challenge the assumption, and secondly it ensures we don't forget the assumption.
Example:
- The sales and dispatch staff will enter the details of their contacts.
- The sales file is up to date and we can load information directly into a new system.

Objectives

The objectives for the project should be measurable. It is a given that the first key objective is to achieve the outcome; however, objectives can also relate to the management of the project.
Answer the questions:
- Business Objectives are ... (What are the objectives for the business?)
- Project Objectives are ... (What are the objectives for the project?)

Example:
Business Objectives
- Reduce examples of reported duplicate contact from an average of 10 per day to 2 per day within 3 months of implementation.
- Reduce customer complaints related to communication from 20 per week to 5 per week.
- Improve sales to 60% of existing customers by an average of 15% over 12 months beginning January next year.

Project Objectives
- Deliver the project within budget.
- Deliver at least 85% of functionality in the first release.
- Complete the first release by end December.
- Ensure all deliverables are quality certified by out QA department.

Critical Success Factors (CSFs)

Some projects have 2 CSFs and others have 20. Some are measurable, some are not. As a general rule there should be between 3 and 8 CSFs and they all should be measurable. Very often the CSFs are contained in the outcomes and objectives; however, not all outcomes and objectives automatically become CSFs. The focus is on the word "Critical."
Think of "Cause" and "Effect." The "Effect" of improving sales is driven by the "Cause" of delivering the project by end December.
Answer the question:
- How will we know the most important outcome and objectives have been met?

Example:
The CSFs for the project are:

- 60% of existing customers improve sales by an average of 15% over 12 months.
- Customer complaints are reduced to 5 per week.

The project is delivered in terms of budget, scope, and timing (assuming).

Summary

The following diagram shows the hierarchy of understanding a program. In many cases components will be identified and agreed out of sequence. For example, the Business Problem may be the first thing identified within a project.

The left hand side contains the negatives we need to overcome, and the right hand side are the achievements we expect to come from undertaking the project.

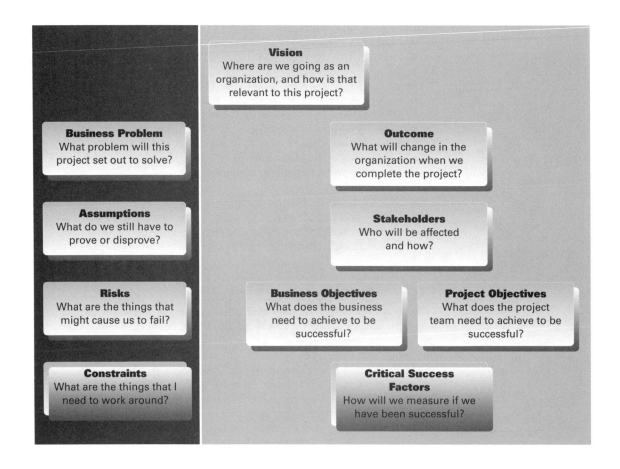

Vision
Where are we going as an organization, and how is that relevant to this project?

Business Problem
What problem will this project set out to solve?

Outcome
What will change in the organization when we complete the project?

Assumptions
What do we still have to prove or disprove?

Stakeholders
Who will be affected and how?

Risks
What are the things that might cause us to fail?

Business Objectives
What does the business need to achieve to be successful?

Project Objectives
What does the project team need to achieve to be successful?

Constraints
What are the things that I need to work around?

Critical Success Factors
How will we measure if we have been successful?

Defining each of these terms is not an exercise in filling in forms. It is critical to the success of the project that the organization is focused on what the project is all about.

More importantly, everyone should see the project in the same light. If there are differences, the project will either meet the expectations of some and not others, or be diluted in the delivery. Defining each of these terms is a critical step in understanding what the project is about, and reaching a successful conclusion.

The Five Myths of Project Breakdown (and What You Can Do About It)

BARRY FLICKER

www.pmboulevard.com

Barry Flicker *is founder of Basic Training, a San Francisco Bay Area-based company that offers a complete curriculum of courses in management and professional development to organizations intent on keeping pace with the rapid transformations of the global economy. He has authored texts on project management, collaborative negotiating, conflict resolution, non-linear problem solving, meeting management, team building, leadership, and effective communication. The hallmark of his approach to all of these subjects teaches people to recognize how their own unchecked assumptions trigger counterproductive behavior. This startling approach to project management has made him one of the most sought after experts in Silicon Valley and throughout the country.*

Could you, or someone you know, be undermining your project's success by clinging to one of five widely held myths about project breakdown? Read on—you might be surprised.

The Ten Most Common Project Complaints

- Everyone enters the project ***running on overload***.
- Rushing leads to ***poorly defined goals*** at the project's inception.
- ***Unrealistic completion dates*** leave the team feeling they've been "set up to fail."
- A sense of urgency causes ***poor communication***.
- Feeling the crunch, the ***planning effort is reduced or skipped entirely***.
- Other departments ***fail to support the project***, creating delays.
- Continued breakdowns trigger ***blame and finger pointing***.
- ***Scope expands*** as customers request additional features.
- ***Endless meetings*** to sort it all out lack focus, run too long, rehash the same territory, are dominated by a few people, and fail to produce or complete action items.
- ***Constant firefighting*** consumes ever more time and effort.

Broken projects and people with colds have a few things in common. In both cases, professionals prescribe "quick fixes" that often prove ineffective and can produce disastrous side effects.

Antibiotics fight bacterial infections, but most colds are viral and unresponsive to the drug. However, their indiscriminate use has sharply reduced their effectiveness.

Technology is the "antibiotic" of project management—upgrade your software, shift from critical path to critical chain, or use Monte Carlo algorithms to calculate your risks, and call us in the morning. Too often, these powerful interventions fail because they have been misapplied.

The list of The Ten Most Common Project Complaints suggests that better communication and inclusion would probably be a better (and cheaper) remedy. But improved communication seems too simple and "touchy-feely" to be taken seriously. On the other hand, technology, like the wonder drugs, is powerful and expensive. Does that necessarily mean effective?

We've just completed a decade-long technological binge. Are you less overloaded now than you were a few years ago? Do you fight fewer fires?

Maybe you think your mounting load of work and stress translates into greater project effectiveness. Think again. In one benchmark study conducted by the Standish Group in 1995, of the $250 billion spent in the U.S. each year on IT projects, $81 billion was wasted on canceled software projects—that's almost one-third. Three years later, in 1998, they calculated the odds of a Fortune 500 software development project coming in on time and on budget—only 25 percent had a prayer. That translated into project overruns and failures totaling $97 billion. And those are just the failures that we know about. The majority of project failures are covered up, ignored, and/or rationalized.

The belief that communication is "touchy-feely" and wastes time is a myth. The belief that stress equals success is a myth. In fact, these are just two of the five myths dominating project thinking that have wasted untold billions. We can no longer afford them. It's time to let them go.

Myth One: We've Got it Covered...

To avoid looking incompetent, we tend minimize or deny project problems. Heck, all projects have glitches. That's the nature of the game. Furthermore, we're convinced we've got it covered—that's myth number one. Whether we're confronting death, addiction, or a career crisis, human beings often try to cope with painful reality by denying it.

This tendency to minimize the nature of a problem or deny its existence makes solving it almost impossible. Therefore, getting past this denial system is the first order of business with any new client, and I have discovered a simple, but highly effective way to accomplish this. I show them The Ten Most Common Project Complaints listed above.

"Does any of this reflect what you've been experiencing?" I ask. With a visible sense of relief the client says, "Yes!"

The relief is two-fold. First, they recognize that we are on the same page; that they are talking with someone who understands what they are up against. The second factor is more subtle, but perhaps more important. The fact that their problems are predictable, suggests that they are not unique to their organization, which, of course, is true. The obvious universality of this list serves to remove the stigma that these breakdowns indicate something essentially flawed about their particular team, department, or company.

These breakdowns occur because of how we are wired up as human beings. The next question is, "Why are they so persistent?" This question surfaces myth number two.

Myth Two: It's the Idiots Out There...

After admitting that we don't have it covered, we blame the breakdown on the failure of others.

Some point the finger at "irresponsible upper management" for assigning arbitrary completion dates that bear little resemblance to reality. Clueless customers often take the hit for constantly expanding scope. Ask an engineer and he'll blame "fast-talking marketers." Ask the folks in marketing and they'll bend your ear with tales of "nay-saying, anal-retentive engineers."

If we strip away all the frustrating details however, we're left with a common denominator. The cause of all of these problems is—"the idiots out there." This explanation presents us with an interesting good news/bad news scenario.

What is the good news? Somebody else is to blame, getting us off the hook. The bad news is that we're always somebody else's idiot. But far more serious, the "idiots out there" explanation makes us victims. We can't change other people—especially if we treat them like idiots.

Therefore, I ask clients to explore the opposite hypothesis with me—that it's something we're doing, or failing to do, that triggers these chronic breakdowns. Of course, the bad news here is that we now become responsible for the breakdowns. However, the good news is—the more squarely we can place ourselves at the root of these problems, the more power we have to change things.

I have distilled the changes we must make in our behavior into four rules. To combat "idiots out there" thinking I remind clients to ***avoid confusion through inclusion***.

This means doing a better job of including our customer, not just at the beginning of the project, but continually so that as things change, both for the customer and within the project itself, we can make the required adjustments together. It also means including the entire core team in the planning process so that everyone develops a sense of ownership for the project early on. Better inclusion during the planning stage also enables us to discover conflicts and potential breakdowns on paper rather than in an implementation crisis.

In principle, everyone agrees that increased inclusion leads to better feedback and that the resulting sense of ownership and empowerment is a good thing. But our beliefs and actions often diverge because of myth number three.

Myth Three: Communication Takes too Long...

We're addicted to action and suspicious of—if not outright hostile to—talk. If you have any doubt about this, just look at our language. You pay someone a high compliment indeed if you call him "a man of action." When was the last time you heard someone praised as a "man of talk?"

Our warp speed world keeps us in a state of constant urgency. Too often we operate under the false belief that if we are not continually doing something opportunity will slip away. Better to "shoot first and ask questions later."

This bias against communicating with one another and taking time to plan before we act underlies every one of the complaints on The Warp

Speed Barrier Checklist. I try to inoculate clients against this tendency for frantic, counter-productive action with the rule that encourages them to *Shift from racing to pacing*.

Effective pacing means that, at certain points, we're going to trade speed for accuracy. Think of it this way: you're racing to a friend's house at 60 miles per hour. You come to a stretch of road on which you know you'll have to make a turn, but you can't remember exactly which street to turn on. If you want to read the street signs to find the right road, you're going to slow down. If you miss the turn, the speed is useless.

You'll probably brake going into the turn as well. In other words, when you're making key connections or changing direction it pays to slow down. When you know the turf or have a wide-open stretch of road, you can open it up.

Involving people takes time. Is it worth it? The all-action-all-the-time model only pays attention to the cost if we do. What gets overlooked is the cost if we don't.

The cost when we don't is quantified by the Standish Group reports. When we *Shift from racing to pacing* we have a better shot at getting the mix between talk and action back in balance. Unfortunately, this balance is made particularly difficult to maintain because of a distorted sense of effectiveness introduced by myth number four.

Myth Four: Stress Equals Success...

I once coached a media distribution company through a major capital improvements project. By following the systems approach we mapped out early on and, aided by an exceptional run of luck, they brought it in on time, on budget, and without a single major glitch. A few months later one of the key contributors told me that, about midway through the project, the project manager became convinced that, despite the glowing numbers, something must be seriously wrong because nobody was "freaking out."

We laughed about this story, but this confusion between stress and productivity is no laughing matter. Over the past twenty years the "no pain, no gain" approach to life has moved from the gym to the workplace with disastrous results. For example, the California Workers' Compensation Institute reports that claims for mental stress increased by almost 700 percent between 1979 and 1989. Work-related stress accounts for $200-300 billion a year in lost productivity and continues to rise.

When we become overwhelmed by constant firefighting and work overload (which many people believe is the definition of project work) the brain goes into emergency mode and starts pumping out cortisol as well catecholamines. "But we do our best work," says Daniel Goleman, author of *Working with Emotional Intelligence*, "at a lower level of brain arousal, when only the catecholamine system is engaged." In other words, the brain chemicals that generate enthusiasm for a challenge are different from those that respond to stress and threat.

Keeping this distinction in mind can make a huge difference in how we manage and motivate people. In between a sense of overload on the one extreme, and boredom on the other, we experience a zone of optimal performance that best engages our biochemistry. And the guideline to help us remember this "sweet spot" in human performance is Work from the Zone. This becomes much easier when we address the fifth and final myth as to what our purpose in project work is to begin with.

Myth Five: Satisfy the Specification by any Means Necessary...

Is delivering a project to specification, on time, and within budget an adequate definition of project success? It's not if our customer is unhappy. In over a decade of project management training and consulting, I have never found a group that didn't have multiple stories of projects that satisfied the numbers but disappointed the customer. It's our version of the old joke in which the operation is a success but the patient died.

The final rule I ask my clients to keep in mind states that ***both the people and the project must be fulfilled***. The other three rules are designed to guide us toward this outcome.

By increasing the inclusion of customers and team members, by pacing our projects and ourselves appropriately, and by remembering how important it is to work from the zone we can satisfy this final guideline. Granted, all these things are easier said than done, but by acknowledging their importance and making them the compass with which we guide the rest of our journey we will be well on our way.

The Face of Project Management

An Interview with Jim Highsmith

An Interview with Jim Highsmith, Cutter Consortium Senior Consultant and Director of Cutter's Agile Project Management Advisory Service. This interview was published on the Cutter Consortium Web site in October 2000 as the consultant of the month feature titled "The Face of Project Management."

Editor's note: Jim Highsmith is a respected thought leader, writer, and consultant in the broad area of systems delivery and particularly the Agile methodology. His comments apply more broadly than just to the e-project segment mentioned in the article. This article should be viewed as a contemporary view of the state of project management.

What Are Some of the Changes in the Current Project Management Environment?

People are beginning to realize that the traditional approaches to project management and software engineering are necessary, but insufficient, for e-projects. E-projects vary in their type and scope, but they generally all require three things:

1. Fast time to market
2. Very high quality (as we hook Web sites into back-end systems, they're doing transaction processing, so they have to be robust)
3. Very agile (the team must be able to respond to frequent changes during the project)

I recently did consulting engagements with two very large system integration companies in Asia (bordering on the largest in the country). In both cases, their projects were traditionally very successful—one company was certified CMM Level 4. But both companies recognized that the e-commerce projects they were going to be doing required a more innovative way of managing those projects. They wanted to maintain some of their traditional approaches, but they knew they needed to implement a different style for e-projects.

I see this as a long-term trend. We're five years into a 20-year transition into e-business. We'll continue to be in an environment where lots of things will be changing, the business models will be very turbulent, and the technology will be changing rapidly. There's a slew of technology that's brand new that we really don't know how to use yet. For example, Java, which has been around for five or six years, is just now enterprise-ready. Likewise, some of this new integration middleware is just in its first iteration.

The number one issue for the implementation of all these great ideas for e-business is pure project management. It's the definitive skill to make those things happen. And we're not talking about traditional project management.

What Should Companies be Focusing on in Terms of Agile Project Management?

I look at three critical skills for the new project management approach: innovation, discipline (to achieve high quality), and adaptability. Of those three, if you don't have innovation, you're dead. Because there is so much new technology, you have to have an environment where people are encouraged to come up with new answers, make mistakes and learn from them, and look beyond the norm.

Traditional practices focus on control; they're based on the premise that projects are fairly predictable. I can lay out a plan and then control that plan. Traditional lifecycles are task oriented. First we do requirements, then we do design, and so on. The project plans are relatively fixed. We know the requirements, we know what we're going to do (or at least we think we do), and the project is expected to go pretty much as planned.

In an e-project environment, the development lifecycle is exploratory in nature. We have a plan, but we don't expect the plan to work out exactly. It's a direction we want to go, rather than a fixed destination. Additionally, the development lifecycle is focused on delivering value to the customer using a feature-driven approach. In short-interval cycles, we deliver something useful (a business feature) to the client, as opposed to starting out by delivering documentation. For example, the first cycle might involve delivering three partial features. We can't explore by looking at documentation—we have to explore by looking at partially completed, actual features.

How Should Companies Doing Traditional Management Begin to Shift Their Focus?

Traditional approaches are based on the idea of control, and they're focused on optimizing—we've done it before, and we're focused on how to do it better. Many e-projects have not been done before, so we need to focus on how we can adapt over the course of a project. However, some of the practices are the same. We still do good project initiation and good project planning—but we don't view the plan the same way.

The hardest thing a group doing traditional development has to come to grip with is the change in perspective. The best impetus for this is fear. The truth is, in most cases, they're already scared—they know what they're currently doing isn't getting the job done. They're just not sure where to go. They're trying new things and looking for the "next practice."

One of the things I stress with organizations trying to make this move is that Agile Project Management is focused on a different problem domain than traditional practices. It's not that traditional practices are wrong—it's that we're tying to solve a different problem. When you get into the details of the new processes, you usually get some resistance because you're telling people to do things differently from what they've traditionally done. But I always return to the idea that we've got to put things in place that foster innovation, creativity, and adaptability to get this thing out the door.

Have You Seen Successes in Companies Using New Project Management Practices?

I've been working with a pharmaceutical company in Canada. They have been building their software like this, both for internal use and external sales, for about five years. I talked to the IT director recently, and he said, "Lots of things have been changing in our organization, some for the good, some for the bad, but we're still using adaptive practices."

However, showing success by traditional measures can be difficult. On these kinds of projects, the measure of success is often very different from those used in the past. What's important is not whether the project came in on time and on budget; it's "Are these projects creating successful products in the marketplace?" These are people on the cutting edge—they're much more interested in getting their projects out the door than in measuring stuff.

Another measure of success for these types of project management practices is taking ad hoc practices and adding some formality. For example, one of the larger banks in New Zealand is using an adaptive approach for their Web-based projects. They realized that their traditional approach to software development wasn't appropriate for their Web-based stuff, and their Web development staff said, "We can't use the traditional stuff for our Web projects, so we're going to do it completely ad hoc." When they implemented adaptive development, they were able to add some structure to their Web-based development.

Similarly, I'm working with two dot-coms. I'm helping them move from an ad-hoc environment to one with some framework and structure. It's not a traditional, highly controlled process, of course—that would be much too heavy for this type of environment.

Editors' note on selected vocabulary terms used here:

Agile   Refers to a contemporary development approach designed to generate systems output faster than the traditional life cycle. Mr. Highsmith is one of the founders of this movement.

CMM   The Capability Maturity Model is a popular vehicle for assessing the maturity of an organization's software process. More details on this can be found at the Software Engineering Institute Web site.

e-project   While there is no universally accepted definition of the term "e-" it is generally implied that the process deals with "webizing" a business. All major companies today are attempting to migrate into this arena. One might think of this as a second generation of the dot-com craze of a few years ago.

CHAPTER 3

Project Success and Failures

Chapter 3 Contents

Chapter Overview

Over the past several years, there has been extensive documentation outlining the details of IT project failures. These surveys indicate that this situation has been problematic for many years. Along with the traditional overrun statistics, there are consistent lists of factors that contribute to both success and failure. The question is if we know why projects fail and why they succeed, then why do they continue to fail? The question that cannot be answered quickly, but its answer lies at the core of the following material.

The list below contains published examples of major project failures that have had significant impact on the organizations mentioned:

- Hershey Foods had to issue two profit warnings during the Halloween and Christmas seasons due to massive distribution problems following a failed ERP system implementation. Hershey shares ended the year down, losing 27% market capitalization. [Steadman]
- FoxMeyer Drug, a $5.1 Billion corporation, collapsed following its ERP system implementation. Bankruptcy trustees filed a $500 million lawsuit against the software vendor and a Big 5 consulting firm. [The Best and the Worst]
- An IRS project to replace the existing Taxpayer Compliance System was in progress for over a decade. This slow completion cost the country $50 billion per year in uncollected tax revenues. [Anthes]
- Two years into a planned five-year, $50 million project to automate the Oregon Department of Motor Vehicles, the project was re-estimated at eight years and $123 million. Even worse, after the pilot rollout, lines at local DMV offices backed up around the block. In response to public outcry, state officials killed the project. [Hayes]

Results such as these are catastrophic in terms of business impact. Generally speaking, project failures are insignificant events and must be minimized. The first problem in overcoming project failure, oddly enough, is that there is disagreement over what constitutes a failed project. Some argue that it should be based on economic criteria only, while others hold to the theory that the project is a failure if it fails to meet the stated requirements within the specified cost and time parameters. Both aspects will be discussed to determine what should be considered in determining project failure.

Failure Based on Economic Criteria

Those that believe project failure is based solely on economic factors rely upon the tangible return on investment (ROI) associated with the project. In other words, if the value stream generated by the project exceeds the investment cost of the project, the project would be judged a success (using traditional time value of money calculations). In addition, assuming the project is completed on time and within budget, but the cost of the project exceeds the return value, it would still be judged a failure. So, in this case the sole measure of success is the financial view.

Failure Based on Requirements, Cost, and Time Parameters

An alternative school of thought is that any project that fails to deliver all features on time and on budget is a failure. Opponents to this theory contend that it is too black and white, too restrictive. There can be extenuating circumstances to mitigate this conclusion. In support of this position, most surveys done on project success do portray other analytical assessments.

For a business to sustain success, it must exhibit control in its management and decision processes. Following the economic criteria theory, a project would be a success even if it were over-time and over-budget as long as the return still exceeds the cost of the initiative. This view does not exhibit a control perspective; it exhibits serendipity. While a project's validity should be compared to its benefits, the benefit stream may actually occur over multiple phases or projects. Complex benefit realization further complicates the allocation of benefits to a particular initiative. Initiatives have to be undertaken to support other enterprise objectives, and some of these may not be financially based, especially projects that are required for government or environmental regulations. Seldom is a global calculation performed for this class of activities. For all of the reasons outlined here, there will always be subjectivity in the grading of success versus failure.

Survey Results

The following project surveys provide statistical insight into the industry view on this topic: (IT Cortex 2004)
- The Robbins-Gioia Survey (2001)
- The Conference Board Survey (2001)
- The KPMG Canada Survey (1997)
- The Chaos Report (1995)

The Robbins-Gioia Survey and the Conference Board Survey concentrated on ERP (Enterprise Resource Planning) implementations, while the others would be characterized as broader in nature.

The Robbins-Gioia Survey. This study was based on the qualitative perception of enterprises in regard to their ERP implementations and included 232 respondents and produced three key findings:

- 51% viewed their ERP implementation as unsuccessful.
- 46% did not believe their organization understood how to use the system to improve the way they conduct business.
- 56% of survey respondents indicated they had a program management office (PMO) in place, and of these respondents, only 36% believed their ERP implementation was unsuccessful.

The Conference Board Survey. This survey consisted of 117 companies who were attempting ERP implementations. The most important findings are as follows:

- 34% were very "satisfied."
- 58% were "somewhat satisfied."
- 8% were unhappy with what they got.
- 40% of the projects failed to achieve their business case within one year of going live.
- The companies that did achieve benefits said that achievement took six months longer than expected.
- Implementation costs were found to average 25% over budget.
- Support costs were underestimated for the year following implementation by an average of 20%.

Even though this survey indicates that almost all executives were at least partially satisfied with the implementation, it was noted that budgets and schedules were greatly exceeded. This fact can bring into question what the definition of "somewhat satisfied" is, or at least the question of whether the executives are actually aware of the overruns.

The KPMG Canada Survey. This general IT survey was sent to 1,450 public and private organizations. Usable response rate was 12%. The key survey findings are as follows:

- 61% of the projects analyzed were deemed to have failed.
- More than 75% exceeded their schedules by more than 30%.
- More than 50% exceeded their budgets by a substantial margin.

Considering Canada was spending $25 billion annually on IT application development in 1997, these figures would indicate that project failures amounted to billions of dollars in wasted resources.

The Chaos Report. This report was compiled by the Standish Group and is the most extensive and quoted survey in the U.S. It is viewed as the landmark study of IT project failure. This survey has been repeated multiple times and that process is ongoing. The report's widely publicized findings are as follows:

- 31.1% of projects will be cancelled before they are completed.
- 52.7% of projects will cost over 189% of their original estimates.
- 16.2% of projects are completed on time and on budget.
- 9% of projects in large companies are on time and on budget.
- 42% of the originally proposed features and functions are included at the largest companies.
- For smaller companies, 78.4% of the software projects are deployed with 74.2% of the original features and functions.

Using results from the 1995 survey, the Standish Group estimated that U.S. companies and government agencies would spend $81 billion for cancelled software projects and an additional $59 billion for projects that were completed, but exceeded their original time estimates. While risk is always an issue in high technology initiatives, many of the 80,000 cancelled projects were low technology initiatives for such systems as a new driver's license database, a new accounting package, and an order entry system. So, project failure is not isolated to high technology initiatives and is more management based than technological as had been thought prior to this.

Business Impact

By analyzing the various project surveys, the magnitude of business impact is on the bottom line. With measured project success conservatively in the range of only 20%, the related losses can be measured into the billions of dollars. Ten years ago, executives seemed to accept this phenomenon as inherent in the technology beast, but that attitude disappeared. Executives are much more sensitive and intolerant to the overruns. Today, careers ride on meeting planned project expectations. Certainly, the importance of a rigorous project management process rises in such an environment.

To counter the poor project performance outlined above there have been numerous methodologies developed, countless books and papers on the subject, and consultants galore who all tout solutions to this problem. What we now understand is that project success can be difficult for even the most experienced professionals. The fact is, a large IT project has conflict and complexity hidden all though the process. Executive management and other stakeholders often still do not understand their role in the project management process. All of these factors converge on the project to create a challenging management environment.

Looking Deeper at Why Projects Fail

Sifting through the sea of fact, opinion, denial, and blame, one can begin to see similarities in root cause for failures and successes. It is within these similarities that improved techniques can be derived. For example, some believe the importance of a formal methodology is paramount in the overall success, while others rate it lower on the scale. Regardless of specific rating factors, the importance of an experienced project manager is recognized as the catalyst for keeping the pieces together.

Naomi Karten took a satirical approach to project failure by imagining the goal was to guarantee failure rather than success. She compiled a list of ten ways to guarantee such failure:

1. Abbreviate the planning process.
2. Don't ask "what if?"
3. Minimize customer involvement.
4. Select team members by seeing who is available regardless of skill.
5. Work people long and hard.
6. Don't inform management of problems.
7. Allow changes at any point.
8. Discourage questions from team members.
9. Don't give customers progress reports.
10. Don't compare project progress with project estimates.

There are three recognized factors that contribute to project failure. One common item strongly linked to failure is conflict. Project managers encounter a variety of conflicts such as inadequate resources, changing organizational direction, project scope definition, disagreement among stakeholder groups, clashes among functional teams, team unity, and ineffective communication, to name just a few. One of the reasons people get into conflict is they do not envision or evaluate all scenarios and, therefore, do not take proper corrective action in a timely manner. [Kohrell] A second key item associated with project failure is that "In managing and developing products, the number one reason for schedule slippages is changing requirements."[Kopelman, Voegtli] The third causal item that is reflected in the surveys is that large projects fail more frequently than small ones. Obviously, size has a lot to do with the ability to have effective communication and it adds exponential technical complexity to the design. Complex communication and design characteristics generate control issues. So, managing size is regarded as one of the key management variables that can impact success.

Establishing Project Control

Just as the Standish Group has gained a leading reputation for identifying the reasons for project failure, they are also well known for their development of success factors for project success. The original CHAOS study, conducted in 1994, identified ten success factors known as the CHAOS Ten, and this data was again updated in 2000. Two articles in this chapter explore these factors in more detail.

Most projects "seem" to fail in the last third of the project. In reality, they fail in the first third of the project. To the untrained eye, projects generally look like they are in good shape until it is too late to do anything about it. The project team does not recognize many problems during the first half of the project because:
- Few, if any, deliverables are due early in the life cycle.
- There is still a "lot" of time left to fix problems.
- Early project optimism still prevails.

Corporate management is also easily fooled early in the project:
- The project team typically promises management a completion date and budget, prior to cost and time estimates becoming available. In other words, actual expenditures still look low in comparison to the total budget.
- Interpretation of project management status reports is generally insufficient or not well understood by management.
- Executives are reluctant to stay close to the details, and the project team only wants to disseminate good news early in the process.

One important key to avoiding project failure is understanding the performance metrics of a project, detecting deviations early, and using appropriate corrective action to move the project back on track.

Summary

Organizations do not purposely develop a culture that is geared to support project failures. More likely, such cultures evolved out of a lack of understanding of the fundamental causal issues. It is often very difficult for traditional business executives to comprehend how the lowly IT project manager can play such an important role in the success of the business. Consider a highly visible example to illustrate this point. Within today's airline industry, imagine what would happen if a critical IT system becomes inoperative or a new system is delivered late. It is pretty clear that such a malfunction would create significant operational maladies. An airline risks shutdown while the technical problem is resolved. Reservation systems, boarding passes, flight scheduling, and Web sites must operate 24×7. For less intensive IT enterprises, a technical malfunction or late project delivery could have an operational or competitive impact. As organizations increase the use of technology, the impact of poor project implementation will look more like the airline industry. Over the past decade, IT projects invaded the core of most business processes, and the related technology is pervasive throughout the organization. Today, selecting the right project targets and then executing these as planned continues to be a tough challenge.

Readings

The following reading, by Poli and Shenhar, titled "Project Strategy: The Key to Project Success," offers a good introduction into the project elements that influence success of the venture. This is a high-level view of key environment type topics.

References

Anthes, Gary. H. "IRS project failures cost taxpayers $50B annually." *Computerworld*, October 14, 1996.

Hayes, Frank. "Beyond Users: Why One Project Failed." *Computerworld*, August 11, 1997. *http://www.computerworld.com/news/1997/story/0,11280,1770,00.html.*

IT Cortex (2004), "Failure Rate," *http://www.it-cortex.com/Stat_Failure_Rate.htm.*

Johnson, Jim, Karen D. Boucher, Kyle Connors, and James Robinson (2001). "Collaborating on Project Success," *http://www.softwaremag.com/archive/2001feb/CollaborativeMgt.html.*

Karten, Naomi. "Ten Ways to Guarantee Project Failure", *http://www.stickyminds.com/sitewide.asp?ObjectId=6370&Function=DETAILBROWSE&ObjectType=COL.*

Kohrell, David. L. "PRE-EMPT CONFLICT: How to Actively Prepare for, Engage and Overcome Project Conflict," *http://www.projectconnections.com/pc/knowhow/member/papers_files/PRE-EMPT-conflict.doc.*

Kopelman, Ori, and Cinda Voegtli. "Powerful Product Visions for Developing Products in Half the Time," *http://www.projectconnections.com/pc/knowhow/member/papers_files/PowerfulProjectVisions.doc.*

Stedman, Craig. "Failed ERP Gamble Haunts Hershey." *Computerworld*, November 1, 1999. *http://www.computerworld.com/news/1999/story/0,11280,37464,00.html.*

"The Best and the Worst—A Look at the Projects that Bombed, the Viruses that Bugged Us and Other Facts from the World of IT," *Computerworld*, December 30, 2002. *http://www.computerworld.com/news/2002/story/011280,74620,00.html.*

Note: The editors acknowledge the research efforts of Alan E. Markowski for the survey material presented in this chapter.

Project Strategy: The Key to Project Success

MICHAEL POLI AND AARON J. SHENHAR

Wesley J. Howe School of Technology Management, Stevens Institute of Technology

Originally published in the 2003 PICMET Conference Proceedings. Reprinted here with permission of Portland International Center for Management and Technology, PICMET, Reference: www.picmet.org.

Reading Overview

This paper introduces and defines the concept of Project Strategy. Nike's "Just Do It!" is the prevailing attitude around projects. Schedule and budget dominate the measures of project success. To take advantage of opportunities, projects must be more than just tactical or operational. Building market share, extending product lines, increasing revenue, satisfying customers, and building for the future are more important measures of project success. Projects should be an active element in the implementation of a company's strategic intent, achieve better results, and increase the company's competitive advantage or value. Project Strategy focuses the project on the desired strategic results. It is an overarching set of guidelines to be used by the project in making decisions and taking action in alignment with corporate, business, marketing, and operational strategies. Existing frameworks and models offer insight in defining Project Strategy.

Introduction

The traditional measures of project success are based upon the "triple constraint," delivering the project on time, within budget and to specification. Doing this is based upon short-term thinking. Nike's "Just Do It!" is the prevailing attitude around projects. Here are the schedule, the budget and the specifications—"Just Do It!" In this reactive mindset, schedule and budget dominate the measures of project success. If we have to trade off anything, we usually trade off specification. Customers do not get the feature/functionality they expected. No wonder they are not satisfied with project results. Project success must be measured differently and projects must be managed differently.

Projects must be managed strategically. They must be more than just tactical or operational. Corporations need to take advantage of the enormous opportunities that projects represent. Project Strategy provides an umbrella or framework that can be used to dynamically guide project actions and decision making as the project environment changes.

Project Success

Project success must be measured on more then the triple constraint criteria of schedule, budget, and specification. Building market share, extending product lines, increasing revenue, satisfying customers, and building for the future are more important measures of project success.

Shenhar developed four Success Dimensions[8] that measure project success over time, both the short-term and long-term. The nearest term measure, immediately after project completion, is Success Dimension #1. It measures project success based upon "Efficiency," whether the project was completed on time and within budget, two of the traditional triple constraint measures.

Within a year of project completion, Success Dimension #2 measures "Impact on the Customer." Was the specification met (the third measure of the traditional triple constraint)? Additionally, Success Dimension #2 measures customer satisfaction and quality.

A year or two after project completion, Success Dimension #3 measures "Impact on the Business." Did the project efforts result in increasing revenue and profits, creating positive ROI and ROE?

In three to five year's time, Success Dimension #4 measures "Building for the Future." Did the project create infrastructure, new core competencies, new market opportunities, or extend product lines?

Given this new perspective on project success, it is necessary to approach projects with a different mindset. The reactive nature of the Nike philosophy of "Just Do It!" is not acceptable. Just having a project plan is not enough. The nature of projects is that they are contingent on the environment. Project success depends upon the ability to adapt to that ever-changing environment. Projects must be proactive and dynamic! There must be a Project Strategy to guide the project.

Project Strategy

Projects should be an active element in the implementation of the company's strategic intent. At the corporate level, there is a corporate strategy embodied in a strategic plan.[2] The business strategy is found in the business plan. The marketing plan is derived from the marketing strategy. The operational plan from the operations plan. All the strategies lead to plans. But the project plan just is. There is no Project Strategy. Project Strategy is missing.

All the strategies and plans have to embrace and build upon the prior strategies and plans. The project plan does not build upon nor embrace the other strategies or plans. Instead it focuses on the tactics of doing tasks and completing deliverables. But for what purpose? To complete the project on time, within budget, and to specification is a short-term perspective. Long-term thinking would be to have the project create competitive advantage or value for the corporation. A Project Strategy is essential to achieving better results and increasing the value obtained from projects.

We define Project Strategy as "The project perspective, direction, and guidelines on what to do and how to do it, to achieve the highest competitive advantage and the best value from the project."[9]

Project Strategy is an overarching set of guidelines to be used by the project in making decisions and taking action throughout the course of the project. It is in alignment with the corporate, business, marketing, and operational strategies.

There are two types of projects: those that are undertaken with the intent of creating products or services for external customers and those that are focused on internal customers. The external customer projects are meant to achieve a competitive advantage for the firm. They provide the revenue, cash flow, and profits. The internal customer projects are meant to create business value for the firm. They provide cost efficiencies, productivity enhancements, and faster response times. They contribute indirectly to competitive advantage. A Project Strategy is required whether projects are focused on external or internal customers.

Asking and answering the questions of Why, What, How, Who, When, and Where at a high-level, the Project Strategy helps the project focus on the desired strategic results, to achieve the highest competitive advantage and the best value from the project results.

Project Frameworks

Existing frameworks and models offer insight in defining the elements of Project Strategy.

At the corporate strategy level, Michael Porter's generic strategies[4] of cost leadership, differentiation, and focus (a niche strategy, combining cost leadership and differentiation) can be used especially with external customer projects.

At the business strategy level, Wheelwright and Clark's framework[1] can be used to assemble a project portfolio, selecting projects based upon project mix and resource usage. The framework classifies projects on the degree of product and process change in the project. Three project types are defined: breakthrough projects where there is extensive product and process change, platform projects where there is moderate product and process change, and derivative projects where there is modest or incremental product and process change.

At the marketing strategy level, the target customer, their characteristics, and a deployment strategy can be determined using Rogers' Technology Adoption Life Cycle.[6] Rogers identifies four customer types and their expectations. The Innovators like to dabble in new technology. The Early Adopters are the visionaries. They see the application, are willing to take the risks and can supply the resources to further develop the technology. The Early Majority are the first customers in the mainstream market.[3] They embrace the technology once the application has been developed and the costs to switch to the new technology have been justified. The rest of the mainstream market comprises members of the Late Majority. They are risk averse and will not embrace the new technology until it has become an industry standard. Finally, there are the Laggards who will resist the new technology no matter what. Waiting for them to adopt the new technology can be a time-consuming and exasperating experience.

Internal customer projects have a better chance of success if they use a deployment strategy that deploys to users according to their customer type in the sequence suggested by the Technology Adoption Life Cycle. Why try to deploy to the Laggards first? That is only setting the project up for disaster and failure. The Innovators can help test the project deliverables. By creating teams of "power" users from within the Early Adopters, the value of the project deliverables can be established. The Early Adopters can provide valuable leadership when it comes time to train the rest of the user population. The success established by the Early Adopters provides the impetus for the Early Majority to accept the project deliverables and to use them on a larger scale. The Early Majority in turn provide the stability that the Late Majority users require.

At the operations strategy level, Porter's Value Chain[5] concept can be used with internal customer projects. Projects can affect the firm's infrastructure: its primary activities such as inbound logistics, operations, outbound logistics, marketing and sales, and service; or its support activities such as human resource management, technology development, and procurement. These projects tend to be focused on internal customers but they can have a significant indirect effect on competitive advantage. Often internal customer projects must be developed in coordination with external customer projects to create the proper organizational support for the effective marketing, distribution, and sales of external products/services.

Shenhar's UCP (Uncertainty, Complexity and Pace) model[7] helps to determine project management style and to assess project risk. On the Technological Uncertainty dimension, Shenhar classifies the project as low-tech with no new technology, medium-tech with some new technology, high-tech with mostly new technology, and super-high-tech with all new technology. Projects are classified as assembly, system, or arrays on the Complexity dimension. Pace is classified as regular, fast competitive, or blitz-critical. Project risk increases as one moves from lowest to highest ranking on each of these dimensions. Taken as a three-dimensional model, the highest risk project would be a super-high-tech, array project being run at blitz-critical pace; the lowest risk project would be a low-tech, assembly project being run at regular pace. Shenhar further offers suggestions on how to adapt one's project management style to the project type, as classified on the UCP dimensions.

Elements of Project Strategy

Project Strategy involves six elements: objective, product definition, competitive advantage/value, business perspective, project definition, and strategic focus. Asking and answering the questions of Why, What, How, Who, When, and Where at a high level helps us to define each of these elements and, in turn, Project Strategy.

Objective. Why are we doing the project? What is the business opportunity? Is the project to create a new product or service with increased sales? Then we need to address Success Dimension #3, Impact on the Business. We can use Porter's generic strategies to guide us in choosing from either a cost leadership, differentiation, or focus strategy. We would choose to set up an externally focused customer project.

If the project addresses Success Dimension #4, Building for the Future, to build infrastructure for the long-term, then we can use Porter's Value

Chain. We can choose among the primary and support activities to instantiate an appropriate internally focused customer project.

Who is the customer? Who are the users? What are their needs? How do we address their needs? What is the deployment strategy? Which users should get the project deliverables first, second, etc.? From the Rogers' framework we can determine the customer type for the customer and the users, their needs, expectations, and deliverables. This enables us to understand how we can address their needs and satisfy them, helping us to be successful on Success Dimension #2.

Product Definition. This element addresses the product definition process. What deliverables are we producing? Is it a product/service? What are we required to make? What are the deliverables that will address the Whole Product that the customer expects? Here we look to the Leavitt framework to define the product, the project deliverables. How are the project deliverables to be defined? The voices of the customers and the users, their needs, and expectations must be addressed. How will we communicate with the customer? Data is needed to assess the efficacy and effectiveness of the proposed project deliverables. What information needs to be collected? How will market data be collected? Was there a competitive analysis—comparing competitors' products and positions? Were there technology, market, and risk assessments? Who will do them? Will we use maps and trends, QFD, or other methods to define requirements and specs?

A product vision, a statement that expresses an emotional appeal of the product and its advantage, is required. This vision needs to be clearly articulated. Who will do so, when, and how? Who will determine if the vision needs to be changed during the project and re-articulated?

Functional requirements and technical specification documents need to be developed. How are the requirements and specifications to be defined? Who and what organizational functions will be involved? How will this cross-functional involvement be managed? What do we expect of top management?

Answers to the above questions further solidify our ability to achieve Success Dimension #2, Impact on the Customer.

Competitive Advantage/Value. The project must identify the specific competitive advantage of the project deliverables (product, process, or service). How good is it? What is the advantage to customers and users over the competitors, over previous products, over alternative solutions?

Will one of the following variables: cost, performance, time of introduction, or another advantage, or a combination of advantages, allow us to be successful on Success Dimension #3, Impact on the Business? Are the project deliverables cost-effective? Why is our solution better? Why would customers prefer our process, product, or service? What is the value to our business? What is the value to the company? How would we benefit? How does it support or fit the company's strategy (separate short- and long-term value).

Business Perspective. This element asks the questions "What are the business expectations? What do we expect?" By establishing high level criteria, we can insure that the project goals will be in alignment with the corporate, business, marketing, and operational strategies. This alignment will address Success Dimension #3, Impact on the Business and Success Dimension #4, Building for the Future.

We must develop a business plan that defines and articulates the strategy and competitive advantage/value that the project seeks. The project manager should be involved in strategy setting and strategic planning sessions that lead to the project launch. Input from the customer, users, and the other project stakeholders should be part of this process.

The competitive advantage/value sought should be clearly defined, articulated, written down, and well communicated to management and team members. All team members should be aware of the competitive advantage/value, understand it, accept it, and work to achieve it.

Project Definition. This element focuses on the project scope, project type, and team selection issues. The scope defines the extent of the project's deliverables and the magnitude of the available resources. The project type classifies the project. We can use Wheelwright and Clark's framework to classify projects as either breakthrough, platform, or derivative. We can define the levels of product and process change required. We can also use Shenhar's framework to classify the project on the UCP to set expectations vis-à-vis project risk. Additionally, we can determine the project management style to be used and how to relate to Success Dimension #1, Efficiency. From the leadership and team viewpoint, we can ask the following: From what level of management should the project manager be selected? What competencies will be needed?

Strategic Focus. This element creates the mindset that will guide the project. It defines the behavior needed to achieve the competitive advantage/value. How should the team behave? What specific guidelines for behavior and decisions should be used to support the strategic focus? What should be done to achieve the best competitive advantage/value?

How will we create a relentless pursuit of competitive advantage/value? A motivated team will enable the project to achieve its goals. What is the strategic focus of the project? Is it clearly associated with the competitive advantage? How will the Project Strategy be articulated, by whom, and when?

How should we characterize the behavior that supports the proper strategic focus? How will we know if this behavior is present? What are our policies on managing and leveraging company competencies, professional expertise, internal synergies, and external alliances? Who will communicate and explain the policy?

How do we ensure that the project manager and team members manage the project with the strategic focus in mind—explicitly, implicitly? What actions should the project manager take to guarantee strategic project success? What actions should others take to guarantee the strategic focus is maintained?

Answers to these questions will ensure that the four Success Dimensions will be properly addressed; that the corporate, business, marketing, and operational strategies will be aligned; and that the expectations for the project will be met.

Conclusions

Projects offer an enormous opportunity for achieving competitive advantage and/or achieving value for the corporation. Projects must be managed strategically. It is proposed that a Project Strategy is necessary to take advantage of these opportunities.

This paper uses existing frameworks to define Project Strategy and in turn define how to align your corporate, business, marketing, and operations strategies and to achieve your strategic intent.

Asking and answering the questions of Why, What, How, Who, When, and Where at a high level, the Project Strategy helps the project focus on the desired strategic results, to achieve the highest competitive advantage and to obtain the best value from the project.

What Is Project Strategy?

Definition: We define Project Strategy as "The project perspective, direction, and guidelines on what to do and how to do it, to achieve the highest competitive advantage and the best value from the project."

Project Strategy involves six elements: Objective, Product Definition, Competitive Advantage/Value, Business Perspective, Project Definition, and Strategic Focus.

Elements of Project Strategy	Question	Details
Objective	Why do we do it?	Who is the customer/user? What is their need? How do we address this need? What is the business opportunity?
Product Definition	What is the product?	What are we producing? Functional requirements. Technical specifications.
Competitive Advantage/Value	How good is it? Why is it better? Why would the customer buy? What is the value for us?	What is the advantage to customer/user over: – Competitors? – Previous products? – Alternative solutions? Product cost/ effectiveness? How would we benefit?
Business Perspective	What do we expect? How to assess success?	Specified success dimensions. Business plan.
Project Definition	How do we do it? What is the project?	Project scope – (SOW). Project type – classification. Resources – time, $, etc.
Strategic Focus	How to behave? What to do to achieve the best CA/V? How to create a relentless pursuit of competitive advantage/value?	Guidelines for behavior. Policy on managing and leveraging: – Company competencies – Professional expertise – Internal synergy – External alliances

References

[1]Clark, K. B., & S. C. Wheelwright (1993). *Managing New Product and Process Development*, The Free Press, New York, NY.

[2]Mintzberg, H., B. Ahlstrand, & J. Lampel (1998). *Strategy Safari*, Simon & Schuster, New York, NY.

[3]Moore, G. (1999). Crossing the Chasm, Revised ed., *Harper Business*, New York, NY.

[4]Porter, M. (1980). *Competitive Strategy*, The Free Press, New York, NY.

[5]Porter, M. (1985). *Competitive Advantage*, The Free Press, New York, NY.

[6]Rogers, E. M. (1995). *Diffusion of Innovations*, 4th ed., The Free Press, New York, NY.

[7]Shenhar, A. J., D. Dvir, T. Lechler, & M. Poli (2002, July). *One Size Does Not Fit All—True for Projects, True for Frameworks*, PMI Research Conference, Seattle.

[8]Shenhar, A. J., O. Levy, D. Dvir, & A. Maltz (2001). *Project Success—A Multidimensional, Strategic Concept.* Long Range Planning, pp. 699–725.

[9]Shenhar, A. J., M. Poli, & T. Lechler (2001). *A New Framework for Strategic Project Management*, Pergamon, Management of Technology: The Key to Prosperity in the Third Millennium, PICMET—Ninth International Conference on Management Technology, Thousand Oaks, CA.

Business Alignment

Chapter 4 Contents

Chapter Overview

The role of IT in the enterprise has been increasing over the past several years. At this juncture, it is a major competitive driver for many organizations. On one side of the management coin, IT expenditures are large and concern senior staff. On the more positive side, many organizations see the value in IT. In the past, business drove IT. Now, there is strategic value in viewing a partnership with both sides supplying needed guidance. This process must be very dynamic, owing to the similar nature of both the IT and business environments. In some situations the organization is making decisions that pull it away from the current IT architecture. In other cases, technology offers opportunities to the enterprise that will support a change in direction.

Alignment is defined as the process of managing IT activities such that IT's value to the enterprise is optimized. This implies a global view of all related activities. In reality, this activity is very political and technically complex to achieve. Defining the value of IT in itself makes the basic process difficult in regard to comparing dissimilar technology proposals. At the political level, this process takes away local freedom to pursue solo applications. In a 1994 survey of 244 companies, Sabherwal and Kirs found a positive correlation between achieving business success and maintaining a positive perception of IT. [Sabherwal] Merkhofer reports from his discussions with business leaders that they "obtain only about 60% of the [IT] value that could be derived from their businesses. The remaining 40% of available value is lost, reportedly, due to errors in decision-making and weaknesses in business systems." [Merkhofer] This suggests that there is significant waste in an ineffective alignment process.

Hirschheim and Sabherwal position the alignment perspective by describing an organizational strategy framework consisting of three types: Defenders, Prospectors, and Analyzers. [Hirschheim] They describe these three organizational attitudes as follows:

- Defender: Defends a stable and predictable but narrow niche in its industry
- Prospector: Continually seeks new opportunities and creates change in the market
- Analyzer: Seeks simultaneously to minimize risk while maximizing opportunities for growth

Each of the strategy types outlined in the preceding anticipates different needs from IT in regard to alignment. Alignment dictates other decisions such as organization structure, resource acquisition, and level of aggressiveness toward changing the business. At one extreme, a Defender type organization needs to be very efficient. The likelihood is that the organization does not have high growth objectives and would attempt to minimize IT expenditures. At the other extreme, the Prospector approach seeks out targets of opportunity and IT would need to be ready to follow such targets with the business. Higher expenditures and more aggressive use of new technologies would follow this strategy. Strategies toward sourcing and organizational structure also have to be considered. This subject is made more difficult because many organizations do not declare what they really are trying to be and, in fact, are schizophrenic in their behavior. Both of these traits can cause a mismatch in internal management goals and a corresponding mismatch in the IT alignment results.

Within the internal mechanics of the alignment decision process, organizations can diverge. One example is the situation where a particular strategic goal is selected for aggressive action, while leaving many other activities in a Defender mode. This situation is essentially an approved management version of the divergence. We can also add a time dimension to this phenomenon, meaning that timing of one proposal does not match another even if both are appropriate technical actions. Beyond these examples, there are also other situations that create internal misalignment and cause IT to be out of synchronization. In order to better identify these issues, it is necessary to have a common communication and status system so that the entirety of efforts can be adequately reviewed.

One of the key underlying facts of the alignment process is that there is not a sufficient level of resources to pursue all proposed ideas. In addition, the organization cannot absorb high levels of change created by excessive initiatives. All organizations have these limitations, but the operational question is: at what point do you curtail spending and where do you allocate scarce resources? All allocations should not be to short-term projects at the exclusion of strategic high-value areas. Many organizations focus only on the short-term initiatives, which will limit their market position over the longer term.

Regardless of one's belief about the correct way to allocate IT resources, it is clear that there needs to be a formal IT decision-making mechanism that adds a degree of management and control, whether at the departmental or enterprise level. The chosen allocation center should be consistent with the organizational goals. This suggests that the way to obtain maximum value is to centralize the allocation of these resources and focus them on management-approved target areas. Some would argue that centralized planning adds a level of bureaucracy, which in turn takes away the agility of the organization to react quickly to business changes. Our professional belief is that a significant portion of this allocation should be both global and strategic.

Vendor Models

It was mentioned earlier that a formal communication system is needed to show all decision stakeholders what the plan is and why it was selected. To aid in the alignment analysis and presentation activities, there are a growing number of consulting organizations and tools designed to help document and support this process. Details on this are available at Gartner and other industry think tank organizations (reference the Gartner and Meta Group Web sites for details).

One tool example is provided by BMC Software with its methodology to measure and support the alignment activity. The product is marketed under the label of Business Service Management. [BMC] In late 2003, the company undertook a survey of approximately 240 respondents to quantify the state of alignment maturity in medium to large organizations. The results of this survey provide a good discussion structure for the topic and some analytical data to show what organizations are actually doing.

The BMC model components consist of 45 IT business alignment practices grouped into four broad areas: plan, model, manage, and measure. Within these groups, the five-stage Gartner maturity measures are applied. They are as follows:

- Chaos: No standard process
- Reactive: Multiple processes/procedures in place; little standardization
- Proactive: Standards and documentation exist; minimal compliance assurance
- Service: Processes are standardized and compliance is managed; some automated tools
- Value creation: Processes have been matured to best practices; continuous improvement and benchmarking in place

After the survey, organizations were measured and evaluated according to these groups. BMC drew six qualitative conclusions that were very interesting:

1. There is a strong relationship between IT-business alignment maturity and the participants' assessment of overall IT efficiency and alignment.
2. Organizations that rated highly on item one also showed positive assessments in managing change.
3. Existence of a strong IT management organization was linked to item one.
4. Integrated metrics and scorecards by mature participants provided consistent management data across all functions.
5. Top performers in the study based on maturity scores were also viewed as top in the qualitative assessments.
6. Overall, the study population did not rate highly in the alignment area, although there were a few who were very mature in this area.

Within the model groupings, there was more process maturity observed in measurement than in modeling capability. The average score was half-way between reactive and proactive, with 70% of the respondents below the proactive state. Large organizations fared better than middle-sized ones in terms of maturity across the model groups.

Quantitative studies of this type add improved understanding of the value related to proper alignment and ultimately of how to accomplish the goal. Space does not allow us to dwell further into the details of this study, but it is worthy of further reading (see the BMC Web site). The key point is that most organizations have not yet achieved mature process levels in the alignment arena, and more management focus is needed to improve the project selection process.

Conclusion

Business alignment is a fundamental management activity that lies above the project management domain. There is an old adage that "garbage in equals garbage out." That is certainly true where a bad project approval decision can lead to nothing but a bad outcome no matter how well it is managed. We have also seen evidence that there is much to be gained in regard to added business value and improved IT perception when this activity is properly carried out. Most organizations can use alignment improvement. We view it as a fundamental activity in the global view of project management.

Readings

Each of the readings presented makes a contribution to our understanding of IT alignment.

Kaplan and Norton discuss the use of a technique that they developed to support alignment efforts in "Plotting Success with Strategy Maps." This approach, based on the balanced scorecard evaluation methodology and strategy maps, can be used to ensure that a business is pursuing a strategy that is focused and internally consistent according to four dimensions (financial, customer, internal, and learning and growth). They argue that such factors are a necessary first step to enable alignment.

In "Choosing the Wrong Portfolio of Projects," Merkhofer discusses common reasons organizations pursuing alignment make wrong choices for their slates of IT projects. Human decision-making biases are one of a number of reasons for ineffective portfolio choices. The article also describes and examines the use of techniques that can enable businesses to make more effective portfolio decisions that align with their particular needs and strategies.

These readings offer varying views on the relationship of IT projects in the business environment. The key point to leave with the reader is that a project is not a standalone entity. It is created to solve a business problem, and its constraints and drivers should be business-goal based. Whenever a project fails to meet these criteria it should be shut down in favor of more profitable alternatives. Also, be aware that this chapter is intended to be introductory. Later chapters go into more detail on this process as they explore the Project Management Office and Project Portfolio Management topics, respectively. This chapter represents the basic theory, while the future view is more oriented toward the actual implementation of the concept.

References

BMC, *www.bmc.com.*

Gartner, *www.gartner.com.*

Hirschheim, Rudy and Rajiv Sabherwal, *"Detours in the Path Toward Strategic Information Systems Alignment,"* California Management Review, Vol. 44, No.1, Fall 2001; 87–108.

Merkhofer, Lee. "Choosing the Wrong Portfolio of Projects: And What Your Organization Can Do About It—Part 3," October 2003, *http://www.maxwideman.com/ guests/portfolio/reason3.htm.*

Meta Group, *www.metagroup.com.*

Sabherwal, Rajiv, and P. Kirs, "The Alignment Between Organizational Critical Success Factors and Information Technology Capability in Academic Institutions," *Decision Sciences,* 25/2 (1994); 301–330.

Plotting Success with "Strategy Maps": A Framework for Aligning Intangible Assets and Processes with the Business Strategy

ROBERT KAPLAN AND DAVID NORTON

Optimize, February 2004, Issue 28

Robert Kaplan is a professor at the Harvard Business School. David Norton is founder and president of the Balanced Scorecard Collaborative.

Since the introduction more than 10 years ago of the Balanced Scorecard methodology for aligning business objectives with IT investments, we've seen successful implementations in countries and cultures around the world by all types of organizations—manufacturing and service, nonprofit and public sector, large and small. Initially proposed as a way to improve companies' performance-management systems, the scorecard has proved to be an effective management tool for rapidly and effectively implementing any organization's strategy. Our new book emphasizes the identification of the most important processes for successful strategy execution and how to link investments in human capital, IT, and organizational culture to enhance these critical processes.

One of the principal reasons for the scorecard's success is its ability to align intangible assets—especially human resources (HR) and IT—to the company's strategy. While the acquisition and management of both physical and financial assets determined competitive success in the 19th and 20th centuries, companies today look more to their intangible assets—their human, information, and organizational capital—to differentiate them from competitors in achieving success for customers and shareholders.

The alignment between intangible assets and business strategy can be illustrated through a framework we call a Strategy Map (see Strategy Map [4.1]). Though we originally introduced the framework in a September 2000 *Harvard Business Review* article, it has been greatly expanded in our new book, *Strategy Maps: Converting Intangible Assets Into Tangible Outcomes* (Harvard Business School Press, 2004). The Strategy Map framework integrates the four perspectives of the Balanced Scorecard concept: financial, customer, internal, and learning and growth.

The expanded Strategy Map concept, paired with the Balanced Scorecard, offers a new way to manage information-capital development and deployment. By shifting the focus away from evaluating information-capital performance by cost and reliability, our approach considers a company's strategic alignment—for example, measuring how information capital contributes to the company's strategic objectives and especially to the differentiating processes identified in the internal perspective of the Strategy Map. Information

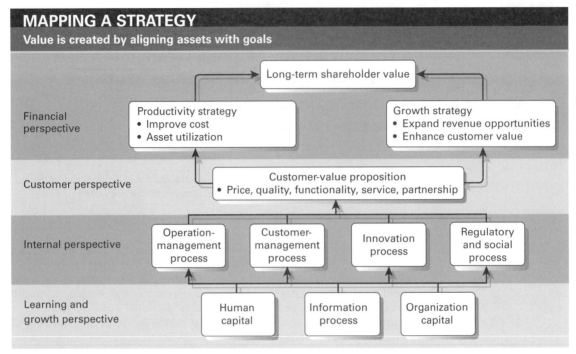

DATA: Kaplan and Norton

4-1 Strategy Map. The alignment between the intangible assets and the business strategy is illustrated through a framework that is called a Strategy Map.

capital must be managed like any other asset, with its value measured by how it contributes to the corporate strategy for creating competitive advantage.

The *financial perspective* describes the tangible outcomes of the strategy in traditional financial terms. Measures like ROI, shareholder value, profitability, revenue growth, and cost per unit are the "lag indicators," or outcomes, that indicate whether the organization's strategy is succeeding or failing. The *customer perspective* defines the value proposition for targeted customers. This proposition provides the context for how intangible assets, such as human resources and IT, create value. If customers value consistent quality and timely delivery, then the skills, systems, and processes that produce and deliver quality products and services are highly valuable to the organization. If the customer values innovation and high performance, then the skills, systems, and processes that create new products and services with superior functionality take on high value. Consistent alignment of actions and capabilities with the customer-value proposition is the core of strategy execution.

The financial and customer perspectives describe the desired outcomes of the strategy. Both perspectives contain many lag indicators. How does the organization create these desired outcomes? The *internal perspective* identifies the critical few processes that are expected to have the greatest impact on the strategy. For example, one organization may increase its internal R&D investments and reengineer its product-development processes so that it can develop high-performance, innovative products for its customers. Another organization, attempting to deliver the same value proposition, might choose to develop new products through joint ventures.

The *learning and growth perspective* identifies the intangible assets that are most important to the strategy. The objectives in this perspective identify which jobs (the human capital), which systems (the information capital), and what kind of climate (the organization capital) are required to support the value-creating internal processes. These assets must be bundled together and aligned to the critical internal processes.

The objectives in the four perspectives are linked by cause-and-effect relationships. Starting from the top is the hypothesis that financial outcomes can be achieved only if targeted customers are satisfied. The customer-value proposition describes how to generate sales and loyalty from targeted customers. The internal processes create and deliver the customer-value proposition. And intangible assets that support the internal processes provide the foundation for the strategy. Alignment of each of these four perspectives is the key to value creation and, hence, to a focused and internally consistent strategy.

Bearing in mind the concepts introduced in the Balanced Scorecard and the Strategy Map, we can now explore in greater detail the specific ways in which information-capital assets can contribute to strategic readiness.

Information capital includes the computing systems, databases, and networks that make information available to employees. Their value can be assessed only in the context of strategy, as we'll illustrate with four generic strategic-value propositions:

- **Low total cost.** The first value proposition is well-demonstrated by companies as diverse as McDonald's, Toyota, and the Vanguard Group. Each of these companies offers its customers the lowest total cost in its category. Companies striving to offer this value proposition should emphasize attractive prices, excellent and consistent quality, good selection, and purchase simplicity.

The most important internal processes for this value proposition are operating processes. IT is vital. Many repetitive, labor-intensive processes can be automated to cut costs, ensure consistent quality, and reduce processing times. But technology also plays a role in delivering continuous process improvements. With timely, easy-to-grasp displays of product and process information, employees can use data-analysis tools to continuously improve cost, quality, and process time.

- **Product leadership.** The product-innovation and product-leadership value proposition, demonstrated by companies such as Mercedes-Benz and Sony, generates products that feature superior speed, accuracy, size, and performance that loyal customers value and willingly pay more to receive.

The companies in this category must excel at innovation in their internal processes. They must anticipate customers' needs and develop products and services in direct response. This segment of companies also probably has superb product-development processes that bring new, high-performance offerings to the market quickly.

IT is most valuable for such companies when it supports internal processes related to product innovation and rapid product development. For example, project teams can benefit from advanced three-dimensional simulations in lieu of physical mock-ups to test alternative product designs. Virtual prototyping is faster and less expensive than traditional prototyping; it accommodates more design cycles and learning. In pharmaceutical research, for example, high-throughput screening and algorithms for combinatorial genetics have become as central to the research effort as biology and chemistry. What's more, IT enhances the communication of knowledge and project experiences across departments.

- **Complete customer solutions.** This value proposition stresses the provision of complete customer solutions. Good examples of companies successfully delivering this value proposition are Goldman Sachs and IBM Consulting. For this value proposition to work, customers should believe that the company understands their needs and can provide a complete set of products and services tailored to them. Companies offering this value proposition emphasize their ability to fulfill all of their customers' solution needs by selling multiple, bundled products and services. They also seek to provide exceptional service before and after the sale, as well as to build and sustain a long-term customer relationship built on trust.

The key internal processes support selecting, acquiring, and creating high satisfaction and loyalty among customers. IT applications for companies following this strategy provide customer data and support analytic calculations that reveal customers' buying patterns.

For example, customer databases and related analytics permit better customer selection through cluster analysis of demographic data and customer-profitability trends; also, database marketing supports the telemarketing process to improve customer acquisition. Additionally, CRM software improves sales effectiveness through sales-force automation and lead management. By combining CRM software with an activity-based costing system, companies can measure customer profitability accurately, suggesting specific actions the company can take to transform unprofitable relationships into profitable ones.

- **System lock-in.** Cisco and Microsoft exemplify this strategy by making the cost of switching to another competing supplier prohibitively expensive for customers. In a system lock-in strategy, a proprietary product, such as a computer operating system or microprocessor hardware architecture, becomes the standard for a given industry. In this case, both buyers and sellers want their products to be consistent with the standard to benefit from the large network of users that have adopted it. The high cost of changing from one company's product to another's can be demonstrated in different ways. For example, customers that choose to buy or sell products on an auction service other than eBay lose access to the vast community of buyers and sellers who use only the eBay site. Customers that switch from a Microsoft Windows computer to an Apple Macintosh lose access to many application programs that run only on the Windows operating system.

Information capital is often at the heart of a system lock-in strategy. The information resource provides the platform used by customers and complementors, or suppliers developing complementary products and services. Ideally, the information platform should be complex enough that competitors can't easily imitate it, but it should have a simple interface that makes customer access easy.

Choosing the Right Information Capital

As shown in the Strategy Map [4-1], information capital is linked to critical internal processes that deliver the customer-value proposition in the four generic business strategies just described (low total cost, product leadership, complete customer solutions, and system lock-in). A well-defined Strategy Map can help executives identify the critical information-capital applications that align to their company's strategy.

Workshops conducted after the company has developed its initial Strategy Map can help with the identification process. In these meetings, participants develop an integrated information-capital plan for each strategic internal process on the map, such as "respond quickly to customers" or "understand potential customer segments."

Workshop attendees are drawn from line-organization units, as well as HR and IT, so that the expertise of IT professionals and other specialists can be brought to bear on the information capital required for each strategy component. The results of these sessions are then shared with the various departments that implement the plan.

After the workshops have identified the critical information-capital applications, managers can assess the strategic readiness of the company's information-capital portfolio of applications to support the strategy. A frequently used approach to determining strategic readiness is a simple numerical scale of one to six that identifies the status of each strategic application.

1. Application exists; functioning well.
2. Application exists; needs minor enhancements.
3. New application under development; on schedule.
4. New application under development; behind schedule.
5. Major enhancement required; not yet initiated.
6. New application required; not yet initiated.

Managers responsible for the information-capital development programs provide the subjective judgments for this measurement system, though the CIO maintains ultimate responsibility for the integrity of the reported numbers. The measurement system focuses attention on the development process to ensure that the best efforts are made to achieve strategic readiness. Managers viewing such a report can determine, at a glance, the strategic readiness of the company's information capital, as well as the areas where more work is needed. The report serves as an excellent tool for monitoring a portfolio of information-capital development programs.

At the other end of the spectrum, many sophisticated IT organizations use more quantitative, objective assessments of their application portfolios. They might survey users to assess their satisfaction with each application or perform analysis to determine the operating and maintenance costs of each application. Some may conduct technical audits to assess the underlying quality of the code, and the operability, documentation, and failure frequency of each application.

From this profile, a company can build strategies for managing the portfolio of existing information-capital assets, just as one would manage a portfolio of physical assets, such as machinery or automobiles. For example, applications with high maintenance levels can be streamlined; applications with high operating costs can be optimized; and applications with high levels of user dissatisfaction can be replaced. This more comprehensive approach is particularly effective for managing a portfolio of applications that are already operational.

90-Day Plan

In three months' time, you can set in motion plans to more tightly tie intangible assets, such as an IT portfolio better customized to meet your company's needs, to the overall corporate success strategy. Here are the steps you can take.

FIRST MONTH: DEVELOP YOUR STRATEGY MAP AND SELECT A VALUE PROPOSITION

- Figure out what draws customers and keeps them committed to your company. The customer-value proposition is the combined effect of many factors: the product or service, price, brand, and customer attention your company offers customers.
- Select your company's differentiating value proposition and develop strategic objectives in the four perspectives outlined in the Balanced Scorecard: learning and growth, internal, customer, and financial.

SECOND MONTH: EXAMINE THE INTERNAL PROCESSES THAT DELIVER THE VALUE PROPOSITION

- Consider the operational, regulatory, R&D, customer-management, and other processes in place at your company. Identify the IT systems and software that will be most critical in enhancing the performance of these processes.
- Measure the extent to which these processes deliver the customer-value proposition and support the productivity goals outlined in the financial perspective of the Balanced Scorecard. A close examination may reveal that some processes need to be overhauled, streamlined, or outsourced.

THIRD MONTH: EVALUATE YOUR IT INFRASTRUCTURE AND SYSTEMS PORTFOLIO

- Ask managers and other stakeholders in your company to report on the status of processes pertinent to their units. Ask them to think about the key internal processes they believe customers most value, such as "Suggest related products for potential up-selling opportunities" or "Tailor marketing campaigns to prospects' needs."
- As you measure the degree to which these processes are met and supported by IT investments, you may learn that some existing applications

aren't really strategic and that some strategic applications are missing from your portfolio.

- If there are discrepancies between what managers would like information capital to help them accomplish and what it actually enables, initiate a program to acquire the missing capabilities to support strategic processes.

Choosing the Wrong Portfolio of Projects: And What Your Organization Can Do About It—Part 3: Finding the Right Metrics

LEE MERKHOFER

This is the third part of a six-part paper explaining the reasons organizations tend to make poor project choices. Part 1 described the common errors and biases in human judgment that distort decision-making. Part 2 described the error of failing to see the forest for the trees, and provided recommendations for establishing a project portfolio management function. This part offers Reason 3, why organizations choose the wrong projects, and describes the need to develop proper metrics for evaluating and selecting projects.

Reason 3: Lack of the Right Metrics

The metrics that an organization uses have a big impact not only on the projects that get chosen but also on the projects that get proposed. "Tell me how you will measure me, and I will tell you how I will behave."[1] Even if the metrics aren't used to create incentives, managers interpret them as indicating what the organization regards as important. Lack of the right metrics is the third reason organizations choose the wrong projects.

INADEQUACY OF FINANCIAL METRICS

Most organizations use financial metrics, for example, return on investment (ROI), return on assets (ROA), internal rate of return (IRR), net present value (NPV), pay-back period, etc. Using these metrics to evaluate candidate projects requires forecasting all of the ways that a project can impact cash flows, which is often difficult to do. The biggest limitation of using such metrics for project prioritization, however, is that they provide, at best, only a partial representation of what is relevant.

Financial metrics, quite simply, don't capture all of the organization's true objectives. For public-sector organizations, this limitation is obvious. Public-sector organizations have non-financial objectives such as protecting public health and the environment, as well as mission-specific objectives. For example, a water utility has a mission that includes serving community water needs. A public school has a mission that includes educating its students. Financial metrics fail to measure the full value of projects that achieve non-financial objectives.

Likewise, the standard financial metrics do not represent the true objectives of private-sector organizations. Management scientists and U.S. business leaders are nearly unanimous in the opinion that the fundamental objective of investor-owned organizations is to maximize shareholder value. With this view, the appropriate metrics for evaluating projects in the private sector are those relevant to forecasting impacts on the market value of the business.

What kinds of metrics reflect impacts on value? Many organizations have trouble answering this question. Organizations tend to measure what is easy to measure, not necessarily what is important. Most organizations use a bottom-up approach. They define interesting metrics, but then can't come up with the algorithms for computing value based on those metrics. Unless there is a way to combine the metrics to determine the value added by projects, the metrics will not be of much help in identifying value-maximizing project portfolios. How can you determine the value added by projects?

Shareholder Value

For publicly held companies, the value assigned by markets is the ultimate measure of the degree to which the company is meeting its business goals. Market valuations are objective and applied consistently across all publicly held companies and markets. If they were not there would be opportunities for arbitrage; that is, one could buy shares of a company at a lower price in one market and simultaneously sell it at a higher price in another market. Seeking higher stock value is clearly important to senior management. A company whose stock is depressed because it is not effectively managing for shareholder value is a candidate for investor takeover.

It is important to understand that managing for shareholder value and managing for profitable cash flows are two very different things. As shown by the figure below, the market value of a company does not equal the risk-adjusted discounted value (NPV) of its projected future earnings. In the literature on real options, the difference is referred to as "option value."

As illustrated, it is not uncommon to find two companies in the same industry such that one has a higher NPV of projected returns but the other has a higher total market value. Market value depends not only on projected future cash flows, but also the how buyers and sellers in the marketplace perceive, among other things, the ability of the business to respond

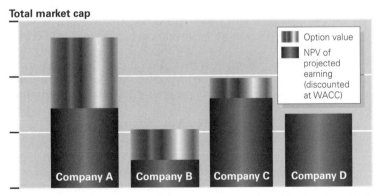

4–3 Figure 3. Company value depends on market perception of "real option value" as well as projected earnings (data for four companies in the same industry).

to future opportunities and avoid future threats. Option value does eventually translate into increased earnings.

However, because it is difficult or impossible to forecast the exact mechanisms by which this will occur, option value and other indirect sources of value will not be represented in accounting forecasts of cash flows. Companies that evaluate projects by estimating impacts on profits alone ignore a significant component of market value.

Stakeholder Value

An alternative view, more popular outside the U.S., is that firms should create value for all stakeholders, not just shareholders. Stakeholder value includes value for employees, suppliers, customers, and the local community. Proponents of more narrow shareholder value argue that organizations that pursue self-interest and economic efficiency will, in fact, be socially responsible and serve all stakeholders.

However, this argument carries the implicit assumption that the markets within which the firm operates are "perfect", with the result that stakeholders other than shareholders are unaffected by the firm's actions. For example, if people are hired, they are merely paid market wages, and if they are laid off, they can immediately get equivalent jobs elsewhere. Similarly, suppliers and consumers can switch to other firms, and taxes to all layers of government will be the same regardless of the firm's operations.

The U.S. economy is well diversified, which makes the "perfect market assumption," a pretty good approximation. However, the recent well-publicized accounting scandals have caused politicians and some U.S. business leaders to question absolute reliance on shareholder value. It may be reasonable, therefore, for even a private sector company to want to explicitly consider impacts on all stakeholders when making company decisions. Including stakeholder value further weakens the argument for using financial metrics as the sole basis for evaluating projects.

Finding the Right Metrics

What kinds of metrics reflect impacts on value? Many organizations have trouble answering this question. Organizations tend to measure what is easy to measure, not necessarily what is important. Most organizations use a bottom-up approach. They define interesting metrics, but then can't come up with the algorithms for computing value based on those metrics. Unless there is a way to combine the metrics to determine the value added by projects, the metrics will not be of much help in identifying value-maximizing project portfolios. How can you determine the value added by projects?

CREATE A VALUE MODEL

The answer is—you need to reverse the process, use a top-down approach and create a value model.[2] The value model describes the various ways that projects create value, for example, shareholder value, stakeholder value, or mission value. Identifying the ways that a project creates value requires judgment. In the case of shareholder value, judgments are similar to those made by careful investors and Wall Street analysts. Since the model is based on judgment, the model's assumptions must be clear so that they can be discussed, debated, and set to reflect best-organizational understanding of what the organization does, how it does it, and how its choices determine the value it creates.

Building a value model is not as difficult as it may sound. Even a fairly sophisticated value model can be constructed in a 2–3 day framing workshop (using techniques based on multi-attribute utility analysis, influence diagramming, and causal modeling). The model captures the understanding of the organization's experts in relevant areas such as R&D, engineering, manufacturing, marketing, sales, customer relations, legal counsel, regulatory affairs, etc. The value model establishes an explicit connection between the characteristics of the business that may be impacted by proposed projects and the value ultimately derived. Figure 4 [4-2] provides an example.

Having a value model is critical to making intelligent project decisions. Project value determines whether the project should be done at all, and whether, after it has been started, it should be continued. But, the value model has other uses as well. For example, a value model provides a way to estimate the value of a day of schedule, the value of a project feature, or the value of a dollar of project cost. The project team or portfolio manager can use the value model to illustrate how a marginal change in resources, say plus or minus 10%, might affect the overall value to be generated. A value model is a means for explaining and justifying the resources required for doing projects.

Once you have a value model, it is relatively easy to define the right project metrics. The desired metrics are "observables"(discussed next) that influence the model's value drivers; that is, those project characteristics and impacts, that is, model parameters that have the greatest influence on value. These typically include forward-looking financial metrics, like NPV, but also factors and considerations on value paths that don't directly impact cash flows. The latter can include indicators of the contribution of the project to the organization's capability and knowledge, customer satisfaction, and even political and regulatory impacts.

Metrics for these other sources of project value must be included along with the financial metrics. Otherwise the value of projects will be underestimated and there will be a bias against doing projects whose benefits cannot readily be expressed as cost savings or revenue increases. Note that metrics need to represent timing, that is, when the project benefits are likely to occur, and the risks, for example, the likelihood that the project will actually produce its anticipated benefits. When all such metrics are specified, the model defines the aggregation equation that allows the value of a project to be expressed in dollar terms. In the case of a privately owned company, for example, this represents the estimated impact of the project on shareholder value.

Metrics as "Observables" and the Clairvoyant Test

To the extent possible, metrics should be observables; that is, characteristics of projects or project outcomes that can be observed and measured in the real world. Since estimating project value requires forecasting the future, metrics don't, obviously, all have to be things we can observe today.

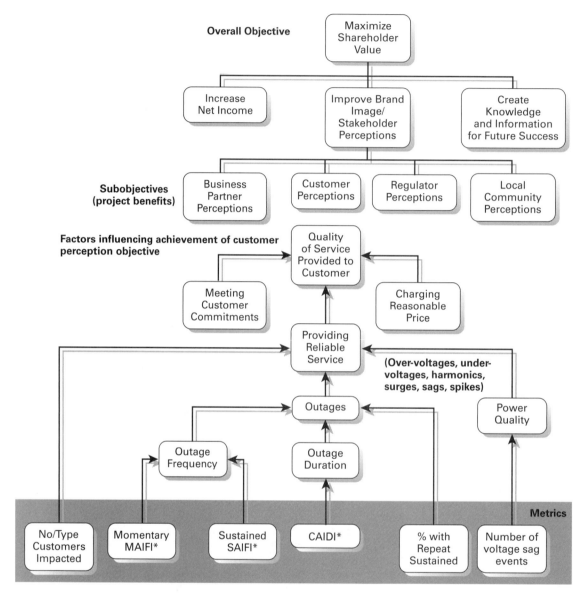

*Measures of electric power distribution system reliability commonly tracked by utilities:
  MAIFI, Momentary average interruption frequency index
  SAIFI, System average interruption frequency index
  CAIDI, Customer average interruption duration index

4–2 Figure 4. Portion of value model linking characteristics and impacts of proposed projects to value creation (electric power delivery company).[3]

Metrics can, for example, include a projected future state of some observable, for example, an improvement in a reliability-of-service statistic important to customer satisfaction.

A useful device for checking whether a metric is observable is the so-called "clairvoyant test" devised by my college mentor, Professor Ron Howard. Before accepting what appears to be a good metric, consider whether a clairvoyant could give an unequivocal value for that metric given that a project decision is made in a specific way. Oftentimes, the clairvoyant test points out inexactness of what initially appears to be a well-defined metric. For example, "customer satisfaction" doesn't pass the clairvoyant test. However, "percent reduction in recorded customer complaints" and "company ranking in the next industry customer satisfaction survey" are metrics that do pass the test.

Metrics that don't pass the clairvoyant test are vague. They create inconsistency and imprecision when used for estimating. More importantly, if the metrics are not observables, they cannot be monitored so that actual values can be compared against estimates. Observable metrics allow project proponents to be held accountable for achieving estimates submitted as part of project proposals, which is essential for minimizing biases and gaming in project forecasts.

Don't Forget Financial Metrics

The traditional financial metrics should be used to determine the direct financial (or "hard") components of project value. Project investment cost is, of course, an important financial metric for any project. Projects that impact operations (for example, projects that create new products or cut costs) produce additional financial impacts that should also be evaluated. Thus, any significant, incremental, period-by-period cash flows that are anticipated to result from such projects should be estimated, either directly as an average or in the form of alternative scenarios. The organization's standard accounting model may then be used to determine the after tax, or unencumbered "free" cash flows, which may be used to compute a project's financial NPV.

Some important principles for estimating financial value in support of project prioritization include:

- Ignore previously paid, sunk costs.
- Include opportunity costs (the opportunity cost of a resource is the value of the net cash flow that could be derived from it if it were put to its best alternative use).
- Include overhead expenses (for example, administrative expenses, managerial salaries, legal expenses, rent) that are directly related to a project. Indirect overhead can, if necessary, be prorated across proposed projects.
- Include "spill over" effects. For example, if a project introduces a new product or service that draws sales from existing products, include such lost revenue in cash flow estimates.
- Interpret expected project cash flows submitted in support of a project proposal as commitments to be achieved by the project manager. If there are cash flow components that are more speculative or for which the project manager cannot be held accountable (for example, because

they are contingent on events beyond the control of the project manager), specify such cash flows separately and assign probabilities.

■ Identify and include any terminal cash flows, for example, cash flows expected from the disposal of assets when the project is terminated.

■ Be consistent in accounting for inflation. For example, using an inflation-adjusted discount rate while ignoring inflation in estimating cash flows would result in a bias against accepting projects.

■ For the purposes of prioritizing projects, remember that the project's financial benefit is its NPV exclusive of its current-period costs.

Be suspicious of long-term, positive NPVs. Keep in mind the economic axiom that excess profits (the source of positive NPV) are zero in a competitive market. For a project to have a positive NPV, it must have some competitive edge—be first, be best, be the only.

Be Careful Using Balanced Scorecards

The majority of currently available, project prioritization and portfolio management software tools provide the capability for defining both financial and non-financial metrics. The tools are often based on the balanced scorecard approach. Balanced scorecards can be effective, but there are problems with the way they are often implemented. First, the scorecards are typically defined so as to trade off achievement of objectives in some arbitrary or subjective way intended to imply balance. That is, "The measures represent a balance between external measures for shareholders and customers and internal measures of critical business processes, innovation, and learning for growth."[4]

But, maximizing value requires efficient business processes, innovation and learning, and customer satisfaction. Why would an organization want to accept less value (for example, lower shareholder value), in order to obtain a higher score (that is, better "balance") on some internal business process? Maximization, and not balance, is the goal.

The second problem is that, contrary to typical scorecard mathematics, it is generally not correct to weight objectives that represent means for achieving more fundamental objectives. For example, suppose we include scorecards for both costs and business processes. But, improving business processes is a means for achieving the more fundamental objective of reducing costs. Thus, a project might get a favorable score on process improvement, but zero weight should be assigned to this score if the value of that process improvement is completely reflected in a favorable score assigned to cost reduction. If the weight is not zero, there will be double counting.

Failure to account for the hierarchical nature of objectives and the consequent overlap is a serious error being made by many who are designing tools for project portfolio management. For example, several Web sites suggest that there are four goals for portfolio management: value maximization, balance, strategic direction, and the right number of projects. In fact there is only one goal: value maximization. The proper balance, strategic direction, and number of projects are whatever is required to maximize value to the organization.

A third problem is that it is generally not correct to add different types of value. This statement, which is well established by value measurement theories such as multi-attribute utility analysis, often comes as a surprise to people accustomed to adding and subtracting money values. In fact, being able to weight and add sources of values is an exception. It requires the condition in which the value of achieving any level of performance on any one objective does not depend on the degree to which any other objective is achieved. Scoring methods are being advocated that involve weighting and adding scores for criteria such as project risk, internal rate of return, time-to-complete, urgency, and many other criteria that fail to pass this test.

It makes no sense, for example, to weight and add a project's score for time-to-complete to weighted scores for other criteria that indicate the value added once the project is completed. Being quick is much more valuable if the project adds a lot of value than if the project adds little or no value. Weight-and-add could only make sense, in this case, if the weights are not constants; that is, if the weight assigned to time-to-complete is a function of the ultimate value of the project.

A sound value model addresses these issues by specifying a logically correct way of quantifying value. Prioritizing projects using a balanced scorecard approach will distort project decisions unless the weights and mathematical form of the aggregation equation are derived consistently with the model of value.

Each Organization Needs Its Own Metrics

Different organizations conduct different types of projects. The metrics for evaluating new product investments by a software vendor, for example, will be different from the metrics needed to evaluate process improvements for a company operating an oil pipeline. Also, different organizations create value in different ways. An electric utility, for example, creates value differently compared to, say, a ballet school. Some organizations will seek to maximize shareholder value, while others will want to value impacts to other stakeholders as well. Thus, each organization will have a different model for how its projects create value and, therefore, will want to use different metrics. There is no one set of project metrics that works for every organization. However, in all cases, good metrics provide a means for computing the value added by projects. Good metrics are observables. And, they are sensitive to project decisions so that they may be used to differentiate the value of alternative project portfolios.

One of the most under-appreciated benefits of having good metrics linked to a defensible value model is improved justification. Author Anthony O'Donnell quotes a portfolio manager at an insurance company that implemented a portfolio management tool: "People would come to me and ask me to do a particular project... I would tell them I couldn't fit it in, but had a hard time articulating why." Metrics now allow him to give concrete reasons for turning away projects. "Their satisfaction immediately went up, and I still didn't do their projects!"[5]

References

[1]Goldratt, Eliyahu. *The Haystack Syndrome*, North River Press, 1991.

[2]The recommendation to develop a value model and, more generally, the views and ideas expressed in this and the next part of this paper are shared by many decision

analysts. See especially "Choosing the Right Metrics for Measuring, Monitoring, and Maximizing Shareholder Value," C. Spetzler and R. Arnold, *www.sdg.com*, May 2003. The book *Value Focused Thinking* by Ralph Keeney describes many of the concepts and techniques for building value models.

[3]The figure is derived from an application described in E. Martin and M. W. Merkhofer, "Lessons Learned—Resource Allocation based on Multi-Objective Decision Analysis," Proceedings of the First Annual Power Delivery Asset Management Workshop, New York, June 3–5, 2003.

[4]Kaplan, R., and D. Norton, *The Balanced Scorecard*, Harvard Business School Press, 1996.

[5]O'Donnell. *"Worth the Effort,"* Insurance Technology, March 4, 2003.

PART TWO

CHAPTERS 5-16

Exploring the *PMBOK*® *Guide*

PART TWO Contents

Part Overview

The profession of project management has matured greatly over the past few years, and a large part of that has been through the work of industry organizations such as the Project Management Institute (PMI). In addition, the growth of the Internet has allowed smaller organizations to proliferate their opinions and best practices to an international readership. This collection of electronic collaboration activities has evolved this discipline from an ill-defined black art in the 1940s into something that is beginning to look like an engineering process. We now know why projects fail, what basic activities are important to the planning and execution process, and various techniques that are useful throughout the project life cycle. The major management issues that continue to be debated today are the sequence of events in the life cycle and the degree of predefinition of requirements. In other words, should requirements be defined before coding, or can that occur iteratively through the execution cycle? Regardless of one's belief on this topic, the essential management issues remain similar to those described in this text.

If we could forecast what projects would look like in the future, there would likely be surprises as to their target and the ways used to achieve that target (that is, tools and basic techniques); however, there would remain a lot of similarity of process to that described here. It is important to recognize that the greatest changes would occur in the characteristics of these future systems. We have already seen the role that software has made in the modern weapons environment. That trend will evolve into the business, home, medical, and transportation arenas. One only has to watch the modern teenager to see that they are going to continue to challenge traditional uses of information technology. Would it have been logical to conclude even 20 years ago that much of our involvement with computers would come in the form of mobile Internet with color, video, music, and few numbers? We think not. Even within more traditional-looking environments such as the automobile, this technology continues to find new uses to enhance functionality. The modern automobile has more code embedded in its internal operating structure than the typical large organization had to run its business 20 years ago, and the projections are for this to accelerate over the next decade. Clearly, we will see this type of trend continue. Nevertheless, the product goal of the future project may be much different, but the underlying processes outlined here will not change in basic concept.

In these future initiatives there will continue to be technical challenges that impact completion plans, requirements to define, resources to manage, and activity in all of the other knowledge areas outlined in the PMI model. So, it is important not to lose sight of the basic project truisms as these new outward goals cloud the management process. The process-clouding caused by new technology and project targets may well be the most difficult concept to keep in mind.

PMBOK® GUIDE

PMI as an international organization has had what is arguably the greatest single organizational impact on formalizing the function of project management. They have made the topic of project management visible to an international audience. One of the key artifacts sponsored by PMI is a document titled *Project Management Body of Knowledge* (*PMBOK® Guide*). [PMI, 2004] Part Two is dedicated to a summary of the key processes and activities described in that document.

Today, organizations seek out individuals with PMI's Project Management Professional (PMP) credentials, which are acquired by taking a background exam on the topics outlined here. Whether you are seeking support information to aid in achieving this goal or are just interested in understanding the tenets of project management, the articles contained here will provide a broad industry perspective on these subjects. Part Two, Chapter 5 that follows offers an overview of the *PMBOK® Guide* and its internal components. Following that, the remaining readings in this Part describe the key knowledge areas in further detail. This exposure is not sufficient for passing the PMP exam, but will provide good support for that task when linked to a review text.

Simply stated, the goal for Part Two is to provide the reader with an easy-to-understand overview of the PMI model, using supporting articles that add understanding to the topics.

Exploring the PMBOK Knowledge Areas and Processes

Chapter 5 Contents

READING 1: Gimme a P!

Chapter Overview

The profession of project management has matured greatly over the past few years largely through the work of the Project Management Institute (PMI) and their international organization. Through its broad scope, PMI has made project management much more visible to an international audience and, as a result, is essentially recognized as the accepted definer of the subject. One of the key definitional artifacts sponsored by PMI is a document titled *A Guide to the Project Management Body of Knowledge (PMBOK® Guide).* [PMI, 2004] This reference document contains a summary of the key concepts and processes involved in executing a project. In this chapter, we will follow that general structure.

Today, organizations are seeking out those individuals with PMI's Project Management Professional (PMP) certification. To acquire this certification, you must have the requisite practical work experiences, formal education in the subject, and then take an exam on the key topics. Whether you are seeking support information to aid in achieving the PMP, or are just interested in understanding the tenets of project management, the articles contained this text will provide a broad view of the *PMBOK® Guide* subject areas and associated management rationale. Figure 5.1 [5-1] shows a high-level general view of project management's body of knowledge scope.

The structure of the *PMBOK® Guide* follows the classic tenets of W. Edwards Deming's approach to quality: Plan-Do-Check-Act. However, the 2004 version *PMBOK® Guide* has added an increased focus on the planning and closeout activities.

In the case of high technology project efforts, formalization of the project initiation is very important because it provides the basis for scope management, which historically has been a major source of project failure. Also, the *PMBOK® Guide* stresses early management consideration of

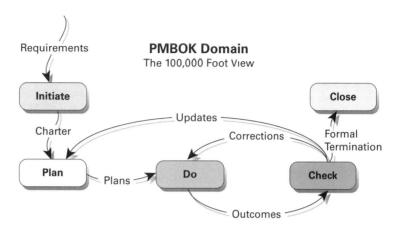

5-1 Figure 5.1 High-level view of PMBOK processes

human resources, procurement, quality, and risk assessment planning in addition to the traditional concerns over schedule and budget. Finally, the project closeout process is emphasized, based on the concept that lessons-learned information would be useful for subsequent projects—supporting the concept of continuous improvement.

The *PMBOK® Guide* partitions a project life cycle into five high-level process groups:

- Initiating
- Planning
- Executing
- Monitoring and Controlling
- Closing

Philosophically, the *PMBOK® Guide* emphasizes formality in the initiation and planning segments. Philosophically, once the appropriate stakeholders have approved a plan, the execution phase focuses on doing what the plan defines. The monitoring and control phase works in parallel with the execution phase and deals with taking appropriate action as deviations are observed in scope, cost, schedule, quality, and communication. The closing process captures relevant information that might be useful for future efforts. When examined from this high-level perspective, the *PMBOK® Guide* describes a deceptively simple concept, but recognizes that this simple view hides significant real-world challenges in executing these processes.

Embedded within these five major process groups are a defined series of nine knowledge areas and 44 associated activities. The nine knowledge-management areas are listed below, along with the *PMBOK® Guide* reference chapter designator:

1. Integration
2. Scope
3. Time
4. Cost
5. Quality

6. Human resources
7. Communications
8. Risk
9. Procurement

Each of the knowledge areas listed previously is further decomposed into groupings of specific activities organized into an evolutionary sequence. Within the major process groupings, there are core and facilitating tasks. The core tasks are essentially done in a defined order on most projects, while the facilitating activities are more dependent on the nature of the project as to how and to what degree they are undertaken.

Selected readings related to each knowledge area will be provided in subsequent chapters. The order of topics presented in the text does not follow the *PMBOK® Guide* chapter-numbering sequence, but we believe the text order is a more logical development sequence for this publication. For example, project initiation and planning (Chapter 7) is separated from the scope management discussion (Chapter 8) in order to focus more on project startup. Our reorganization is a stylistic repackaging change and does not affect the content of the total package. The important item to emphasize is the recognition that the various knowledge area activities occur throughout the project life cycle.

More information regarding the *PMBOK® Guide*, project manager certification (PMP), and PMI can be found at *www.pmi.org*.

Readings

The single reading in this chapter is a background presentation from David Liss, titled "Gimme a P!" This reading traces the evolution of the *PMBOK® Guide* and describes the use of a set of tasks and processes that should be used in a flexible manner based on the needs and characteristics of the project. Many think of the *PMBOK® Guide* as a bible of instructions to be followed rigorously for all projects. To be a successful project manager, it is important instead to use it as a conceptual reference. The challenge for the project manager is to learn how to adapt the theoretical PMI model to real-world situations.

Reference

PMI, A Guide to the Project Management Body of Knowledge (PMBOK® Guide) 2004 Edition, Project Management Institute, Inc. 2004.

Gimme a P!

DAVID LISS

www.gantthead.com/article.cfm?ID=51367

David Liss is the subject matter expert for Gantthead's Portfolio Manage-ment department.

No, *PMBOK® Guide* is not a new sports shoe by Reebok specifically made to enable project managers to jump higher, talk faster, and keep projects on budget in scope and on time. It is, however, considered by many to be the gospel of project management, the complete listing of the rules of the road for project managers. I have worked on projects where PMBOK, or *A Guide to the Project Management Body of Knowledge (PMBOK® Guide)*, to be precise, was quoted and referred to as THE oracle by which we would manage projects to the letter, allowing no room for variation.

This got me wondering. Was this the intention of the *PMBOK® Guide* and its author? How should I interpret and use this guide as I manage my projects? What kind of flexibility do I have as a project manager to use methods that aren't described in the *PMBOK® Guide*? What can I do about my nasty dandruff problem? And my breath could choke a horse. (Wait a second. I digress . . .)

So, as a public service to fellow project managers across the country, around the world, and in galaxies far, far away, I went straight to the source and spoke to the man who helped pull together all versions of the *PMBOK® Guide*. That man is Steve Fahrenkrog, Project Management Professional (PMP), the Standards Manager for the Project Management Institute (PMI). We talked; I kept my mouth closed and my ears opened. I learned. Hopefully, so will you.

The *PMBOK® Guide* is a product of PMI, an organization founded in 1969 based on the idea that management practices surrounding projects have common structures regardless of industry. The first iteration of what we now refer to as the *PMBOK® Guide* began in 1983 and was first published as a special report on ethics, standards, and accreditation (The ESA Baseline Report) in the August 1983 issue of *Project Management Journal*. This report resulted in PMI's initial accreditation and certification program. In 1987, the PMI Board of Directors approved a second standards document published in the August 1986 issue of *Project Management Journal*. This document added sections to discuss a basic framework for project management, risk management, and contract/procurement management and was the first to capture the critical body of knowledge for all of the *PMBOK® Guide*.

In 1996, the first version of the guide was published, with an updated version published in 2000. The fourth version of the document and the second edition of the *PMBOK*® *Guide* are perceived by many to be the de facto global standard for project management. Best of all, you can download an excerpted version of the guide here.

So, how does the guide define a project and project management, anyway? Page four of the 2000 edition defines a project as a "temporary endeavor undertaken to create a unique product or service. Temporary means that every project has a definite beginning and a definite end. Unique means that the product or service is different in some distinguishing way from all other products or services." The guide proceeds to define project management as "the application of knowledge skills, tools, and techniques to project activities to meet project requirements. Project management is accomplished through the use of the processes such as initiating, planning, controlling, and closing. The project team manages the work of the projects, and the work typically involves competing demands for: scope, time, cost, risk, and quality; stakeholders with differing needs and expectations; (and) identified requirements."

But is this book really the gospel that must be strictly and stringently adhered to, or is it a guide? "The book is a guide intended to offer a descriptive standard of generally accepted principles for project management that describes what is done rather than being a prescriptive standard that describes what should be done," says Fahrenkrog. "All of the standards expressed in the *PMBOK*® *Guide* are intended to allow for the flexible execution of projects using methods and practices that have shown value over time."

Further, he added, "The *PMBOK*® *Guide* (sic) is designed to provide a flexible structure and a common lexicon for talking about projects to help people communicate using commonly accepted terminology to facilitate communication for project management professionals."

In other words, this structure is intended to help all project managers speak more easily with each other.

The guide states that "The primary purpose of the document is to identify and describe that subset of the *PMBOK*® *Guide* that is generally accepted. Generally accepted means that the knowledge and practices described are applicable to most projects most of the time, and that there is widespread consensus about their value and usefulness. Generally accepted does not mean that the knowledge and practices described are or should be applied uniformly on all projects; the project management team is always responsible for determining what is appropriate for any given project. Project management is a relatively young profession, and while there is substantial commonality around what is done, there is relatively little commonality in the terms used."

Fahrenkrog gave this interpretation: "What this does not mean is that the structures described should be applied in the same way for all projects. The focus is on the commonality of activities amongst different types of projects, whether the project involves software development with a project length of six months or building construction with a project duration of 10 years. Each project and all projects have the same core elements. Both projects would be well served to develop a scope of work statement, a project schedule, and cost estimate. Most projects should also have a Work Breakdown Structure, but that doesn't mean all projects should. Very small projects may not require all of these activities. The project management team will always determine what is appropriate for any given project. What is appropriate will vary for a six-month IT project or a 10-year construction project to build a highway. For example, no accession plan may be needed in a short-term project, but it may be critical in a project of five to 10 years where retirement and job changes by critical staff could dramatically impact project completion if it happens five years into a 10-year project."

According to Fahrenkrog, the *PMBOK® Guide* focuses on the commonality of project constructs that most projects need for success. "The guide is written on a high level, the 10,000-foot view of the project. It is up to the project team to add, subtract, or supplement the processes and practices expressed, based on the specific circumstances and needs of their particular project."

While the *PMBOK® Guide* does assist project managers by defining general knowledge, standards, and practice, it does not include concepts regarding general management, engineering, systems engineering, and other knowledge and practice areas. These areas are deemed to be out of scope for the Guide. Also, according to Fahrenkrog, you will not find cutting edge stuff in the guide, and ideas and concepts that have fallen out of favor are not in the current version of the *PMBOK® Guide*. PERT charts are no longer considered applicable to most projects most of the time. In addition, there are no recommendations for software. An example of a new idea is the Project Management Office. While the PMO is acknowledged in the guide, it is not considered to have gained widespread general acceptance as a concept by PMI. The thought is that there is no general agreement on where the PMO fits within an organization, what its specific duties are, and what it should accomplish.

The *PMBOK® Guide* is an effort to set standards for project managers. Fahrenkrog would contrast this to ISO 9000, which is a quality assurance standard that touches on some PM requirements. Six Sigma also has a quality focus. IEEE has a standard for software development and only speaks about the application of project management in the context of software development. Therefore, ipso facto and ergo, these other acronyms and methodologies only touch on the periphery of project management.

To Fahrenkrog, the true value of the *PMBOK® Guide* processes are the ability that they give to provide consistency and repeatability across project types in various industries and in a framework provided in the *PMBOK® Guide* to level the playing field for project management and performance.

"If you want to rely on spectacular people doing spectacular things to be successful, or if you have average people and you want to achieve spectacular success, you need to have repeatable processes," he says. "The value of the *PMBOK® Guide* processes is that they demonstrate a generally accepted group of practices so that people can be successful more of the time. The objective is to try to build consistency of process so that organizations can execute their strategic direction through successful delivery of projects."

To Fahrenkrog, the most common mistakes people make in using the *PMBOK® Guide* processes lie in misunderstanding the process groups described in Chapter Three. He says that these process groups are often not correctly understood as a process for project teams to execute projects.

"New project managers often utilize these concepts too literally rather than to judiciously use the methodology in the execution of projects."

The Knowledge Areas (described in Chapters 4 through 12) are a way to co-locate like concepts for ease of discussion and elaboration. Initiating, planning, executing, controlling, and closing process groups are utilized and repeated throughout the project lifecycle. Project lifecycles tend to be industry-specific and will vary per the type of business that they represent. Feedback with process controls must be used to ensure proper execution according to plan and that processes exist to monitor and control and close each project phase. The process groups described must be able to be used over and over again.

So, it seems that in the end, the *PMBOK® Guide* is intended to be just that, a *guide* to give you—the project manager—a basic structure for repeatability of process and *guidelines* for managing projects across various industries with different and unique project lifecycles. I am reminded of a legal explanation I got once about the letter and the spirit of the law. In many instances, without fine or fear of imprisonment, you have the discretion and the flexibility to comply with what the most relevant rules and procedures are that apply to your particular circumstances. As you manage your projects, don't let anyone bully you into applying *PMBOK® Guide* standards to the letter. But, just in case, keep plenty of spirits around. Personally, I recommend tequila.

Integration Management

Chapter 6 Contents

Chapter Overview

The material in this chapter mirrors Chapter 4 of the *PMBOK® Guide*. This knowledge area subject matter is broadest in its scope and actual implementation, compared to other knowledge areas. Students studying for the PMP often find this topic the hardest to comprehend in that it deals more with "fuzzy" experience-based decision-making and process customization than that found in other knowledge areas such as cost, risk, or quality. The third edition of the *PMBOK® Guide* contains considerably expanded underlying details on this topic by adding four additional defined specifications to the earlier three processes documented in the second edition.

Chapter 4 of the *PMBOK® Guide* offers an excellent starting definition for this activity:

> *The Project Integration Management knowledge area includes the processes* and *activities* needed to identify, define, combine, unify, and coordinate the various processes and *activities* of *project management* within the *Project Process Groups*. In the *project management* context, integration includes characteristics of unification, consolidation, articulation, and integrative actions that are crucial to project completion, successfully meeting *stakeholder* needs, and managing their expectations. Integration, in the context of managing a *project*, is making choices about where to concentrate *resources* and *effort* on any given day, anticipating potential issues, dealing with the issues before they become critical, and coordinating the *work* for the overall project good. The integration effort also involves making trade-offs among competing *objectives* and alternatives. The project management processes are usually presented as discrete components with well-defined interfaces, while, in practice, they overlap and interact in ways that cannot be completely detailed in the *PMBOK Guide*. [PMI, 78]

One key implication is that the various component parts of the other *PMBOK® Guide* knowledge areas and processes interact. For example, output of risk assessment can affect schedules, which in turn can impact cost and HR items. So, the major function of the integration knowledge area is to ensure that all of the project management pieces are coordinated into a coherent whole from initiation through the life cycle to closure.

The seven integrative processes defined by the *PMBOK® Guide* are as follows:

1. **Develop Project Charter:** Developing a project charter that formally authorizes the project or a project phase
2. **Develop Project Scope Statement (Preliminary):** Developing the preliminary project scope statement that provides a high-level scope narrative
3. **Develop Project Management Plan:** Identifying the actions necessary to define, prepare, integrate, and coordinate all subsidiary plans into a Project Management Plan
4. **Direct and Manage Project Execution:** Executing the work defined in the Project Management Plan to achieve the project's objectives
5. **Monitor and Control Project Work:** Monitoring and controlling the processes required to initiate, plan, execute, and close a project to meet the performance objectives defined in the Project Management Plan
6. **Integrated Change Control:** Reviewing all change requests, approving changes, and controlling changes to the deliverables and organizational process assets
7. **Close Project:** Finalizing all activities across all of the Project Process Groups to formally close the project or phase [PMI, 78]

Develop Project Charter and Develop Preliminary Scope Statement are key processes within the project initiation phase. They basically authorize the project to move forward and provide approved definition of the proposed scope. Further discussion of these processes is in Part Two, Chapter 7 and Part Two, Chapter 8. The process of integrating the subordinate activities into a single coherent Project Plan is undertaken in the planning process and is described in Develop Project Management Plan. This activity integrates the planning segments associated with the knowledge processes of scope, schedule, cost, risk, communications, staffing, and procurement. The resulting deliverable containing this composite information is called a Project Management Plan. It is important to note that, once approved, this plan establishes tracking parameters such as cost, budget, and functionality. These parameters can only be changed through a process defined in the Integrated Change Control Process. The Execution phase follows approval of the project plan and is focused on carrying out the specifications outlined in the approved plan. Emerging issues that do not follow the plan are routed to another process for formal review and approval. The integrative activity to support ongoing review is titled Direct and Manage Project Execution. The following are sample management events associated with this activity:

- Perform the required project objectives.
- Staff, manage, and train the project team.
- Manage risks and implement risk response activities.
- Implement changes that were previously approved.

- Implement corrective action items that were identified and approved.
- Implement preventive actions as authorized.
- Implement approved defect repairs identified through quality inspection and audits.
- Produce work status information.

Collect and document lessons learned, and implement approved process improvement activities.

Section 4.4 of the *PMBOK® Guide* contains more details of the integration process list, but this summary should give sufficient general understanding of the intentions in this area. The control process operates in parallel with other project phases and is designed to monitor the life cycle process and take corrective action as necessary. The *PMBOK® Guide* defines this process in Monitor and Control Project Work. This activity serves to oversee activities occurring through the entire life cycle of the project from initiation through closing. The monitoring activity includes collection, measurement, and dissemination of performance information. Its basic goal is to identify areas that require special management attention and to communicate appropriate status to the stakeholders. This process receives data regarding any deviations observed and deals with that data in a proactive mode. Typical data items monitored include requested changes, defect prevention, ongoing risk assessment, task completion status, budget information, and other proposed process improvement actions.

Closely linked to the monitoring and control process is a change control activity. One should assume that no project is going to run from the initial plan to closure stages without a change. Therefore, it is necessary to track and manage this activity closely. To ensure that the project does not experience significant scope creep, the change management process is one of the most important overall project management activities. The *PMBOK® Guide* requires a formally approved management process that is designed to capture all change requests and manage their disposition from creation through resolution (either approval and implementation, or rejection). The key objective is to control what changes get approved and ensure that those that are approved get processed properly. This process is titled Integrated Change Control. A related vocabulary term used by the *PMBOK® Guide* is configuration management, which is defined as "any documented procedure used to apply technical and administrative direction and surveillance to …" various system attributes. Configuration management and change management are the major components of the Integrated Change Control process.

The final integrative process defines steps for formally closing the project, either as a result of normal completion or abnormal termination. This process is titled Close Project. There are four output tasks defined for the closure process. These are:

1. **Administrative closure:** All administrative actions related to the project team, deliverables, and stakeholder approvals
2. **Contract closure:** The actions required to formally close all contracts associated with the project
3. **Deliverables:** Formal turnover of all project deliverables

4. **Organizational assets:** Proper filing of all project artifacts, including customer acceptance of the results, closure documents, lessons learned, and other project files [PMI, 100]

The tasks represent many project management activities that are not often formally performed in the traditional project. There are three key management philosophies embedded in the formal integrative processes. These include:

1. Plan and document the proposed scope of the project and obtain management approval for that scope.
2. Execute the planned project according to the approved plan; a defined change control process must formally approve any changes.
3. Formally close out the project and file the historical results for use by other subsequent projects.

These are important tenets of the *PMBOK® Guide*, and these concepts are particularly important for high technology and strategic-type projects. There are dissenting opinions regarding this approach that need to be recognized. One project management school of thought believes that the project scope must evolve in daily involvement with key stakeholders—that is, there must be a rolling scope definition. Thus, the concept of a detailed plan before execution would be rejected using this approach. Also, many project managers will question the overhead defined by these guidelines as being excessive. We believe that the project manager will have to face both of these positions and seek some form of resolution. One has to believe that some degree of prior planning formality brings value. Various research sources from Berkeley, Software Engineering Institute, and others have shown that organizations that consistently follow the processes as described in this text will produce higher quality products in less time with better managed risk. This outcome does not occur instantly, but results from a sustained organizational change process supported by executive management. Anything less will result in compromise of the approach. The one process issue outlined that is broadly supported by most groups is the need for formal change management. One critical management principle is that you cannot control something for which there is no plan. So, avoiding the formal planning process raises critical questions as to whether you are managing the project or just executing it and hoping it turns out okay.

Moving Forward to the Knowledge Areas

As we move away from the integration process view, the subsequent chapters will narrow focus toward more detailed knowledge topics. Part Two, Chapters 7 through 16 will explore in more detail the remaining nine *PMBOK® Guide* knowledge areas that essentially make up the project components that will need to be integrated. We can look at this latter set of items as feeding the integration process and vice-versa. As we move into these more detailed areas, do not lose sight of the fact that each knowledge area potentially interacts with all of the others. Also, because a project is a dynamic activity, one should expect the best of plans to change during execution. Unanticipated risks will occur, quality issues will emerge, and pressure for project scope creep will be continual. Many more "issues" will emerge to create stress on the project team. To deliver the desired project goals successfully, it will be necessary to apply sophisticated technical and management judgment through every stage and in each of these component areas. The tools and techniques described throughout this text are designed to aid in that process. None of this material by itself will make you a better project manager, but it collectively will provide time-tested guidance and processes that will help organize the problem into more manageable views. IT projects must adopt more formal management approaches for its future project activities and the PMBOK knowledge topics that essentially make up the project components that will need to be integrated. One can look at this latter set as feeding the integration process and vice-versa.

Readings

In the theory part of this discussion we have reviewed the formal definition of process integration processes. The reading selected for this chapter comes from the DoD system development sector. Here, we extract a chapter (14), titled "System Integration," from the *Guidelines for Successful Acquisition Management (GSAM)*. [DoD] The approach described here views the integration process as both the project management integration and the physical product integration processes that occur within the organization. In many cases, it is hard to separate the management process from that related to the work tasks which create the output. The *PMBOK® Guide* tends to focus on the management portion of this activity, but we feel that both of these segments are important for the project manager. DoD reference repositories such as this offer a wealth of open source information related to the topics of system development. The reading shown here contains a checklist of questions related to this project phase. Similar checklists are contained in this source for other knowledge areas, and they would be useful topics to review (see the Web site reference for this). Checklists provide good reminders of issues to review prior to leaving a particular project phase. Any item that cannot be answered in the affirmative should be reviewed by the project team in an open discussion to decide how to move forward. The full text of the GSAM offers various checklists to aid in reviewing other project phases.

Reference

DoD Guidelines for Successful Acquisition Management. *www.stsc.mil.hill.af/resources/tech_docs/gsam4.html.*

System Integration

This material is provided with the approval of the U.S. Air Force Software Technology Support Center, Hill AFB, Utah. This is Chapter 14 of their Guidelines for Successful Acquisition Management *manual. Figure numbers have been left in original form. The full text can be found at* www.stsc.hill.af.mil/resources/tech%5docs/gsam4.html.

> *"Like a jigsaw puzzle: you have to make the pieces fit without getting out the scissors."*
>
> —Dr. Karl Maurer—On translating Greek sentences[1]

Introduction

It may have happened late on Christmas Eve, or it could have been almost any other time. You bought or received something with the some assembly required caveat attached. You spent untold time trying to assemble something that was supposed to be easily assembled, but couldn't see how the pieces fit together. Even after humbling yourself to the point of referring to the instruction manual, the puzzle remained a mystery, and was only solved through trial and error, repeated calls to the manufacturer, or the help of a friend who had already gone through the test. Think of the people who had to design the diabolical contraption in the first place, having to find or design each part and make all of them work together.

System integration is the successful putting together of the various components, assemblies, and subsystems of a system and having them work together to perform what the system was intended to do. It follows the coding phase in the development life cycle, as shown in Figure 14.1 [6-1], and is intertwined with the testing.

While it may sound like the final assembly of the parts of a system, successful system integration involves almost every aspect of the project and reaches from the very beginning into and through the maintenance phase of a system's life cycle. Figure 14.2 [6-2] shows the actual integration, where the system comes together, many of the results of successful integration, and several of the activities that are required for successful integration.

Successful system integration results from the proper implementation of project activities shown on the left side of Figure 14.2 [6-2]. The primary requirement and driver is systems engineering (see Chapter 13 [in *Guidelines for Successful Acquisition Management*]). When systems engineering is employed throughout the project, successful system integration is one of the primary outcomes. This includes requirements definition, functional

Requirements	Design	Coding & Unit Test	Integration & Test	Acceptance	Deployment

6-1 Figure 14.1 Integration's Place in the Development Life Cycle

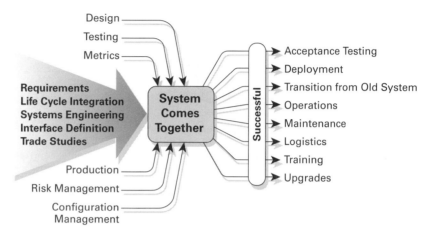

6-2 Figure 14.2 System Integration Inputs and Results

analysis, synthesis, trade studies, careful interface definition, true life cycle integration, etc. In addition to the activities associated with systems engineering, correct employment of other activities such as configuration management, design, risk management, and testing are essential to ensuring all the pieces fit together during integration.

Testing goes hand in hand with integration because it is through testing that we determine whether or not the assemblies, subsystems, and systems operate as they should after integrating them. Testing and integration are part of the development process. If there were no testing, the results of system integration would remain an unknown until acceptance testing.

Process Description

As with almost everything else, system integration begins with planning. Because system integration is the logical consequence of systems engineering and other activities, the integration plan is usually a composite of those portions of other plans which pertain to it, as shown in Figure 14.3 [6-3].

The integration process was shown in abbreviated form in conjunction with testing in Chapter 12, Figure 12-7, [in *Guidelines for Successful Acquisition Management*]. That drawing has been expanded in Figure 14.4 [6-4] to depict integration and testing more realistically as a series of integrations and tests. Testing is used to assure developers that the integrated product is properly functional. Integrated modules that fail testing are sent back for debugging and rework.

When tests fail, the test results are analyzed to determine the cause of failure. The components that make up the module being tested are then

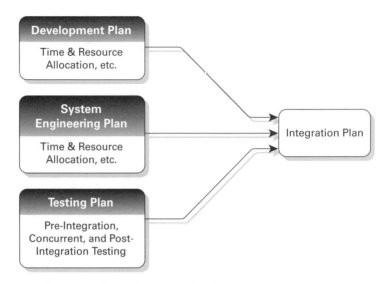

6-3 Figure 14.3 System Integration Planning

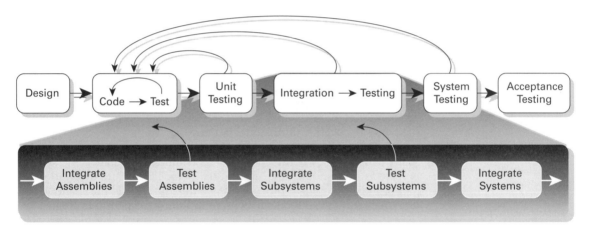

6-4 Figure 14.4 System Integration Process

sent back for debugging and recoding by the developers. If there appears to be a problem with the design, and not with the coding, the module is sent back to design for resolution. When the problem appears to be solved, the integration is repeated and the module is tested again. After rework, all lower-level integration and test cycles should be repeated before repeating the higher-level integration. This is part of the regression testing process and detects any new errors that may slip in due to "fixing" other problems.

Integration is iterative and progressive, with each level of integration building from and on top of the previous level of integration. This iterative, progressive nature is shown in Figure 14.5 [6-5]. Components are integrated into assemblies, and the assemblies are tested for functionality. Successful testing is followed by the integration of subsystems, which are also

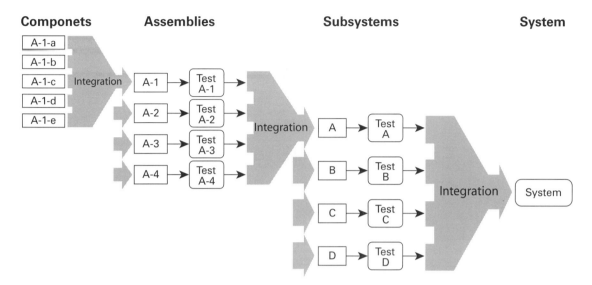

6-5 Figure 14.5 Iterative, Progressive Nature of Integration

tested for correct functionality. Finally, the subsystems are integrated into the complete system, which is then tested for functionality. While three levels of integration are shown in Figures 14.4 [6-4] and 14.5 [6-5], it is only representative and in a real project there will probably be additional iterations of integration and testing, depending on the complexity of the system.

Integration and testing are part of the development process and are used to ensure all the various pieces work together in performing their higher-level functions.

INTERFACES

An absolute essential to any integration effort is complete knowledge of all interfaces. This includes interfaces between components, assemblies, and subsystems, and between the system and other systems it will need to work with. This is depicted in Figure 14.6 [6-6]. Defining interfaces and maintaining those definitions is a primary responsibility of systems engineering.

COMPLETE SYSTEM INTEGRATION

Most systems consist of both hardware and software. These two are sometimes looked at as complete systems in and of themselves, but they cannot function independently of each other. While they may be called the hardware and software systems, in the system level view they should both be considered as elements of the real, complete system. Development of these two elements may proceed concurrently, with their integration also proceeding concurrently. However, it may be necessary for the hardware to already be in place and operational before the software can be developed, integrated, and tested. Ideally, both elements will be ready for integration into the final system at the same time. If one has to wait on the other, there will likely be problems with schedule, funding, and manpower.

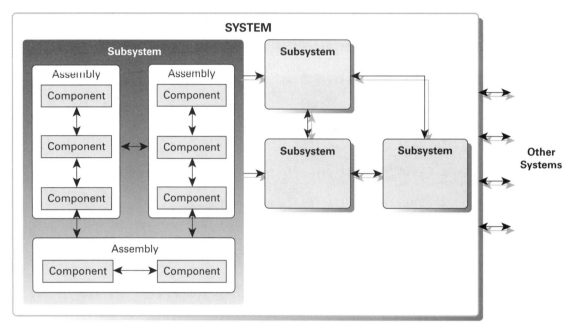

6-6 Figure 14.6 Interfaces Between System Parts and Between Systems

The integration of software and hardware elements into a complete system is shown in Figure 14.7 [6-7].

Figure 14.7 also shows two other system elements: people and support systems. While these other elements may not need to be in place during the development integration, they nonetheless are part of the complete system. For a system to be successfully implemented and used, these other elements must be in place and functioning correctly. The system integration plan must also consider these oft forgotten parts and monitor their establishment. They cannot be left as a follow-on effort. Failure to consider and prepare for all system elements from the beginning will leave the new system crippled or useless.

System Integration Checklist

This checklist is provided to assist you in understanding the system integration issues of your project. If you cannot answer a question affirmatively, you should carefully examine the situation and take appropriate action.

BEFORE STARTING PROJECT

1. Have you implemented systems engineering as an integrated life cycle effort ?
2. Do your test plans include and support integration efforts?
3. Does your development plan allocate adequate time and resources for system integration efforts, including rework time?
4. Are the interfaces between components, assemblies, subsystems, and systems defined in adequate detail?

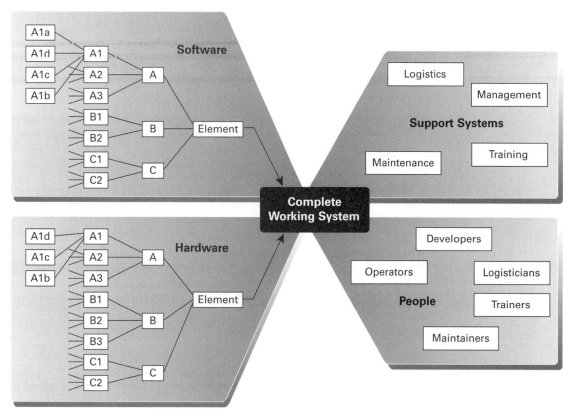

6-7 Figure 14.7 System Elements

5. Will hardware be available for testing software during integration?
6. Is there a contingency plan if the schedule slips and if the integration schedule is compressed?
7. Are all elements of the system included in the integration plan?
8. Is all documentation current and available for reference?

DURING CODE INTEGRATION

9. Is there an efficient rework cycle in place to fix problems found during integration testing?
10. Are "fixed" modules or components integrated and retested at all levels of integration up to the level where the problem was found?
11. Is the people element (operators, maintainers, logisticians, trainers, etc.) being prepared to work with the system when it is deployed?
12. Is the support systems element (logistics, maintenance, training, etc.) being prepared to support the new system when it is deployed?
13. Are you following an iterative, progressive integration process?
14. Are experienced integrators involved with the integration?
15. Are area/subject matter experts involved with the integration?

16. Is adequate time being allowed for integration, testing, rework, reintegration, and retesting?

17. Are all necessary resources being made available for integration?

18. Is adequate testing being performed on integrated units (assemblies, subsystems, elements, system) to ensure that there are no surprises during acceptance testing?

19. Are you updating documentation during rework?

20. Are integration and system test errors being traced back to requirements and design? And if so, are the requirements and design being updated?

Reference

[1]Maurer, Dr. Karl, "Quotes From Greek Class": *www.angelfire.com/ga/dracodraconis/ greekquotes.html.*

Supplementary Resources

Department of Energy (DOE). Software Engineering Methodology, Chapter 8: *http://cio.doe. gov/sqse/sem_toc.htm* Crosstalk Magazine: *www.stsc.hill.af.mil/crosstalk/.*

"C++ Component Integration Obstacles": *www.stsc.hill.af.mil/crosstalk/1997/05/ swanson.asp.*

Guide to Software Engineering Body of Knowledge, especially Appendix D: *www.swebok.org.*

NASA Systems Engineering Handbook: http://ldcm.gsfc.nasa.gov/library/library.htm.

Software Engineering Institute: *www.sei.cmu.edu.*

System Engineering Fundamentals, 2001, Defense Acquisition University, download at: *www.dau.mil/pubs/gdbks/sys_eng_fund.asp.*

Systems Engineering Guide, Version 1.1, 5 April 1996, ASC/EN–SMC/SD: *http://web1. deskbook.osd.mil/reflib/DAF/073GZ/001/073GZ001DOC.HTM.*

Project Initiation and Planning

Chapter 7 Contents

Chapter Overview

Activities related to project initiation and planning are actually part of the Integration Management area. However, this topic is so important for achieving project success that it has been selected for special focus. In Part I.3, this book presented information showing that a major source of project failure is a lack of a rigorous and formalized project initiation process. Poor planning and inadequate requirements contribute to such failures. The validity of this statement may not be obvious to many at this point. For now, recognize that an initiative started without consensus of the stakeholders will likely result in future disagreements and high risk of less-than-desirable results. One might ask, "What is the big deal in getting started and letting the requirements evolve?" Why is it not reasonable to bring together dollars and human resources and expect the desired output to result? In reality, poor planning and inadequate requirements are common in project ventures. From project initiation, the negative effects of these early issues can persist throughout project duration and contribute to project shortcomings or failures.

One of the underlying villains in project confusion is the pressure to quickly begin working on the deliverables (and therefore finish on time). This action is often accompanied by securing quick management approval for a level of budget and human resources from a friendly and often hurried sponsor. The problem that often occurs with this approach is that the resulting project scope does not fit the allocation level. In turn, this approach causes a combination of the triple constraint set (time, budget, and functionality) to get out of kilter. Project stakeholders have different interests in the outcome of the project. Some are concerned about budget; some schedule; and many others functionality. The definition of project satisfaction then is a compromise between these various points of view. A consensus among stakeholders should occur before the project gets started and not dynamically along the way. Failure to achieve consensus yields future frustration for the groups that do not get what they want. A second possible limitation scenario is the creation of a "shadow" project that does not have proper management approval. After a time period, this type of project becomes visible, yet management does not support it. Both approaches are fraught with failure potential that can be avoided by a reasonable initiation process. In all project situations, it is important for the business users, IT, and senior management stakeholders to approve the schedule, budget, and general functionality of the envisioned project, recognizing that early schedules and predictions are more target estimates than bull's-eyes. Employees using good project management practices will review these expectations along the way and make adjustments in an orderly manner.

Initiation is the first *PMBOK® Guide* knowledge area and is designed to start the project off on the right foot. First, it uses a project charter definition to formally authorize the defined initiative; this action links to subsequent management steps in the project. In this initial step a link is established between the project and strategic and tactical objectives of the organization. In this step, a formal leader is also identified and provisions made for acquisition of team members. One subtle point about project initiation is that the process also applies to multiple stages within the project life cycle. This point is described in the *PMBOK® Guide*, which states that there should be key evaluation points at which status is reviewed and official management approval granted before the project moves forward to the next step. In other words, projects that have begun do not have a lifetime contract and should be cancelled if the projected cost-benefit proposition goes awry during development. These secondary decision points are often called stage gates or go/no-go points. The preparation process for these reviews is similar to the original justification for the project, except that in the follow-on stages project documentation is updated rather than begun.

There are two key process artifacts produced at the completion of the two steps described here, as follows:

Initiation creates a project charter that minimally contains a description of the business need, the desired deliverables, and a formal approval to proceed by appropriate management.

Planning creates an integrated plan outlining in greater detail the various projected aspects of the proposed effort. Articles in this section will deal with these topic areas in more detail.

A major point in this chapter is that the initiation process and its related planning activities are fundamental activities that should not be shorted to save time.

Readings

The first reading in this chapter is "How to Create a Clear Project Plan in Six Easy Steps," by Elizabeth and Richard Larson. In this reading, you will find a prescription for the steps in the process and some key vocabulary. As the authors indicate, this is an easy process but one often neglected in the rush to get started.

Douglas Arnstein provides a good overview of the initiation and planning stages in his reading, "Gaining Visibility and Commitment on Technology Projects." He walks through the entire initiation and planning process from the first day a project manager is given the task. Note in this reading that IT was not involved in the initial planning process, or in the sizing activity. Rather, the project manager was given a vague specification, complete with due date and no defined resources. We have named initiation processes of this type *Project Titanic*. Keep in mind the key point here: A project should be formulated with involvement from all key knowledge (stakeholder) sources, and a resulting Project Charter should represent a feasible plan based on requirements scope being balanced against schedule and resource availability. Failure to accomplish this balance early in the life cycle places the project under great stress through the rest of the cycle.

We leave this chapter with one parting thought—as Yogi Berra, the great Yankee catcher, is reported to have said, "If you don't know where you are going, that's where you will end up." Whether Yogi actually said this or not, the point is that management principles require that you have a goal, and the concept of control is based on a plan that defines the goal. This principle is manifested here in the form of a Project Charter or a Statement of Work (usually for contracted work). Don't underestimate the value of this step!

How to Create a Clear Project Plan in Six Easy Steps

ELIZABETH LARSON, PMP AND RICHARD LARSON

Elizabeth Larson and Richard Larson, co-principals of Minneapolis-based Watermark Learning, have over 25 years each of experience in business, project management, business analysis and training/consulting. Contact Elizabeth Larson at elarson@WatermarkLearning.com or Rich Larson at rlarson@ WatermarkLearning.com or call 952-921-0900.

One of the critical factors for project success is having a well-developed project plan. Here is a six-step approach to creating a project plan. It not only provides a roadmap for project managers to follow, but also acts as the project manager's premier communications and control tool throughout the project.

Step 1: Explain the project plan to key stakeholders and discuss its key components.

Unfortunately, the "project plan" is one of the most misunderstood terms in project management. Hardly a fixed object, the project plan is a set of living documents that can be expected to change over the life of the project. Like a roadmap, it provides the direction for the project. And like the traveler, the project manager needs to set the course for the project, which, in project management terms, means creating the project plan. Just as a driver may encounter road construction or new routes to the final destination, the project manager may need to correct the project course as well.

A common misconception is that the plan equates to the project timeline, which is only one of the components of the plan. The project plan is the major work product from the entire planning process, so it contains all the planning documents. For example, a project plan for constructing a new office building needs to include not only the specifications for the building, the budget, and the schedule, but also the risks, quality metrics, environmental impact, etc.

Components of the project plan include:

- *Baselines:* These are sometimes called performance measures because the performance of the entire project is measured against them. They are the project's three approved starting points for scope, schedule, and cost. These provide the stakes in the ground, and are used to determine whether or not the project is on track during execution.
- *Baseline management plans:* These include documentation on how variances will be handled throughout the project.
- *Other work products from the planning process*: These include plans for risk management, quality, procurement, staffing, and communications.

Step 2: Define roles and responsibilities.

Identifying stakeholders—those who have a vested interest in either the project or the project outcome—is challenging and especially difficult on large, risky, high-impact projects. There are likely to be conflicting agendas and requirements among stakeholders, as well as different slants on who needs to be included. For example, the stakeholder list of the city council for which a new office building is being constructed could differ from that of an engineering consulting firm. It would certainly include the developer who wants to build the office complex, the engineering firm that will build the office building, citizens who would prefer a city park, consultants to study the environmental impacts, the city council itself, etc. The engineering firm may have a more limited view. It is important for the project manager to get clarity and agreement on what work needs to be done by whom, as well as which decisions each stakeholder will make.

Step 3: Develop a scope statement.

The scope statement is arguably the most important document in the project plan. It is used to get common agreement among the stakeholders about the project definition. It is the basis for getting the buy-in and agreement from the sponsor and other stakeholders and decreases the chances of miscommunication. This document will most likely grow and change with the life of the project. The scope statement should include:

- Business need and business problem.
- Project objectives, stating what will occur within the project to solve the business problem.
- Benefits of completing the project, as well as the project justification.
- Project scope, stated as which deliverables will be included and excluded from the project.
- Key milestones, the approach and other components as dictated by the size and nature of the project.

It can be treated like a contract between the project manager and sponsor, one that can only be changed with sponsor approval.

Step 4: Develop the project baselines.

Scope baseline. Once the deliverables are confirmed in the scope statement, they need to be developed into a work breakdown structure (WBS) of all the deliverables in the project. The scope baseline includes all the deliverables produced on the project, and therefore identifies all the work to be done. These deliverables should be inclusive. Building an office building, for example, would include a variety of deliverables related to the building itself, as well as such things as impact studies, recommendations, landscaping plans, etc.

Schedule and cost baselines.

1. Identify activities and tasks needed to produce each of the deliverables identified in the scope baseline. How detailed the task list needs to be depends on many factors, including the experience of the team, project risk and uncertainties, ambiguity of specifications, amount of buy-in expected, etc.
2. Identify resources for each task, if known.
3. Estimate how many hours it will take to complete each task.
4. Estimate cost of each task, using an average hourly rate for each resource.

5. Consider resource constraints, or how much time each resource can realistically devote to this one project.

6. Determine which tasks are dependent on other tasks, and develop critical path.

7. Develop schedule, which puts all tasks and estimates in a calendar. It shows by chosen time period (week, month, quarter, or year) which resource is doing which tasks, how much time each task is expected to take, and when each task is scheduled to begin and end.

8. Develop the cost baseline, which is a time-phased budget, or cost by time period.

This process is not a one-time effort. Throughout the project, you will most likely be adding to and repeating some or all of these steps.

Step 5: Create baseline management plans.

Once the scope, schedule, and cost baselines have been established, create the steps the team will take to manage variances to these plans. All these management plans usually include a review and approval process for modifying the baselines. Different approval levels are usually needed for different types of changes. Not all new requests will result in changes to the scope, schedule, or budget, but a process is needed to study all new requests to determine their impact to the project.

Step 6: Communicate!

One important aspect of the project plan is the communications plan. This document states such things as:

- Who on the project wants which reports, how often, in what format, and using what media.
- How issues will be escalated and when.
- Where project information will be stored and who can access it.
- What new risks have surfaced and what the risk response will include.
- What metrics will be used to ensure a quality product is built.
- What reserves have been used for which uncertainties.

Once the project plan is complete, it is important that its contents be delivered to key stakeholders. This communication should include such things as:

- Review and approval of the project plan.
- Process for changing the contents of the plan.
- Next steps—executing and controlling the project plan and key stakeholder roles/responsibilities in the upcoming phases.

Destination Success

Developing a clear project plan takes time. The project manager will probably be tempted to skip the planning and jump straight into execution. However, the traveler who plans the route before beginning a journey ultimately reaches the intended destination more quickly and more easily than the disorganized traveler who gets lost along the way. Similarly, the project manager who takes time to create a clear project plan will follow a more direct route toward project success.

Gaining Visibility and Commitment on Technology Projects

DOUGLAS M. ARNSTEIN

President, Absolute Consulting Group, Inc.

Introduction

I have seen it too often. A technology project gets off to a rocky start, jumps into the middle of a solution, and limps along while all parties hope that it will eventually get straightened out. What results are delays, changes in direction, re-work, cost increases, and occasionally project cancellation. Depending on the size of your institution, your technology project is vying for attention with hundreds of others within your organization. Most likely, the resources assigned to your project are also working on other projects for other project managers. Throw in daily distractions such as production problems, management fire drills, projects that need just 'a little bit' of attention, and dozens of e-mails and voice messages, and it is easy to see how your project can get lost in the 'noise'. I am going to present some practical suggestions as to how you can gain visibility for your project, and how you can obtain commitment from project Stakeholders and participants by using the project planning process and the Project Plan as tools for success. This presentation will provide tips, tool examples, and real-world experiences for differentiating your project from its start to help you meet your ultimate objective: to get the right project done right.

Getting Started: Using the Planning Phase to Gain Visibility and Commitment

The first step in gaining visibility and commitment is to develop a Project Charter and Scope Statement with the Project Sponsor. This document is the vehicle by which you start gathering data about the project, aligning the project with organizational goals, and defining the boundaries of the project. If your organization is high on the Project Management Maturity Model, it is likely that the sponsor organization will have developed a Project Charter and Scope Statement. If that is not the case, your first objective is to interview the Project Sponsor and have him/her articulate the business drivers, project mission, project objectives, other internal organizations with a stake in the outcome, and his/her definition of what constitutes completion of the project. There is much written about this document in project management literature which I will not reiterate here. Here is what I have found to be effective for technology projects.

Keep the document short and direct. Start with the following sections: Introduction, Project Description and Justification, including Business Drivers, Constraints, Stakeholders, Deliverables, Project Objectives for Time, Cost,

Quality, and Scope, Project Resource Roles and Responsibilities, Preliminary Resource Identification, Assumptions, Dependencies, and Issues. This information allows you to begin to coordinate with groups needing to participate on the project. As you assemble the project Core Team, use group work sessions to solicit their input to expand the document beyond the information provided by the Project Sponsor. A tip for the Project Charter and Scope Statement is to use numbered lists for all sections other than the narrative Introduction and Project Description and Justification. These lists provide the relevant information in an easy-to-read manner that facilitates group review of the document.

Review the document first with the Project Sponsor and Sponsor Division Management. This forum gives them the opportunity to validate the project mission and objectives. It engages their support and participation to direct the project from its inception. It lets them know that their input is valued, raising their level of tangible and intangible project ownership. After updating and refining the document with the Sponsor feedback, the second review is with the Project Sponsor and other primary Stakeholders outside the Sponsor Division. It is their first opportunity to hear some detail about the project, understand the impact to their respective areas, and provide feedback to the project about any aspect of the Charter and Scope. This review also presents the opportunity to identify critical success factors for working with their functional areas. This information will prove invaluable as you continue the planning process and design the project.

The next step in developing the Project Plan is to conduct a Stakeholder Analysis. It is an excellent way to engage the project Core Team and elicit their commitment to the project by having them participate. According to the *PMBOK*: Stakeholders are individuals and organizations who are involved in or may be affected by project activities. It is important to the success of the project to understand what they think about the project and how they define success. I have yet to conduct a Stakeholder Analysis without learning something unexpected from an individual Stakeholder that altered some deliverables or affected the project scope of work. What I want to know from each Stakeholder is:

1. Does he/she agree with the project objectives as defined in the Charter and Scope Statement?
2. What does he/she define as the project scope?
3. What does he/she view as project risks?
4. How does he/she define Critical Success Factors for the project?
5. How would he/she define project quality?
6. What, how, and how frequently does he/she want to hear about the project?

Talking to Stakeholders is just that. This is not an e-mail exercise. If you are unable to sit face-to-face with a Stakeholder, use the telephone. Assign each Core Team member several Stakeholder interviews. There are no rules other than to get their feedback. I have used group and solo, directed and non-directed interviews successfully. For non-directed interviews, I merely ask the questions above. For directed interviews, I create an interview sheet with the lists of Project Objectives and Project Scope from the Charter and Scope Statement, share it with the Stakeholder, and solicit concurrence and feedback. For the question topics above that were not part of the Charter and Scope, I ask the open-ended questions. To assist with the evaluation of the feedback, it is important to obtain the same information from all interviewees.

Upon completion of the Stakeholder Analysis, the Core Team evaluates the data and determines whether any Stakeholder feedback should be assimilated into the Project Charter and Scope Statement. The rest of the information will be used to design the project and build the Project Plan. Specifically, Stakeholder feedback will be used in the Risk Management Plan, Quality Management Plan, and Communication Plan sections of the Project Plan. Between developing the Project Charter and Scope Statement and conducting the Stakeholder Analysis, you have given your project visibility, engaged key participants, gained consensus, and started building the Core Team's commitment to the project.

The Project Plan

According to the *PMBOK*, the Project Plan is a formal, approved document used to manage and control project execution. It defines the 'What, Why, Who, When, Where, and How' of your project. It is a text document not to be confused with the Project Task Schedule or Work Breakdown Structure (WBS). Some organizations seldom produce one. This would be true of organizations that skip directly into requirements definition upon starting a project. It is a major oversight to skip this deliverable because regardless of the size of your project, it documents the manner in which the project intends to achieve its objectives. It also helps other internal and external organizations understand what they will need to do and when to support the project.

There is much available literature about Project Plans that I do not intend to survey here. I will present what has worked well for me [when] managing technology projects. The Project Plan should include the following sections: Introduction, Project Charter and Scope Statement, Milestones, Resource Plan, Scope Management and Change Control, Quality Management, Communication Plan, Communication Matrix, and Deliverables Responsibility Matrix. In addition, it could also include sections on Risk Management, Funding, Issues, as well as a preliminary Project Task Schedule or WBS. Any information that you as the project manager feel is relevant to the management and control of the project should be included. The contents of the Project Plan should be controlled by the size and complexity of the project. However, anytime you consider skipping a section, you should rationalize your decision based on what the project could lose by omitting it.

Although the project manager has primary responsibility for producing the Project Plan, it is an excellent team-building exercise for the Core Team. Participating in the Project Plan development gains their commitment early in the project because they can contribute to and influence project processes. Include staff from the Project Sponsor organization and other key functional areas impacted by your project if they are not already members of the Core Team. The Project Plan will be more readily accepted if it is developed as a partnership between the business and technology organizations.

Project Plan Components: Their Purpose and What They Accomplish

THE INTRODUCTION

It is useful to include a short Introduction to the readers of the document that details the Background and Purpose of the document, its structure, the Intended Audience, and the reader's obligations. One of the obligations should be to require formal approval from project Stakeholders, and that should be directly stated.

PROJECT CHARTER AND SCOPE STATEMENT

The Project Plan will be distributed to a wider audience than may have participated in the Project Charter and Scope Statement and Stakeholder Analysis exercises. I have found it beneficial to incorporate the completed Project Charter and Scope Statement in its entirety as the next section. This gives project newcomers a brief, comprehensive overview of the project and sets the stage for the rest of the Project Plan.

MILESTONES WITH PROJECTED DATES

This section uses a combination of significant events and the list of key deliverables developed in the Project Charter and Scope Statement and sets forth projected beginning and ending dates for each. This information sets expectations as to when components of the project work are to be started and completed. At this early stage of the project, these may merely be best estimates based on the Project Sponsor's required implementation dates. Regardless, this information is helpful to project Stakeholders as they begin thinking about resources they will have to provide and when.

RESOURCE PLAN

This section identifies project resource roles and responsibilities. It describes the project organization and how the project will interact with the day-to-day organization. Every organization is unique in the way it organizes projects, and this section will reflect the particulars of your organization. At a minimum, one should provide specific role and responsibility information for the Project Sponsor, the Project Manager, the Project Core Team, any Management Oversight or Steering Committees, and specific Business and Technical resources known to be required for the project. This information should also include project reporting hierarchies and matrix relationships developed for the duration of the project. The more information that can be provided, the more likely you will obtain resources with the correct skills to support the project. I list each role, the responsibilities of the role, the skills required, and the projected start date for the resource. In many projects, the Project Sponsor and/or Project Manager know which individuals are critical to the project's success and have already assigned them to the effort. In these cases, it is appropriate to name the specific individuals.

PROJECT ORGANIZATION CHART

As an adjunct to the Resource Plan, a visual representation of the project team is a helpful tool. It clearly and succinctly communicates the relationships between the project players [7-1]. Your project may have two views of these

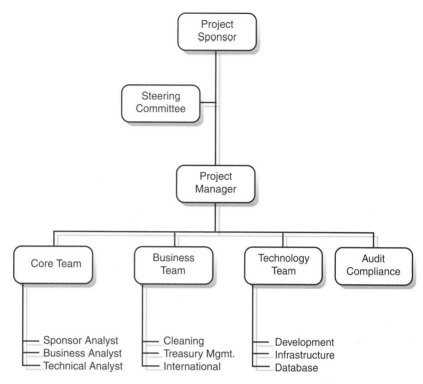

7-1 Project Organization Chart—Team View

relationships. Often the Project Core Team views their roles and relationships somewhat differently than other internal or external organizations. In this case, two project organization charts may be in order, one representing the internal project view, the other representing the external view. For example, the Project Core Team may align itself by the functions that the individuals play on the project, but to the external view [7-2], those same individuals represent business interests of different areas within the financial institution. Having two views of the project is often the best way to communicate these differences.

SCOPE MANAGEMENT AND CHANGE CONTROL

Change is inevitable. Change can hurt your project. The Scope Management and Change Control section documents how your project will manage change. There is much industry literature about Scope Management that I will not present here. I will address the 'how to' of Scope Management. It is critical to identify your project's process for submitting, logging, approving, and adopting Change Requests. By defining this process now, you are communicating the same rules to all project participants and Stakeholders. By including the Core Team members in defining the process, you are also reinforcing that this is their project. All change is not created equal. Projects deal with both trivial and significant change from day one. Projects must also keep moving in order to accomplish the ultimate

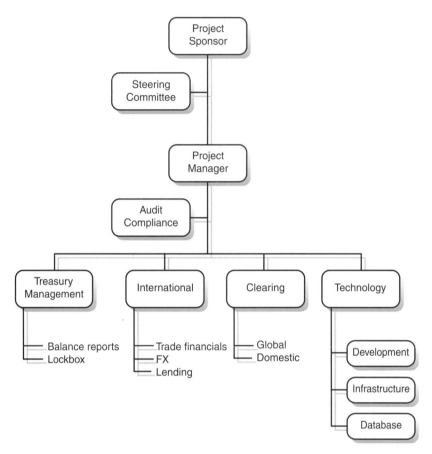

7-2 Project Organization Chart—External View

objectives in the scheduled time, and it is often difficult to engage critical Stakeholders quickly to address every Change Request that is submitted. A tool that I have used successfully to address this issue is to use a Change Control Variance to manage scope.

A Change Control Variance is a set of measurements applied to Project Cost, Schedule, Scope, and Quality. These measurements can be used to define a 'two-tier' process to approve Change Requests. For any Change Request that does not exceed the variance criteria, the Project Core Team is empowered to make the approve/deny decision. Anything that exceeds the variance criteria requires Management to approve/deny the request. An example of a Project Cost Variance would be, 'if the Change Request requires additional staff exceeding one-half staff month ($7,000) in order to meet the implementation date'. An example of a Project Scope Variance would be, 'any Change Request reduces the scope of the project or eliminates tasks'. Defining this two-tier process proved to be another beneficial planning task that brought the Core Team together and engaged Management's support by letting them finalize the variance criteria.

QUALITY PLAN

There has been much focus on project quality lately. Sometimes in a technology project, the definition of quality can be elusive; however, quality can be found and defined. During the Stakeholder Analysis you received feedback from Stakeholders regarding project quality. The Core Team should be able to come up with other ideas. Generally, quality can be defined for an end deliverable, such as the software product, or it can be applied to a process. From a product perspective, quality can be measured in several ways. It can be developing reusable code, defining throughput performance, or integrating the software with organizational infrastructure standards. As for process quality, it can be defined as how the project will conduct a given process so as to produce quality project results. For example, in a Y2K testing project, one financial institution defined quality as having the end users participate in the test planning effort and conduct the actual testing since they knew the system and how they used it best.

The Quality Plan is where your project defines its quality objectives, and its plan for achieving them. These objectives can be defined in Quality Categories. For example, individual deliverables may have their own Quality definitions. In the example above, one could define a category for 'Conducting a quality test of the final software product'. Within this category, it is essential to define how the project will measure testing quality. These measurements can be objective or subjective, which should be noted. In addition, each quality definition must have a Responsible owner for ensuring that it is accomplished. These concepts are illustrated in [7-3] Exhibit 3. The final component of the Quality Plan is scheduled reviews to ensure that the project followed the quality directives. For example, in the definition of a quality testing effort, the project may want to review the quality definition measurements after completion of the Test Plan and Test Scripts, and then again after the completion of the actual Test Execution [7-3].

RISK MANAGEMENT PLAN

This section articulates the project's early understanding of risk. I will not delve into the specifics of risk assessment, but I would like to discuss the appropriate level of activity to spend on it at this point in the project life cycle. Naturally, the project size and complexity will be the main drivers of this activity. The objective at this stage is to identify the risk response development that you want to formally build into the project execution processes. In order to do so, the project team must identify and quantify the risks as normal. In the quantification step, it is important to develop common probability and severity criteria so that all risks can be objectively evaluated to the extent possible. This facilitates the use of a Risk Matrix on which you can plot the identified risks in a 3 by 3 (Low, Medium, High) grid with an x axis of Severity and a y axis of Probability. Once plotted, focus the early risk response development on the Medium-High and High-High risks. These risks may require additional planning or the design of tasks built into the WBS. Include the Risk Matrix and a summary of the findings in this section of the Project Plan. Bear in mind that this is not a substitute for continuing your Risk Management activities throughout the project life cycle [7-4].

Category and Quality Definition	Measurement	Responsible
1. Developing and executing a meaningful test of…		
a) User involvement in testing scope and planning	Objective	John B.
b) User involvement in test execution	Objective	Susan F.
c) Clearly documented tests scripts including: Inputs, Outputs, and Expected Results	Subjective	Paul G.
d) Measure actual test results against expected results	Objective	Paul G.
e) Script-level test sign-off (tester, separate reviewer)	Objective	Maria S.
f) Test plans document "who/what/where/when/how"	Subjective	Paul G.
g) Acceptance criteria clearly defined and measurable	Objective	Susan F.
h) Maintain a problem-tracking system	Objective	John B.
i) Acceptance criteria measured and met	Objective	Paul G.
j) Progress measurement	Objective	John B.
k) Instituting a formal review process	Objective	John B.

7-3 Quality Plan Category and Definitions

Probability				
H	RA6			RA8
M			RA1, RA2, RA4	RA5, TA2
L	RA7		TA3, TA4, TA5	RA3, TA1

Severity

7-4 Risk Matrix

COMMUNICATION PLAN

If you want your project to succeed and be visible throughout its life cycle, communicate, communicate, communicate, and then communicate some more. The Communication Plan section documents the information that you intend to capture and disseminate about project activities. Depending on the practices within your organization, some of it may be predefined, yet other forms may be dictated by the wishes of the Stakeholders or developed by the Core Team. Information captured may include task schedule status, action items, issues, milestone progress, deliverables, deliverable status, meeting minutes or outcomes, and vendor communications. Information disseminated may include deliverables, status reports, current project task schedules, status meeting materials, milestone progress reports, and vendor communications. Certain information loses timeliness quickly, so thought needs to be put into the frequency of distribution for all of your project's communication vehicles. In today's distributed world, there are numerous viable options for receiving and distributing information. When choosing the ones appropriate to your project, listen to what the recipients want. Give them what they want the way they want it. It will elicit their support for the duration of the project. It is a Core Team exercise to define the proposed audience for each vehicle, the frequency of distribution, and the distribution media. After reviewing the completed Project Plan, you can expect that some project participants and Stakeholders will request changes to the Communication Plan. These changes should be accommodated.

Define your project's document standards in the Communication Plan. These include: how you will differentiate document drafts from approval copies, how you will manage version control, how you will identify revisions from prior versions of documents, where you will store hard copy and electronic document versions, how you will prevent unauthorized updates to completed documents, and what you will do with the document repositories after the project has ended. Having the Core Team define these standards makes this another activity that contributes to team commitment.

COMMUNICATION MATRIX

This matrix is a visual representation of the information collected and documented in the Communication Plan. It is a simple tool to develop, easy to read, and it conveys a significant amount of information on one page. The information presented is the Stakeholders, the communication vehicles, the frequency of the distribution, and the media on which the information will be distributed. The Stakeholders are listed along the top of the x axis, and the communication vehicles are listed along the y axis. For each row along the y axis, list the frequency and media of the vehicle and then place an 'X' in the column for each Stakeholder receiving the information [7-5].

DELIVERABLES/RESPONSIBILITY MATRIX

This matrix has the same format as the Communication Matrix, but is focused solely on the Deliverables. Like the Communication Matrix, it is easy to read and conveys a significant amount of information. However, it is not quite as easy to develop because there can be conflict over Deliverable ownership

	Frequency	Media	Name Project Manager	Name Project Sponsor	Name Product Management	Name Information Technician

1. Status Reporting
   Meeting Outcomes
   Action Item Log
   Issue Log
   Project Task Schedule
	Weekly	Electronic	X		X	X

2. Milestone Progress Report	Bi-weekly	Electronic	X	X	X	X
3. Vendor Communications	Upon receipt	Paper	X	X	X	
4. Status Meeting	Weekly	Conference	X		X	X
5. Steering Committee Meeting	Monthly	Conference	X	X		

7-5 Communication Matrix

and approval responsibilities. The purpose of this matrix is to document for each Deliverable the project participants responsible for creating the deliverable, actively supporting the creation, reviewing it, and approving it. Stakeholders are listed along the top of the x axis, and the Deliverables are listed along the y axis. For each row along the y axis, list the target date for Deliverable completion and then place one of five values in the column to identify each Stakeholder's responsibility for the Deliverable. These values represent Primary responsibility for deliverable creation, Support responsibility, Review responsibility, Approval of the Deliverable, or 'blank' for no responsibility.

There can be honest disagreements about Deliverable responsibilities, especially for Approvals. Negotiating acceptable outcomes for the Stakeholders involves engaging their participation in resolving the issue. In respect to assigning responsibilities to individual Deliverables, there should be only one Primary owner for creating a Deliverable. I recommend keeping the number of Approvers for a Deliverable to the essential minimum. Too many Approvers can stall the project at critical times, and collecting Approval signatures gets exponentially more difficult the more Approvers there are. However, do not exclude Stakeholders who have a legitimate need to Approve a Deliverable [7-6].

PROJECT TASK SCHEDULE/WBS WITH PRELIMINARY RESOURCE IDENTIFICATION

Depending on how much is known about the project at this stage, include the Project Task Schedule or WBS in the Project Plan. In many projects the objectives are to implement known technologies within well-understood

Key: P = Primary creator A = Approver of outcome R = Reviewer of outcome S = Supporter of delivery creation	Target Date	Name Project Manager	Name Project Sponsor	Name Product Management	Name Information Technician
1. Project Plan	1/15/00	P	SA	A	A
2. Business Requirements	2/28/00	R	A	P	A
3. Technical Design	4/15/00	R	R	A	P
4. Code and Unit Test	7/31/00	R		A	P

7-6 Deliverables Responsibility Matrix

environments and the scope of work is clear from the beginning. In these situations, it may be straightforward to work with the Core Team to construct the Project Task Schedule or WBS at this stage and present it with identified resources or responsible functional areas for each task. If you are in a situation that is not well defined, document what you know about the schedule or WBS to the extent possible. The more information presented, the better Stakeholders will understand the impact to their respective areas.

FINALIZING THE PROJECT PLAN

Congratulations, you have accomplished a significant amount of work producing the Project Plan. Once your review draft has been completed, distribute it to all project participant groups and Stakeholders and schedule group reviews. Depending on the number of project participants and Stakeholders, you may need to conduct several reviews to cover the entire document with everyone. During these reviews, listen carefully to the feedback and negotiate appropriate changes to the document. Upon completion of the reviews, update the document, identifying the revisions as you defined them in the document standards section of the Communication Plan and re-distribute the Project Plan for approval. All Stakeholders should approve the Project Plan in writing. Post the signatures in the project repository.

It is now a matter of executing the plan. I carry the Project Plan with me and refer to it often throughout the project. I use it to keep participants focused on the agreed-upon project mission and objectives. When disputes arise about scope or deliverables, the Project Plan is an excellent source for revisiting the planning decisions. If a request falls outside the agreed-upon scope, a quick review of the Scope Management and Change Control section sets forth the project's defined process for addressing new requests.

Wrap Up

I have described the project planning process that I have effectively used on technology projects to produce a Project Plan. I have demonstrated how the project planning process can engage project participation and commitment from the Sponsor, Stakeholders, and direct participants. I have described a collaborative planning process that encourages input and ownership from groups affected by the project outcomes. These activities are not complicated. Conducting them gives your project early visibility with the organizations that will be instrumental in achieving your objectives. When you are through with this process, all interested parties will have a clear understanding of the What, Why, Who, When, Where, and How of your project. Happy project planning!

Scope Management

Chapter 8 Contents

Chapter Overview

We view the concept of project scope as being a foundation idea. It establishes the base for much of the subsequent management activities. Material for this section is heavily linked to Chapter Five of the *PMBOK*® *Guide*. The *PMBOK*® *Guide* defines scope as "the sum of the products and services to be provided as a project." Scope is a critical concept in that it consumes resources and time. If scope is allowed to grow, then it follows that budget and schedule overruns will likely occur. Many project managers believe that scope management is the most important management responsibility to keep a project in planned bounds.

There are five defined *PMBOK*® *Guide* activities constituting the Scope knowledge area. These are the following:

- 5.1 Scope Planning
- 5.2 Scope Definition
- 5.5 Create WBS
- 5.6 Scope Verification
- 5.7 Scope Control

The 5.X reference numbers refer to Chapter 5 of the *PMBOK*® *Guide* where Scope Management details are discussed. The first three scope activities occur during the planning phase, while the last two are defined as part of the monitoring and control phases.

SCOPE PLANNING

Scope planning establishes the degree of management formality that a project is to have.

The output of this step is a Scope Management Plan, which provides guidance regarding how project scope will be managed by the project management team.

In addition, the Scope Management Plan contains design strategy for creation of the following project elements:

- Project WBS.
- Change Control process to be used.
- Formal deliverables verification and acceptance process.

The level of management formality for these elements is variable, based on the project's size, complexity, and importance, and this formality will be reflected in the ground rules defined in this step.

SCOPE DEFINITION

Scope definition is an activity used to produce a detailed project scope statement outlining major deliverables, assumptions, and constraints. This activity is a further elaboration of the preliminary scope definition, defined in the *PMBOK® Guide*, produced during the Initiating phase (see Section VI[HJ1]). At this second point, more information is known and the preliminary assumptions and constraints can be examined in greater detail. The major output of this activity is a detailed scope statement defining the deliverables and the work tasks required to create the specified deliverables. This document provides definitive guidance for all participants in the team and establishes a baseline for scope. In addition to the deliverables view, scope definition also relates to other topics such as task definition, project resources, and stakeholders objectives. Schedule and resource accuracy is still limited at this stage, but defined range values are important for project sizing purposes.

In addition to the basic project deliverables and resource estimates, there are other important considerations to be defined at this stage. A summary of these considerations is as follows:

- Process for accepting the output products.
- Statements to define what is included in the project and what is excluded.
- Project constraints that affect the team's options (for example, budgets, schedule, technical resources, equipment, etc.).
- Assumptions that were made during the plan development (for example, a common one states that the planned resources will be made available on the schedule indicated).
- A preliminary risk assessment, which will be updated during subsequent planning steps.
- Initial project organization showing team members and stakeholder roles.
- Approval processes to be employed during the project.

These items are documented in the project management plan which, in turn, is supplemented in content by other knowledge area activities occurring in parallel during the planning phase and beyond. The project plan will be maintained as a common repository of goals and objectives for the project, and it should reflect both the initial plan baseline as well as approved changes during the course of project execution. Any additions, modifications, or revisions to the project plan will be processed through the formal change control process and reflected in the plan.

CREATE WBS

The work breakdown structure (WBS) is a deliverables-oriented hierarchy of subproject components that organizes and defines the total work effort of the project. The WBS is a tangible representation of the detailed project scope statement, and it specifies the work to be accomplished by the project. The work elements defined in the WBS assist the stakeholders in viewing the overall goal of the project. Work elements are subdivided from high-level aggregations to low-level work units that can be accomplished in reasonable time periods; for example, 80 hours or 2–4 weeks in duration.

Kerzner defines a work package as a "natural subdivision of cost accounts." [Kerzner] Work packages appear at the lowest level of the WBS and represent work to be accomplished by a single organizational group. These components are the lowest point in the project structure where work is estimated, scheduled, and tracked. The basic role of the WBS is to identify and document major deliverables of the project, including project management deliverables and those deliverables acquired by contract. Some of the design characteristics of a WBS are as follows:

- Major deliverables or project phases are typically shown at the first level of the structure.
- An associated WBS dictionary documents details of the various elements of the structure, including work packages.
- Work package definition includes a statement of work, associated activities, and any defined milestones. In addition, other relevant project information can be stored here.
- It is common to label the WBS structure with a numbering system that allows cross-references to other project views such as accounting and schedule.

SCOPE VERIFICATION

Scope verification is the process of obtaining stakeholders' formal acceptance of completed project scope. The *PMBOK® Guide* segregates the processes of verification from control. "Scope verification differs from quality control in that it is primarily concerned with *acceptance of the work results*, whereas quality control is primarily concerned with the *correctness of the work results.*" [PMI, 103] Questions related to this point will appear on every PMP exam, and the differences in the two processes are not completely discrete. One way to segregate the two processes is to recognize that the verification process involves reviewing defined deliverables to ensure that they were satisfactorily completed. This is a user view of the output, rather than a measure of quality achieved. Quality control involves the internal measurement and corrective action process focused on adequacy of the process and its associated output. It may be possible for a marginal or out-of-bounds quality process to produce verifiable output from the user view. The quality and verification processes occur in parallel and are collectively intended to ensure both acceptance of the output and correctness (quality).

SCOPE CONTROL

Scope control is "concerned with influencing the factors that create scope changes, assuring all requested changes are processed according to the project integrated change control, and managing the actual changes when they occur." [PMI, 119] Closely related to scope control is the change control system, which, in *PMBOK® Guide* terms, is a formally defined process. This methodology requires that project changes are restricted until they have been through the approved change control steps. Change control is designed to ensure that all project stakeholders are aware of the proposed changes and appropriate groups have been appropriately involved in the decision process. As an example, the addition of a new task might well add risk, cost, schedule, and quality issues to the overall project, as well as other impacts. If this change is approved without proper coordination and review, the results could be disastrous. The change control process is not intended to curtail change because it is recognized that change is inevitable. However, it is intended to ensure that the change is orderly and adds value to the outcome. Scope control output is managed through the Integrated Change Control (ICC) knowledge area. [PMI, 121] The relationship between these two activities can be confusing. Stated simply, the scope control activity recommends changes as a result of its project oversight. For example, a schedule overrun is observed and corrective action is identified by the scope control activity. This information is documented and passed to the ICC where decision resolution occurs (that is, accept or reject the proposal). If it is accepted, it is up to the scope control process to ensure that the change is undertaken as planned. As a byproduct of these actions, the scope control process updates project plans, the WBS, and any other asset information related to the activity. Mature project organizations also formalize lessons learned from such changes and use this information to improve subsequent project activities.

Readings

The readings presented in this chapter are intended to provide a tutorial view on the topic of scope management. The first and second readings in this section are by Rich Schiesser. The first is titled "Change Management—Part I," and it describes the first nine steps of the thirteen required for planning, designing, implementing, and maintaining a robust change management process. Then, in "Change Management—Part II," Schiesser discusses the tenth step, which consists of the actual design of the process and includes the prioritization of changes. The third reading, "Work Breakdown Structure (WBS)," provides a good fundamental view of the work breakdown structure. The author, James Chapman, is one of the dedicated knowledge contributors to the industry and writes on a broad variety of IT topics.

Reference

Kerzner, Harold. *Project Management,* 8th Ed, John Wiley and Sons, 2003.

Change Management—Part I

RICH SCHIESSER

July 29, 2004, Pearson Education, Inc. InformIT, *http://www.informit.com/guides/ content.asp?g=it_management&seqNum=26.*

Reading Overview

This is the first of a three-part series on change management, one of the most critical processes within IT management. A recent survey of 240 senior IT directors at the May 2004 IT Directors' Forum listed change management as the biggest challenge in IT that year. This section introduces the major aspects of this important infrastructure activity. I begin with the definition of change management and explain the subtle but significant difference between change control and change management. Next, I summarize the 13 steps required to design and implement an effective change management process.

The first nine of these steps are preparatory to process design. I discuss each these steps in the remaining portion of this section. Part II will describe in detail step ten, which comprises the actual design of a change management process. Part III will cover the remaining three steps of implementing and maintaining the process, along with a method to assess the change management environment of an IT infrastructure.

Definition of Change Management

Change management is a process to control and coordinate all changes to an IT production environment. Control involves requesting, prioritizing, and approving changes; coordination involves collaborating, scheduling, communicating, and implementing changes.

A change is defined as any modification that could impact the stability or responsiveness of an IT production environment. Some shops use the terms change management and change control synonymously, but there is an important distinction between the two expressions. Change management is the overall umbrella under which change control and change coordination reside. Unfortunately, to many people the term change control has a negative connotation that warrants some further discussion.

To many IT technicians, change control implies restricting, delaying, or preventing change. But to system, network, and database administrators, change is an essential part of their daily work. They view any impediments to change as something that will hinder them as they try to accomplish their everyday tasks. Their focus is on implementing a large number of widely varying changes as quickly and as simply as possible. Since many of these are routine, low-impact changes, technicians see rigid approval cycles as unnecessary, non-value-added steps.

This apparent dichotomy is a challenge to infrastructure managers initiating a formal change management process. They need the individuals who will be most impacted by the process and are the most [suspicious] of it to buy into the process. This is why marketing a change management process properly by pointing out its benefits, and by gaining early buy-in by those most affected by it, is so important.

Steps to Implementing a Change Management Process

There are 13 steps required to implement an effective change management process; they are listed in Figure 1 [8-1]. I discuss each step in some detail and augment where appropriate with examples and forms.

1. Identify executive sponsor.
2. Assign a process owner.
3. Select a cross-functional process design team.
4. Arrange for meetings of the cross-functional process design team.
5. Establish roles and responsibilities for members supporting the design team.
6. Identify the benefits of a change management process.
7. If change metrics exist, collect and analyze them; if not, set up a process to do so.
8. Identify and prioritize requirements
9. Develop definitions of key terms.
10. Design the initial change management process.
11. Develop policy statements.
12. Develop a charter for a change review board (CRB).
13. Use the CRB to continually refine and improve the change management process.

Step 1: Identify an Executive Sponsor

An effective change management process requires the support and compliance of every department in a company that could affect change to an IT production environment. This includes groups within the infrastructure such as technical services, database administration, network services, and computer operations; groups outside of the infrastructure such as the applications development departments; and even areas outside of IT such as facilities.

An executive sponsor must garner support from, and serve as a liaison to, other departments; assign a process owner; and provide guidance, direction, and resources to the process owner. In many instances, the executive sponsor is the manager of the infrastructure, but he or she could also be the manager of the department in which change management resides, or [be] the manager of the process owner.

Step 2: Assign a Process Owner

As I mentioned previously, one of the responsibilities of the executive sponsor is to assign a process owner. The ideal process owner will possess a variety of skills and attributes to accomplish a variety of tasks. These tasks include assembling and leading teams, facilitating brainstorming sessions, conducting change review meetings, analyzing and distributing process

Priority	Requirement
High	1. Need to define workflows.
	2. Need to develop a notification process.
	3. Need to establish rules and responsibilities for the communication process.
	4. Need to determine *when* to communicate *what* to *whom*.
	5. Include IT planning group in initial change implementation review.
	6. Include IT planning group in final change implementation review.
Medium High	7. Need to establish initial base metrics; should include count of total changes made and how many were emergency changes.
	8. Must be enforceable.
	9. Should be reportable.
	10. Leverage existing tools (no requirements for new tools initially).
	11. Ensure management buy-in; communicate process to various staffs.
	12. Include service metrics.
	13. Include process metrics.
	14. Develop management reporting and trending reports.
Medium	15. Initially concentrate only on infrastructure changes.
	16. Process should be scalable.
	17. Include resolution process (that is, conflicts with scheduling or priorities).
	18. Include escalation process.
	19. Empower staffs to enforce policy statements.
	20. Start small, with just infrastructure and operations initially.
Medium Low	21. Establish a systems management department.
	22. Make process easy to comply with and difficult to circumvent; consider rewards for compliance and penalties for avoidance or circumvention.
	23. Agree on a change coordination process definition.
	24. Establish change coordination process policy statements.
	25. Include a priority scheme for scheduling and implementing.
	26. Keep the process simple.
	27. Establish a marketing strategy (what's in it for me [WII-FM]).
Low	28. Eventually extend out to enterprise architecture and planning group.
	29. Present the process in a very positive manner.
	30. Eventually integrate with problem management.

8-1 Figure 1. Steps Required to Develop a Change Management Process

metrics, and maintaining documentation. High on the list of desirable attributes are the abilities to promote teamwork and cooperation and to effectively manage highly diverse groups.

Step 3: Select a Cross-Functional Process Design Team

The success of a change management process is directly proportional to the degree of buy-in from the various groups that will be expected to comply with it. One of the best ways to ensure this buy-in is to assemble a process design team consisting of representatives from key functional areas. The process owner, with support from the executive sponsor, will select and lead this team. It will be responsible for completing several preparatory steps leading to the design of the initial change management process.

Step 4: Arrange for Meetings of the Cross-Functional Process Design Team

This sounds routine but it actually is not. The diversity of a well-chosen team can cause scheduling conflicts, absentee members, or misrepresentation at times of critical decision making. It is best to have consensus from the entire team at the outset as to the time, place, duration, and frequency of meetings. The process owner can then make the necessary meeting arrangements to enact these agreements.

Step 5: Establish Roles and Responsibilities for Members of the Process Design Team

Each individual having a key role in the support of the process design team should have clearly stated responsibilities. The process owner and the cross-functional design team should propose these roles and responsibilities and obtain concurrence from the individuals identified.

Step 6: Identify the Benefits of a Change Management Process

One of the challenges for the process owner and the cross-functional team will be to market the use of a change management process. If an infrastructure is not used to this type of process, this will likely not be a trivial task. Identifying and promoting the practical benefits of this type of process can help greatly in fostering its support. Figure 2 [8-2] lists some examples of common benefits of a change management process.

Step 7: If Change Metrics Exist, Collect and Analyze; If Not, Set Up a Process to Do So

An initial collection of metrics about the types and frequencies of change activity can be helpful in developing process parameters such as priorities, approvals, and lead times. If the existing environment is not producing meaningful metrics, then process design team members should gather some initial set of metrics, even they must collect them manually.

Step 8: Identify and Prioritize Requirements

One of the key preparatory tasks of the cross-functional design team is to identify and prioritize requirements of the change management process. Prioritizing is especially important because budget, time, or resource constraints may prevent all requirements from being met initially. The Strategic Management portion of this guide contains techniques for effectively brainstorming and prioritizing requirements. In Table 1 [not included in this text], I present some examples of prioritized requirements from a composite of prior clients.

1. *Visibility.* The number and types of all changes logged will be reviewed at each week's CRB meeting for each department or major function. This shows the degree of change activity being performed in each unit.

Term	Definition
Change management	The overall process of *controlling* and *coordinating* changes for an IT infrastructure environment.
Change control	The requesting, prioritizing, and approving of any requested *production change* prior to the *change coordination* required for its implementation.
Change coordination	The collaboration, scheduling, communication, and implementation of any requested *production change* to the operations environment to ensure that there is no adverse impact to any production systems and minimal impact to customers. The initial scope of the change coordination process does not include any changes implemented by personnel outside of the infrastructure department.
Production change	Any activity, of either a *planned* or *emergency* nature, that could potentially impact the stability or responsiveness of a company's IT *production environment*.
Planned change	A mandatory change to the *production environment*, which is scheduled at least 24 hours in advance.
Emergency change	An urgent, mandatory change requiring manual intervention within 2 hours to restore or prevent interruption of accessibility, functionality, or acceptable performance to a *production application* or to a support service.
Production environment	Any hardware, software, or documentation (electronic or hard copy) component that directly supports a *production application*.
Production application	Any IT application software system designated as necessary for a company to conduct normal business. This includes all nondevelopment applications and all *critical production applications*.
Critical production applications	Any IT application software system designated as critical for a company to conduct essential business functions. These functions include generating revenue; acquiring, retaining, and delivering services to customers; providing employees' benefits and wages; and paying suppliers.

8-2 Figure 2. Benefits of a Change Management Process

2. *Communication.* The weekly CRB meeting is attended by representatives from each major area. Communication is effectively exchanged among board members about various aspects of key changes, including scheduling and impacts.
3. *Analysis.* Changes that are logged into the access database can be analyzed for trends, patterns, and relationships.

4. *Productivity.* Based on the analysis of logged changes, some productivity gains may be realized by identifying root causes of repeat changes and eliminating duplicate work. The reduction of database administration change is a good example of this.

5. *Proactivity.* Change analysis can lead to a more proactive approach toward change activity.

6. *Stability.* All of the above benefits can lead to an overall improvement in the stability of the production environment. Increased stability benefits customers and support staff alike.

Step 9: Develop Definitions of Key Terms.

Change management involves several key terms that should be clearly defined by the design team at the beginning to avoid confusion and misunderstandings later on. Table 2 [not included in this text] offers some common terms and definitions used by several clients. Planned and emergency changes are especially noteworthy.

This concludes the first of the three-part series on change management. As mentioned previously, Part II will continue with a detailed description of step ten, which comprises the actual design of a change management process. Part III will cover the remaining three steps of implementing and maintaining the process, along with a method to assess the change management environment of an IT infrastructure.

References

ComputerWeekly.com, Change Management Is Biggest Challenge This Year, June 22, 2004.

Jones, John, DeAnne Aguirre, and Matthew Calderone, "Resilience Report-Strategy+ Business," Booz Allen Hamilton, February, 2004.

Schiesser, Rich, *IT Systems Management*, Prentice Hall, 2002.

Change Management—Part II

RICH SCHIESSER

August 5, 2004, Pearson Education, Inc. InformIT. *http://www.informit.com/guides/printerfriendly.asp?g=it_management&seqNum=27*.

Change Management: Process Design

This is the second of a three-part series on change management. Part I described the first nine steps of the 13 required for planning, designing, implementing, and maintaining a robust change management process. This section discusses the tenth step, which consists of the actual design of the process and includes the prioritization of changes, action matrices for approving and communication changes, and a sample change request form.

Designing the Initial Change Management Process

As mentioned in Part I, there are 13 steps needed to implement an effective change management process. Figure 1 [8-3] lists these steps.

This section will focus on step 10, which focuses on the design of the initial change management process. I use the term 'initial' because the process is very much a living entity that expands and alters its scope as infrastructure environments change. Several of my clients decided to pilot their new change management processes using just a small subset of their total IT department changes to get a feel for how the process is going to work. One financial company decided to only process infrastructure hardware changes at the outset. They soon realized that software changes also needed to be included to prevent undocumented and untested changes from jeopardizing system stability. Many companies elect to pilot infrastructure changes first and to add applications development changes later. In my experience, I recommend starting slow and small but to include all departments on the design team who will eventually be participating in the final process.

Step 10: Design the Initial Change Management Process.

This is one of the key activities of the cross-functional team because this is where the team proposes and develops the initial draft of the change management process. The major deliverables produced in this step are a priority scheme, a change request form, a review methodology, and metrics.

The priority scheme should apply to both planned changes and emergency changes (these two categories should have been clearly defined in the previous section). A variety of criteria should be identified to distinguish different levels of planned changes. Typical criteria include quantitative

1. Identify executive sponsor.

2. Assign a process owner.

3. Select a cross-functional process design team.

4. Arrange for meetings of the cross-functional process design team.

5. Establish roles and responsibilities for members supporting the design team.

6. Identify the benefits of a change management process.

7. If change metrics exist, collect and analyze them; if not, set up a process to do so.

8. Identify and prioritize requirements.

9. Develop definitions of key terms.

10. Design the initial change management process.

11. Develop policy statements.

12. Develop a charter for a change review board (CRB).

13. Use the CRB to continually refine and improve the change management process.

8-3 Figure 1. Steps Required to Develop a Change Management Process

items such as the number of internal and external customers impacted, as well as the number of hours to implement and back out the change. The criteria could also include qualitative items such as the degree of complexity and the level of risk.

Some shops employ four different levels of planned changes to offer a broader variety of options. Many shops just starting out with formalized change management begin with a simpler scheme of only two levels. Table 1 [8-4] lists some quantitative and qualitative criteria for four levels of planned changes, and Table 2 [8-5] does the same for two levels.

I have worked with some clients who prefer only the two-level priority scheme, others who prefer only the four-level scheme, and still others who start out with a two-level scheme and then revise it over time to three or four levels. The type of priority scheme an organization uses depends on factors such as how experienced they are with infrastructure processes, the number of changes executed each week, the number and variety of customers, the number and variety of applications, and the ratio of emergency to planned changes. Smaller, less diverse shops usually start with a lower level of priority scheme than larger, more complex shops that use higher-level priority schemes.

After the team determines priority levels, it will need to develop lists of actions to be taken depending on the level of planned or emergency change. These actions include such items as who will approve changes, when the approvals will be made, and who will be notified about the change. Table 3 [8-6 on page 129] shows some sample actions for planned

Descriptors	Priority Level			
	1	2	3	4
Narrative descriptors	Very high Substantial Significant Substantial "A"	High Major Important Principle "B"	Medium Moderate Standard Nominal "C"	Low Minor Optional Time-permitting "D"
Percent of total external customers impacted	>90%	50%–90%	10%–49%	<10%
Type of total external customers impacted	Customers of critical applications	Customers of high-priority applications	Customers of medium-priority applications	Customers of low-priority applications
Percent of internal users impacted	>90%	50%–90%	10%–49%	<10%
Type of internal users impacted	Customers of critical applications	Customers of high-priority applications	Customers of medium-priority applications	Customers of low-priority applications
Critical applications impacted	Yes	No	No	No
Noncritical application downtime required	Yes	Yes	No	No
Amount of additional budget required	>$10,000	<$10,000	0	0
Hours to implement	>8	5–8	1–4	<1
Back out plan required	Yes	Yes	No	No
Hours to back out	>4	<4	n/a	n/a
Broadness of scope	Very high	High	Medium	Low
Extent of impact	Very high	High	Medium	Low
Degree of complexity	Very high	High	Medium	Low
Level of risk	Very high	High	Medium	Low
Strategic value	Very high	High	Medium	Low

8-4 **Table 1.** Criteria for Four Levels of Planned Changes

changes by impact level and time frame. An IT department will customize these actions to suit its individual needs. Similarly, Figure 2 [8-7 on page 129] describes sample actions for emergency changes.

The team next develops a change request form. Two characteristics are always present in such a form: simplicity and accessibility. The form needs

	Impact Level of Planned Changes	
Criteria	**High**	**Low**
Any impact to subscribers	Yes	No
Percent of total external customers impacted	>25%	<25%
Type of total external customers impacted	Customers of critical applications and high- and medium-priority applications	Customers of low-priority applications
Percent of internal users impacted	>50%	<50%
Type of internal users impacted	Customers of critical applications and high- and medium-priority applications	Customers of low-priority applications
Critical applications impacted	Yes	No
Noncritical application downtime required	Yes	No
Amount of additional budget required	>$1000	<$1000
Hours to implement	>4	<4
Back out plan required	Yes	No
Broadness of scope	High	Low
Extent of impact	High	Low
Degree of complexity	High	Low
Level of risk	High	Low
Strategic value	High	Low

8-5 Table 2. Criteria for Two Levels of Planned Changes

to be simple enough to use that minimum explanation is required, yet thorough enough that all pertinent information is provided. The form also needs to be easily accessible to users, preferably through a company's intranet or in a public e-mail folder on a shared drive. Change requests should be stored in a database, preferably a relational database, for subsequent tracking and analysis. Figure 3 [8-8 on page 130] shows a sample change request form.

A recent client of mine involved in law enforcement developed an in-house electronic form for change management that is now widely used in his organization on their intranet. The client has enhanced the form, called eChange, to include electronic signatures, automatic distribution, and provisions for feedback and help commands. If you are interested in

	Impact Level/Time Frame		
Actions	**Low/Anytime**	**High/Prior to Review Meeting**	**High/After Review Meeting**
Types of approvals required	Supervisor of implementer	Supervisor plus two board members or representatives, preferably one familiar with change and one familiar with impact	Change Review Board (CRB)
Advance approval time	1 hour	1 day	At CRB meeting
Advance notification time	n/a	1 day	1 day
Groups to be notifed	n/a	Customers impacted	Customers impacted
Preferred time of change	Anytime	Not prime shift	Not prime shift
Back out plan required	No	Yes	Yes

8-6 Table 3. Action Matrix for Planned Changes

1. If not an emergency change, then follow the actions in the action matrix for planned changes.
2. Implementer or recovery team representative notifies all appropriate parties, including the support center of the emergency change.
3. Recovery team should initiate recovery action within 2 hours.
4. Recovery team should determine problem status update interval for support center.
5. If status interval is exceeded, recovery team representative updates support center.
6. Support center to notify all appropriate parties of the update.
7. Repeat steps #5 and #6 until problem is resolved.
8. Support center issues final resolution to all appropriate parties.
9. Implementer logs activity as an emergency change.
10. CRB issues final disposition of the emergency change at the next meeting of the CRB.
11. Change manager records the board's disposition of the change into the emergency change request record.

8-7 Figure 2. Action Procedure for Emergency Changes

Information Technology Change Request Form

Requester _____ Request Date _____ Priority ____

Summary Description of Change _____

_____

Customers Impacted _____

Systems Impacted _____

Expected Start Date/Time of Change _____ Estimated Duration _____

Actual Date/Time of Change _____ Actual Duration _____

Detailed Description of Change _____

_____

_____

_____

_____

For Low-Priority Changes, Requester's Manager's Approval _____

Disposition of Change _____

For High-Priority Changes, CRB Approval _____

Back Out Plan in Place? _____ Downtime Required? _____

Estimated Time to Back Out? _____ Downtime Notices Sent Out? _____

Final Disposition of Change _____

8-8 Figure 3. Sample Change Management Request Form

more information on this home-grown enhancement, please contact me and I will put you in touch with him.

The next part of this step involves the establishment of metrics for tracking, analyzing, and trending the number and types of planned and emergency changes occurring every week. Shops with robust change management processes place special emphasis on the analysis of these metrics, particularly the ratio of emergency to planned changes.

The final task for the cross-functional team is to devise a methodology for reviewing all changes. Most shops constitute a Change Review Board (CRB) that meets weekly to review the prior week's changes and to discuss upcoming changes. Steps 11 and 12 of this process discuss policy statements and the charter of the CRB, respectively. Part III of this series covers both of these steps in more detail, along with step 13 on how to use the CRB to continually improve the change management process.

References

ComputerWeekly.com, Change Management Is Biggest Challenge This Year, June 22, 2004.

Jones, John, DeAnne Aguirre, and Matthew Calderone, "Resilience Report-Strategy+ Business," Booz Allen Hamilton, February, 2004.

Schiesser, Rich, *IT Systems Management*, Prentice Hall, 2002.

Work Breakdown Structure (WBS)

JAMES R. CHAPMAN

Introduction to the WBS

A Work Breakdown Structure is a results-oriented family tree that captures all the work of a project in an organized way. It is often portrayed graphically as a hierarchical tree, however, it can also be a tabular list of "element" categories and tasks or the indented task list that appears in your Gantt chart schedule. As a very simple example, Figure 1 [8-9] shows a WBS for a hypothetical banquet.

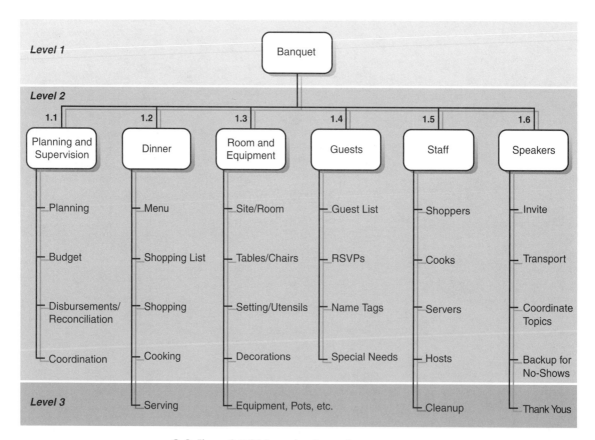

8-9 **Figure 1.** WBS Example—Banquet

Large, complex projects are organized and comprehended by breaking them into progressively smaller pieces until they are a collection of defined "work packages" that may include a number of tasks. A $1,000,000,000 project is simply a lot of $50,000 projects joined together. The Work Breakdown Structure (WBS) is used to provide the framework for organizing and managing the work.

In planning a project, it is normal to find oneself momentarily overwhelmed and confused, when one begins to grasp the details and scope of even a modest-size project. This results from one person trying to understand the details of work that will be performed by a number of people over a period of time. The way to get beyond being overwhelmed and confused is to to break the project into pieces, organize the pieces in a logical way using a WBS, and then get help from the rest of your project team.

The psychologists say our brains can normally comprehend around 7–9 items simultaneously. A project with thousands or even dozens of tasks goes way over our ability to grasp all at once. The solution is to divide and conquer. The WBS helps break thousands of tasks into chunks that we can understand and assimilate. Preparing and understanding a WBS for your project is a big step toward managing and mastering its inherent complexity.

The WBS is commonly used at the beginning of a project for defining project scope, organizing Gantt schedules, and estimating costs. It lives on, throughout the project, in the project schedule and often is the main path for reporting project costs. On larger projects, the WBS may be used throughout the project to identify and track work packages, to organize data for *Earned Value Management (EVM)* reporting, and for tracking deliverables, etc.

History of the WBS

The WBS was initially developed by the U.S. defense establishment, and it is described in Military Standard (MIL-STD) 881B (25 Mar 93) as follows: "A work breakdown structure is a product-oriented family tree composed of hardware, software, services, data and facilities.... [it] displays and defines the product(s) to be developed and/or produced and relates the elements of work to be accomplished to each other and to the end product(s)."

It requires some mental discipline to develop a product-oriented or deliverable-oriented grouping of project elements adding up to comprise the entire project scope. Intuitively, we tend to start out with a task-oriented approach. This is OK for very small projects where extensive project management controls will not be used. The task-oriented approach is easy to understand, because we can easily think of projects as a collection of tasks. A task-oriented WBS can be developed by beginning with a simple "to-do" list and then clustering the items in a logical way. The logical theme could be project phases, functional areas, or major end-products.

If your organization will be collecting historical data to form a cost database, you should try to select a standard approach consistent with the organization's long-term data collection needs.

A sample WBS is shown in the figure that follows [8-10] on the next page.

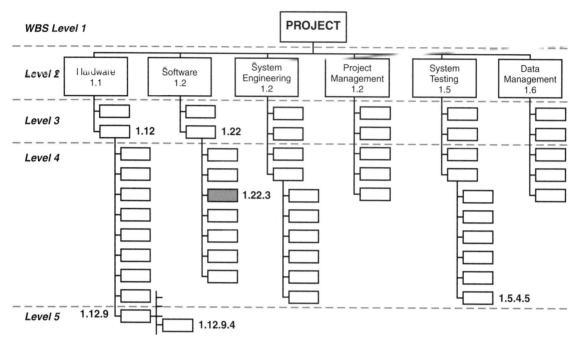

WBS Level 1

Level 2

Level 3

Level 4

Level 5

8-10 WBS Format for System Development Projects

Additional level 2 elements not shown here might include development of environment support, logistics and training, and installation and startup. This next link will take you to a skeleton *sample WBS* for a software and hardware system development project, and you can also download a zipped version of the corresponding MS-Project 2002 (.mpp) file.

A WBS for a large project will have multiple levels of detail, and the lowest WBS element will be linked to functional area cost accounts that are made up of individual work packages. Whether you need three levels or seven, work packages should add up through each WBS level to form the project total.

Product or Process Oriented?

The WBS was initially defined as a product-oriented family tree, however subsequent definitions have introduced more flexibility—so a WBS can also be deliverable or process oriented. Your WBS can be built on nouns or verbs. If the results of your project are primarily verbs, then a verb-based or process-based WBS may make more sense. If your WBS is to be product or deliverable oriented, then you can start by thinking of the WBS as a parts list for the ultimate end-items of your project. This link will give a simple illustration of a *product or process* based WBS orientation. These differences are not shown to tell you what is the right way for your project, but just to familiarize you with the distinctions, so you can think about them and choose what's best for your project.

WBS Numbering

WBS elements are usually numbered, and the numbering system may be arranged any way you choose. The conventional numbering system is shown in the figure. The shaded box shown in the above slide could be numbered 1.2.2.3, which would tell you it was in the second box in level 2, the second box in level 3, and the third box in level 4.

WBS Dictionary

If a WBS is extensive and if the category content is not obvious to the project team members, it may be useful to write a WBS dictionary. The WBS dictionary describes what is in each WBS element, and it may also say what is not in an element, if that is unclear. Here is a sample of a WBS dictionary description:

WBS Element 1.5.4.5.—Systems Integration Test Equipment Planning—This element includes the effort to identify requirements and specify types and quantities of test equipment needed to support the System Integration and Test process. It does not include the design or procurement of such equipment, which is covered in Element 1.5.4.6.

Mapping WBS for Cost Management

In a product-oriented WBS, functional categories of work may form "cost accounts" within a WBS element. Cost account managers are responsible for a functional area's contribution to a WBS element. Cost accounts from several departments or functions may combine into one WBS element.

Internal department planning for a cost account will be made up of individual work packages. A work package will typically have its own budget and schedule. Work packages should be small enough to be executed by individuals or small groups in a single department, and they should be of relatively short schedule duration. A small project might define a maximum work package size as two weeks of effort. Larger projects will assemble larger work packages that can be appropriately managed and controlled.

The project manager will have to decide to what degree employment of various details of WBS implementation will benefit the efficient management of the project. On a very small project, a formal WBS may serve no useful purpose, but it can become valuable if project size or complexity start to increase.

As an organization's project management environment matures, or as larger size and complexity are encountered, application of the WBS concept can evolve from an ad hoc list of tasks, to time-phased activity lists, task lists clustered by project deliverables and services, or an end-product–focused WBS fed by cost accounts and work packages [8-11].

If you are using MS-Project or a similar project management software application, you may encounter the WBS as a vertical list with indents to show structure. This will be compatible with the Gantt View data entry screens. While some software packages provide a separate WBS view, you could prepare your WBS in the vertical format using a word processor, and then cut and paste your WBS into your project management software package.

WBS Elements

8-11 WBS Elements

Program and Contract WBSs

A top-level WBS for a large program is sometimes called a Program WBS (PWBS) or Program Summary WBS (PSWBS). If a project involves several organizational participants or contractors, guidance for one contractor can be provided in a Contract WBS (CWBS). The project manager may provide a high-level CWBS for each developer, perhaps to level 2 or level 3. The developer will then fill in the details of lower WBS levels to reflect the work to be accomplished and the data flow in that organization.

Organizational Standards

Your organization may want to decide on a standard WBS format or group of formats, use these across all projects, and communicate definitions widely so everyone will be speaking the same language. This can save re-learning project lessons and can lay the groundwork for successful data gathering to aid future cost estimates.

WBS Implementation

When you set up a project WBS, think about how you will be using it later in the project. Try to consider how you will organize the WBS, schedule format, manager assignments, and charge numbers, in your early project planning. These days, the WBS in smaller projects ends up automatically being the indent structure in your Gantt schedule, so pay attention to those indents, and make sure that is the WBS you want for rolling up costs in your project, especially if you will be using EVM. It will be helpful if you can map the charge numbers, managers, and task groups to each other. This will help you track costs and progress for each manager. If your project schedule will on MS-Project, you may want to insert "text" columns into your schedule (Gantt View) for project charge numbers and manager names.

If your project charge numbers cannot be linked to groups of tasks assigned to specific managers, you will have no way to provide performance measurement feedback to managers.

Some project management environments have definite conventions for grouping items in a WBS. The best method is to have a WBS that works for your particular project environment. The WBS should be designed with consideration for its eventual uses. Your WBS design should try to achieve certain goals:

- Be compatible with how the work will be done and how costs and schedules will be managed.
- Give visibility to important or risky work efforts.
- Allow mapping of requirements, plans, testing, and deliverables.
- Foster clear ownership by managers and task leaders.
- Provide data for performance measurement and historical databases.
- Make sense to the workers and accountants.

There are usually many ways to design a WBS for a particular project, and there are sometimes as many views as people in the process. Experience teaches that everyone takes a slightly different slice of the apple, so make sure WBS arguments seeking metaphysical certainty are quickly brought to closure. Simple practicality, combined with enlightened trial and error, usually is the best approach.

Generating a WBS from Microsoft Project

There is a third-party add-on software application for MS-Project called *WBS Chart Pro* that will convert your Gantt chart task list with indents into a standard WBS graphic in a few clicks. You can also use this application to create a WBS and transfer it back to MSP. I have found this software very valuable in organizing project work into a WBS, reviewing the scope of proposed projects, and helping managers visualize the WBS implicit in their MS-Project schedules.

PMI Practice Guide for WBS

The Project Management Institute (PMI) has a document, Project Management Institute Practice Standard for Work Breakdown Structures, that provides examples of WBS formats commonly used in several different project areas, construction, defense, etc. From the PMI Web site, upper-right corner, click Publications & Information Resources, then click Bookstore. A key word search for Work Breakdown Structure will bring up this standard and other references.

CHAPTER 9

Quality Management

Chapter 9 Contents

Chapter Overview

Few management topics have sparked as much thought and excitement in the field of management as quality. All American consumers experienced quality concepts in the auto wars of the past several years as we watched the Japanese competitors extract market share from traditional American car builders. Names such as Honda and Toyota became familiar household terms as a result of demonstrated quality difference from their U.S. counterparts. Ironically, the Japanese experience was led by American consultants who could not find willing participants at home. Edward Deming is the name most associated with this international movement. However, other pioneers such as Philip Crosby and Ishikawa also helped mature the movement. Crosby particularly got management attention with his phrase that "quality is free." His work convinced many organizations to make the commitment to quality and ignore the initial implementation overhead. As the quality movement eventually became recognized, the U.S. government sponsored the Baldridge Award to reward organizations that had made the most progress in their quality initiatives. This award was an attempt to make the movement visible and stimulate U.S. organizations to become more competitive. The manufacturing organizations that were able to remain in business during this period did, in fact, make significant improvements. However, it is still recognized that the Japanese generally remain ahead in their use of disciplined quality processes.

Running in parallel to this movement in the durable manufacturing segment was the recognition inside IT organizations that their typical development processes did not produce adequate output quality. The most noticeable implication was the number of measured discrepancies in completed software compared to that found in comparative rigorously managed processes. The U.S. programmer would typically produce code with five errors per 1,000 lines of code, while a Japanese counterpart would do the same job with fewer than one error per 1,000 lines of code. Also, the U.S. process would consume 25% or more of the development cycle, mostly caused by the activity related to filtering out the bad code. Thus it came to be recognized in IT organizations, just as in the manufacturing segment, that quality needs to be built into the product and not simply inserted later through inspection.

The U.S. Department of Defense and the Software Engineering Institute (SEI) have been notable in pioneering processes and measurement techniques to document the positive results of standardized processes and early error detection. Prior to the new focus on quality, the IT process was equivalent to the traditional automobile industry: inspect the final product, identify all of the errors, and then work to repair the damage. In the modern approach, a quality system is designed to start with worker attitude toward the product, build quality into the product early in the process, and filter out errors as early as possible before they become expensive to find and repair. Another aspect of the modern approach is to define the level of quality desired. In other words, quality is not an absolute term and there is recognition that quality requires resources to achieve. So, there must be a proper balance between these two variables.

Beyond the basic quality methods used in the code production process, there was an increased view that quality is an organizational attitude. This implies that processes should be continually improved. Therefore, the definition of process quality will also change as improvements are installed. Many organizations developed quality programs in the attempt to infuse this culture into their fabric. Programs such as *Zero Defects, Six Sigma,* and *Quality Is Free* represent this phase of the movement.

The *PMBOK® Guide* approaches the quality initiative along the lines described above. Three specific activities are defined in Chapter 8 of this document. These are:

- 8.1 Quality Planning: Identifying which quality standards are relevant to the project and determining how to satisfy them.
- 8.2 Perform Quality Assurance: Applying the planned, systematic quality activities to ensure that the project employs all processes needed to meet requirements.
- 8.3 Perform Quality Control: Monitoring specific project results to determine whether they comply with relevant quality standards and identifying ways to eliminate causes of unsatisfactory performance (PMI, 179).

There is a subtlety in processes 8.2 and 8.3. The term quality assurance deals with the confirmation that the product meets user requirements, while quality control determines how well the process is working compared to standards. Recognize that a process could be out of control and still meet user requirements. Much has been written about the U.S. quality movement over the past several years. Our selected articles simply scratch the surface on this topic. Authors such as Schwalbe, Kerzer, and others should be consulted for more on this subject.

Readings

Readings presented in this section show different facets of the quality issue, either through examining the importance of quality to organizations or through the means that managers should use to ensure that their organizations deliver quality products. In the first reading, "The 10 Most Powerful Principles for Quality in Software and Software Organizations," Thomas Gilb presents a set of principles based on best practices. He argues that these principles will help managers improve the quality of the software their teams deliver. In the second reading, "An Early Start to Testing: How to Test Requirements," Suzanne Robertson discusses how many software problems stem from incomplete, vague, missing, or wrong requirements. To address this problem, she presents a set of tests for evaluating requirements before developers begin trying to satisfy them with physical software products. This reading maps to the earlier point that errors in definition need to be identified as early as possible. In this case, the key is to link testing to requirements so that user expectations can be better met.

Keep in mind as you read through the readings in this section and others that quality is more than producing good code. It is an improved process; it is a happier customer; it could even be making an existing set of code run better as a result of user training. Think of it as an organizational attitude and not a better coding language or development tool.

The 10 Most Powerful Principles for Quality in Software and Software Organizations

TOM GILB

The software industry knows it has a problem: The industry's maturity level with respect to "numbers" is known to be poor. While solutions abound, knowing which solutions work is the big question. What are the most fundamental underlying principles in successful projects? What can be done right now? The first step is to recognize that all your quality requirements can and should be specified numerically. This does not mean "counting bugs." It means quantifying qualities such as security, portability, adaptability, maintainability, robustness, usability, reliability, and performance. This article presents 10 powerful principles to improve quality that are not widely taught or appreciated. They are based on ideas of measurement, quantification, and feedback.

All projects have some degree of failure, compared with initial plans and promises. Far too many software projects fail totally. In the mid 1990s, the U.S. Department of Defense (DoD) estimated that about half of its software projects were total failures [1]. The civil sector is no better [2]. So what can be done to improve project success? This article outlines 10 key principles of successful software development methods that characterize best practices.

These 10 principles have been selected because there is practical experience showing that they really gain control over qualities and their costs. They have a real track record spanning decades of practice in companies like IBM, Hewlett Packard, and Raytheon. They are not new: They are classic. But the majority of our community is young and experientially new to the game, so my job is to remind the industry of the things that work well. Your job is to evaluate this information and start getting the improvements that your management wants in terms of quality and the time and effort needed to get them.

"Those who do not learn from history are doomed to repeat it" [3].

Principle 1: Use Feedback

The practice of gaining experience from formal feedback methods is decades old, and many appreciate its power. However, far too many software engineers and their managers are still practicing low feedback methods, such as waterfall project management (also known as Big Bang or Grand Design). Even many textbooks and courses continue to present low feedback methods. This is not done in conscious rejection of high feedback methods but from ignorance of the many successful and well-documented projects that have detailed the value of high feedback methods.

141

Methods using feedback succeed; those without feedback seem to fail. Feedback is the single most powerful principle for software engineering. (Most of the other principles in this article support the use of feedback.) Feedback helps you get better control of your project by providing facts about how things are working in practice. Of course, the presumption is that the feedback comes early enough to do some good; rapid feedback is the crux. We need to have the project time to make use of the feedback (for example, to radically change direction, if that is necessary). Four of the most notable rapid high-feedback methods are discussed in the following sections.

DEFECT PREVENTION PROCESS

The Defect Prevention Process (DPP) equates to the Software Engineering Institute's Capability Maturity Model® (CMM®) Level 5 as practiced at IBM from 1983 to the present [4]. The DPP is a successful way to remove the root causes of defects. In the short term (one year) about a 50 percent defect reduction can be expected; within two to three years, about a 70 percent reduction (compared to the original level) can be experienced; and in five to eight years, about a 95 percent defect reduction is possible [5].

The key feedback idea is to decentralize the initial causal analysis activity by investigating defects back to the grassroots programmers and analysts. This gives you the true causes and acceptable, realistic change suggestions. Deeper cause analysis and measured process-correction work can then be undertaken outside of deadline-driven projects by the more specialized and centralized process improvement teams.

There are many feedback mechanisms. For example, same-day feedback is obtained from the people working with the specification, and early numeric process change-result feedback is obtained from the process improvement teams.

INSPECTION METHOD

The Inspection Method originated at IBM in work carried out by M. Fagan, H. Mills (cleanroom method), and R. Radice (CMM inventor) [6]. Originally, it primarily focused on bug removal in code and code-design documents. Many continue to use it this way today. However, inspection has changed character in recent years. Today, it can be used more cost-effectively by focusing on measuring the significant defects on upstream specifications. Furthermore, sample areas often only need to be inspected rather than processing the entire document [7]. For example, the defect level measurement should be used to decide whether the entire specification is fit for release downstream to be used for a go/no-go decision-making review or for further refinement (test planning, design, or coding).

The main Inspection Method feedback components are as follows:

- Feedback to author from colleagues regarding compliance with software standards.
- Feedback to author about required levels of standards compliance in order to consider their work releasable.

EVOLUTIONARY PROJECT MANAGEMENT

Evolutionary Project Management (Evo, which originated in large scale within cleanroom methods) has been successfully used on the most demanding space and military projects since 1970 [8, 9]. The DoD changed its software engineering standard MIL-STD-2167A to an Evo standard (MIL-STD-498), which derived succeeding public standards, (for example, the Institute of Electrical and Electronics Engineers). The reports (op. cit.), along with my own experience, are that Evo results in a remarkable ability to deliver on time and on budget, or better, compared to conventional project management methods [2].

An Evo project is consciously divided into small, early, and frequently delivered stakeholder result-focused steps. Each step delivers benefits and builds toward satisfaction of the final requirements. Step size is typically weekly or 2 percent of total time or budget. This results in excellent regular and realistic feedback about the team's ability to deliver meaningful, measurable results to selected stakeholders. The feedback includes information on design suitability, stakeholders' reactions, requirements' trade-offs, cost estimation, time estimation, people resource estimation, and development process aspects.

STATISTICAL PROCESS CONTROL

Statistical Process Control [10], although widely used in manufacturing [11], is only used in software work to a limited degree. Some use is found in advanced inspections [5, 12]. The Plan Do Study Act cycle is widely appreciated as a fundamental feedback mechanism.

Principle 2: Identify Critical Measures

It is true of any system—your body, an organization, a project, software, or service product—that there are several factors that can cause a system to die. Managers call these critical success factors. If you analyzed systems looking for all the critical factors that cause shortfalls or failures, you would get a list of factors needing better control. They would include both stakeholder values (such as serviceability, reliability, adaptability, portability, and usability) and the critical resources needed to deliver those values (that is, people, time, money, and data quality). For each critical factor, you would find a series of faults that would include the following:

- Failure to systematically identify all critical stakeholders and their critical needs.
- Failure to define the factor measurably. Typically, only buzzwords are used and no indication is given of the survival (failure) and target (success) measures.
- Failure to define a practical way to measure the factor.
- Failure to contract measurably for the critical factor.
- Failure to design toward reaching the factor's critical levels.
- Failure to make the entire project team aware of the numeric levels needed for the critical factors.
- Failure to maintain critical levels of performance during peak loads or on system growth.

Our entire culture and literature of software requirements systematically fails to account for the majority of critical factors. Usually, only a handful, such as performance, financial budget, and deadline dates, are specified. Most quality factors are not defined quantitatively at all. In practice, all critical measures should always be defined with a useful scale of measure. However, people are not trained to do this and managers are no exception. The result is that our ability to define critical breakdown levels of performance and manage successful delivery is destroyed from the outset

Principle 3: Control Multiple Objectives

You do not have the luxury of managing qualities and costs at whim. With software development, you cannot decide to manage just a few of the critical factors and avoid dealing with the others. You have to deal with all the potential threats to your project, organization, or system. You must simultaneously track and manage all the critical factors. If not, then the forgotten factors will probably be the very reasons for project or system failure.

I have developed the Impact Estimation (IE) method (Table 1 [9-1]) to enable tracking of critical factors; however, it does require that critical objectives and quantitative goals have been identified and specified. Given that most software engineers have not yet learned to specify all their critical factors quantitatively (Principle 2), this next step, tracking progress against quantitative goals to enable control of multiple objectives (this principle), is usually impossible.

IE is conceptually similar to Quality Function Deployment [13], but it is much more objective and numeric. It gives a picture of reality that can be monitored [14, 15] (Table 1 [9-1]). It is beyond the scope of this article to provide all the underlying detail for IE. To give a brief outline, the percentage estimates in Table 1 [9-1] are based, as far as possible, on source-quoted, credibility—evaluated, objective, documented evidence. IE can be used to evaluate ideas before their application, and it can also be used, as in Table 1 [9-1], to track progress toward multiple objectives during an evolutionary project. In Table 1 [9-1], the Actual Difference and Total numbers represent feedback in small steps for the chosen set of critical factors that management has decided to monitor. If the project is deviating from plans, this will be easily visible and can be corrected in the next step.

Principle 4: Evolve in Small Steps

Software engineering is by nature playing with the unknown. If we already had exactly what we needed, we would reuse it. When we choose to develop software, there are many types of risk that threaten the result. One way to deal with this is to tackle development in small steps, one step at a time. If something goes wrong, we will immediately know it. We also have the ability to retreat to the previous step, a level of satisfactory quality, until we understand how to progress again.

It is important to note that the small steps are not mere development increments. The point is that they incrementally satisfy identified stakeholder requirements (Figure 1 [9-2]). Early stakeholders might be salespeople needing a working system for demonstration, system installers/help desk/service/testers who need to work with something, or early trial users.

The duration of each small step is typically a week or so. The smallest widely reported steps are the daily builds used at Microsoft, which are

	STEP 1 Plan A: (Design: X, Function: —Y)	STEP 1 Actual	STEP 1 Difference (— is bad; + is good)	STEP 1 Total	STEP 2 Plan B: (Design: Z, Design: F)	STEP 2 Actual	STEP 2 Difference	STEPS 1 and 2 Total	STEP 3 Next Step Plan
Reliability 99%–99.9%	50% ±50%	40%	−10%	40%	30% ±20%	20%	−10%	60%	0%
Performance 11 sec–1 sec	80% ±40%	40%	−40%	40%	30% ±50%	30%	0	70%	30%
Usability 30 min–30 sec	10% ±20%	12%	+2%	12%	20% ±15%	5%	−15%	17%	83%
Capital Cost 1 million	20% ±1%	10%	+10%	10%	5% ±2%	10%	−5%	20%	5%
Engineering Hours 10,000	2% ±1%	4%	−2%	4%	10% ±2.5%	3%	+7%	7%	5%
Calendar Time	1 wk	2 wk	−1 wk	2 wk	1 wk	0.5 wk	+0.5 wk	2.5 wk	1 wk

9-1 Table 1. Example of an Impact Estimation Table

useful-quality systems. They cumulate to six- to 10-week shippable quality milestones [16].

Principle 5: A Stitch in Time Saves Nine

Quality control must be done as early as possible, from the earliest planning stages, to reduce the delays caused by finding defects later. There needs to be strong specification standards (such as all quality requirements must be quantified) and rigorous checking to measure that the rules are applied in practice. When the specifications are not of some minimum standard (like ">1 major defect/page remaining"), then they must be edited until they become acceptable, including the following:

- Use inspection sampling to keep costs down, and to permit early, i.e., before specification completion, correction and learning.
- Use numeric exit from development processes such as Maximum 0.2 Majors per page.

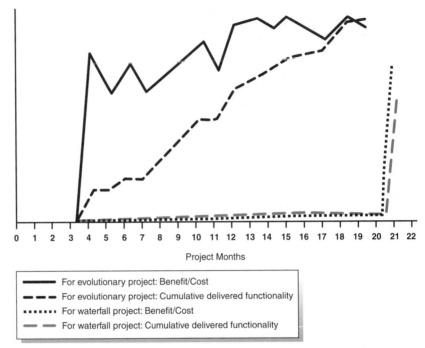

Project Months

———	For evolutionary project: Benefit/Cost
— — —	For evolutionary project: Cumulative delivered functionality
·······	For waterfall project: Benefit/Cost
— —	For waterfall project: Cumulative delivered functionality

Note: One advantage of Evo is that you can focus on delivering high-value increments to critical stakeholders early. The upper line represents high value at early stages (17).

9-2 Figure 1. Evolutionary vs. Waterfall Comparison

It is important that quality control by inspection be done very early for large specifications, for example, within the first 10 pages of work. If the work is not up to standard, then the process can be corrected before more effort is wasted. I have seen half a day of inspection (based on a random sample of three pages) show that there were about 19 logic defects per page in 40,000 pages of air traffic control logic design. The same managers who had originally approved the logic design for coding carried out the inspection with my help. Needless to say, the project was seriously late.

In another case I facilitated (United States, 1999, jet parts supplier), eight managers sampled two pages out of an 82-page requirements document and measured 150 major defects per page. Unfortunately, they had failed to do such sampling three years earlier when the project started, so they had already experienced one year of delay; they told me they expected another year delay while removing the injected defects from the project. This two-year delay was accurately predictable given the defect density they found and the known average cost from major defects. They were amazed at this insight, but agreed with the facts. In theory, they could have saved two project years by doing early quality control against simple standards: clarity, unambiguity, and no design in requirements.

These are not unusual cases. I find them consistently all over the world. Management frequently allows extremely weak specifications to go unchecked into costly project processes. They are obviously not managing properly.

Principle 6: Motivation Moves Mountains

Motivation is everything! When individuals and groups are not motivated positively, they will not move forward. When they are negatively motivated (fear, distrust, and suspicion), they will resist change to new and better methods. Motivation is a type of method. In fact, there are many large and small items contributing to your group's sum of motivation. We can usefully divide the motivation problem into four categories:

- The will to change.
- The knowledge to change direction.
- The ability to change.
- The feedback about progress in the desired change direction.

Leaders (I did not say managers) create the will to change by giving people a positive and fun challenge and the freedom and resources to succeed. During the 1980s, John Young, CEO of Hewlett Packard, inspired his troops by saying that he thought they needed to aim to be measurably 10 times better in service and product qualities by the end of the decade. He did not demand it. He supported them in doing it. They reported getting about 9.95 times better, on average, in the decade. The company was healthy and competitive during a terrible time for many others.

The knowledge of directional change is critical to motivation; people need to channel their energies in the right direction! In the software and systems world, this problem has three elements, two of which have been discussed in earlier principles. They are as follows:

- Measurable, quantified clarity of the requirements and objectives of the various stakeholders (Principle 2).
- Knowledge of all the multiple critical goals (Principle 3).
- Formal awareness of constraints such as resources and laws.

These elements are a constant communication problem because of the following:

- We do not systematically convert our directional changes into crystal-clear measurable ideas; people are unclear about the goals and there is no ability to obtain numeric feedback about movement in the right direction. We are likely to say we need a robust or secure system, and less likely to convert these rough ideals into concrete, measurable, defined, agreed-upon requirements or objectives.
- We focus too often on a single measurable factor (such as percent built or budget spent) when reality demands that we simultaneously track multiple critical factors to avoid failure and to ensure success. We do not understand what we should be tracking, and we do not get enough rich feedback.

Principle 7: Competition Is Eternal

Our conventional project management ideas strongly suggest that projects have a clear beginning and a clear ending. In our competitive world, this is not as wise a philosophy as one W. Edwards Deming suggests,

"Eternal process improvement is necessary as long as you are in competition" [11]. We can have an infinite set of milestones or evolutionary steps of result delivery and use them as we need; the moment we abandon a project, we hand opportunity to our competitors. They can sail past our levels of performance and take our markets.

The practical consequence is that our entire mindset must always be on setting new ambitious numeric stakeholder value targets both for our organizational capability and our product and service capabilities (Figure 2 [9-3]).

Continuous improvement efforts in the software and services area at IBM, Raytheon, and others [4, 5, 18] show that we can improve critical cost and performance factors by 20 to one, in five- to eight-year time frames. Projects must become eternal campaigns to get and stay ahead.

Principle 8: Things Take Time

"It takes two to three years to change a project, and a generation to change a culture" [11].

Technical management needs to have a long-term plan for improving the critical characteristics of their organization and their products. Such long-term plans need the ability to be tracked numerically and stated in multiple critical dimensions. At the same time, visible short-term progress toward those long-term goals should be planned, expected, and tracked (Figure 3 [9-4]).

Principle 9: The Bad with the Good

Any method (means, solution, or design) you choose will have multiple quality and cost impacts whether you like them or not! In order to get a correct picture of how good any idea is for meeting our purposes, we must do the following:

- Have a quantified, multidimensional specification of our requirements, our quality objectives, and our resources (people, time, or money).
- Have knowledge of the expected impact of each design idea on all these quality objectives and resources.

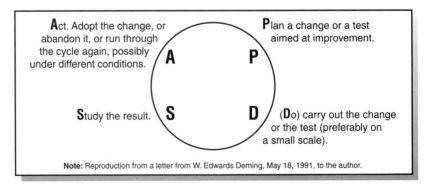

Note: Reproduction from a letter from W. Edwards Deming, May 18, 1991, to the author.

9-3 Figure 2. The Shewhart Cycle for Learning and Improvement—the PDSA Cycle

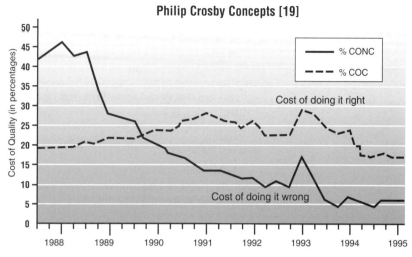

Cost of quality = CONC (cost of nonconformance) + COC (cost of conformance)
CONC = Cost of fix and check fix
COC = Appraisal and prevention
Project cost = {Cost of quality + Cost of performance}
Cost of performance = {Planning, documentation, specification}

Note: In the case of Raytheon process improvements (Dion, 1995), many years of persistent process change for 1000 programmers were necessary to drop rework costs from 43% of total software development costs to below 5%.

9-4 Figure 3. Cost of Quality vs. Time: Raytheon 95—the Eight-Year Evolution of Rework Reduction

- Evaluate each design idea with respect to its total—expected or real—impact on our requirements, the unmet objectives, and the unused cost budgets.

We need to estimate all impacts on our objectives. We need to reduce, avoid, or accept negative impacts. We must avoid simplistic one-dimensional arguments. If we fail to use this systems engineering discipline, then we will be met with unpleasant surprises of delays and bad quality, which seem to be the norm in software engineering today. One practical way to model these impacts is using an IE table (see Table 1 [9-1]).

Principle 10: Keep Your Eyes on Where You Are Going

"Perfection of means and confusion of ends seem to characterize our age," said Albert Einstein.

To discover the real problem, we have only to ask of a specification: Why? The answer will be a higher level of specification, nearer the real ends. There are too many designs in our requirements!

You might say, why bother? Isn't the whole point of software to get the code written? Who needs high-level abstractions? Cut the code! But somehow that code is late and of unsatisfactory quality. The reason is often lack of attention to the real needs of the stakeholders and the project. We need these high-level abstractions of what our stakeholders need so that we can focus on giving them what they are paying us for! Our task is to design and deliver the best technology to satisfy their needs at a competitive cost.

One day, software engineers will realize that the primary task is to satisfy their stakeholders. They will learn to design toward stakeholder requirements (multiple simultaneous requirements). One day we will become real systems engineers and realize there is far more to software engineering than writing code.

Conclusion

Motivate people toward real results by giving them numeric feedback frequently and the freedom to use any solution that gives those results. It is that simple to specify. It is that difficult to do.

References

[1]Jarzombek, Stanley J. "The 5th Annual Joint Aerospace Weapons Systems Support, Sensors, and Simulation Symposium (JAWS S3)." Proceedings, 1999.

[2]Morris, Peter W. G. The Management of Projects. Ed. Thomas Telford. London, 1994.

[3]Santayana, George. *The Life of Reason.* Amherst: Prometheus Books, 1903.

[4]Mays, Robert. *Practical Aspects of the Defect Prevention Process.* (Gilb, Tom, and Dorothy Graham. Software Inspection. Addison-Wesley, 1993. Chapter 17 written by Mays).

[5]Dion, Raymond, et. al. The Raytheon Report. Pittsburgh: Software Engineering Institute, 1995, *www.sei.cmu.edu/publications/documents/95.reports/95.tr.017.html.*

[6]Fagan, Michael E. "Design and Code Inspections." IBM Systems Journal 15.3 (1976): 182–211. Reprinted 38.2, 3 (1999): 259–287, *www.almaden.ibm.com/journal.*

[7]Gilb, Tom, and Dorothy, Graham. *Software Inspection.* Addison-Wesley, 1993. Japanese Translation, Aug. 1999.

[8]Mills, Harlan D. IBM Systems Journal. 1980. Also republished IBM Systems Journal, Nos. 2 and 3, 1999.

[9]Cotton, Todd. "Evolutionary Fusion: A Customer-Oriented Incremental Life Cycle for Fusion." Hewlett-Packard Journal 47.4 (Aug. 1996): 25–38.

[10]Shewhart, Deming, Juran 1920s.

[11]Deming, W. Edwards. Out of the Crisis. Cambridge: MIT CAES Center for Advanced Engineering Study, 1986.

[12]Florac, William A., Robert, E. Park, and Anita, D. Carleton. Practical Software Measurement: Measuring for Process Management and Improvement. Pittsburgh: Software Engineering Institute, *www.sei.cmu.edu.*

[13]Akao, Yoji. *Quality Function Deployment: Integrating Customer Requirements into Product Design.* Cambridge: Productivity Press, 1990.

[14]Gilb, Tom. *Principles of Software Engineering Management.* Boston: Addison-Wesley, 1988.

[15]Gilb, Tom. *Competitive Engineering.* United Kingdom. Addison-Wesley, 2000, *www.resultplanning.com.*

[16]Cusumano, Michael A., and Richard, W. Selby. *Microsoft Secrets: How the World's Most Powerful Software Company Creates Technology, Shapes Markets, and Manages People.* The Free Press (a division of Simon and Schuster), 1995.

[17]Woodward, Stuart. "Evolutionary Project Management." IEEE Computer Oct. 1999. 49–57.

[18]Kaplan, Craig, Ralph Clark, and Victor, Tang. *Secrets of Software Quality, 40 Innovations From IBM*. McGraw Hill, 1994.

[19]Crosby, Philip B. *Quality Is Still Free: Making Quality Certain in Uncertain Times*. McGraw Hill, 1996.

About the Author

Tom Gilb has been a freelance consultant since 1960 and is the author of nine books, including Software Metrics, Principles of Software Engineering Management, Software Inspection, *and the forthcoming* Competitive Engineering. *Gilb teaches and consults worldwide with major multinational clients including Nokia, Ericsson, Motorola, HP, IBM, BAE Systems, Philips, Sony, Canon, Intel, and Microsoft and does pro bono training and consulting for the Department of Defense, United Kingdom, NATO, and the Norwegian Defense.*

[®]*Capability Maturity Model and CMM are registered in the U.S. Patent and Trademark Office.*

An Early Start to Testing: How to Test Requirements

SUZANNE ROBERTSON

This paper was presented to EuroSTAR '96, Amsterdam December 2–6, 1996.

Reading Overview

We accept that testing the software is an integral part of building a system. However, if the software is based on inaccurate requirements, then despite well-written code, the software will be unsatisfactory. The newspapers are full of stories about catastrophic software failures. What the stories don't say is that most of the defects can be traced back to wrong, missing, vague, or incomplete requirements. We have learnt the lesson of testing software. Now we have to learn to implement a system of testing the requirements before building a software solution.

This paper describes a set of requirements tests that cover relevance, coherency, traceability, completeness, and other qualities that successful requirements must have. The tests have their starting point with the criterion that each requirement has at least one quality measure. This measure is used to test whether any given solution satisfies, or does not satisfy, the requirement.

Requirements seem to be ephemeral. They flit in and out of projects, they are capricious, intractable, unpredictable, and sometimes invisible. When gathering requirements, we are searching for all of the criteria for a system's success. We throw out a net and try to capture all these criteria. Using Blitzing, Rapid Application Development (RAD), Joint Application Development (JAD), Quality Function Deployment (QFD), interviewing, apprenticing, data analysis, and many other techniques [6], we try to snare all of the requirements in our net.

The Quality Gateway

As soon as we have a single requirement in our net we can start testing. The aim is to trap requirements-related defects as early as they can be identified. We prevent incorrect requirements from being incorporated in the design and implementation where they will be more difficult and expensive to find and correct. [5]

To pass through the quality gateway and be included in the requirements specification, a requirement must pass a number of tests. These tests are concerned with ensuring that the requirements are accurate, and do not cause problems by being unsuitable for the design and implementation stages later in the project.

I will discuss each of the following requirements tests in a stand-alone manner. Naturally, the tests are designed to be applied to each of the requirements in unison.

Make the Requirement Measurable

In his work on specifying the requirements for buildings, Christopher Alexander [1] describes setting up a quality measure for each requirement:

> *"The idea is for each requirement to have a quality measure that makes it possible to divide all solutions to the requirement into two classes: those for which we agree that they fit the requirement and those for which we agree that they do not fit the requirement."*

In other words, if we specify a quality measure for a requirement, we mean that any solution that meets this measure will be acceptable. Of course it is also true to say that any solution that does not meet the measure will not be acceptable.

The quality measures will be used to test the new system against the requirements. The remainder of this paper describes how to arrive at a quality measure that is acceptable to all the stakeholders.

Quantifiable Requirements

Consider a requirement that says "The system must respond quickly to customer enquiries." First we need to find a property of this requirement that provides us with a scale for measurement within the context. Let's say that we agree that we will measure the response using minutes. To find the quality measure we ask: "under what circumstances would the system fail to meet this requirement?" The stakeholders review the context of the system and decide that they would consider it a failure if a customer has to wait longer than three minutes for a response to his enquiry. Thus "three minutes" becomes the quality measure for this requirement.

Any solution to the requirement is tested against the quality measure. If the solution makes a customer wait for longer than three minutes, then it does not fit the requirement. So far so good: we have defined a quantifiable quality measure. But specifying the quality measure is not always so straightforward. What about requirements that do not have an obvious scale?

Non-Quantifiable Requirements

Suppose a requirement is "The automated interfaces of the system must be easy to learn." There is no obvious measurement scale for "easy to learn." However, if we investigate the meaning of the requirement within the particular context, we can set communicable limits for measuring the requirement.

Again we can make use of the question: "What is considered a failure to meet this requirement?" Perhaps the stakeholders agree that there will often be novice users, and the stakeholders want novices to be productive within half an hour. We can define the quality measure to say "a novice user must be able to learn to successfully complete a customer order transaction within 30 minutes of first using the system." This becomes a quality measure, provided a group of experts within this context is able to test whether the solution does or does not meet the requirement.

An attempt to define the quality measure for a requirement helps to rationalise fuzzy requirements. Something like "the system must provide good value" is an example of a requirement that everyone would agree with, but each person has his own meaning. By investigating the scale that must be used to measure "good value" we identify the diverse meanings.

Sometimes by causing the stakeholders to think about the requirement we can define an agreed quality measure. In other cases we discover that there is no agreement on a quality measure. Then we substitute this vague requirement with several requirements, each with its own quality measure.

REQUIREMENTS TEST 1

Does each requirement have a quality measure that can be used to test whether any solution meets the requirement?

Keeping Track

Figure 1 [9-5] is an example of how you can keep track of your knowledge about each requirement.

By adding a quality measure to each requirement we have made the requirement visible. This is the first step to defining all the criteria for measuring the goodness of the solution. Now let's look at other aspects of the requirement that we can test before deciding to include it in the requirements specification.

Description: Short (1 sentence) description of the requirement

Purpose: Why is this requirement considered to be important?

Owner(s): Who raised this requirement?

Quality Measure: Unambiguous test for whether a solution meets the requirement

Value: Customer value 1 (frill) 10 (essential)

Type: Functional or nonfunctional?

Unique identifier: Tag for tracking the requirement

Dependency: Existence/change dependencies on the requirements

---

9-5 Figure 1. This requirement's micro spec makes your requirements knowledge visible. It must be recorded so that it is easy for several people to compare and discuss individual requirements and to look for duplicates and contradictions.

Coherency and Consistency

When a poet writes a poem he intends that it should trigger off rich and diverse visions for everyone who reads it. The requirements engineer has the opposite intention: he would like each requirement to be understood in the same way by every person who reads it. In practice, many requirements specifications are more like poetry, and are open to any interpretation that seems reasonable to the reader. This subjectivity means that many systems are built to satisfy the wrong interpretation of the requirement. The obvious solution to this problem is to specify the requirement in such a way that it is understood in only one way.

For example, in a requirements specification that I assessed, I found the term "viewer" in many parts of the specification. My analysis identified six different meanings for the term, depending on the context of its use. This kind of requirements defect always causes problems during design and/or implementation. If you are lucky, a developer will realize that there is inconsistency, but will have to re-investigate the requirement. This almost always causes a ripple effect that extends to other parts of the product. If you are not lucky, the designer will choose the meaning that makes most sense to him and implement that one. Any stakeholder who does not agree with that meaning then considers that the system does not meet the requirement.

REQUIREMENTS TEST 2

Does the specification contain a definition of the meaning of every essential subject matter term within the specification?

I point you in the direction of abstract data modeling principles [7] which provide many guidelines for naming subject matter and for defining the meaning of that subject matter. As a result of doing the necessary analysis, the term "viewer" could be defined as follows:

Viewer

> *A person who lives in the area which receives transmission of television programs from our channel.*
>> *Relevant attributes are:*
>>> *Viewer Name*
>>> *Viewer Address*
>>> *Viewer Age Range*
>>> *Viewer Sex*
>>> *Viewer Salary Range*
>>> *Viewer Occupation Type*
>>> *Viewer Socio-Economic Ranking*

When the allowable values for each of the attributes are defined, it provides data that can be used to test the implementation.

Defining the meaning of "viewer" has addressed one part of the coherency problem. We also have to be sure that every use of the term "viewer" is consistent with the meaning that has been defined.

REQUIREMENTS TEST 3

Is every reference to a defined term consistent with its definition?

Completeness

We want to be sure that the requirements specification contains all the requirements that are known. While we know that there will be evolutionary changes and additions, we would like to restrict those changes to new requirements, and not have to play "catch-up" with requirements that we should have known about in the first place. Thus, we want to avoid omitting requirements just because we did not think of asking the right questions. If we have set a context [10, 11] for our project, then we can test whether the context is accurate. We can also test whether we have considered all the likely requirements within that context.

The context defines the problem that we are trying to solve. The context includes all the requirements that we must eventually meet: it contains anything that we have to build, or anything we have to change. Naturally if our software is going to change the way people do their jobs, then those jobs must be within the context of study. The most common defect is to limit the context to the part of the system that will be eventually automated [3]. The result of this restricted view is that nobody correctly understands the organization's culture and way of working. Consequently, there is a misfit between the eventual computer system and the rest of the business system and the people that it is intended to help.

REQUIREMENTS TEST 4

Is the context of the requirements wide enough to cover everything we need to understand?

Of course this is easy to say, but we still have to be able to test whether or not the context is large enough to include the complete business system, not just the software. ("Business" in this sense should mean not just a commercial business, but whatever activity—scientific, engineering, artistic—the organization is doing.) We do this test by observing the questions asked by the systems analysts: Are they considering the parts of the system that will be external to the software? Are questions being asked that relate to people or systems that are shown as being outside the context? Are any of the interfaces around the boundary of the context being changed?

Another test for completeness is to question whether we have captured all the requirements that are currently known. The obstacle is that our source of requirements is people. And every person views the world differently according to his own job and his own idea of what is important, or what is wrong with the current system. It helps to consider the types of requirements that we are searching for:

- Conscious Requirements
  - Problems that the new system must solve

- Unconscious Requirements
  - Already solved by the current system

- Undreamed of Requirements
  - Would be a requirement if we knew it was possible or could imagine it

Conscious requirements are easier to discover because they are uppermost in the stakeholders' minds. Unconscious requirements are more difficult to discover. If a problem is already satisfactorily solved by the current system, then it is less likely for it to be mentioned as a requirement for a new system. Other unconscious requirements are often those relating to legal, governmental, and cultural issues. Undreamt of requirements are even more difficult to discover. These are the ones that surface after the new system has been in use for a while. "I didn't know that it was possible; otherwise I would have asked for it."

REQUIREMENTS TEST 5

Have we asked the stakeholders about conscious, unconscious, and undreamed-of requirements?

Requirements engineering experience with other systems helps to discover missing requirements. The idea is to compare your current requirements specification with specifications for similar systems. For instance, suppose that a previous specification has a requirement related to the risk of damage to property. It makes sense to ask whether our current system has any requirements of that type, or anything similar. It is quite possible, indeed quite probable, to discover unconscious and undreamed-of requirements by looking at other specifications.

We have distilled experience from many projects and built a generic requirements template [12] that can be used to test for missing requirement types. I urge you to look through the template and use it to stimulate questions about requirements that otherwise would have been missed. Similarly, you can build your own template by distilling your own requirements specifications, and thus uncover most of the questions that need to be asked.

Another aid in discovering unconscious and undreamed-of requirements is to build models and prototypes to show people different views of the requirements. Most important of all is to remember that each stakeholder is an individual person. Human communication skills are the best aid to complete requirements [2].

REQUIREMENTS TEST 5 (ENLARGED)

Have we asked the stakeholders about conscious, unconscious, and undreamed-of requirements? Can you show that a modeling effort has taken place to discover the unconscious requirements? Can you demonstrate that brainstorming or similar efforts have taken place to find the undreamed-of requirements?

Relevance

When we cast out the requirements gathering net and encourage people to tell us all their requirements, we take a risk. Along with all the requirements that are relevant to our context, we are likely to pick up impostors. These irrelevant requirements are often the result of a stakeholder not understanding the goals of the project. In this case, people, especially if they have had bad experiences with another system, are prone to include requirements "just in case we need it." Another reason for irrelevancy is personal bias. If a stakeholder is particularly interested or affected by a subject, then he might think of it as a requirement even if it is irrelevant to this system.

REQUIREMENTS TEST 6

Is every requirement in the specification relevant to this system?

To test for relevance, check the requirement against the stated goals for the system. Does this requirement contribute to those goals? If we exclude this requirement, then will it prevent us from meeting those goals? Is the requirement concerned with subject matter that is within the context of our study? Are there any other requirements that are dependent on this requirement? Some irrelevant requirements are not really requirements; instead they are solutions.

Requirement or Solution?

When one of your stakeholders tells you he wants a graphic user interface and a mouse, he is presenting you with a solution not a requirement. He has seen other systems with graphic user interfaces, and he wants what he considers to be the most up-to-date solution. Or perhaps he thinks that designing the system is part of his role. Or maybe he has a real requirement that he has mentally solved by use of a graphic interface. When solutions are mistaken for requirements then the real requirement is often missed. Also the eventual solution is not as good as it could be because the designer is not free to consider all possible ways of meeting the requirements.

REQUIREMENTS TEST 7

Does the specification contain solutions posturing as requirements?

It is not always easy to tell the difference between a requirement and a solution. Sometimes there is a piece of technology within the context and the stakeholders have stated that the new system must use this technology. Things like: "the new system must be written in COBOL because that is the only language our programmers know," and "the new system must use the existing warehouse layout because we don't want to make structural changes" are really requirements because they are genuine constraints that exist within the context of the problem.

For each requirement ask "Why is this a requirement?" Is it there because of a genuine constraint? Is it there because it is needed? Or is it the solution to a perceived problem? If the "requirement" includes a piece of technology, and it could be implemented by another technology, then unless the specified technology is a genuine constraint, the "requirement" is really a solution.

Stakeholder Value

There are two factors that affect the value that stakeholders place on a requirement. The grumpiness that is caused by bad performance, and the happiness that is caused by good performance. Failure to provide a perfect solution to some requirements will produce mild annoyance. Failure to meet other requirements will cause the whole system to be a failure. If we understand the value that the stakeholders put on each requirement, we can use that information to determine design priorities.

REQUIREMENTS TEST 8

Is the stakeholder value defined for each requirement?

Pardee [9] suggests that we use scales from 1 to 5 to specify the reward for good performance and the penalty for bad performance. If a requirement is absolutely vital to the success of the system then it has a penalty of 5 and a reward of 5. A requirement that would be nice to have but is not really vital might have a penalty of 1 and a reward of 3. The overall value or importance that the stakeholders place on a requirement is the sum of penalty and reward. In the first case a value of 10, in the second a value of 4.

The point of defining stakeholder value is to discover how the stakeholders really feel about the requirements. We can use this knowledge to make prioritization and trade-off decisions when the time comes to design the system.

Traceability

We want to be able to prove that the system that we build meets each one of the specified requirements. We need to identify each requirement so that we can trace its progress through detailed analysis, design, and eventual implementation. Each stage of system development shapes, repartitions, and organizes the requirements to bring them closer to the form of the new system. To insure against loss or corruption, we need to be able to map the original requirements to the solution for testing purposes.

REQUIREMENTS TEST 9

Is each requirement uniquely identifiable?

In the micro spec in Figure 1 we see that each requirement must have a unique identifier. We find the best way of doing this is simply to assign a number to each requirement. The only significance of the number is that it is that requirement's identifier. We have seen schemes where the requirements are numbered according to type or value or whatever, but these make it difficult to manage changes. It is far better to avoid hybrid numbering schemes and to use the number purely as an identifier. Other facts about the requirement are then recorded as part of the requirements micro spec.

Order in a Disorderly World

We have considered each requirement as a separately identifiable, measurable entity. Now we need to consider the connections between requirements and to understand the effect of one requirement on others. This means we need a way of dealing with a large number of requirements and the complex connections between them. Rather than trying to tackle everything simultaneously, we need a way of dividing the requirements into manageable groups. Once that is done we can consider the connections in two phases: the internal connections between the requirements in each group; and then the connections between the groups. It reduces the complexity of the task if our grouping of requirements is done in a way that minimizes the connections between the groups.

Events or use cases provide us with a convenient way of grouping the requirements [4, 8, 11]. The event/use case is a happening that causes the system to respond. The system's response is to satisfy all of the requirements that are connected to that event/use case. In other words, if we could string together all the requirements that respond to one event/use case, we would have a mini-system responding to that event. By grouping the requirements that respond to an event/use case, we arrive at groups with strong internal connections. Moreover, the events/use cases within our context provide us with a very natural way of collecting our requirements.

Figure 2 [9-6] illustrates the relationships between requirements. The event/use case is a collection of all the requirements that respond to

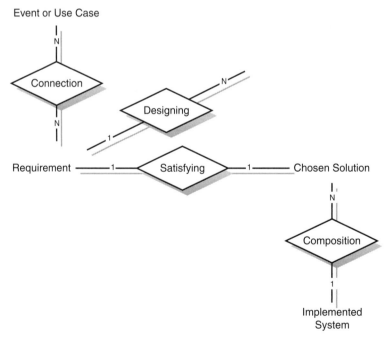

9-6 Figure 2. The Event/Use Case provides a natural grouping for keeping track of the relationships between requirements.

the same happening. The n-to-n relationship between Event/Use Case and Requirement indicates that while there are a number of Requirements to fulfill one Event/Use Case, any Requirement could also contribute to other Events/Use Cases. The model also shows us that one Requirement might have more than one Potential Solution but it will only have one Chosen Solution.

The Event/Use Case model provides us with a number of small, minimally-connected systems. We can use the event/use case partitioning throughout the development of the system. We can analyze the requirements for one event/use case, design the solution for the event/use case, and implement the solution. Each requirement has a unique identifier. Each event/use case has a name and number. We keep track of which requirements are connected to which events/use cases using a requirements tool or spreadsheet. If there is a change to a requirement we can identify all the parts of the system that are affected.

REQUIREMENTS TEST 10

Is each requirement tagged to all parts of the system where it is used? For any change to requirements, can you identify all parts of the system where this change has an effect?

Conclusions

The requirements specification must contain all the requirements that are to be solved by our system. The specification should objectively specify everything our system must do and the conditions under which it must perform. Management of the number and complexity of the requirements is one part of the task.

The most challenging aspect of requirements gathering is communicating with the people who are supplying the requirements. If we have a consistent way of recording requirements, we make it possible for the stakeholders to participate in the requirements process. As soon as we make a requirement visible we can start testing it and asking the stakeholders detailed questions. We can apply a variety of tests to ensure that each requirement is relevant, and that everyone has the same understanding of its meaning. We can ask the stakeholders to define the relative value of requirements. We can define a quality measure for each requirement, and we can use that quality measure to test the eventual solutions.

Testing starts at the beginning of the project, not at the end of the coding. We apply tests to assure the quality of the requirements. Then the later stages of the project can concentrate on testing for good design and good code. The advantages of this approach are that we minimize expensive rework by minimizing requirements-related defects that could have been discovered, or prevented, early in the project's life.

References
[1]Alexander, Christopher. *Notes On The Synthesis Of Form*. Harvard Press. Cambridge, Massachusetts, 1964.

[2]Gause, Donald and Gerald Weinberg. *Exploring Requirements*. Dorset House. New York, 1989.

[3]Jackson, Michael. *Software Requirements and Specifications*. Addison-Wesley, London, 1996.

[4]Jacobson, Ivar. *Object-Oriented Software Engineering*. Addison-Wesley. 1992.

[5]Jones, Caspar. *Assessment and Control of Software Risks*. Prentice Hall, 1994.

[6]Maiden, Neil and Gordon Rugg. Acre: Selecting Methods for Requirements Acquisition. Software Engineering Journal, May 1996.

[7]Mellor, Steve and Sally Schlaer. *Object-Oriented Systems Analysis: Modelling the World in Data*. Prentice Hall, New Jersey, 1988.

[8]McMenamin, Steve and John Palmer. *Essential Systems Analysis*. Yourdon Press. New York, 1984.

[9]Pardee, William J. *How To Satisfy & Delight Your Customer*. Dorset House. New York, 1996.

[10]Robertson, James. On Setting the Context. The Atlantic Systems Guild, 1996. *www.atlsysguild.com/Site/James/Context.html*.

[11]Robertson, James and Suzanne. *Complete Systems Analysis: the Workbook, the Textbook, the Answers*. Dorset House. New York, 1994.

[12]Robertson, James and Suzanne. Requirements Template. The Atlantic Systems Guild. London, 1966.

Risk Management

Chapter 10 Contents

Chapter Overview

Of the nine PMBOK knowledge areas, Risk Management is likely the most foreign and least used by the IT community. For that reason, in this chapter we are including more material on this topic. Most project practitioners rationalize and discuss each of the other eight knowledge areas in more substance and detail than Risk Management. The normal approach is to handle the risk situation as it occurs rather than spend time in the planning or pre-development phases to deal with risk. In defense of this mode of operation, we believe that the process of understanding mechanically how to analyze and manage risk is just now reaching a usable stage of maturity in the IT project world. This is somewhat surprising in that IT projects are noted for their complexity and risk. Yet, formal risk assessments are seldom seen in project plans. The initial step in moving toward a more formalized risk management environment is to identify the potential sources of negative events and then address those events with appropriate tactics for mitigation.

Notice in Figure 1 [10-1] that the risk assessment process flows iteratively through three major stages (essentially equivalent to the *PMBOK*® *Guide* view). In the course of managing a project, this process would be continually monitored and updated.

The *PMBOK*® *Guide* defines six major risk processes: planning, identification, qualitative analysis, quantitative analysis, response planning, and monitoring and control. As the project unfolds, there is a continual monitoring of event status and timely correction actions are taken. Risk management is an ongoing process, and it is not known when using the *PMBOK*® *Guide* whether a correct decision was made regarding an event until it is completed or passed. The *PMBOK*® *Guide* defines project risk as "... an

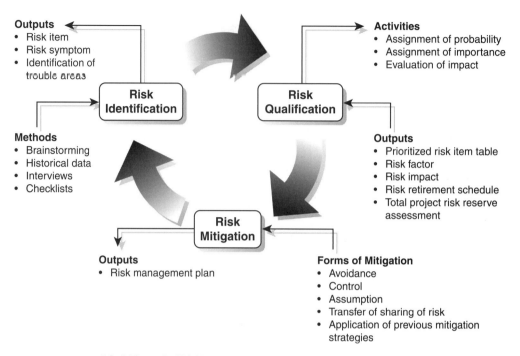

10-1 Figure 1. Risk Management Process

uncertain event or condition that, if it occurs, has a positive or a negative effect on at least one project objective." [*PMI* 2000]

Risks are categorized as either known or unknown; they tend to fall into broad groupings around technical, project management, organizational, or external factors. The most obvious risk in a project is that of not achieving the estimated task parameters (cost and schedule). Assume that estimates show that it will take X to perform a task, only to find out later that it took 2X. Negative repercussions on the project result when cost and schedule estimates are too low. The failure of a vendor to deliver in a timely fashion can have a similar impact. These are just a couple of the typical risk situations that can occur during the course of project execution. A good risk assessment process reviews a broader set of events and establishes strategies to deal with them appropriately.

One of the major players in the field of industry standards is the non-profit Committee on Sponsoring Organizations (COSO). This organization is currently providing needed definition and leadership in the areas of internal control and risk management. Toward that end they have formalized vocabulary and operational strategies regarding these topics. [COSO] Publications from COSO and other standards bodies are periodically released. The interested reader should identify the major standards bodies and track current thinking on key topics. As an example of evolutionary changes, COSO started out focused primarily on internal controls but later added risk management to their scheme. The project manager needs to be aware of such changes as they execute the project life cycle.

Readings

Readings presented in this chapter provide a breadth of viewpoints on the topic of risk management. Unfortunately, space limitations prevent a thorough exploration of this subject. Nevertheless, the readings presented do provide a solid foundation.

The first reading, "Psst—Want to Take a Risk?," walks through the risk management steps. One of the most important points offered here is the list of probable risk types. This would make a good checklist for use in starting the risk identification process. Also, the authors show an introductory example of risk quantification. The second reading "Risk Management (Is Not) for Dummies," comes from the military perspective, but the message is global. This reading outlines steps to consider regarding accomplishing risk management at both the system and enterprise levels. In the third reading, "Enterprise Risk Management: A Framework for Success," the authors introduce the concept of structuring the risk management process at the enterprise level. This provides another perspective regarding how this topic is evolving. The *PMBOK® Guide* focuses its risk view at the project level, but standards bodies are now moving that view upward to encompass the whole organization. Given that perspective, the project view would have to evolve into this broader perspective in the future.

Each of the presented sources provides a different perspective on this complex topic. There are many other authors who could have been selected, but we believe that this group sets the proper stage for understanding the importance of the topic in project management. Once this process has been energized within an organization, there are various assessment and control tools that can be used to analyze and present results. Various tools and templates are described on vendor- and project-related Internet sites (see our listing of Web sites in the Appendix). These support sources will assist in carrying out a risk management process. Be aware that there are many third-party vendors selling support products for this knowledge area, but also recognize that the tool selection step should be the final consideration for any of the knowledge areas.

Reference

COSO, Committee of Sponsoring Organizations of the Treadway Commission, Reference *www.coso.org*.

READING 1

Psst—Want to Take a Risk?

REX LOVELADY, PMP, AND A. ANDREW ANDERSON

Abstract

Any project manager has the responsibility to make formal judgments and timely decisions that will lead the project to successful completion within cost and on schedule—a difficult task in an environment that is continually changing and filled with uncertainty and risk. Managing risk is an integral part of managing a project, even in the absence of a formal risk management process. A more disciplined approach, however, enhances the ability of the project manager to more effectively deal with the project unknowns and uncertainty. It provides a means to identify project risks and to develop strategies, which either significantly reduce them or take steps to avoid them altogether.

Introduction

Organizational survival in today's world is achieved by pursuing opportunity within a spectrum of uncertainty, and projects are typically launched to take advantage of these opportunities. Thus, the whole point of undertaking a project is to achieve or establish something new, to venture, to take chances, so risk has always been an intrinsic part of project work. However, in today's markets, with heavy competition, advanced technology, and tough economic conditions, risk has assumed significantly greater proportions. The goals of risk management, therefore, are to identify project risks and develop strategies which either significantly reduce them or take steps to avoid them altogether. At the same time, steps should be taken to maximize associated opportunities. In essence, it involves planning which minimizes the probability and net effects of things going wrong, and carefully matches responsibility to residual risks, which are unavoidably retained. It is a very constructive and creative process.

Preliminary Work

Before risks can be identified, mitigated, or managed at all, certain preliminary work must be accomplished in order to form the foundation for structured project information. These preliminary steps encompass the identification of work scope, schedule, resources, cost elements, and performance measures.

One of the most effective methods of defining work scope is the development of the Work Breakdown Schedule (WBS). The WBS displays the products, services, and data items to be developed for the project in a hierarchical arrangement that relates the WBS elements to each other and to the end product. It provides essential definition for schedule and cost baselines, change control mechanisms, cost tracking, contractual actions, and logical execution of work. The project WBS clearly and explicitly identifies all project deliverables from which to base project estimates for schedules, resources, costs, and performance measures.

The WBS is the essential element necessary for defining a project's activities and formalizing this information into a schedule. From a planning perspective, schedules forecast work to be accomplished during the project's life cycle. This provides the structure for critical milestone decision points, establishes the framework for accountability of time-phased resources and budgets, and establishes the basis for assessing schedule, cost, business, and technical risk.

Once there is agreement on the project schedule, budget, technical specifications, and required resources, these elements of the project are baselined. This baseline forms the foundation for measuring project performance, managing risk, and calculating resource availability and consumption. When the actual data is collected, validated, and compared to the baseline plan, the schedule and cost variances can be identified, investigated, and resolved. It is in this area that project risks are identified, mitigated, and managed. A risk database is used as a means to manage the risk data and to provide reports.

Baseline Thresholds—Step 1

With a solid foundation and source of project information established, the next logical step is the development of a project's minimum and maximum baseline thresholds for the purposes of measuring project performance and identifying project risks. This involves the development of qualitative and quantitative performance parameters identified in the areas of schedule, resources, and cost. It essentially lays out the acceptable variances between what was planned (baseline) and what is actually being reported. Performance parameters could be established, for example, in the following areas.

SCHEDULE

- Timeframes (activity & milestone dates—actual vs. baseline).
- Critical path (identification of positive and negative float).
- Schedule variance (BCWP-BCWS).

RESOURCES

- Level of effort (required skill sets & numbers of people).
- Required hours (allotted vs. expended).
- Availability (individual & organization).

COST

- Dollars (BCWS, BCWP, ACWP).
- Cost variance (BCWP, ACWP).
- Burn rate (dollars vs. hours).

The establishment of baseline thresholds provides a means to measure schedule, resources, and cost performance, and aids in the identification of project risks which could possibly impact the planned completion of the project.

Risk Identification—Step 2

Risk identification is the process that systematically selects all possible sources of risk, assesses the probability of occurrence, and quantifies the project impact in terms of schedule, resources, cost, and technical performance. Risk identification techniques include questionnaires, interviews with key personnel, structured "brainstorming" workshops, and examination of project plans, schedules, and network logic diagrams. The project risks are then populated into a relational database or other electronic formats (tables, spreadsheets, etc.), which saves time, improves accuracy, and facilitates analysis and reporting of the information. The identification of risk by identifying risk types within specific work or business areas enhances the ability to analyze and manage project risk.

Risk types are categories from which risks can be identified and described. They also aid in identifying dependencies between risks during analysis. The following list depicts the most probable risk types to be considered in a program or project:

1. Requirements
2. Performance
3. Technology
4. Complexity
5. Reliability
6. Safety
7. Security
8. Skills/Resources
9. Experience
10. Communication
11. Contractual
12. Operations
13. Management
14. Information
15. Support
16. Procurement
17. Schedule
18. Cost

Any or all of these risk types can be associated with a specific work area or business area. Each business area should be analyzed for risk, and assessed against other business areas for risk impact and integrated mitigation steps. This facilitates integration with the project control process and enables accounting of the risk itself when it is assigned its own schedule activity number or cost account number. Policy, technical (Web, hardware, software, interfaces, architecture, etc.), training, GOTS/COTS, systems development, and implementation illustrate possible business areas within a project.

A risk manager is assigned for each identified risk and is responsible for ensuring that mitigating actions are defined and performed. Some actions may be applicable to more than one risk, and the database captures these linkages and eliminates the redundancy of risk elements. A risk matrix methodology is used to get consensus of the probability of occurrence and the criticality of impact to the project. Calculations of a Probability-Impact (P-I) score for each risk are performed, allowing for each risk to be prioritized and ranked by severity or by category of impact on the schedule, resources, cost, and technical performance. This provides a tailored list of risks that are the most critical and that are relevant to each area of responsibility. Given that the project risks are now defined, the next step is to develop the levels of acceptable risk for the project.

Acceptable Risk Parameters—Step 3

Risk parameters are nothing more than thresholds that depict levels of risk acceptability to the project. Risks are described using predefined scales of probability and impact as depicted in the table below [10-2]. Within each scale, a quantitative and qualitative assessment is made to assess the magnitude of each risk element within each risk area, magnitude meaning the severity of risk based on the acceptable scale.

Scale	Probability	Schedule (Months)	Cost Performance ($)
Very High (Red) (Lose major functions, failure to achieve primary mission, or systems not accepted)	90%	>10%	>10%
High (Yellow-Red) (Lose major requirements or have system degradation)	70%	5%–10%	5%–10%
Medium (Yellow) (Degrade major requirement or lose many minor requirements)	50%	2%–5%	2%–5%
Low (Green-Yellow) (Lose a minor requirement)	30%	1%–2%	1%–2%
Very Low (Green) (Minor requirement degradation)	10%	0%–1%	0%–1%

10-2

Risk Analysis Process—Step 4

Once the risks and parameters are identified, the next logical step is to develop an analytical process by which project risks and impacts are evaluated. This analysis can be simple or complex. At this stage of the project, the suggestion is to move toward a simple analytical process in which risk is assessed within the project. The forum in which this is to take place is the weekly and monthly project team meeting. Each risk manager should be prepared to discuss the projects associated with schedule, resources, and cost.

In preparation for the project team meetings the risk manager should assess the level of risk for each activity and its impact to the overall project. Risk elements should be assessed against schedule, resource, and cost thresholds. A risk assessment matrix should be developed which captures the answers to the following questions:

Schedule—How does each risk element impact the approved schedule as it pertains to activity, float, critical path, and project completion date?

Resources—How does each risk element impact the resources assigned to each activity?

Cost—How does each risk element impact the allotted funding?

Other—How does risk impact other areas, events (internal/external) and/or issues relative to the project?

The risk manager should be watchful of potential risks that may surface, based upon the predetermined risk areas, and perform an analysis of their potential and/or real impact to the project.

Risk Mitigation Planning—Step 5

Risk mitigation planning involves the response taken to control risks facing a project. The process includes reporting, reviewing, developing, and prioritizing responses to risks, and continuing risk identification and analysis on a regular basis. This planning process monitors the progress and effectiveness of risk reduction. It also determines the cost of mitigation strategies and any secondary risks associated with such strategies. The overall objective is to contain, reduce, and plan for project risks as far in advance as possible.

Risk mitigation should be conducted using only available resources and within a reasonable period of time. The planning effort should include specific corrective actions to be taken and deadlines to which the actions will be measured. Each stakeholder will provide status and updates to the risk mitigation process as required. Once the risk mitigation planning process is complete, the final activity is to input the data into the risk management database.

Risk Documentation and Reporting Requirements—Step 6

The documentation of risk should be performed at every major step of the project. Risk documentation should begin with the weekly project status updates. During these weekly updates, the subject of risk should be addressed so that current risk elements can be assessed, and new risk elements can be identified, analyzed, mitigated, and entered into the risk management database. Risk reporting formats, quantities, and frequencies should be discussed and approved. Risk documentation and reporting is a dynamic and continuous process and should become part of the weekly routine of managing the project.

Summary

Risk is inherent in all projects. With careful planning and good management, however, some inherent risks in the project management process can be substantially reduced or virtually eliminated, thus increasing the probability of project success. The following tasks contribute to an effective risk management program:

1. Thorough and realistic appraisal of the project concept and project scope definition.
2. Observing good project management practices in the project planning and development phase, including realistic estimation of time and cost.
3. Examining the uncertainty and risk inherent in the project, and identifying ways of mitigating this risk.
4. Preparing contingent action plans and work-arounds.
5. Developing sound procurement strategies designed to optimize performance, supported by an appropriate organizational structure and responsibility distribution.
6. Assigning specific responsibility for risk in a way that motivates by recognizing that risk and reward are often linked as one.
7. Examining contract documents for risk identification, general clarity, and potential source of understanding.
8. Seeking innovative but practical solutions to offset potential areas of risk.

Risk Management (Is Not) for Dummies

LT. COL. STEVEN R. GLAZEWSKI

Air Force Institute of Technology

Reading Overview

Software program managers crave a silver bullet in the form of a comprehensive checklist of things to watch so the program does not suffer from bad surprises. Highlighted in this reading are some prime examples from almost 15 years' experience acquiring software in Department of Defense programs, from identifying broad areas where software risks tend to hide, to describing an eight-step risk management process. While there are no silver bullets to be found, there are a few golden nuggets if you make the focused effort to look!

What is risk management? We have all heard the saying, "Give a man a fish, and you feed him for a day. Teach a man to fish, and you feed him for a lifetime." Let me revise that from a risk management standpoint: "Put out a manager's fires, and you help him for a day. Teach a manager fire prevention, and you help him for a career." If a manager understands good risk management, he can worry about things other than firefighting.

Unfortunately, most people who look for risk management help are seeking to know the steps to put fires out. After all, being a good firefighter has its rewards! Take a look at your organization's person-of-the-quarter listing for the past few years. Who is on it? Typically listed is the person who put out the worst fire. What about people who avoided the fires in the first place? Therein lie the problems with good risk management: people who avoid fires do not get noticed, and the risks they avoid do not get documented.

> Risks that are well understood and controlled tend not to become full-blown problems, and thus are rarely documented in risk databases.

Risks that are well understood and controlled tend not to become full-blown problems, and thus are rarely documented in risk databases. To this day, some people mistakenly believe the millions of dollars spent on Year 2000 mitigation were wasted because "nothing bad happened." This is the irony: If people die or property is destroyed, then preventative measures are deemed inadequate; if nobody is hurt and nothing is destroyed, then preventative measures are deemed valueless!

We can do a lot of damage in the name of process and standardization. Some things lend themselves well to both, such as building a car on an assembly line. Some things do not, such as creative, knowledge-based work like design and management. Yet we sometimes delude ourselves by creating templates for something like a risk management plan. Look carefully at such templates: 80 percent of the outline tends to be boilerplate or context setting. The meat is contained in sections that comprise only 20 percent of the table of contents entries. What does the template tell you about those meaty sections? Almost nothing! The real meat of a risk management plan—assembling a qualified team, devising ways to discover risks, devising methods of quantifying or categorizing the risks, and monitoring the risks—cannot be completed by simply following a checklist.

In contrast, template instructions for the non-meaty sections tend to be far more explicit (e.g., "state your funding authorization by appropriation for each fiscal year"). Usually, this information is readily available and easily culled from program management plans, status reports, organizational charts, etc. We delude ourselves into thinking that a plan is 80 percent complete when in fact we are just getting started.

There is a subtle yet critical message implied in the above: Nobody can give you a simple risk checklist. The reality is, when people want to learn/know how to do risk management, they are looking for Dick-and-Jane instructions for the meaty 20 percent. That is, they are specifically looking for detailed steps on those things that cannot be determined in advance by someone who is not intimately familiar with the project and its domain and environment. Simply put, they are looking for steps, words like "go to the financial department and get last month's numbers and look for expenditures that lag the fiscal year spending plan." They do not want tasks like "monitor the expenditures to verify claimed accomplishments." The message I get is, "Do not tell me what to think about or investigate, tell me exactly who to see, exactly what to ask, exactly what to record, and exactly what to do about it. Don't make this hard—just tell me exactly what to do."

There can be value added from a template. But this is far more likely when the template is based on a process or procedure that is absolutely relevant to the program. For example, if you are managing an avionics modernization project, your risk plan template should come from another avionics modernization project. Not only that, but also the template should have been assessed and revised by the last project. This feedback loop is critical! If there was no feedback, then you have no idea if the template's prior users benefited from it or not. In the worst case, the very template you propose to use may have hindered their ability to discover, quantify, categorize, prioritize, and manage project risks—and you do not know that! Ideally, the prior users reviewed and updated their risk management plan throughout their project, and all of their lessons learned were captured—you should do this, too.

Speaking of lessons learned, I am often asked for databases of risks, or more simply, where an interested party should look for risks experienced in past programs. The answer always disappoints the inquirer for two reasons. First, the historical data that exists is typically a list of problems, not risks. Risks are undesirable events that could happen: The concern over possible glitches associated with Year 2000 is a great example. Problems are risks that came to fruition. Problems are well documented in post-mortem analyses. But good risk management—risk that did not turn into problems—is forgotten.

Second, risks—and even problems—experienced by past programs are tuned for the environment that existed for that program and the unique circumstances of that program. What may have been a high priority risk for a past program may not be worth your investment of resources to monitor or track. Most people who request lessons learned do not really want a database anyway. They want the 15 or 20 items from the database that are most likely to happen to them. And they do not want to read hundreds of items to find those 15 to 20 nuggets. They are really asking me for a five-minute answer to a two-week question.

That is not to say that there is no value added in researching history. My experiences show that there is a fertile ground for finding risks—we know this because problems have consistently arisen from these areas. I have learned to focus some risk identification energy on three areas (if they are present in a project): test and integration hardware, interfaces, and reused code.

Test and integration hardware tends to be a capacity-constraining resource. If you have a system or software integration lab (SIL), you have a potential resource conflict. Many efforts in the program seem to demand SIL time simultaneously, and usually the software developers do not have top priority. I worked on a program where the same test hardware was used to validate test software and to test hardware that was about to be sold to the government. Needless to say, the chance to generate revenue trumped the software developer's needs until we were able to prove that the impending delays to the project would negatively affect the contractor's bottom line by more than a little delay in cash flow. While working on a different program, I discovered that the developer's detailed schedules required over 30 hours per day in the SIL to meet the schedule. Scheduling tools are great, but they fail when you disable or ignore the resource conflict warnings.

Interfaces are historically a source of error, and therefore risk. One significant example was the Mars Climate Orbiter that crashed into the planet in 1999 because one group coded as if the measurement were in feet, while the other coded as if it were in meters. Most bugs in a program are problems found while integrating modules or communicating between objects. On a grander scale in systems of systems, the biggest risks are where the independently built systems must interface. System test engineers always praise a good interface control document (ICD) more than the project managers bemoan the ICD's cost. We have a proverb that "good fences make good neighbors" and the same is true in software: If everyone knows the boundary conditions and interfaces, things go much smoother. The hard part is resisting the temptation to cut or minimize the typically large expense of creating good ICDs. ICDs are used for inter-system interfaces, but there are analogous—and equally valuable—design products that should describe the intra-system interfaces in detail.

Reused code, which includes commercial off-the-shelf code, is often sold to the program as a means of drastically reducing development and test costs. Code reuse can certainly reduce costs, but only within the very narrow circumstances where you make absolutely no changes to the code, and you use it for exactly and only the purpose for which it was designed. Many potentially dangerous commercial products like pesticides now carry a standard warning such as "Use of this product in a manner other than described below is a violation of federal law." Yes, the spray is flammable—no, you should not use it to light your barbeque grill. A similar warning should accompany all attempts to reuse code, albeit only a warning that it violates sound reuse strategy, and maybe the laws of good sense. It is not a bad idea to reuse code, but you have to accept the limitations when you do. If your plans call for reusing code and you are assuming substantial time and cost savings or test simplification, you had better not tinker with the reused code (or code products) in any way, or you violate your plan/assumption and incur risk.

Of course, the risk manager must look beyond these three areas, and must apply knowledge of the project's details to determine whether any of those three areas are applicable and worthy of investing resources.

Risk management is much like being the manager of a mutual fund or a stock analyst on Wall Street. Risk managers are asked to peer into the future—to make predictions with better-than-average accuracy—to not only be right, but to know what to do when they are right. Risk management goes beyond predicting risk; it also demands planning to handle the risk once it materializes. (As a side note, think of how well paid mutual fund managers and Wall Street stock analysts are, especially the successful ones!)

How do fund managers and analysts become successful? They dig into the details of a company. They may not have complete data because the company may not release any more than the minimum required by law. Yet the manager can assemble current information about this particular company, as well as information from its recent and not-so-recent past. Information can be gathered about similar companies over time, and about the segment of the economy that affects this company. This information can then be used to make an educated guess at future earnings, profits, and trends. In other words, they develop detailed knowledge about the specific company, and compare it with a solid general knowledge about the industry and the economy. This helps them more accurately foresee profitability, which can then be used to make sound investment decisions.

This is the essence of risk management! The risk manager combines detailed knowledge of the project with general knowledge of the technical domain and the acquisition environment to foresee potential undesirable events, and to plan and take actions accordingly.

Asking a complete novice to do risk management is, well, risky. Risk management involves thoughtful, determined, and creative work to implement the following eight-step process.

Step 1: Get Time to Do Risk Management

If you are spending 95 percent of your time doing day-to-day operations, you do not have enough time to sit and think (or plan or just be creative). You need slack time—that is, time away from operations—to plan and think. For a great discussion on why, read Tom DeMarco's book *Slack* [1]. It even contains a few chapters on risk management. Sometimes, this seemingly simple step can be the hardest part. Next comes the creative part.

Step 2: Plan Your Risk Management Program

What method will you use to discover/elicit risks? Who will help? (*Hint*: you need those people who are intimately familiar with the project, the domain, and the environment.) What are the desired outputs of your risk analysis? How will you categorize or quantify risk? What information must be recorded for each risk? Who will use the data and how? Now comes more creativity (problem solving) and some tedium.

Step 3: Identify Risks

Gather the team and identify potential risks. Remember that the team should consist of people with lots of project and domain experience. These people tend to be senior members and are very busy, so these identification sessions should be short and controlled. Excellent administrative support is absolutely necessary! So is follow-up and coordination of results. For each risk identified, the team should describe what data they need to assess the risk. Much of that data will probably not be available at this meeting, which is okay. This first session is identification only.

Step 4: Assess Risks

The risk team does risk assessment. It involves a facilitator doing lots of research and legwork before another meeting with the experts. Once the data is available and pre distributed, the team can reconvene to assess probabilities and impacts, determine indicators that a risk may be coming true, and prioritize the risks according to the documented procedure. The indicators are used to select metrics so the decision maker can be proactive when choosing whether to implement handling strategies.

Step 5: Plan to Handle Risks

With the decisionmaker and the team, decide how each risk will be handled. Determine what, if any, mitigation efforts are prudent; what alternative approaches or procedures are available; and/or how to share the risk. It is a good idea to identify thresholds (or trigger points) associated with the metrics selected in Step 4 so it is easier to initiate action.

Step 6: Monitor Risks

Conduct operations and periodically check to see if any of the risks show signs of turning into problems, or if any of the risks change because of the dynamics of project and environment. This period could be daily or weekly or something different, depending on how dynamic the project and environment are.

Step 7: Account for Changes in the Environment and Project

Periodically go back to Step 3. This period could be weekly or monthly or something different, depending on how dynamic the project and environment are.

Step 8: Improve Your Risk Management Process

Periodically go back to Step 2. This period could be quarterly or annually or something different, depending on how successful your program is at giving sufficient notice of things that may go wrong. This is the part that everyone hates, but it is the critical feedback loop that improves the process—for you and for the next project that uses your project as a template.

General Ideas

Here are some general ideas on risks. They must be general because I do not (and cannot) know the details of every reader's situation.

If you cannot assign a probability, assess an impact, or draft a unique action plan, then the risk you have identified is too generic, or not a risk at all. For example, stating that the risk is "our budget will get cut" is meaningless because you cannot say what the impact is or what you would do about it. A better risk would be "next year's budget will be cut by 5 percent, which means we cannot fully fund long-lead spares." Document why you chose the numbers you did. Why 5 percent and not 8 percent or 2 percent? Why impact spares and not tech orders?

If a risk is a near-certainty, then it is not a risk, it is something that the project's execution plan should already address. Does it?

Risks should be prioritized according to an agreed-upon scheme. The risk team may track 100 risks. Project managers may only have time to track the top 10. Of those, the senior acquisition officials probably have time and attention for only the top two or three. Know how these lists will be derived. Are they based on probability of occurrence? Are they based on severity of impact if they do occur? Are they based on some combination of the two?

A top 10 list should have exactly 10 items. Having 15 different No. 1 priority items may look good when spreading the wealth for performance review bullets, but it does nothing for helping senior people prioritize their time and the favors they would like to call in.

Good risk descriptions include indicators, or some method of foreseeing that the risk may actually be coming true. The better these indicators are, the better you can prepare the contingency plans.

Finally, there are many approaches and processes to manage risk. An Internet search will turn up dozens. But remember the rule of domain applicability: If the risk management process was built by those making and assembling automobiles, it may not be well suited for a different environment such as software development. Risk management, when done correctly, consumes the time of the most experienced, most project-knowledgeable people who also happen to be the busiest and highest-paid. However, the cost and effort to prevent a fire is almost always far less than the cost and effort to rebuild after the fire is out.

Note

The views expressed in this article are those of the author and do not necessarily reflect the official policy or position of the Air Force, Department of Defense, or the U.S. government agency.

Reference

Demarco, Tom. *Slack: Getting Past Burnout, Busywork, and the Myth of Total Efficiency.* Broadway, 9 Apr. 2002.

About the Author

Lt. Col. Steven R. Glazewski is currently an instructor at the School of Systems and Logistics at the Air Force Institute of Technology (AFIT/LS) located at Wright-Patterson AFB, OH. He teaches Professional Continuing Education courses in software project planning and execution, and software system maintenance as part of the Software Professional Development Program. Glazewski has more than 18 years in weapon system acquisition. He is an Institute of Electrical and Electronics Engineers Computer Society Certified Software Development Professional. The author will be leaving this assignment on October 1, 2005. After that time, direct inquires to the Air Force Institute of Technology, 3100 Research BLVD, Pod 3, Kettering, OH 45420-4022.

Enterprise Risk Management: A Framework for Success

FRANK MARTENS AND LUCY NOTTINGHAM

Reading Overview

In today's uncertain and volatile business world, the need to manage risk more coherently, comprehensively, and economically through effective enterprise risk management is more critical than ever. Up until now, however, enterprise risk management as a concept has suffered from a decided lack of support, due in large part to a lack of understanding and competing enterprise risk management theoretical frameworks, the claim that "intangible" enterprise risk management benefits skew traditional investment analysis, and, last but not least, a lack of experience amongst those translating enterprise risk management theory into practical value.

Mindful of these challenges, the Committee of Sponsoring Organizations of the Treadway Commission (COSO)—a private sector group dedicated to improving financial management through effective risk management, internal control and corporate governance—launched a landmark initiative in 2001 to build a commonly agreed-upon framework for enterprise risk management.

PricewaterhouseCoopers was asked to lead COSO's project to research and develop a comprehensive enterprise risk-management framework. During this intensive process, the team sought input from many sources within the global business community. The framework described here is currently being circulated for public comment. For more detailed information and to offer relevant comments, please visit *www.coso.org*.

What Is Enterprise Risk Management?

Every enterprise must cope with factors that create uncertainty. Enterprise risk management is a comprehensive, systematic approach for helping all organizations, regardless of size or mission, to identify events, and measure, prioritize, and respond to the risks challenging the projects and initiatives they undertake. Enterprise risk management enables an organization to determine what level of risk it can—or wants to—accept as it seeks to build shareholder value.

Uncertainty is a double-edged sword: It creates both risks and opportunities, which can either erode or enhance value. Enterprise risk management offers a framework for effectively managing uncertainty, responding to risk, and exploiting opportunities as they arise.

Managing risk more successfully enables organizations to achieve their performance and profitability targets, prevent the loss of resources, and ensure effective reporting and compliance. In short, enterprise risk management helps an organization attain its goals while avoiding pitfalls and surprises along the way. Enterprise risk management offers a number of compelling benefits.

> Enterprise risk management helps an organization attain its goals while avoiding pitfalls and surprises along the way.

ALIGNING RISK APPETITE AND STRATEGY

Risk appetite is the degree of uncertainty an enterprise is willing to accept to reach its goals. Risk appetite is a key factor in evaluating strategic options. Enterprise risk management helps management consider risk appetite when setting goals that align with overall corporate strategy, and managing risks related to that strategy.

LINKING GROWTH, RISK, AND RETURNS

Enterprise risk management enhances the capacity to identify events and assess risks, and set risk tolerances consistent with growth and return objectives.

IMPROVING RISK RESPONSE

Enterprise risk management provides tools for identifying and deciding among different risk responses, from acceptance and sharing to reduction or avoidance.

REDUCING OPERATIONAL SURPRISES AND LOSSES

Enterprise risk management helps organizations recognize potential adverse events, assess risks, and establish responses, thereby reducing surprises and related costs or losses.

MANAGING ENTERPRISE-WIDE RISKS

Every organization faces multiple risks that affect different functions and operations. Enterprise risk management emphasizes the interrelated impact of risks and supports integrated solutions for managing them.

EXPLOITING OPPORTUNITIES

By considering the full range of potential events—rather than just risks—enterprise risk management ensures that management can identify and take advantage of positive events quickly and efficiently.

RATIONALIZING RESOURCES

Enterprise risk management creates more robust risk information, which allows management to deploy resources more effectively, thereby reducing overall capital requirements and improving capital allocations.

Enterprise Risk Management: The New Framework

Enterprise risk management is not limited to one event or circumstance. It is a dynamic process that unfolds over time and permeates every aspect of an organization's resources and operations. It involves people at every level and requires applying a portfolio view of risk across an entire enterprise. By embedding risk management techniques in its day-to-day operations, an enterprise is better equipped to identify events affecting its goals and manage risks in ways that are consistent with its risk appetite.

As a process, risk management has eight interrelated components. Together, they form a comprehensive framework for action.

INTERNAL ENVIRONMENT

An enterprise's internal environment is the foundation of its risk management framework. This environment influences how strategies and goals are set; activities are structured; and risks are identified, assessed, and acted upon. Internal environment has many building blocks: ethical values, personnel, management's operating style, and risk management philosophy and culture.

An enterprise's risk appetite is an important part of the internal environment and affects strategy setting. A range of strategies can be pursued to help an enterprise achieve its desired growth and return targets; each strategy has different risks associated with it. Enterprise risk management helps management select a strategy consistent with its risk appetite.

OBJECTIVE SETTING

Enterprise risk management offers management a process for setting objectives, for ensuring that those objectives are aligned with strategic goals, and that those goals are consistent with risk appetite. An enterprise's objectives are viewed from four perspectives:

- Strategic: related to high-level goals and mission.
- Operations: related to efficiency, performance and profitability.
- Reporting: related to internal and external reporting.
- Compliance: related to compliance with laws and regulations.

EVENT IDENTIFICATION

Uncertainties abound. No enterprise can know definitively if or when certain events will occur or what their results will be. Through the event identification process, management considers factors, both internal and external, that might affect its strategy and achievement of objectives.

In some cases, it may be useful to group potential events into categories. By aggregating events horizontally across an entity and vertically within operating units, management develops an understanding of the interrelationships between events, gaining enhanced information as a basis for risk assessment.

RISK ASSESSMENT

This process focuses on both the likelihood and impact of potential events and their effects on objectives. While a single event's impact might be minimal, a sequence of events can amplify its significance.

Risk assessment employs both qualitative and quantitative methods—and evaluates potential uncertainties as they unfold, whether they are internally or externally generated.

RISK RESPONSE

Once risks have been identified and categorized, management evaluates possible responses and their effects. Options are weighed in relation to both risk appetite and cost vs. benefit models. For effective risk management, managers must select a risk response that is within the parameters of risk tolerance.

Risk responses typically fall into four categories: avoidance, sharing, reduction, and acceptance. Management considers actions based on the response categories cited above. Once management selects a risk response, it shifts into action, developing an implementation plan to respond to, and then reassess residual risk.

CONTROL ACTIVITIES

These policies and procedures ensure that risk responses are carried out efficiently. Since each enterprise has its own set of objectives and implementation techniques, control activities will differ. Controls also reflect the environment and industry in which an enterprise operates, as well as its internal structure, history, and culture. General controls encompass IT infrastructure and management, security management, and software. Application controls are designed to ensure completeness, accuracy, and validity of data capture and processing.

INFORMATION AND COMMUNICATION

Information is needed at all levels of an organization to identify, assess, and respond to risk. Pertinent information from both internal and external sources must be captured and shared in a form and timeframe that equips personnel to react quickly and efficiently. Effective communication also involves the exchange of relevant data with external parties, such as customers, vendors, regulators, and shareholders.

Effective enterprise risk management relies on both historical and current data. Historical data tracks actual performance against targets, identifies trends, correlates results, and forecasts performance. Historical data also provides early warning signals concerning potential risk-related events. Current data gives management a real-time view of risks inherent in a process, function, or unit. This enables an organization to alter its activities as needed in keeping with its risk appetite.

MONITORING

Monitoring ensures that the components of enterprise risk management are applied at all levels. Monitoring occurs in two ways: on an ongoing basis or via one-time evaluations. Ongoing monitoring is performed in real time, responds to changing conditions, and is embedded in operations. Since one-time evaluations take place after the fact, problems are targeted more quickly by ongoing monitoring systems.

Using the enterprise risk management framework outlined here can increase senior management's and the board's confidence that they will achieve those objectives.

All risks that affect an organization's ability to develop and execute its goals—whether they represent potential problems or opportunities—should be reported to those positioned to take action. Protocols should be established to identify what information is needed at a particular level for effective decision making.

Enterprise risk management is definitely a dynamic process. For it to work, all eight of the components described here must be present and functioning smoothly. Clearly, however, no risk management procedures, no matter how well designed and executed, can guarantee results. Nevertheless, using the enterprise risk management framework outlined here can increase senior management's and the board's confidence that they will achieve those objectives.

About the Author

Frank Martens is a Senior Manager in PricewaterhouseCoopers Global Risk Management Solutions practice in Vancouver, Canada. He has over 15 years of experience in risk management, enterprise risk management, and governance-related services in a wide range of companies. Frank has a Bachelor of Commerce degree from the University of British Columbia and is a member of the Institute of Chartered Accountants of British Columbia.

Lucy Nottingham is a Manager in PricewaterhouseCoopers Global Risk Management Solutions practice in Boston and has prepared a number of reports on enterprise risk management. Prior to joining PricewaterhouseCoopers, Lucy was research associate with The Conference Board of Canada. She has a B.A. from McGill University and an M.A. from Carleton University in Ottawa.

Procurement Management

Chapter 11 Contents

Chapter Overview

The role of procurement in the project scene has increased significantly with the enchantment of third-party technical contracting, mostly in the form of cheap offshore providers from India, Malaysia, and Russia. Because of this trend, we are splitting the discussion of procurement into two sections. This section will discuss the general *PMBOK® Guide* Procurement Management process overview and the related material sourcing side of procurement.

Management of the procurement process continues to be a major concern of project managers due to its potential positive or negative impact on the project goals. For companies dealing in commodity goods, the costs associated with acquiring or purchasing such products make up a considerable portion of their costs of goods sold. The ability to reduce those procurement costs can markedly improve profits, so sourcing and contract management are critical to those situations. The positive potential offered by effective procurement management also extends to purchasing or acquiring resources from high technology suppliers and skilled services from third-party providers. Thus, the processes described in this section are applicable to a wide range of organizations seeking to enhance the management of their procurement practices.

Several activities fall within the scope of procurement management. For this discussion, we will consider the points of view of both the buyer and the seller of goods or services. The interfacing activities are the same, regardless of perspective. As a starting point, it is necessary to make a determination as to which sets of goods and services to potentially acquire from external sellers. This decision triggers the establishment of a procurement plan based upon those decisions. Though the activities associated with procurement management are relatively universal among organizations, the nature of what is being acquired affects the complexity of the process.

PMBOK® Guide View of Procurement

The *PMBOK® Guide* defines six basic procurement processes as follows: [PMI, 269]

1. **Plan Purchases and Acquisitions:** Determining what to purchase or acquire and determining when and how.
2. **Plan Contracting:** Documenting products, services, and results requirements and identifying potential sellers.
3. **Request Seller Responses:** Obtaining information, quotations, bids, offers, or proposals, as appropriate.
4. **Select Sellers:** Reviewing offers, choosing among potential sellers, and negotiating a written contract with each seller.
5. **Contract Administration:** Managing the contract and relationship between the buyer and seller, reviewing and documenting how a seller is performing or has performed to establish required corrective actions and provide a basis for future relationships with the seller, managing contract-related changes, and, when appropriate, managing the contractual relationship with the outside buyer of the project.
6. **Contract Closure:** Completing and settling each contract, including the resolution of any open items, and closing each contract applicable to the project or a project phase.

PLAN PURCHASES AND ACQUISITIONS

The project team identifies which products or services could be best provided by outside sources. This activity involves various analytical techniques and expert judgment. External procurement affords opportunities to acquire resources that either cannot be supplied by the internal organization, or can be acquired externally at a lower price. However, there is a degree of trust that must exist between the buyer and the seller, and there may be environmental or legal issues that limit this activity.

The output of this process is a Procurement Management Plan that will list various specifications for the upcoming acquisition activity. A sample of these includes:

- Types of contracts to be used
- Standardized procurement documents
- Constraints and assumptions that could affect purchases
- Risk assessment issues
- Procurement metrics to be used

The level of formality for this plan is variable and should be adjusted to fit the needs of the project. Once completed, the Procurement Management Plan becomes a subsidiary plan to the master Project Plan.

PLAN CONTRACTING

In the course of carrying out the procurement planning process there is a formal set of documentation and support activities that should be performed, starting at the initial bidding and continuing through the contract closure. The Plan Contracting process prepares the documents needed to support the supplier selection activities that follow. The primary output from this process is the creation of various procurement documents that will be sent to prospective sellers. Common names for these documents are request for proposal (RFP), invitation to bid, and request for quotation (RFQ), among others. These documents are used to define the item to be acquired and assist in the evaluation process.

REQUEST SELLER RESPONSES

This procurement activity obtains responses from the prospective sellers. From this activity, qualified sellers will be identified and procurement packages prepared. The procurement package will identify in sufficient detail how the seller is to make their formal bid. The seller response to this is a proposal outlining how they intend to support the request.

SELECT SELLERS

This process receives the bids from the approved seller list and applies decision criteria to those responses in order to identify the winning bidder or bidders. This process can be iterative if the responses were not suitable, or misunderstanding resulted in the misinterpretation of the bid documentation. The intended output is a contract award to the winning bidder.

CONTRACT ADMINISTRATION

During the course of executing the identified deliverables, it is the duty of both parties to ensure compliance with the terms of the agreement. This activity is particularly critical in regard to change management and performance tracking. In order to accomplish these activities effectively, careful consideration must be given to a formal change management process and an equally formal performance reporting definition. Other activities that should be defined are the payment terms, claims administration for contested items, and a records retention policy for the seller's work products.

CONTRACT CLOSURE

We have seen previously the role that project closure has in its lessons learned. In this situation, the major goal is to verify that all work contracted was delivered in an acceptable form. Usually, a formal letter pertaining to this is a contractual requirement. Also, there should be a review of any contested items and a final review of the contractual specifications related to closure. All contractual documents should be properly archived to the contract files. Any lessons learned during the contract should be documented and passed on to the project lessons learned process.

The PMI procedures seem overly regimented to many project managers, but failure to document this process can lead to significant grief for the project team later. Poor terms and conditions create the potential for later buyer/seller disagreement. Poor contractual terms can lead to similar issues. As with most projects, there is seldom a major acquisition that goes from concept to delivery without some change emerging. This must be anticipated in the contractual relationship.

Readings

This section presents two readings that offer managerial advice on how to improve procurement practices to world-class levels. The first article, "Contracting and Procurement," comes from a Department of Energy publication titled "Project Management Practices." This source provides a valuable foundation outlining how to handle procurement and contract administration effectively. The material contained here is similar to that outlined in the *PMBOK® Guide*.

In the second article, "Procurement Transformation: A Holistic Approach to Best Practice Procurement," Richard Laub and his Accenture colleagues focus on the benefits of an approach to transforming procurement practices. Also, an underlying theme is that personnel expertise in this field is needed to manage this process.

The process of acquiring goods and services from third parties continues to take on increased significance in the contemporary world. Use of external suppliers brings both potential advantages and disadvantages, which must be understood in order to make effective use of the strategy. We will see more of the human side of third-party sourcing in Chapter 18.

Contracting and Procurement

Project Management Practices, Chapter 15, Department of Energy Archives.
http://www.science.doe.gov/SC-80/sc-81/PDF/pract15.pdf

Editor's Note: Paragraph numbers have been changed for inclusion in this book.

Project contracting and procurement management include the processes required to acquire goods and services from outside the performing organization. For the purposes of this discussion, it does not include the acquisition of capital assets. These processes include:

- Procurement planning: what to procure and when.
- Solicitation planning: product requirements and identifying potential sources.
- Solicitation: obtaining quotations, bids, offers, or proposals, as appropriate.
- Source selection: awarding the bid.
- Contract administration: the relationship with the seller.
- Contract closeout: completion and settlement of the contract, including resolution of any open items.

These processes interact not only with each other, but with processes in other knowledge areas. Each process may involve effort from one or more individuals or groups of individuals based on the needs of the project. Process interactions are an integral part of the contracting and procurement process.

Project procurement management is discussed from the perspective of the buyer in the buyer-seller relationship.

The *seller* will typically manage their work as a project. In such cases:

- The *buyer* becomes the customer and is a key stakeholder for the seller.
- The seller's project management team must be concerned with all the processes of project management.
- The terms and conditions of the contract become a key input to many of the seller's processes. The contract may contain the input (e.g., major deliverables, key milestones, cost objectives) or it may limit the project team's options (e.g., buyer approval of staffing decisions is often required on design projects).

11.1 Procurement Planning

Procurement planning is the process of identifying which project needs can be best met by procuring products or services outside the project organization, and includes consideration of whether to procure, how to procure, what to procure, how much to procure, and when to procure. Procurement planning should also include consideration of potential subcontracts, particularly if the buyer wishes to exercise some degree of influence or control over subcontracting decisions. The project management team shall seek support from specialists in the disciplines of contracting and procurement when needed.

When the project does not obtain products and services from outside the organization, the processes from solicitation planning through contract closeout would normally not be performed. This is most often associated with research and development projects, and on many smaller, in-house projects when the cost of finding and managing an external resource may exceed the potential savings.

11.1.1 INPUTS TO PROCUREMENT PLANNING:

- Scope statement: The scope statement describes current project boundaries and provides important information about project needs and strategies that must be considered during procurement planning.
- Product description: The description of the product provides important information concerning any technical issues or concerns that need to be considered during procurement planning.
- Procurement resources: An estimate of the resources needed to support the project.
- Market conditions: The procurement planning process shall consider what products and services are available in the marketplace. Also, are multiple sources of information available?
- Constraints: Constraints are factors that limit the buyer's options. One of the most common constraints for DOE projects is the availability and timing of funds.

11.1.2 TOOLS AND TECHNIQUES FOR PROCUREMENT PLANNING

- Make-or-buy analysis: This technique can be used to determine whether a particular product can be produced cost-effectively by the performing organization, or if it should be procured.

The make-buy process may compare the cost of construction forces on site (when available), implementing a project or portion of a project, versus buying the services with fix-priced subcontracts. The guiding principles to a make-or-buy analysis process include:

- The process is auditable to ensure financial analysis guidelines are consistent.
- The process yields qualified sources with the lowest evaluated cost.
- The process is unbiased, i.e., estimates of "make" cost and "buy" cost are prepared by independent organizations.
- The process is nonexclusionary. Activities will not be performed in-house solely because of qualitative criteria.
- The Project Manager should initiate the make-or-buy analysis during the conceptual phase prior to CD-2.
- Expert Judgment: Expert judgment will often be required to assess the inputs to this process.
- Contract Type Selection: Different types of contracts are more or less appropriate for different types of purchases. Contracts generally fall into one of three broad categories:

- Fixed Price or Lump Sum Contracts: This category of contract involves a fixed total price for a well-defined product.
- Cost Reimbursable Contracts: This category of contract involves payment (reimbursement) to the seller for actual costs. Cost reimbursable contracts often include incentives for meeting or exceeding selected project objectives, such as schedule targets or total cost.
- Unit Price Contracts: The seller is paid a preset amount per unit of service, and the total value of the contract is a function of the quantities needed to complete the work.

11.1.3 OUTPUTS FROM CONTRACTING AND PROCUREMENT PLANNING

- Contracting and Procurement Management Plan: The contracting and procurement management plan (an element of the PEP) shall describe how the remaining procurement processes (from solicitation planning through contract closeout) will be managed. For example:
  - What type of contracts will be used?
  - Will independent estimates be needed as evaluation criteria?
  - Will standardized procurement documents be needed, and how will multiple providers be managed?
  - How will procurement be coordinated with other project aspects such as scheduling and performance reporting?

The plan should include a listing of contracts/procurements required including a listing of key dates (e.g., date of issuance of approved specification, procurement start, receipt of approved requisition package by Procurement, contract award date, product delivery date, intermediate milestones, etc.).

- Statement(s) of Work: The statement or scope of work (SOW) describes the procurement in sufficient detail to allow prospective sellers to determine if they are capable of providing the item. "Sufficient detail" may vary based on the nature of the item, the needs of the buyer, or the expected contract form.

The statement of work shall be as clear, complete, and concise as possible. The SOW should include a description of any collateral services required, such as performance reporting, spare parts, or post-project operational support for the procured item. In some applications, there are specific content and format requirements for a SOW.

A recommended practice is to require the successful bidder to prepare a document that describes their understanding of the scope of work. This document must be submitted prior to initiation of work and then reviewed with the buyer to assure a complete understanding of the work to be performed and the product expected.

11.2 Solicitation Planning

Solicitation planning involves preparing the documents needed to support solicitation of bids, quotes, or proposals.

11.2.1 INPUTS TO SOLICITATION PLANNING

- Contracting and Procurement Management Plan.
- Statement(s) of work.
- Project schedule: Solicitation planning shall be closely coordinated with the project schedule.

11.2.2 TOOLS AND TECHNIQUES FOR SOLICITATION PLANNING

- Standard Forms: Standard forms may include contracts, descriptions of procurement items, or standardized versions of all or part of the needed bid documents.
- Expert Judgment: Expert judgment should be sought and used as needed.

11.2.3 OUTPUTS FROM SOLICITATION PLANNING

- Contracting and Procurement Documents: Contracting and Procurement documents are used to solicit proposals from prospective sellers. Common names for different types of procurement documents include Invitation for Bid (IFB), Request for Proposal (RFP), Request for Quotation (RFQ), Invitation for Negotiation, and Contractor Initial Response.

  Contracting and procurement documents shall be structured to facilitate accurate and complete responses from prospective sellers, and should always include the relevant statement of work, a description of the desired form of the response, and any required contractual provisions (e.g., a copy of a model contract or nondisclosure provisions). Some or all of the content and structure of contracting and procurement documents may be defined by regulation. Procurement documents shall be rigorous enough to ensure consistent, comparable responses, but flexible enough to allow consideration of seller suggestions for better ways to satisfy the requirements.

- Evaluation Criteria: Evaluation criteria are used to rate or score proposals. They may be objective or subjective, and are often included as part of the procurement documents.

- Evaluation criteria may be limited to purchase price if the contract/procurement item is known to be readily available from a number of acceptable sources When this is not the case, other criteria must be identified and documented to support an integrated assessment. For example:

  - Understanding of need—as demonstrated by the seller's proposal.

  - Overall or life cycle cost—will the selected seller produce the lowest total cost (purchase cost plus operating cost)?

  - Technical capability—does the seller have, or can the seller be reasonably expected to acquire, the technical skills and knowledge needed?

  - Management approach—does the seller have, or can the seller be reasonably expected to develop, management processes and procedures to ensure a successful project?

- Financial capacity—does the seller have, or can the seller reasonably be expected to obtain, the financial resources needed?
- Past performance—does the seller have a past history of performance/ nonperformance and will the seller provide "best value" for the projects.

11.3 Solicitation

Solicitation involves obtaining information (bids, proposals) from prospective sellers on how project needs can best be met. Most of the effort in this process is expended by the prospective sellers, normally at no cost to the project.

11.3.1 INPUTS TO SOLICITATION

- Contracting and Procurement Documents.
- Qualified Seller Lists (QSLs): Most organizations maintain lists or files with information on prospective sellers, known as qualified seller lists (QSLs). A QSL is a composite of quality-related information for suppliers, obtained from various sources. If QSLs are not available, the project team shall develop its own sources. General information is widely available through library directories, relevant local associations, trade catalogs, and similar sources. Detailed information may require site visits or contact with previous customers.

11.3.2 TOOLS AND TECHNIQUES FOR SOLICITATION

- Bidder Conferences: Bidder conferences are meetings with prospective sellers prior to preparation of a proposal. They are used to ensure that all prospective sellers have a clear, common understanding of the procurement. Responses to questions may be incorporated into the procurement documents as amendments.
- Advertising: Existing lists of potential sellers can often be expanded by placing advertisements in general circulation publications such as newspapers or in specialty publications such as professional journals. The DOE requires public advertising of subcontracts on a government contract.

11.3.3 OUTPUTS FROM SOLICITATION

- Proposals: Proposals are seller-prepared documents that describe the seller's ability and willingness to provide the requested product. They are prepared in accordance with the requirements of the relevant procurement documents.

11.4 Source Selection

Source selection involves the receipt of bids or proposals and the application of the evaluation criteria to select a provider. This process is seldom straightforward.

- Price may be the primary determinant for an off-the-shelf item, but the lowest proposed price may not be the lowest cost if the seller proves unable to deliver the product in a timely manner.

■ Proposals are often separated into technical (approach) and commercial (price) sections with each evaluated separately.
■ Multiple sources may be required for critical products. In this case, past performance should be considered.
■ Rank and order proposals to establish a negotiating sequence.

On major procurement items, this process may be iterated. A short list of qualified sellers will be selected based on a preliminary proposal, and then a more detailed evaluation will be conducted based on a more detailed and comprehensive proposal.

11.4.1   INPUTS TO SOURCE SELECTION

■ Proposals.
■ Evaluation Criteria.
■ Organizational Policies: Any and all of the organizations involved in the project may have formal or informal policies that can affect the evaluation of proposals.

11.4.2   TOOLS AND TECHNIQUES FOR SOURCE SELECTION

■ Contract Negotiation: Contract negotiation involves clarification and mutual agreement on the structure and requirements of the contract prior to signing of the contract. To the extent possible, final contract language should reflect all agreements reached. Subjects covered generally include, but are not limited to, responsibilities and authorities, applicable terms and law, technical and business management approaches, contract financing, and price.

This process should obtain goods and services of the required quality, at the lowest possible cost, in accordance with the specified schedule and consistent with the terms and conditions. Preparation is the primary key to successful negotiation.

The following guidelines should lead to successful negotiation:

• Develop a negotiation plan outline. Preparing and planning goals, tactics, and strategy are most important.

• Choose a negotiation team and include only required disciplines.

• Agree, in advance, upon realistic cost/commercial/technical objectives as well as a negotiation plan.

• Be informed regarding the suppliers/contractors and their representatives.

• Negotiate in DOE or requestor facilities to increase "control" over the process.

• Negotiate only with supplier/contractor representatives who have the authority to make commitments or concessions.

• Let the lead negotiator control the negotiation. Their duty is to control any sudden changes, surprises, breakdowns in bargaining, and other nondirectional situations.

• Weighting system: A weighting system is a method for quantifying qualitative data in order to minimize the effect of personal prejudice on source selection. Most systems involve: (1) assigning a numerical weight to each of the evaluation criteria, (2) rating the prospective sellers on each criterion, (3) multiplying the weight by the rating, and (4) totaling the resultant products to compute an overall score.

- Screening System: A screening system involves establishing minimum performance requirements for one or more of the evaluation criteria.

- Independent Estimates: When needed, the project shall prepare/ provide independent or government estimates as a check on proposed pricing. Significant differences from these estimates may be an indication that the SOW was not adequate or that the prospective seller either misunderstood or failed to respond fully to the SOW.

11.4.3 OUTPUTS FROM SOURCE SELECTION

- Contract: A contract is a mutually binding agreement which obligates the seller to provide the specified product and obligates the buyer to pay for it. A contract is a legal relationship subject to remedy in the courts.

  Although all project documents are subject to some form of review and approval, the legally binding nature of a contract usually means that it will be subjected to a more extensive approval process. In all cases, a primary focus of the review and approval process should be to ensure that the contract language describes a product or service that will satisfy the need identified. In the case of major projects undertaken by public agencies, the review process may even include public review of the agreement.

11.5 Contract Administration

Contract administration is the process of ensuring that the seller's performance meets contractual requirements. On larger projects with multiple product and service providers, a key aspect of contract administration is managing the interfaces among the various providers. The legal nature of the contractual relationship makes it imperative that the project team be acutely aware of the legal implications of actions taken when administering the contract.

- Project work release systems to authorize the contractor's work at the appropriate time.
- Performance reporting to monitor contractor cost, schedule, and technical performance.
- Quality control to inspect and verify the adequacy of the contractor's product.
- Change control to ensure that changes are properly approved and that all those with a need-to-know are aware of such changes.

Once a contract is awarded, a Notice to Proceed is issued. The Notice to Proceed is a formal notification to the contractor that work may begin. However, mobilization does not occur until after initial submittal requirements are met.

Submittal requirements for contracts may be found in the specification or scope of work and in the special conditions/general provisions of the procurement package. The procurement package should define the submittal schedule. Submittals may require approval prior to the start of construction or fabrication. The timing of these submittals is important because of their potential impact on the schedule.

Preparing submittals involves the following activities:

- A submittal identification tracking system should be established.
- The submittal review process should be clearly defined, and implemented.
- A submittal log should be used to establish the system/component review matrix, description of item, date received, date transmitted to review organization, date comments returned, resolution, and date of final approval.
- Submittals must accurately represent the equipment specified, delivered, and installed at the construction site.
- Each organization should provide timely turnaround of submittals. An agreement of standard turnaround time should be obtained.
- A single point of contact for processing of submittals should be established to ensure timely receipt, review, and approvals. This applies to both the project and reviewing personnel/organizations.
- Because contract administration also has a financial management component, payment terms should be defined within the contract and should involve a specific linkage between progress and compensation.

Construction contracts should require the subcontractor to have an approved schedule prior to starting construction activities. Supplemental schedules may be required for the project duration, that is, thirty days or four weeks rolling. These schedules should identify, at a minimum, the milestone dates defined in the subcontract agreement. Examples of milestone dates are construction start, mechanical complete (system operable), and physical complete (all punch list items complete). Preparing schedules involves the following activities:

- The overall project schedule should include the dollar values associated with each activity. These values should sum to the total amount of the subcontract.
- Supplemental schedules should be required that identify and include milestone dates that are specified in the contract documentation.
- The contractor's schedule should provide a Work Breakdown Structure (WBS) bar chart and "S" curve resource-loaded schedule. This schedule should highlight the contractor's critical path.
- The contractor's baseline contract schedule should always be maintained. Any negotiated baseline schedule changes should be incorporated into the baseline schedule in a timely manner.

When work activities are completed, and verified by the project, payment requests may be submitted and approved. Progress payments are based on the values loaded into the schedule, minus retainage, which is usually ten percent of the requested amount.

The Project Manager and responsible project controls personnel should track invoices submitted versus payments to the contractor. The accounting system must capture the delta in actual and invoiced cost to accurately report contractor costs against performance.

Contract administration also has a financial management component. Payment terms shall be defined within the contract and should involve a specific linkage between progress and compensation.

11.5.1 INPUTS TO CONTRACT ADMINISTRATION

- Contract.
- Work Results: The seller's work results—which deliverables have been completed and which have not, to what extent are quality standards being met, what costs have been incurred or committed, etc.
- Change Requests: Change requests may include modifications to the terms of the contract or to the description of the product or service to be provided.

  During the execution of a subcontract, the need to change the contract may occur. This may be the result of a request and agreement. Requests for changes must be submitted in writing. Once negotiated between the supplier and procurement representative, a change order will be issued. Upon issuance of the change order, the contract has been officially amended.

  The key issue that all Project Managers face through the course of a project is managing change. Project Managers should remain aware of the following when managing change:

  - Close management and control of change can help ensure project success.

  - Changes to contracts/procurement documentation baselines must be by approved documentation through the authorized representative (procurement).

  - Change documentation must provide an adequate description of the change's impacts to baseline contract cost and schedule supported by an independent cost estimate.

  - The contractor should be forced to submit claims in a timely manner.

  - The Project Manager should be involved in the negotiation of any major changes.

Sellers must be monitored to ensure that all work is in compliance with contract requirements. The project must keep the subcontractor on schedule, enforce safety procedures, approve payment, educate the subcontractor on site procedures, and perform many other tasks as part of the payment process.

11.5.2 TOOLS AND TECHNIQUES FOR CONTRACT ADMINISTRATION

- Contract Change Control System: A contract change control system defines the process by which the contract may be modified, and includes the paperwork, tracking systems, dispute resolution procedures, and approval levels necessary for authorizing changes. The contract change control system should be integrated with the project change control system.

- Performance Reporting: Performance reporting provides information about how effectively the seller is achieving the contractual objective. Contract performance reporting should be integrated with overall project performance reporting.
- Payment System: Payments to the seller are usually handled by the accounts payable system of the performing organization. The system must include appropriate reviews and approvals by the project management team.
- Incentive: Some contracts are amenable to incentives as a method of rewarding performance. If used, this technique must be carefully controlled and monitored to assure the process adds value.

11.5.3   OUTPUTS FROM CONTRACT ADMINISTRATION

- Correspondence: Written documentation of certain aspects of buyer/ seller communications, such as telephone conversations and meeting minutes.
- Contract Changes: Changes (approved and unapproved) are used as appropriate to upgrade the PEP or other relevant project documentation.
- Payment Requests: This assumes that the project is using an external payment system. If the project has its own internal system, the output here would simply be "payments."
- Historical Records: Historical records of the subcontractor's performance starting from award and proceeding through closeout must be maintained. Also, a collection of factually documented observations and records for the project's protection is kept in the event legal actions (claims) are brought against the project by the seller.

11.6   Contract Closeout

Contract closeout is similar to administrative closure in that it involves both product verification and administrative closeout. The contract terms and conditions may prescribe specific procedures for contract closeout. Early termination of a contract and termination for the convenience of the government are special cases of contract closeout.

11.6.1   INPUTS TO CONTRACT CLOSEOUT

- Contract Documentation: Contract documentation includes, but is not limited to, the contract itself along with all supporting schedules, requested and approved contract changes, any seller-developed technical documentation, seller performance reports, financial documents such as invoices and payment records, and the results of any contract-related inspections.

11.6.2   TOOLS AND TECHNIQUES FOR CONTRACT CLOSEOUT

Procurement Audits: A procurement audit is a structured review of the procurement process from procurement planning through contract administration. The objective of a procurement audit is to identity successes and failures and lessons learned.

- Acceptance Walkdown or Inspection: The procurement documents must specify the process for turnover and acceptance of the equipment or service.

  The project team and customer representatives must be involved in walkdowns and acceptance of equipment from contractors. After completion and turnover, the subcontractor is relieved from further responsibility except in three circumstances:
  - Latent Defects—A defect existed at the time of acceptance but was not discoverable through reasonable inspection.
  - Fraud—The subcontractor's intent was to deceive the project.
  - Warranties—Continue for a specified time from the date the mechanical completion certificate is completed.

  These items must be managed to ensure DOE's interests are protected.

11.6.3 OUTPUTS FROM CONTRACT CLOSEOUT

- Contract File: A complete set of indexed records should be prepared for inclusion with the final project records.
- Formal Acceptance and Closure: The person or organization responsible for contract administration should provide the seller with formal written notice that the contract has been completed. Requirements for formal acceptance and closure are usually defined in the contract.

Procurement Transformation: A Holistic Approach to Best Practice Procurement

RICHARD LAUB, ROB WOODSTOCK, AND MARTIN SJÖBERG
Accenture

Imagine a self-financing solution that could transform your company's procurement capabilities, realize savings, and sustain improvement over time. By combining human performance with strategic sourcing, process excellence, and deep category knowledge, procurement transformation will help companies realize greater benefits from their procurement programs.

Just a few years ago, e-procurement was viewed as the simplest route into the brave new world of e-commerce and, in terms of balancing risk against potential benefits, a no-brainer. But in a recent survey with 30 e-procurement pioneers, Accenture learned that many of these early adopters were still in the pilot phase of their implementations. Even the few that had fully implemented their systems were still significantly short of their original usage targets. Despite admitting to some substantial cost overruns, particularly in the area of e-requisitioning, most of the companies surveyed expressed satisfaction with the progress they had made and the savings they had realized, and were confident that they would ultimately achieve their original objectives. Accenture found only one organization out of the 30 surveyed that admitted their e-procurement initiative had completely failed to meet expectations.

Despite these optimistic findings from pioneers, the fact that so few had moved beyond the pilot stage meant that the jury was still out on key aspects of the e-procurement case. This has done little to dispel a growing perception that the enthusiasm for e-procurement in the late '90s was based on a naive trust in the ability of a magic bullet to resolve complex and long-standing procurement problems.

The same could be said of strategic sourcing. By focusing on total cost of ownership and taking into account quantitative and qualitative processes, as well as service improvements, strategic sourcing has been shown to facilitate better internal and external customer service. These improvements not only reduce costs, but also directly increase revenue. However, the suspicion has grown that many strategic sourcing programs have delivered results that, while initially impressive, are unsustainable in the long-term. This is due at least in part to a failure to transfer the expertise of the external consultants, who renegotiated the original contracts, to the client's own procurement team.

These impressions were confirmed when Accenture's recent survey asked respondents what they could have done differently. Many of the companies interviewed actually became involved with e-procurement in

> A reliance on systems and technology alone will not provide optimum business results. A holistic approach that places human expertise at the core of the procurement model is a requirement for world-class procurement.

response to senior management pressure to do something—almost any-thing—with an "e" in front of it. So, business cases were often limited or nonexistent. For example, the study concluded that "companies focused on building working catalogs, rather than on ensuring that underlying sup-plier contracts would produce a compelling business case," and "auctions resulted in business failure even though the technology worked well." The report argued that the key to success lies, as always, in being business-driven rather than technology-driven.

Most significant was the recognition that these early e-procurement initiatives had often run into trouble in the implementation phase—resul-ting in cost overruns of 20 to 30 percent of the implementation budget, which were already 40 percent or 50 percent of the total because they failed to recognize the human factor. They had underestimated or ignored both the fundamental contribution made by human expertise to the procure-ment process and the potential disruption e-procurement implementation could wreak on organizational structures.

This does not mean that e-procurement can't deliver valid, measurable benefits. E-Requisitioning offers the potential for increased contract com-pliance, increased buyer productivity, and better quality information. Simi-larly, e-sourcing has delivered improved market intelligence, reduced purchase prices, and compressed cycle times [see 11-1].

On the downside, as we have witnessed, are the very real problems en-countered in implementation. In the case of e-requisitioning, implementa-tion costs can amount to as much as 70 percent of total cost. Unforeseen or underestimated problems interfacing with legacy systems are the most com-mon cause of difficulties. Despite these technical problems, the most intra-ctable difficulties seem to center on people issues. A total of 21 percent of the companies surveyed reported user acceptance difficulties, while many more acknowledged that users take far longer than expected to embrace and adapt to new technology. Given that the majority of the companies sur-veyed had not advanced beyond the pilot stage, more attention needs to be devoted to cultural change issues and change management procedures when projects advance to full implementation. Even then, e-requisitioning systems seldom fully address more than 20 percent of an organization's indirect spend and deliver benefits that are difficult to quantify.

Similarly, in e-sourcing, the area where the companies in Accenture's survey seem to have achieved the most success initially, there are real con-cerns about an increasing reliance on auctions impacting supplier relation-ships, and whether price benefits are sustainable over the long-term. Even companies that had sought to share costs and risks through participation in e-marketplaces continue to encounter difficulties of supplier and cus-tomer adoption, supplier content integration, and integration with their own ERP systems.

In light of the growing body of research and anecdotal evidence, there is an urgent need to rebalance the procurement value creation model, repla-cing what has become a traditional focus on one-off systems or strategic sourcing initiatives with a holistic view that places the human factor at its core. Such a model would include, as a key resource, highly skilled buyers with expertise in procurement processes and deep category knowledge. The role of the organization would be to deploy that resource to maximum

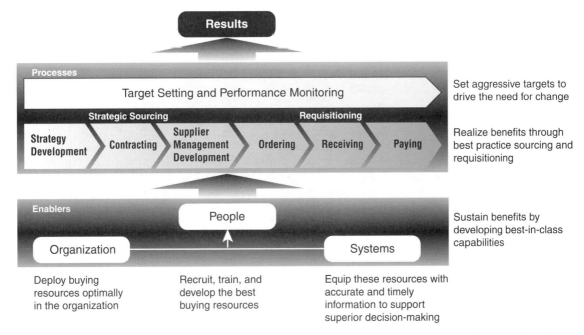

11-1 A procurement transformation program rests upon re-engineering all the drivers of procurement value creation.

internal and external effect, using technology to provide the necessary information for the procurement team to exploit its expertise and enhance its own productivity.

This expert buyer model, which combines process excellence with deep category knowledge, demands that buyers focus on a limited set of categories and are somewhat protected from operational demands. Similarly, the value of their expertise can only be maximized when categories requiring similar buying techniques are grouped together. It follows that a successful personnel strategy requires the development of an organizational structure that is both category-focused and capabilities-driven.

In such a context, technology still has an important role to play, but only to the extent that it supports and enhances the ability of the organization to deploy, support, and exploit the buyer's expertise. Increasingly tight financial resources must be focused on the option that is most likely to deliver the greatest sustained benefit, and technologies must be matched to the needs of specific spend segments. With senior management no longer dazzled by the "e" factor, funding will only be available for projects that promise measurable results in rigorously developed business cases. Moreover, those promised results will only be delivered if the focus shifts from simply making the technology work to achieving the rapid user adoption on which they depend.

Accenture has coined the term "procurement transformation" to describe this holistic approach. Whereas strategic sourcing and e-procurement deliver step changes in performance (which tend to fade over time since they fail to sustain the best practice processes they are based on), real transformation occurs when an organization invests in recruiting and developing top-flight professionals to manage its categories.

To that end, procurement transformation starts with an experience-based diagnostic that is designed to identify and prioritize cost-saving opportunities. The diagnostic is used to assess the procurement capability of the organization in terms of its processes, human resources, and organization structure and systems, as well as develop the business case and define an implementation plan. That intensive eight-week phase is the preliminary step to prepare for a 15- to 24-month implementation, in which strategic sourcing and capability development proceed in parallel. In essence, strategic sourcing drives the realization of the benefits identified in the business case by applying successive waves of best practice sourcing processes. These savings in turn fund the development of best-in-class capabilities, which ensure that the benefits are sustained and further enhanced in the longer term. Not the least attractive aspect of the approach is that, if correctly managed, it should be entirely self-financing [see 11-2 and 11-3].

Read more about best practices in "Better Metrics Improve Performance" by Larry Lapide et al. in *Project Management Practices* **on the Web at** *www. lapide.ASCET.com.*

The purpose of the diagnostic phase is to develop a transformation plan tailored to the specific needs of the individual organization. As such, it comprises detailed analysis of the total spend portfolio and of the organization's procurement capabilities in terms of its processes, organization and human performance, and technology, including its existing e-procurement systems. That analysis provides the basis for the identification of potential improvements and the means by which those improvements may be realized. This forms the basis for the development of a business case and implementation plan. After the initial diagnosis phase, the client can then structure the program according to the identified opportunities, choosing either to embark on the full transformation journey or to focus the program around a few key modules. Either way, the program is driven by the business case and is focused on results.

Once the diagnostic phase is complete and the recommendations accepted, strategic sourcing and capability development run in parallel throughout the remainder of the transformation project. On the strategic sourcing side, the focus is on total cost of ownership—where commodities are prioritized and executed in successive waves of spend categories as part of a coordinated program, rather than a series of line projects. In the specific area of supplier development and management, the aim is to identify and prioritize the relatively small number of suppliers that have the most significant impact on cost and service performance. Supplier confidence and cooperation is best fostered by the organization that is willing to change and improve its own performance; there shouldn't be any "sacred cows," and organizations should embrace out-of-the-box thinking.

Key to the capability development phase is the development of best practice target setting and performance monitoring processes, which will ensure that the realization of previously identified benefits are tracked and sustained. The ultimate aim must be to ensure common goals by developing measures that are consistent both vertically and horizontally across the organization. Arguably the most important parameter to measure is the organization's ability to learn, change, and continuously improve. Procurement transformation is a process that demands the involvement,

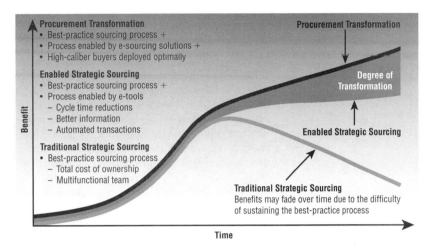

11-2 The procurement transformation journey combines strategic sourcing with the development of world-class procurement capabilities to sustain benefits over time.

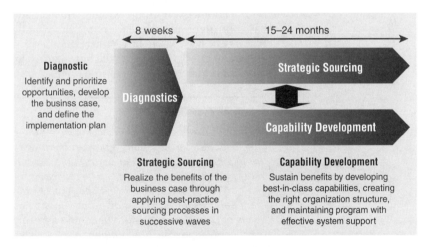

11-3 The procurement transformation delivery model begins with an experience-based diagnostic, followed by the parallel delivery of savings and capabilities.

> Arguably the most important parameter to measure is the organization's ability to learn, change, and continuously improve.

commitment, and sponsorship of senior management, and the participation and agreement of all other levels within the organization. Arguably the most important parameter to measure is the organization's ability to learn, change, and continuously improve.

Target setting and performance monitoring provide the framework where organizational design, human performance, and systems issues can be addressed. The optimal organization for procurement transformation is one that is based on spend segmentation and is logically designed around these segments. The resulting structure gives the required focus on categories and enables the implementation of specific solutions by category. Such an organizational design allows for proper identification of key processes and tasks, and in turn feeds into logical roles and job descriptions. It recognizes that no one organizational model can meet the needs of all organizations or, indeed, the differing needs within any one. The design also strikes a balance between external leverage and internal responsiveness. Most important, by creating a category-focused model, it provides the environment within which buying expertise can be developed.

That buying expertise is the focus of the human performance component of capability development. Its aim must be to attract, retain, and develop the best people by determining the competency levels needed for the different roles within procurement, identifying where gaps exist between current and targeted levels, and developing the necessary strategies for filling them. That requires the early involvement of the human resources department to ensure consistency with wider policies and procedures, and an objective assessment of capabilities by neutral and experienced outsiders. It also requires strong and effective communication in order to carefully manage expectations.

Finally, there is no suggestion that any of this can be achieved without an investment in systems. However, the aim must be to determine how to best leverage the current technology investment, and to take advantage of new technology options. System investments need to be selective and based on rigorous business cases. The overall aim is to increase the effectiveness of the expert buyer through the provision of better information and more effective tools, while automating transactions and reducing the need for human involvement in low-value tasks.

About the Author

Richard Laub, a partner in Accenture's Supply Chain Management Service Line, oversees the company's procurement work in Europe. He joined Accenture in 1999 and has worked on multiple procurement engagements across a variety of activity sectors. He can be reached at richard.laub@accenture.com.

Rob Woodstock is a senior manager in Accenture's Supply Chain Management Service Line, focusing on procurement. Rob's experience in procurement spans outsourcing, e-procurement, and strategic sourcing. He has delivered a number of large-scale procurement programs over his nine years at Accenture, and can be reached at rob.woodstock@accenture.com.

Martin Sjöberg is a manager in Accenture's Supply Chain Management Service Line in France. Most recently, he worked in the Accenture Supply Chain Center of Excellence in London on sourcing and procurement. He can be reached at martin.sjoberg@accenture.com.

Time Management

Chapter 12 Contents

Chapter Overview

A project schedule is the most visible deliverable for a project, and schedule tracking is the measure most frequently used to represent the overall health of the effort. We view a project as a collection of tasks oriented toward the desired objective. In many ways, the time estimate for a task represents an amalgamation of other knowledge areas' impact on the overall schedule. For example, the level of output quality required will affect the time estimated for the task. Likewise, skill levels assumed to execute the effort would change a time estimate, because higher skill would be assumed to produce the output more quickly. So, the issue of time management becomes one of making decisions regarding the various internal aspects of the project. Those decisions will result in the project completion, sooner or later. It is up to the project manager to make the appropriate trade-offs to successfully accomplish the objective.

The *PMBOK® Guide* defines time management as the collection of processes required to ensure timely completion of the project. There are four time-management-related activities identified as part of the project planning process:

- Activity definition
- Activity sequencing
- Activity duration estimating
- Schedule development

Simply stated, this aspect of the overall management structure is designed to identify the project tasks to be performed, sequence those tasks, and estimate the corresponding time duration. The final planning step involves reworking these four steps until a feasible project plan is achieved. A fifth time activity is referenced in the *PMBOK*® *Guide* under the label of Schedule Control. We will discuss this last activity in Chapter 14, "Communications Management."

Activity Definition

The role of the Work Breakdown Structure (WBS) was discussed earlier in Part II, Chapter 8. As the overall scope is decomposed into smaller and smaller work efforts, a definable aggregation of effort is identified. In the vernacular of the WBS, these lower-level aggregations would be called a work package. A general guideline for a work package is that it would be performed by a single organizational group and would be a manageable size. The rule of thumb for this aggregation is that it would be no larger than 40 hours of work and two weeks duration. The theory of time management says that, by dealing with work elements of this size, it is possible to do a better job of estimating and tracking results. So, out of the work package, one or more tasks would be defined. The combination of work packages and the corresponding task collection are the fundamental time- and cost-management elements.

In a network planning model, the normal task would be effort driven. A staffing level assumption would be made, and the duration estimate for the task would derive. It might be possible to add or subtract resources and change the duration estimate accordingly. Another factor in estimating the duration of an activity is the potential for non-human resources to be required for the task. These requirements are called material resources. As a simple example, if you were digging a ditch, you would allocate at least one person and a shovel (assuming that it was necessary to schedule shovels). For many task types, it is necessary to include both human and material resource estimates to derive time duration for the task. A third aspect of task definition is called level of effort, meaning that some amount of resource would be required for the duration of the project. A fourth example is to estimate task duration on a per unit basis and define the task estimate later when the number of units is known. In all of these examples, the requirement is to estimate time duration based on these various task characteristics.

Activity Sequencing

The WBS is a good starting point for defining tasks, but it does not necessarily define the correct order of execution. Most project efforts would have what is defined as a technological sequence, meaning that there is an ideal order for the task pieces to be executed. As an example, if you were building a house, the roof would clearly not be the first task. Based on experience, there is a well-established sequence for house building and other physical construction activities. In the case of software development, the technical sequence is not so firm, but there are clearly prerequisite tasks. From the project manager's technical knowledge, there would be a task sequence developed. In some cases, the sequence chosen is somewhat arbitrary. It could be based on availability of resources, geographical considerations, or customer preferences. What is important to recognize about task or activity sequencing is that it does determine the resulting schedule. So, if one wishes to shorten a project, they would either have to select tasks on the critical path to shorten (likely by spending more resources on that task) or change the sequence and work in more parallel paths. For construction projects, one can see that doing work inside on a rainy day might save days on the schedule later. In this case, there is a substitution of the order (inside for outside). In a software type project, the effect could be accomplished by moving a critical task forward to take advantage of an idle resource. The important point that one needs to recognize is that task sequencing is a dynamic process and not one done once statically during initial planning.

Activity Duration Estimating

Some project task durations are very predicable and time estimates for these tasks would be quite simple. However, there are many other situations where a time estimate is recognized as a range rather than a single discrete value. One of the critical early management decisions for a project is whether to view the task list as deterministic or probabilistic. Oftentimes a project schedule is shown as single-valued, when in fact it is highly probabilistic. This approach results in a schedule that will most likely be overrun when the proper view would have given a more clear understanding of that potential. In the classic network management model, the term CPM applies to situations where the time estimate is discrete. The equivalent probabilistic model is PERT, where task times are viewed as having three values: most likely, optimistic, and pessimistic. Over the years since their inception in the 1950s, the underlying applications of these two modeling approaches have become fuzzy. Today, few project managers could offer a clean delineation of the assumptions of one model versus the other. Today, CPM would often be defined as the "critical path method." Both PERT and CPM have a critical path, thus confusion. Also, the lack of comfort with the PERT probability equations has made the CPM model more popular in spite of its lack of congruence to the real world of uncertain task times. Our bias says that estimating task ranges and managing their probabilistic result is an important project management responsibility.

There is extensive research literature related to estimating for various types of project situations. At the application level, the basic choice is to view the project estimate as a top-down or a bottom-up approach. If the requirements are sufficiently vague, one likely approach is to compare the perceived effort to some other one that is judged to be similar. This is called analogous estimating. Obviously, this approach is designed to produce a ballpark-level estimate. A similar approach is one called Delphi, in which multiple "experts" are asked to provide a sequence of estimates with group review after each one. With each iteration, the group answers are shared and they typically converge as individual logic is shared and analyzed. Moving toward more improved accuracy is the use of forecasting metrics. These approaches come in various forms. One of the most popular is function points (FPs). The advantage of FPs is that a reasonable estimate can be produced with a small number of high-level system attributes. Finally, the most accurate estimating approach is one based on lower-level system attributes. This family of approaches is called parametric estimating. More information on each of these approaches can be found in the various articles included in this chapter.

Schedule Development

If one identifies tasks, creates a sequence for those tasks, and estimates the duration of the tasks, a project schedule emerges. In a simplistic view, the tasks would be linked bars of a defined length stacked together. The total length of the set would be the schedule. However, the actual process of developing a schedule requires more work. Two scenarios are typical as a result of the initial schedule. The most common one would be that the calculated schedule is determined to be too long from the user or management viewpoint. In this case, if the project manager is charged with improving the schedule, several options are available. These options are as follows:

- Add resources to the critical path, thereby shortening the schedule
- Increase the skill level of the team (quicker task estimates)
- Rearrange the task sequence to cut the critical path length
- Decrease the project scope (fewer tasks)

The first two options would increase the project budget, while the latter two might not adversely affect the budget.

A second scenario would be that the resulting budget was deemed too high. Finally, the worst situation occurs when both the schedule and the budget are deemed excessive. At this point, the schedule development problem becomes career-threatening to the project manager. Essentially, the only way to accomplish both time and cost reduction at the same time is to reduce the scope of the project. Too often, the decision is made to move forward by arbitrarily cutting the schedule and budget without a scope change. Our belief is that adjustments can be formulated along the way. Failure to resolve a proper balance between time, cost, and output objective early in the planning process is a serious blunder for the project manager. At the very least, this situation needs to be formally highlighted early and reviewed at each key milestone point. Estimates made early in the initiation process need to be recognized as having a range value, while an estimate made at the end of the formal planning cycle would be more accurate and justifiable. The definition of Project Titanic occurs when a project is assigned a firm budget and due date before requirements are defined. Unfortunately, this project approach is not an uncommon occurrence.

Readings

The six readings chosen for this chapter are intended to describe a broad scope outlining some of the more common theories and mechanics associated with the time management activity. In the first reading, Jan Warkoczewski's discussion of "The Prerequisites for Good Estimates" provides a good attitudinal starting point for the estimating process. In the second reading, "Software Cost Estimation in 2002," Capers Jones summarizes the general state of software estimating. He traces the history of automated cost estimation and then summarizes 10 "generic features" that commercial estimating tools perform.

In the third reading, Kathleen Peters describes some of the higher-level issues related to estimating in "Software Project Estimation." She calls this approach "Software Project Estimation 101." This reading contains a good overview of the theoretical estimating process. A good summary of related problem issues is also included.

The fourth reading, titled "Fundamentals of Function Point Analysis," deals with the mechanics for calculating function points as an initial software-sizing strategy. Function points are frequently used to obtain size estimates early in the development process when there is limited information on more specific sizing parameters. The fifth reading is authored by Professor Eberhard Rudolph of the School of Computing and Information Technology at Griffith University, Brisbane, Australia. His article, "Tool Based Estimating Tutorial," is a very readable overview of this topic taken from his published lecture notes. This article traces a parametric estimating process, when one has more specific sizing information regarding how the product is to be developed (that is, methodology, staff, etc.). Calculations resulting from this approach would normally be the most accurate of all methods described.

The sixth reading in this series shifts focus to project scheduling. In this reading, we once again go to the academic community. Professor Mark Kelly, McKinnon Secondary College, Victoria, Australia, published lecture notes on network management tools. Scheduling models based on PERT and CPM are fundamental planning tools for the project manager. This presentation should be viewed as an introductory tutorial on the topic. Much of this activity today is accomplished using computerized models such as Microsoft Project, but the underlying theory and mechanics are as described by Professor Kelly.

The process of arriving at an accurate, feasible, and approved schedule is fundamental to project success. Each of the readings in this chapter offers a different perspective on this process; collectively they develop an enlightened view of key scheduling techniques and issues. More information on project estimating and other related time-management topics can be found at many professional Web sites. See the Appendix for a starting place to explore this subject in greater detail. We conclude this chapter with a final philosophical thought. Management theory says that control does not exist without a plan. The process of constructing the project schedule is fundamental to producing a plan. It encompasses all of the planning assumptions. The control process would operate from this baseline.

Curiosity: Prerequisite for Good Estimates

JAN WARKO

February 5, 2001

What Makes for a Good Estimate?

In a nutshell, I believe it's curiosity, and the ability to ask questions until your curiosity and your team's curiosity is satisfied. To keep the questions coming, ask your estimators (yourself included) to 'live' the estimates. Help them understand the importance of their estimate in the context of the project. "If we had to present our estimate in an hour and couldn't change it, in what way would your estimate or assumptions change?" Or, "If you had to bet your job on the accuracy of your estimate, would anything change? Why?" Curiosity killed the cat, as the saying goes. Lack of curiosity can kill your project just as easily.

Getting a handle on estimating terminology is also essential. Effort and duration play key roles in schedule estimates (check your *PMBOK® Guide* or any number of other project management documents for the official definitions.

- I like to think of effort as the amount of time an activity or task would take if one person did the task at a 100% productivity level for 24 hours a day, 7 days a week. The effort portion of the estimate is the place to take into consideration a resource's productivity and experience level (ask questions, and/or document your assumptions).
- Duration is that same amount of work identified in your effort estimate, but placed in the context of the client's calendar and the length of the standard workday. Duration is the place to take into consideration calendar events specific to each resource, such as vacations, holidays, nonstandard work schedules, additional work commitments, or other items affecting availability. (Again, ask. This can be one of the more enjoyable aspects of project planning.)

In some circumstances, the estimate for a task is based solely on the duration aspect (for example, coordinating all participants' busy calendars to schedule the acceptance sign-off meeting means waiting three weeks to close the project). Basing an estimate solely on effort is valid only for those of us lucky enough to have an interruption factor of zero. For the tasks performed by humans, the best schedule estimate should take into consideration both effort and duration (plus a little bit of gut feeling and intuition).

Cost estimates address the resource's rate over the life of the project and the frequency at which that rate is incurred. Cost estimates for resources should take into consideration internal staff, external staff, travel, and equipment. Check out Mark Durrenberger's "You Can't Negotiate Cost" article in the September 2000, issue of *pm Network* magazine for a relevant discussion of the role of negotiation in the estimating process.

What's a Good Approach to Developing an Estimate?

Here are some tactics I take into consideration every time I estimate. Skipping one or more is not recommended, but sometimes unavoidable; be sure to capture the elements you bypass in your assumptions and other aspects of your risk management plan. Estimates should:

Match work plans to the numerous client constraints regarding existing or planned processes, quality, risk (including issues and assumptions), results, scope, and, of course, schedule and cost. In other words, estimates are based on clear and open communication about every aspect covered by the knowledge areas of the *PMBOK® Guide*. A full understanding of the scope (both product and project) and risk are most essential.

I can't say enough about assumptions. A wise man knows what he doesn't know, and he also knows when he's made an assumption. Document assumptions regarding your basis for estimating and regarding those things that may affect the estimate (especially those factors that are out of the control of the team). Not only will your change management plan be more robust, re-estimating your project in light of changes will be a breeze.

Be based on a clear understanding of the work to be accomplished. Once again, the scope is critical in developing a good estimate, as is the nature and size of the components supporting the project and the skills required to deliver the results. Estimates aren't accurate if the project's objective isn't known, or is known but not widely understood.

Be based on a clear understanding of the commitment level to the project. Commitment to the project's work plans and supporting estimates has a direct relationship with the degree of certainty about the project's result and the project processes that will be followed.

Involve the right people, including the person(s) doing the work and the person(s) responsible for project delivery. Whenever possible, use qualified resources who:

- Are experts in the application area.
- Are experienced with the technology that will be used to deliver project results.
- Are trained in the process the project will follow.
- Have produced work plans and estimates on a regular basis

There is absolutely no substitute for the judgment and knowledge gained from doing a similar project in the past.

Be iterative. I've found the following iteration points to be consistently valuable:

- At a high level, to exercise the project approach and expected performance.
- At a level of detail that is sufficient enough to make project commitments with logical resources. Assume an average skill level until the next step.
- At a level of detail that provides a solid foundation for managing project performance against schedule and cost, requiring specific, named resources.

- At each status meeting, as agreed to in the communication plan, to keep abreast of changes to and progress of the project

Consider each resource's effectiveness/productivity. So many things contribute to a human resource's effectiveness. The list includes, but is not limited to:

- Project organization (size; number of locations; type).
- Organization's culture.
- Skill, experience, motivation, initiative, and attitude.
- Development environment.
- Size and complexity of the solution being developed.
- Schedule considerations, such as overtime or securing specialized resources.
- Customer characteristics (where they are located and the nature of the client).
- Project elapsed time (risk of burnout).
- Physical working environment (risk of burnout).

Is an estimate provided outside the context of the work to be done and the people doing the work a good estimate? I suggest this would be a good guess, not a good estimate. You are guessing when:

- There isn't any relevant experience (that is, new technology and/or new clients and/or new project type, etc.). Estimates created without relevant experience tend to be off by approximately 35 percent.
- When the project manager doesn't ask questions or otherwise satisfy his/her curiosity.
- A consensus approach is used, which can sometimes result in an educated guess in the context of a work plan review workshop, but does not produce an average.

When you're estimating, you're communicating. As an added bonus, the more you estimate projects of different sizes and complexity levels, the better your estimating becomes and the better your projects perform. If your estimates and corresponding actuals are captured in your Project Review, other projects' estimates may be more accurate. Who thought estimating could benefit so many people?

Software Project Estimation in 2002

CAPERS JONES

The first automated software cost estimation tools were developed independently by researchers in major corporations and military groups in the 1960s. Commercial software cost estimation tools began to be marketed in the 1970s. By 2002, about 50 commercial software cost estimation tools were marketed in the United States and another 25 in Europe. Although standard projects can now be estimated with fairly good accuracy, there are always new technologies that require improvements in estimating tools.

Research on software cost estimation started independently in a number of companies and military organizations that built large software systems. Formal research into software cost estimation became necessary when software applications and systems software began to go beyond 100,000-source code statements in size. This size plateau was reached by several organizations in the 1960s.

The main issue that led to formal research programs for software cost estimation was the difficulty encountered in completing large software applications on time and within budget. A secondary issue was the fact that when deployed, software applications often contained significant numbers of bugs or defects. The evolution of software estimation tools is described in articles by Boehm [1], [2] and Jones [3] (each of which describes the state-of-the-art tools at the time of publication). A time line of the evolution of software estimation tools is shown in Figure 1 [12-1].

As of 2002, about 50 commercial software estimation tools were marketed in the United States. The major features of commercial software estimation tools include the following basic abilities:

- Sizing logic for specifications, source code, and test cases.
- Phase-level, activity-level, and task-level estimation.
- Support for both function point metrics and the older lines-of-code (LOC) metrics.
- Support for specialized metrics such as object-oriented metrics.
- Support for backfiring or conversion between LOC and function points.
- Support for software reusability of various artifacts.
- Support for traditional languages such as COBOL and FORTRAN.
- Support for modern languages such as Java and Visual Basic.
- Quality and reliability estimation.

Additional features found in some but not all software estimation tools include the following:

- Risk and value analysis.
- Estimation templates derived from historical data.

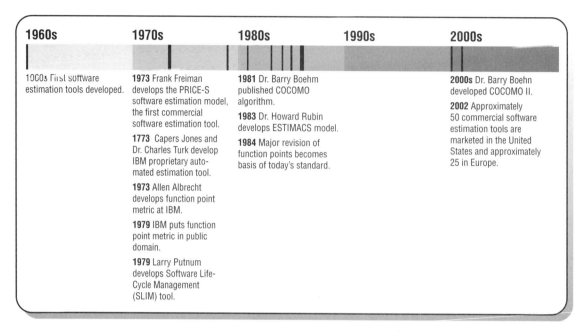

1960s

1960s First software estimation tools developed.

1970s

1973 Frank Freiman develops the PRICE-S software estimation model, the first commercial software estimation tool.

1773 Capers Jones and Dr. Charles Turk develop IBM proprietary automated estimation tool.

1973 Allen Albrecht develops function point metric at IBM.

1979 IBM puts function point metric in public domain.

1979 Larry Putnum develops Software Life-Cycle Management (SLIM) tool.

1980s

1981 Dr. Barry Boehm published COCOMO algorithm.

1983 Dr. Howard Rubin develops ESTIMACS model.

1984 Major revision of function points becomes basis of today's standard.

1990s

2000s

2000s Dr. Barry Boehn developed COCOMO II.

2002 Approximately 50 commercial software estimation tools are marketed in the United States and approximately 25 in Europe.

12-1 Figure 1. Evolution of Software Estimating Tools

- Links to project management tools such as Artemis or Microsoft Project.
- Cost and time-to-complete estimates mixing historical data with projected data.
- Currency conversions for international projects.
- Inflation calculations for long-term projects.
- Estimates keyed to the Software Engineering Institute's Capability Maturity Model® (CMM®).

Modern software cost estimation tools are now capable of serving a variety of important project management functions. However, there are still some topics that are not yet fully supported, even by state-of-the-art software estimation tools. Some of the topics that may require manual estimation include the following:

- Conversion and nationalization costs for international projects.
- Fees for trademark and copyright searches.
- Acquisition costs for commercial off-the-shelf packages.
- Deployment costs for enterprise resource planning applications.
- Litigation expenses for breach of contract if a project is late or over budget.

For ordinary software projects, automated estimation tools can now predict more than 95 percent of the associated effort and cost with fairly good accuracy. But projects that must be converted for sale in many countries, or that run on multiple hardware and software platforms, will have expenses outside the scope of most commercial software estimation tools. The legal expenses are also outside their scope if a software project is subject to litigation such as breach of contract or theft of intellectual property.

A Large Tool Family

The phrase project management tools has been applied to a large family of tools whose primary purpose is sophisticated scheduling for projects with hundreds or even thousands of overlapping and partially interdependent tasks. These tools are able to drop down to very detailed task levels and can even handle the schedules of individual workers. A few examples of tools within the project management class include Artemis Views, Microsoft Project, Primavera, and the Project Manager's Workbench.

The software cost estimation industry and the project management tool industry originated as separate businesses. Project management tools began appearing around the 1960s, about 10 years before software cost estimation tools. Although the two were originally separate businesses, they are now starting to join together technically.

Project management tools did not originate for software, but rather originated for handling very complex scheduling situations where hundreds or even thousands of tasks needed to be determined and sequenced, and where dependencies such as task completion might affect the start of subsequent tasks.

Project management tools have no built-in expertise regarding software, as do software cost estimation tools. For example, if you wish to explore the quality and cost impact of an object-oriented programming language such as Smalltalk, a standard project management tool is not the right choice. By contrast, many software cost estimation tools have built-in tables of programming languages and will automatically adjust the estimate based on which language is selected for the application.

Although there are scores of software cost estimation tools on the market, there are 10 generic features that many software estimation tools can perform:

FEATURE 1: SIZING SPECIFICATIONS, SOURCE CODE, AND TEST CASES

The first step in any software estimate is to predict the sizes of the deliverables that must be constructed. Before about 1985, software cost estimation tools did not include sizing logic. For these older tools, the user had to provide size information. Size data were expressed in LOC for estimation tools developed before the publication of function point metrics.

After function points became available in 1978, size could be expressed using either function points or LOC metrics, and converted between the two. As of 2001, sizing is a standard feature in more than 30 commercial software cost estimation tools.

The advent of function point metrics has eased the burden on software size estimation. Function point totals can be derived from software requirements long before any code is written. Once the function point size of an application is known, then many artifacts can also be sized. These include, but are not limited to, the following:

1. Specification volumes.
2. Source code volumes.
3. User documentation volumes.
4. Numbers of test cases.
5. Numbers of possible bugs or errors.

Another important sizing aspect is dealing with the rate at which requirements creep and hence make projects grow larger during development. If the function point totals for an application are measured at the requirements phase and again at delivery, the two values can be used to calculate the monthly rate of growth.

After the requirements are initially defined, the observed rate of requirements creep is from 1 percent to more than 3 percent per calendar month during the design and coding phases. The average rate of requirements creep is about 2 percent per month based on analysis of several thousand applications during benchmark and baseline studies.

Function points are not the only sizing method available, of course. Some estimation tools also offer templates derived from common kinds of software applications. Many estimation tools allow users to provide their own size data, if they wish, using either LOC metrics or function points or both. Refer to Kan [4] for a discussion of software metrics used in estimation.

In the United States, the function point metric by IBM, and now maintained by the International Function Point Users Group (IFPUG), is most commonly used for software estimates. Version 4.1 of the IFPUG counting rules is assumed in this article [5]. For a discussion of the accuracy of software function point counting, refer to Kemerer [6].

FEATURE 2: SELECTING PROJECT ACTIVITIES

Once the initial sizes of various deliverables have been approximated, the next step is to determine which specific activities will be carried out for the project being estimated. Activity selection is one of the major areas where software cost estimation tools excel. There are some 25 common activities that might be performed for a software project, but only large military applications will normally perform all 25. For a discussion of activities and how they vary, see Jones [7]. Table 1 [12-2] (see page 217) illustrates some of the variances in activity patterns for four different types of projects.

Since variations in the activities performed can affect overall costs, schedules, and productivity rates by significant amounts, it is important to match activities to the project being estimated. More than 100 percent differences in work effort have been observed for projects of exactly the same size due to variations in the activities performed. In general, military projects and systems software projects perform more activities than management information systems or Web applications of the same size.

FEATURE 3: ESTIMATING STAFFING LEVELS AND SPECIALISTS

Although staffing, effort, costs, and schedules are all important for the final estimate, a typical place to start estimating is with staffing levels. There are significant variations in staffing levels based on team experience, application size, reusable materials, and other factors.

One of the trickier aspects of estimating the staffing for large applications is the fact that sometimes as many as 35 different occupation groups might be working on a large project at the same time. A list of 20 common software occupation groups observed on large software systems is shown in Table 2 [12-3].

Activities Performed	Web Projects	MIS Projects	System Projects	Military Projects
01 Requirements	3%	7.5%	4%	7%
02 Prototyping	10%	2%	2%	2%
03 Architecture		0.5%	1.5%	1%
04 Project plans		1%	2%	1%
05 Initial design		8%	7%	6%
06 Detail design		7%	6%	7%
07 Design reviews			2.5%	1%
08 Coding	25%	20%	20%	16%
09 Reuse acquisition	5%		2%	2%
10 Package purchase		1%	1%	1%
11 Code inspections			1.5%	1%
12 Ind. verif. and validation				1%
13 Configuration mgmt.		3%	1%	1.5%
14 Formal integration		2%	2%	1.5%
15 User documentation	5%	7%	10%	10%
16 Unit testing	25%	4%	5%	5%
17 Function testing	17%	6%	5%	5%
18 Integration testing		5%	5%	5%
19 System testing		7%	5%	6%
20 Field testing			1.5%	3%
21 Acceptance testing		5%	1%	3%
22 Independent testing				1%
23 Quality assurance			2%	1%
24 Installation and training		2%	1%	1%
25 Project management	10%	12%	12%	15%
Total	**100%**	**100%**	**100%**	**100%**

12-2 **Table 1.** Software Activity Variations [md] Percentage of Staff Effort by Activity (Assumes applications of about 1,000 function points in size or larger)

Since each of these specialized occupations may work for only part of a project's life cycle, and since each form of specialization can have very different salary and bonus packages, it is not a trivial task to handle staffing estimates for large software applications when multiple specialists are utilized.

FEATURE 4: ESTIMATING SOFTWARE WORK EFFORT

The term *work effort* defines the amount of human work associated with a project. The amount of effort can be expressed in any desired metric such as work hours, work days, work weeks, work months, or work years. Usually, small projects of up to perhaps 1,000 function points utilize hours for expressing effort, but the larger projects in excess of 10,000 function points normally utilize days, weeks, or months as the unit of measure.

Common Software Occupation Groups Involved in Large Applications

1. Architects (software, systems)
2. Configuration Control Specialists
3. Cost Estimation Specialists
4. Database Administration Specialists
5. Function Point Specialists (certified)
6. Globalization and Nationalization Specialists
7. Graphical User Interface Specialists
8. Integration Specialists
9. Library Specialists (for project libraries)
10. Maintenance Specialists
11. Project Managers
12. Project Planning Specialists
13. Quality Assurance Specialists
14. Systems Analysis Specialists
15. Systems Support Specialists
16. Technical Translation Specialists
17. Technical Writing Specialists
18. Testing Specialists
19. Web Development Specialists
20. Web Page Design Specialists

12-3 **Table 2.** Common Software Occupation Groups

For example, in the United States the nominal workweek is five days of eight hours each, or 40 hours total. Yet the number of effective work hours per day is usually only about six due to coffee breaks, staff meetings, etc. The number of workdays per year will vary with vacations and sick leave, but averages about 220 days per year in the United States. However, in Europe, vacation periods are longer, while in other countries such as Mexico and Japan, vacation periods are shorter than in the United States.

This kind of knowledge can only be determined by accurate measurements of many real software projects. This explains why software estimation vendors are often involved in measurement studies, assessments, and benchmark analysis. Only empirical data derived from thousands of software projects can yield enough information to create accurate estimation algorithms using realistic work patterns. For discussions of how software effort varies in response to a number of factors, refer to Putnam and Myers [8] or Jones [9].

FEATURE 5: ESTIMATING SOFTWARE COSTS

The fundamental equation for estimating the cost of a software activity is simple in concept, but very tricky in real life:

$$\text{Effort} \times (\text{Salary} + \text{Burden}) = \text{Cost}$$

A basic problem is that software staff compensation levels vary by about a ratio of 3-to-1 in the United States and by more than 10-to-1 when considering global compensation levels for any given job category. For example, here in the United States there are significant ranges in average compensation by industry and also by geographic region. Programmers in a large bank in midtown Manhattan or San Francisco will average more than $80,000 per year, but programmers in a retail store environment in the rural South might average less than $45,000 per year.

There are also major variations in the burden rates or overhead structures that companies apply in order to recover expenses such as rent, mortgages, taxes, benefits, and the like. The burden rates in the United States can vary from less than 15 percent for small home-based enterprises to more than 300 percent for major corporations. When the variance in basic staff compensation is compounded with the variance in burden rates, the overall cost differences are notable indeed. For a discussion of software cost variations, refer to Jones [10].

FEATURE 6: ESTIMATING SOFTWARE SCHEDULES

Estimating software schedules has been a troublesome topic because most large software projects tend to run late. Close analysis of reported schedule errors indicates three root causes for missed schedules: 1) conservative or accurate schedule projections are arbitrarily overruled by clients or senior executives; 2) creeping requirements are not handled proactively; and 3) early quality control is inadequate, and the project runs late when testing begins.

Formal schedule estimation is an area where cost estimation tools and project management tools frequently overlap. Often the cost estimation tool will handle high-level scheduling of the whole project, but the intricate calculations involving dependencies, staff availability, and resource leveling will be done by the project management tool.

A basic equation for estimating the schedule of any given development activity follows:

$$\text{Effort}/\text{Staff} = \text{Time Period}$$

Using this general equation, an activity that requires eight person-months of effort and has four people assigned to it can be finished in two calendar months, i.e.:

$$8 \text{ Months}/4 \text{ People} = 2 \text{ Calendar Months}$$

> "In real life, schedule estimating is one of the most difficult parts of the software estimation process."

In real life, schedule estimating is one of the most difficult parts of the software estimation process. Many highly complex topics must be dealt with, such as the following:

- An activity's dependencies on previous activities.
- Overlapping or concurrent activities.
- The critical path through the sequence of activities.
- Less than full-time staff availability.
- Number of shifts worked per day.
- Number of effective work hours per shift.
- Paid or unpaid overtime applied to the activity.
- Interruptions such as travel, meetings, training, or illness.
- Number of time zones for projects in multiple cities.

It is at the point of determining software schedules when software cost estimation tools and project management tools come together. The normal mode of operation is that the software cost estimation tool will handle sizing, activity selection, effort estimation, cost estimation, and approximate scheduling by phase or activity. Then the software cost estimation tool will export its results to the project management tool for fine-tuning, critical path analysis, and adjusting the details of individual work assignments.

FEATURE 7: ESTIMATING DEFECT POTENTIALS

One reason software projects run late and exceed their budgets may be that they have so many bugs they cannot be released to users. A basic fact of software projects is that defect removal is likely to take more time and cost more than any other identifiable cost element.

The fact that software defect levels affect software project costs and schedules is why automated software cost estimation tools often have very powerful and sophisticated quality-estimation capabilities.

Quality estimates use two key metrics derived from empirical observations on hundreds of software projects: defect potentials and defect removal efficiency. The defect potential of a software project is the total number of defects that are likely to be encountered over the development cycle during the first 90 days of usage. Defect removal efficiency refers to the percentage of defects found and removed by the developers before release to customers.

Based on studies published in the author's book *Applied Software Measurement* [7], the average number of software errors in the United States is about five per function point (Table 3 [12-4]). Note that software defects are found not only in code, but also originate in all of the major software deliverables in the approximate quantities listed in Table 3 [12-4].

These numbers represent the total number of defects that are found and measured from early software requirements throughout the remainder of the software life cycle. However, knowledge of possible defects is not the complete story. It is also necessary to predict the percentage of possible defects that will be removed before software deployment.

FEATURE 8: ESTIMATING DEFECT REMOVAL EFFICIENCY

Many kinds of defect removal operations are available for software projects. The most common types include requirements reviews, design reviews, code inspections, document editing, unit test, function test, regression test, integration test, stress or performance test, system test, external Beta test, and customer acceptance test. In addition, specialized forms of defect removal may also occur, such as independent verification and validation, independent tests, audits, and quality assurance reviews and testing.

In general, most forms of testing are less than 30 percent efficient. That is, each form of testing will find fewer than 30 percent of the errors that are present when testing begins. Of course a sequence of six test stages such as unit test, function test, regression test, performance test, system test, and external Beta test might top 80 percent in cumulative efficiency.

Formal design and code inspections have the highest defect removal efficiency levels observed. These two inspection methods average more than 65 percent in defect removal efficiency and have topped 85 percent.

U.S. Averages:
Defects for Function Point

Defect Orgins	Defects per Function Point
Requirements	1.00
Design	1.25
Coding	1.75
Document	0.60
Bac fixes	0.40
Total	5.00

12-4 Table 3. U.S. Averages in Terms of Defects per Function Point (Circa 2001)

Before releasing applications to customers, various reviews, inspections, and testing steps utilized will remove many but not all software defects. The current U.S. average is a defect removal efficiency of about 85 percent, based on studies carried out among the author's client companies and published in Software Assessments, Benchmarks, and Best Practices [9], although the top projects approach 99 percent.

The number and efficiency of defect removal operations have major impacts on schedules, costs, effort, quality, and downstream maintenance. Estimating quality and defect removal is so important that a case can be made that accurate software cost and schedule estimates are not possible unless quality is part of the estimate.

FEATURE 9: ADJUSTING ESTIMATES IN RESPONSE TO TECHNOLOGIES

One of the features that separates software estimation tools from project management tools is the way estimation tools deal with software engineering technologies. There are scores of software design methods, hundreds of programming languages, and numerous forms of reviews, inspections, and tests. There are also many levels of experience and expertise on the part of project teams.

Many software estimation tools have built-in assumptions that cover technological topics like the following:

- Requirements-gathering methods.
- Specification and design methods.
- Software reusability impacts.
- Programming language or languages used.
- Software inspections.
- Software testing.

Software estimation tools can automatically adjust schedule, staffing, and cost results to match the patterns observed with various technologies. For additional information on such topics, refer to Putnam [11], Roetzheim and Beasley [12], and Jones [9].

FEATURE 10: ESTIMATING MAINTENANCE COSTS OVER TIME

In 2001, more than 50 percent of the global software population was engaged in modifying existing applications rather than writing new applications.

Although defect repairs and enhancements are different in many respects, they have one common feature. They both involve modifying an existing application rather than starting from scratch with a new application.

Several metrics are used for maintenance estimation. Two of the more common metrics for maintenance and enhancement estimation include: 1) defects repaired per time interval; and 2) assignment scopes or quantities of software assigned to one worker.

The *defects repaired per time interval* metric originated within IBM circa 1960. It was discovered that for fixing customer-reported bugs or defects, average values were about eight bugs or defects repaired per staff month. There are reported variances of about 2 to 1 around this average.

The term assignment scope refers to the amount of software one maintenance programmer can keep operational in the normal course of a year, assuming routine defect repairs and minor updates. Assignment scopes are usually expressed in terms of function points, and the observed range is from fewer than 300 function points to more than 5,000 function points with an average of around 1,000 function points.

Future Trends in Software Estimation

Software technologies are evolving rapidly, and software cost estimation tools need constant modifications to stay current. Some future estimating capabilities can be hypothesized from the direction of the overall software industry.

As corporations move toward Internet business models, it is apparent that software cost estimation tools need expanded support for these applications. While the software portions of Internet business applications can be estimated with current tools, the effort devoted to content is outside the scope of standard estimates. The word content refers to the images and data that are placed in Web sites.

As data warehouses, data marts, and knowledge repositories extend the capabilities of database technology, it is apparent that database cost estimation lags behind software cost estimation. As this article is written, there is no data-point metric for ascertaining the volumes of data that will reside in a database or data warehouse. Thus, there are no effective estimation methods for the costs of constructing databases or data warehouses or for evaluating data quality.

For companies that are adopting enterprise resource planning (ERP), the time and costs of deployment and tuning are multiyear projects that may involve scores of consultants and hundreds of technical workers. Here, too, expanded estimating capabilities are desirable since ERP deployment is outside the scope of many current software cost estimation tools.

Other features that would be useful in the future include value estimation, litigation estimation, and enhanced support for reusable artifacts.

Refer to Jones [3], Boehm [2], and Stutzke [13] for additional thoughts on future estimation capabilities.

Conclusions

Software cost estimation is simple in concept, but difficult and complex in reality. The difficulty and complexity required for successful estimates exceed the capabilities of most software project managers. As a result, manual estimates are not sufficient for large applications above roughly 1,000 function points in size.

Commercial software cost estimation tools can often outperform manual human estimates in terms of accuracy and always in terms of speed and cost effectiveness. However, no method of estimation is totally error free. The current best practice for software cost estimation is to use a combination of software cost estimation tools, coupled with software project management tools, under the careful guidance of experienced software project managers and estimation specialists.

References

[1]Boehm, Barry. *Software Engineering Economics*. Englewood Cliffs, NJ: Prentice Hall, 1981.

[2]Boehm, Barry, et al. "Future Trends, Implications in Software Cost Estimation Models." *CrossTalk*, Apr. 2000: 4–8.

[3]Jones, Capers. "Sizing Up Software." *Scientific American Magazine*, Dec. 1998: 74–79.

[4]Kan, Stephen H. *Metrics and Models in Software Quality Engineering*. Reading, Mass.: Addison-Wesley, 1995.

[5]International Function Point Users Group. *Counting Practices Manual*. Release 4.1. Westerville, Ohio: IFPUG, May 1999.

[6]Kemerer, C. F. "Reliability of Function Point Measurement–A Field Experiment." Communications of the ACM 36 (1993): 85–97.

[7]Jones, Capers. *Applied Software Measurement*. 2nd ed. New York: McGraw-Hill 1996.

[8]Putnam, Lawrence H., and Ware Myers. *Industrial Strength Software–Effective Management Using Measurement*. Los Alamitos, Calif.: IEEE Press, 1997.

[9]Jones, Capers. *Software Assessments, Benchmarks, and Best Practices*. Boston, Mass.: Addison Wesley Longman, 2000

[10]Jones, Capers. *Estimating Software Costs*. New York: McGraw-Hill, 1998.

[11]Putnam, Lawrence H. *Measures for Excellence–Reliable Software On Time, Within Budget*. Englewood Cliffs, N.J.: Yourdon Press-Prentice Hall 1992.

[12]Roetzheim, William H., and Reyna A. Beasley. *Best Practices in Software Cost and Schedule Estimation*. Saddle River, N.J.: Prentice Hall PTR, 1998.

[13]Stutzke, Richard D. "Software Estimation: Challenges and Research." *CrossTalk*, Apr. 2000: 9–12.

About the Author

Capers Jones is chief scientist emeritus of Artemis Management Systems and Software Productivity Research Inc., Burlington, Mass. Jones is an international consultant on software management topics, a speaker, a seminar

*leader, and an author. He is also well known for his company's research pro-
grams into the following critical software issues: Software Quality: Survey of
the State of the Art; Software Process Improvement: Survey of the State of the
Art; Software Project Management: Survey of the State of the Art. Formerly,
Jones was assistant director of programming technology at the ITT Programming Technology Center in Stratford, Conn. Before that, he was at IBM for
12 years. He received the IBM General Product Division's outstanding contribution award for his work in software quality and productivity improvement
methods.*

Software Project Estimation

KATHLEEN PETERS

Effective software project estimation is one of the most challenging and important activities in software development. Proper project planning and control is not possible without a sound and reliable estimate. As a whole, the software industry doesn't estimate projects well and doesn't use estimates appropriately. We suffer far more than we should as a result, and we need to focus some effort on improving the situation.

Underestimating a project leads to understaffing it (resulting in staff burnout), underscoping the quality assurance effort (running the risk of low-quality deliverables), and setting too short a schedule (resulting in loss of credibility as deadlines are missed). For those who figure on avoiding this situation by generously padding the estimate, overestimating a project can be just about as bad for the organization! If you give a project more resources than it really needs without sufficient scope controls, it will use them. The project is then likely to cost more than it should (a negative impact on the bottom line), take longer to deliver than necessary (resulting in lost opportunities), and delay the use of your resources on the next project.

Software Project Estimation 101

The four basic steps in software project estimation are:
1. Estimate the size of the development product. This generally ends up in either Lines of Code (LOC) or Function Points (FP), but there are other possible units of measure. The pros and cons of each are discussed in some of the material referenced at the end of this report.
2. Estimate the effort in person-months or person-hours.
3. Estimate the schedule in calendar months.
4. Estimate the project cost in dollars (or local currency).

ESTIMATING SIZE

An accurate estimate of the size of the software to be built is the first step to an effective estimate. Your source(s) of information regarding the scope of the project should, wherever possible, start with formal descriptions of the requirements—for example, a customer's requirements specification or request for proposal, a system specification, a software requirements specification. If you are [re-]estimating a project in later phases of the project's lifecycle, design documents can be used to provide additional detail. Don't let the lack of a formal scope specification stop you from doing an initial project estimate. A verbal description or a whiteboard outline are sometimes all you have to start with. In any case, you must communicate the level of risk and uncertainty in an estimate to all concerned, and you must re-estimate the project as soon as more scope information is determined.

Two main ways you can estimate product size are:

1. By analogy. Having done a similar project in the past and knowing its size, you estimate each major piece of the new project as a percentage of the size of a similar piece of the previous project. Estimate the total size of the new project by adding up the estimated sizes of each of the pieces. An experienced estimator can produce reasonably good size estimates by analogy if accurate size values are available for the previous project and if the new project is sufficiently similar to the previous one.

2. By counting product features and using an algorithmic approach such as Function Points to convert the count into an estimate of size. Macro-level "product features" may include the number of subsystems, classes/modules, and methods/functions. More detailed "product features" may include the number of screens, dialogs, files, database tables, reports, messages, and so on.

ESTIMATING EFFORT

Once you have an estimate of the size of your product, you can derive the effort estimate. This conversion from software size to total project effort can only be done if you have a defined software development lifecycle and development process that you follow to specify, design, develop, and test the software. A software development project involves far more than simply coding the software—in fact, coding is often the smallest part of the overall effort. Writing and reviewing documentation, implementing proto-types, designing the deliverables, and reviewing and testing the code take up the larger portion of overall project effort. The project effort estimate requires you to identify and estimate, and then sum up all the activities you must perform to build a product of the estimated size.

There are two main ways to derive effort from size:

1. The best way is to use your organization's own historical data to deter-mine how much effort previous projects of the estimated size have taken. This, of course, assumes: (a) your organization has been docu-menting actual results from previous projects; (b) that you have at least one past project of similar size (it is even better if you have several proj-ects of similar size as this reinforces that you consistently need a certain level of effort to develop projects of a given size); and (c) that you will follow a similar development lifecycle, use a similar development methodology, use similar tools, and use a team with similar skills and experience for the new project.

2. If you don't have historical data from your own organization because you haven't started collecting it yet or because your new project is very different in one or more key aspects, you can use a mature and gener-ally accepted algorithmic approach such as Barry Boehm's COCOMO model or the Putnam Methodology to convert a size estimate into an effort estimate. These models have been derived by studying a signifi-cant number of completed projects from various organizations to see how their project sizes mapped into total project effort. These "industry

data" models may not be as accurate as your own historical data, but they can give you useful ballpark effort estimates.

ESTIMATING SCHEDULE

The third step in estimating a software development project is to determine the project schedule from the effort estimate. This generally involves estimating the number of people who will work on the project, what they will work on (the Work Breakdown Structure), when they will start working on the project, and when they will finish (this is the "staffing profile"). Once you have this information, you need to lay it out into a calendar schedule. Again, historical data from your organization's past projects or industry data models can be used to predict the number of people you will need for a project of a given size and how work can be broken down into a schedule.

If you have nothing else, a schedule estimation rule of thumb [McConnell 1996] can be used to get a rough idea of the total calendar time required:

$$\text{Schedule in months} = 3.0 * (\text{effort} - \text{months})1/3$$

Opinions vary as to whether 2.0 or 2.5 or even 4.0 should be used in place of the 3.0 value—only by trying it out will you see what works for you.

ESTIMATING COST

There are many factors to consider when estimating the total cost of a project. These include labor, hardware and software purchases or rentals, travel for meeting or testing purposes, telecommunications (e.g., long-distance phone calls, video-conferences, dedicated lines for testing, etc.), training courses, office space, and so on.

Exactly how you estimate total project cost will depend on how your organization allocates costs. Some costs may not be allocated to individual projects and may be taken care of by adding an overhead value to labor rates ($ per hour). Often, a software development project manager will only estimate the labor cost and identify any additional project costs not considered "overhead" by the organization.

The simplest labor cost can be obtained by multiplying the project's effort estimate (in hours) by a general labor rate ($ per hour). A more accurate labor cost would result from using a specific labor rate for each staff position (e.g., Technical, QA, Project Management, Documentation, Support, etc.). You would have to determine what percentage of total project effort should be allocated to each position. Again, historical data or industry data models can help (Figure 1 [12-5]).

WORKING BACKWARD FROM AVAILABLE TIME

Projects often have a delivery date specified for them that isn't negotiable—"The new release has to be out in 6 months," or "The customer's new telephone switches go on-line in 12 months and our software has to be ready then." If you already know how much time you have, the only thing you can do is negotiate the set of functionality you can implement in the time available. Since there is always more to do than time available, functionality has to be prioritized and selected so that a cohesive package of software can be delivered on time.

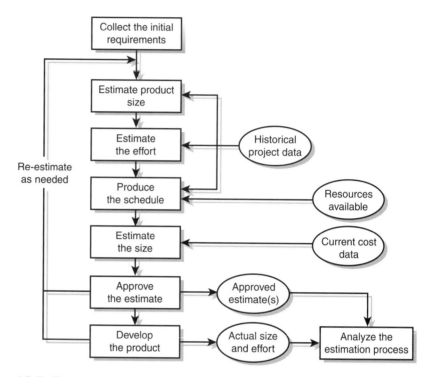

12-5   **Figure 1.** The Basic Project Estimation Process

Working backward doesn't mean you skip any steps in the basic estimation process outlined earlier. You still need to size the product, although here you really do have to break it down into a number of pieces you can either select or remove from the deliverable, and you still need to estimate effort, schedule, and cost. This is where estimation tools can be really useful. Trying to fit a set of functionality into a fixed timeframe requires a number of "what if" scenarios to be generated. To do this manually would take too much time and effort. Some tools allow you to play with various options easily and quickly.

UNDERSTANDING AN ESTIMATE'S ACCURACY

Whenever an estimate is generated, everyone wants to know how close the numbers are to reality. Well, the bottom line is that you won't know exactly until you finish the project—and you will have to live with some uncertainty. Naturally, you will want every estimate to be as accurate as possible given the data you have at the time you generate it. And of course you don't want to present an estimate in a way that inspires a false sense of confidence in the numbers.

What do we mean by an "accurate" estimate? Accuracy is an indication of how close something is to reality. Precision is an indication of how finely something is measured. For example, a size estimate of 70 to 80 KLOC might be both the most accurate and the most precise estimate you can make at the end of the requirements specification phase of a project. If you simplify your size estimate to 75000 LOC it looks more precise, but in reality it's less accurate. If you offer the size estimate as 75281 LOC, it is precise to one LOC, but it can only be measured that accurately once the coding phase of the project is completed and an actual LOC count is done.

If your accurate size estimate is a range, rather than a single value, then all values calculated from it (e.g., effort, schedule, and cost) should be represented as a range as well. If, over the lifetime of a project, you make several estimates as you specify the product in more detail, the range should narrow and your estimate should approach what will eventually be the actual cost values for the product or system you are developing (Figure 2 [12-6]).

Of course, you must also keep in mind other important factors that affect the accuracy of your estimates, such as:

- The accuracy of all the estimate's input data. (The old adage, "Garbage in, Garbage out," holds true.)
- The accuracy of any estimate calculations (e.g., converting between Function Points and LOC has a certain margin of error).
- How closely the historical data or industry data used to calibrate the model match the project you are estimating.
- The predictability of your organization's software development process.
- Whether or not the actual project was carefully planned, monitored, and controlled, and no major surprises occurred that caused unexpected delays.

UNDERSTANDING THE TRADEOFFS

Once you've generated a project estimate, the real work begins—finding some combination of functionality, schedule, cost, and staff size that can be

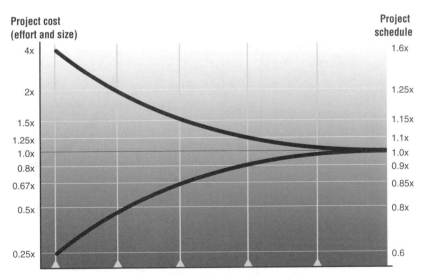

12-6 **Figure 2.** Estimate Convergence Graph. Source: "Rapid Development" (McConnell 1996); Adapted from "Cost Models for Future Life Cycle Processes: COCOMO 1.0" (Boehm et al. 1995).

accepted by management and customers! This is where a solid understanding of the relationships between these variables is so important, and where being armed with different project estimates illustrating the tradeoffs is very useful for establishing the limits.

Here are a few facts of life you need to remember during the estimate "adjustment" phase:

- If you lengthen the schedule, you can generally reduce the overall cost and use fewer people. Sometimes you only have to lengthen the schedule by a few weeks to get a benefit. Usually, management and customers don't want a long delay, but see how much "extra" might be acceptable. Many people don't consider generating an estimate option that lengthens the schedule to see what effect it has unless they are driven to it in an attempt to reduce cost or staff size.

- You can only shorten a schedule three ways. You can reduce the functionality (reducing the effort by doing less), increase the number of concurrent staff (but only if there are tasks you could now do in parallel to take advantage of this), or keep the number of staff constant, but get them to work overtime.

If you can't reduce the functionality, choosing one of the two remaining alternatives is going to cost you. It might cost you a lot more than you can afford to pay depending on just how much you want to shrink the schedule (Figure 3 [12-7]). And it might not work! Remember the "adding people to a late project only makes it later" rule? Well, the same principle applies here—you can add more people, but the amount of work also goes up

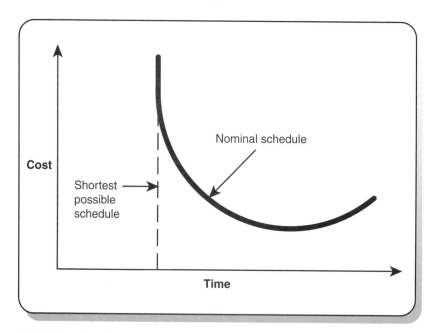

12-7 **Figure 3.** Relationship between cost and schedule on a software project. Source: "Rapid Development" (McConnell 1996). The cost of achieving the nominal schedule is much less than the cost of achieving the shortest possible schedule.

because you now have additional communication and management overhead. If you rely on a lot of overtime to reduce the schedule, you have to remember that productivity may increase in the short term, but will go down over the long term because people will get tired and make more mistakes.

- There is a shortest possible schedule for any project and you have to know what it is. You can only shrink a schedule so far given the functionality you are required to implement, the minimum process you have to follow to develop and test it, and the minimum level of quality you want in the output. Don't even think of trying to beat that limit!

- The shortest possible schedule may not be achievable by you. To achieve the shortest possible schedule, your project team had better all be highly skilled and experienced, your development process had better be well defined and mature, and the project itself has to go perfectly. There are not many organizations that can hope to make the shortest possible schedule, so it's better not to aim for this. Instead, you need to determine what your shortest achievable schedule is (also known as the "nominal" schedule). Data from past projects is your best source of information here.

- Always keep in mind the accuracy of the estimate you are attempting to adjust. If your schedule estimate is currently "5 to 7 months," then a small change, for example, 2 weeks, either way doesn't mean much yet. You can only adjust the schedule in increments that have some significance given the accuracy of the estimate.

It's interesting to observe the reactions of people learning to estimate projects who are asked to do a number of different estimates for a project using a variety of options. When they analyze the results, most people are startled by the consequences of different tradeoffs. For example, the following tables provide 3 different estimate options for a 75 KLOC project:

The difference between the nominal schedule and the shortest schedule for the project is only a little over two months, but to achieve the shortest schedule, the peak staff has to increase by almost 10 people and the cost increases by over $870,000! These results should cause someone to ask if a 2-month decrease in the schedule is worth the cost, and if 10 additional people can be found in time to help achieve it. For some projects, a schedule decrease may be required at any cost; for others, it won't be.

Not all projects have such dramatic differences between estimate options, but the size-effort-schedule-staff-cost relationship follows some basic rules that you can't circumvent. Having various options available as you discuss a project estimate ensures everyone involved can see those basic rules in action and can make properly informed decisions (Figure 4 [12-8]).

THE TROUBLE WITH ESTIMATES

While effective software project estimation is absolutely necessary, it is also one of the most difficult software development activities. Why is it so hard?

The following lists some of the things that make it hard—and they're things that we need to overcome:

- Estimating size is the most difficult (but not impossible) step intellectually, and is often skipped in favor of going directly to estimating a

Nominal Plan	
Management Metric	**Planning Value**
Effort (staff months)	40
Schedule (calendar months)	12.4
Cost	$605,868
Peak Staff (people)	4.8
Average Staff (people)	3.2
Shortest-Schedule Plan	
Management Metric	**Planning Value**
Effort (staff months)	97
Schedule (calendar months)	10.0
Cost	$1,479,170
Peak Staff (people)	14.6
Average Staff (people)	9.8
Least-Cost Plan	
Management Metric	**Planning Value**
Effort (staff months)	14
Schedule (calendar months)	16.2
Cost	$212,131
Peak Staff (people)	1.3
Average Staff (people)	0.9

12-8 Figure 4. Three different estimates for a 75 KLOC Project

schedule. However, if you haven't thought through what you are being asked to build you really don't have a good base from which to predict a schedule or to evaluate how scope changes may affect the schedule.

■ Customers and software developers often don't really recognize that software development is a process of gradual refinement and that estimates made early in a project lifecycle are "fuzzy." Even good estimates are only guesses, with inherent assumptions, risks, and uncertainty, and yet they are often treated as though they are cast in stone. What can help is offering estimates as a range of possible outcomes by saying, for example, that the project will take 5 to 7 months instead of stating it will be complete on June 15. Beware of committing to a range that is too narrow as that's about as bad as committing to a definite date! Alternatively, you could include uncertainty as an accompanying probability value by saying, for example, that there is an 80% probability that the project will complete on or before June 15.

■ Organizations often don't collect and analyze historical data on their performance on development projects. Since the use of historical data is the best way to generate estimates for new work, it is very important to establish some fundamental project metrics that you collect for every project.

■ It is often difficult to get a realistic schedule accepted by management and customers. Everyone wants things sooner rather than later, but for any project there is a shortest possible schedule that will allow you to include the required functionality and produce a quality output. You have to determine what you can do in a given period of time and educate all concerned about what is and what is not possible. Yes, the impossible has been known to happen from time to time, but it's rare and very costly, and we count on it far more than it is prudent to do so!

Maintenance and Enhancement Projects vs. New Development

The software industry does far more maintenance and enhancement work on existing products than completely new development. Most maintenance projects are a combination of new development and adaptation of existing software. Although the estimation steps outlined above can still apply to maintenance and enhancement projects, there are some special issues that have to be considered, such as:

- When sizing new development for a maintenance project, you have to keep in mind that inserting this new functionality will only be feasible if the product's existing architecture can accommodate it. If it cannot, the maintenance effort must be increased to rework the architecture.
- It's tricky to attempt to size adaptation work in the same manner as new work. An experienced individual estimating maintenance effort by analogy is a more common approach than attempting to size adaptation work in LOC or Function Points and then converting size to effort (although approaches to this have been discussed; for example, see [Putnam 1992]).
- Estimation models that are calibrated to produce effort and schedule estimates for new development projects assume everything is created from scratch. This isn't the case for maintenance projects where you are modifying a certain amount of existing documentation, code, test cases, etc. Using these models may tend to over-estimate maintenance projects.
- Often, maintenance work has fixed delivery dates (e.g., a maintenance release every 6 months or once a year) and is done by a fixed number of people (i.e., an allocated maintenance team), so estimates have to deal with fitting work into a fixed timeframe with a constant staffing level.

Some existing estimation models do attempt to address maintenance concerns. At the moment though, there is a lot more support, guidance and discussion available regarding new development estimation than there is on maintenance and enhancement estimation. Hopefully this will change because so much help is needed in this area.

ESTIMATING SMALL PROJECTS

Many people work on small projects, which are generally defined as a staff size of one or two people and a schedule of less than six months. Existing industry-data project estimation models are not calibrated from small projects and so are of little or no use here unless they can be adequately adjusted using an organization's small project historical data.

Estimates for small projects are highly dependent on the capabilities of the individual(s) performing the work and so are best estimated directly by those assigned to do the work. An approach such as Watts Humphrey's Personal Software Process (PSP) [Humphrey 1995] is much more applicable for small project estimation.

ESTIMATING A "NEW DOMAIN" PROJECT

How do you estimate a project in a new application domain where no one in your organization has any previous experience? If it's a leading-edge (or "bleeding-edge") project, no one else has any previous experience, either. The first time you do something, you are dealing with much more uncertainty and there is no way out of it except to proceed with caution and manage the project carefully. These projects are always high risk, and are generally underestimated regardless of the estimation process used [Vigder 1994]. Knowing these two facts, you must: (a) make the risks very clear to management and customers; (b) avoid making major commitments to fixed deadlines; and (c) re-estimate as you become more familiar with the domain and as you specify the product in more detail.

Selecting a project lifecycle which best accommodates the uncertainty of new-domain projects is often a key step that is missing from the development process. An iterative life cycle such as the Incremental Release Model where delivery is done in pieces, or the Spiral Model where revisiting estimates and risk assessment is done before proceeding into each new step, are often better approaches than the more traditional Waterfall Model.

SOME ESTIMATING TIPS

- Allow enough time to do a proper project estimate—rushed estimates are inaccurate, high-risk estimates! For large development projects, the estimation step should really be regarded as a mini-project.
- Where possible, use documented data from your organization's own similar past projects. It will result in the most accurate estimate. If your organization has not kept historical data, now is a good time to start collecting it.
- Use developer-based estimates. Estimates prepared by people other than those who will do the work will be less accurate.
- Use at least one software estimation tool. Estimation tools implement complex models that would take significant time to learn to apply manually. They also make sure you don't forget anything, and allow you to tune an estimate quickly and relatively painlessly.
- Use several different people to estimate and use several different estimation techniques (using an estimation tool should be considered as one of the techniques), and compare the results. Look at the convergence or spread among the estimates. Convergence tells you that you've probably got a good estimate. Spread means that there are probably things that have been overlooked and that you need to understand better. The Delphi approach or Wideband-Delphi technique [Boehm 1981] can be used to gather and discuss estimates

using a group of people, the intention being to produce an accurate, unbiased estimate.

■ Re-estimate the project several times throughout its lifecycle. As you specify the product in more detail, your estimates should begin to approach what you will actually use to complete the project.

■ Create a standardized estimation procedure that all involved can and do buy into. That way you can't argue about the outputs, only the inputs, and your effort is spent productively understanding the scope and cost drivers for the project.

■ Focus some effort on improving your organization's software project estimation process. As each project is completed, compare actuals to estimates—how well did you do in predicting the project's effort and schedule? What did you miss? Where could you improve?

SOFTWARE PROJECT ESTIMATION TOOLS

Estimation tools may be stand-alone products or may be integrated into the functionality of larger project management products. Estimation tools may just support the size estimation process, or just the conversion of size to effort, and schedule and cost, or both. Project management tools have been discussed in an earlier ADS newsletter (November 1997). Tools that support just size estimation include LOC counters, Function Point analysis programs, and even requirements capture and management applications. This section of this report just focuses on estimation tools that are stand-alone products and support the conversion of size to effort, etc.

No estimation tool is the "silver bullet" for solving your estimation problems. They can be very useful items in your estimation toolkit, and you should seriously consider using one (or more), but their output is only as good as the inputs they are given, and they require you to have an estimation and software development process in place to support them. Beware of any vendor claiming their tool is able to produce estimates within +/− some small percentage of actuals unless they also highlight all the things you must be able to do in a predictable manner and what must go right during a project to ensure an estimate can be that accurate.

There are a variety of commercial and public domain estimation tools available. Searching for software project estimation tools on the Web isn't as straightforward as one might expect. A mix of keywords and search engines needs to be used to discover about 80% of the tools, and Web sites where tool lists were available identified the rest. Web-based information on the capabilities and pricing of the tools is variable and occasionally very superficial, so some phone calls and e-mail should be used to augment what is gleaned from the Web.

The following provides a summary of the important features and criteria you should consider when evaluating a software project estimation tool. Figure 5 [12-9] provides a context for the discussion.

PRICE

Commercial estimation tools can be categorized as either "for rent" (you pay an annual fee) or "for purchase" (one-time fee), and they come in price ranges: affordable ($1000 or less), mid-range ($1001–$5000), or

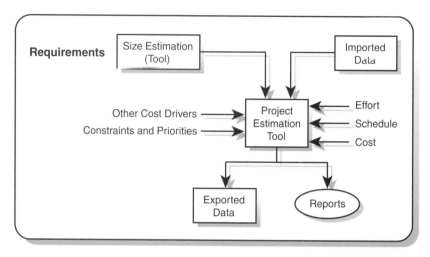

12-9 **Figure 5.** Estimation Tool Context

expensive ($5001 to $20000 or more). Probably only larger organizations or large projects would consider the mid-range or high-priced tools. The tools under $1000 implement non-proprietary models published by others (e.g., COCOMO) and may lack some of the functionality and extensive support of the expensive options, but can still generate more than adequate estimates.

PLATFORM AND PERFORMANCE

Does it run on your current hardware/software? Does it run on more than one platform? How much RAM and disk space is required? Will its database handle the amount of historical data and the size and number of project estimates you will be entering?

EASE OF USE AND DOCUMENTATION

Can you generate an initial project estimate easily the first time you use the tool, or do you have to study the underlying model in detail for days, first learning all the acronyms and struggling with attribute definitions? Can you tailor your estimates easily? Do the user manual and help text provide an understanding how to use the tool to generate project estimates, as well as a simple list of what general functionality the tool possesses? Is sample project data available?

NETWORKING CAPABILITY

Is there a common, shared database so that multiple users can access and add to the historical project data, and view or update estimates (assuming this is important to you)?

UPGRADES

Model data shouldn't be static—as new programming languages and new development paradigms appear, and as different kinds of development projects are studied, updates to the model data in the tool should be made. Does the vendor make model updates available to customers? Is the vendor committed to making continuous enhancements that offer new functionality and support new platforms, etc.? What do these upgrades cost?

SUPPORT

It is important to understand that although estimation tools are becoming more affordable and easier to use, the model(s) they implement are quite complex and you may have questions or need some guidance now and then. Does the vendor provide technical support and a means for asking "how to" questions? Does the vendor offer estimation training courses that extend beyond just how to use the tool, or can they recommend supporting courses and training/reading material?

HOW SCOPE/SIZE IS SPECIFIED

Flexibility is the key—you may start out estimating a project's size a certain way, but as you learn more about the specification of a particular product or as you become more skilled at estimating and branch out into other sizing techniques, you want a tool that supports your needs.

What options does the tool provide regarding specifying the size estimate? Can you enter either LOC or Function Points? Can you specify GUI components, number of classes/methods, or modules/functions? Is the size value entered merely as a single number (e.g., 55000 LOC; 345 Function Points), a range of numbers (e.g., Low: 45000 LOC; Expected: 55000 LOC; High: 65000 LOC), or can the size estimate be divided into a number of "modules" or "work packages" that you estimate in whichever way suits that particular component?

ESTIMATION MODEL(S) SUPPORTED

Some tools use one or more proprietary models where little detailed information is published; others use non-proprietary models where you can purchase a book and/or download detailed information from the Web to learn more. It takes a lot of resources to develop a sophisticated model of software development, so it's not surprising that there are only a handful of models.

Regardless of how much you can learn about the tool's internal algorithms, what you must determine is whether or not the estimates generated by the tool are useful in estimating your organization's type of software development projects. Parametric models typically have a bias—for example, some suit a military development process, while others suit commercial development. The only way to quickly become confident that a tool can give you valuable results is to obtain an evaluation or demo copy and estimate previous projects where actuals are known. Compare the estimates from the tool with what you know about previous projects and see if the results are "in the ballpark."

Assess whether the tool allows you to capture historical information on your past projects and how it requires you to enter it. Some tools can be calibrated to your projects only by modifying the underlying model data (i.e., you have to derive the values yourself); others allow you to simply enter project metrics like actual size, effort, and schedule, and then the tool derives the model data changes.

Does the tool support the estimation of maintenance and enhancement projects? Does it have support for object-oriented, COTS, software re-use or other issues important to your projects?

OTHER COST DRIVERS

The models generally allow you to specify values for a number of cost, or productivity drivers (e.g., staff capabilities and experience, lifecycle requirements, use of tools, etc.) in order to tailor the estimate to your organization and your project's particular situation. What cost drivers are available, and are the values you can set them to useful for your situation?

CONSTRAINTS AND PRIORITIES

Does the tool allow you to specify constraints (e.g., Maximum Schedule = 12 months; Peak Staff = 10) when calculating an estimate? Does the tool allow you to specify priorities (e.g., "Shortest possible schedule has highest priority"; "Lowest number of staff has highest priority") when calculating an estimate?

OUTPUTS GENERATED

Look for a tool that has functionality that shows options, probabilities, and ranges. Tools using Monte Carlo simulation to generate estimates with different probabilities provide interesting insight into the volatility of the development process.

Reports should help you clearly present and discuss estimate options with customers and management. What kinds of reports are generated, and are they useful to you? Can you obtain a softcopy of the reports so that you can add material to them or include them easily in other project documents you generate?

IMPORT/EXPORT CAPABILITY

Possible imports include things like module-by-module size estimates, historical project data, and updated model data. Possible exports include schedule, WBS, and staffing information to project management software like MS-Project or to a spreadsheet program like Excel.

Conclusion

There is no quick fix that will immediately make us better estimators and users of estimates. Effective estimates come about as a result of process definition and improvement, education and training, good project management, use of proper tools and techniques, measurement, sufficient resources, and sheer hard work. Depending on the situation when you start, and how long a typical project lasts in your organization, it could be several years before you've had enough time and project cycles to establish the basics from which better estimates are consistently made. Trying to set up everything in a week is equivalent to trying to build Rome in a day.

But don't be discouraged by this! There are things you can do right now to make a difference to your current project, and there are actions you can take to make your next project better.

Assuming you are past the planning stage of your current project and you have little time to spare, here are some important actions you can take on this project to start improving your estimation process:

- Re-estimate the project at several key stages (e.g., after completion of requirements specification, after completion of architectural design, after completion detailed design).
- At the end of the project, record the actual values (or get as close as you can) for size, effort, schedule, cost, and staffing. Start your historical database.
- At the end of the project, review your estimate(s)/actuals and evaluate what you did right and how you might improve in the future. Use what you learn here the next time you estimate.

Here are some important actions you can take for your next project:

- Review the current state of your software development process—is it chaotic, or does it have some order and structure that you generally follow? If it is chaotic to start with, or your process breaks down under pressure and you expect that to happen on this project, then any estimate you make had better take that into account. Even better, try to reduce the amount of chaos. Establishing a predictable development process isn't something you can do overnight, but every little bit of work you do in this area will help allow for better estimates and better project control.
- Create a first draft of an estimation procedure document and follow the procedure when estimating. See what works and what doesn't, and adjust as necessary. Note that there are templates around for creating such a document so you don't have to start from scratch. Allow enough time to do proper project estimates.
- Decide when you should re-estimate the project and put tasks/milestones for re-estimation into the project plan.
- Start the education of managers and customers regarding the accuracy of estimates. Offer estimates as ranges, and explain the uncertainty and risks associated with them.
- Follow as many of the other estimation tips given earlier in this report as you can.

Try to make time to:

- Work on defining, documenting, and/or improving your software development process. A clearly defined, predictable development process is required so that your project estimates can be made on a firm development foundation. There are document templates and process definition guidelines, consultants, and courses available to help you in this.
- Investigate project estimation tools and use one (or more).

Small improvement steps, taken with care and attention, will lead you down the road to better project estimation and planning. In fact, taking small steps is often the only way to ensure permanent change occurs.

References
General Reading (includes Estimation and Project Planning)

DeMarco, Tom, *Controlling Software Projects*, Prentice-Hall, 1982.

Goether, Wolfhart B., Elizabeth K. Bailey, and Mary B. Busby, Software Effort and Schedule Measurement: A framework for counting Staff-hours and reporting Schedule Information, CMU/SEI-92-TR-021, 1992, *http://www.sei.cmu.edu/publications/documents/92.reports/92.tr.021.html*.

Humphrey, Watts, *A Discipline for Software Engineering*, Addison-Wesley, 1995.

McConnell, Steve, *Rapid Development—Taming Wild Software Schedules*, Microsoft Press, 1996.

McConnell, Steve, *Software Project Survival Guide*, Microsoft Press, 1998.

Vigder, M.R. & A.W. Kark, Software Cost Estimation and Control, 1994, *http://www.sel.iit.nrc.ca/abstracts/NRC37116.abs* (full text available).

Sizing Lines of Code

R. Park, Software Size Measurement: A framework for counting source statements, CMU/SEI-92-TR-20, 1992, *http://www.sei.cmu.edu/publications/documents/92.reports/92.tr.020.html*.

Function Points

A function point FAQ: *http://ourworld.compuserve.com/homepages/softcomp/fpfaq.htm*.

Dreger, Brian, *Function Point Analysis*, Prentice-Hall, 1989.

Garmus, David & David Herron, *Measuring the Software Process*, Yourdon Press, 1996.

International Function Point Users Group (IFPUG) Web site: *http://www.ifpug.org*.

Jones, Capers, *Applied Software Measurement: Assuring Productivity and Quality*, McGraw-Hill, 1991.

Jones, Capers, What are Function Points? 1997, *http://www.spr.com/library/0funcmet.htm*.

Symons, Charles, *Software Sizing and Estimating: Mark II Function Point Analysis*, John Wiley, 1991.

Estimation Models

Boehm, Barry, *Software Engineering Economics*, Prentice-Hall, 1981 (original COCOMO).

COCOMOII Web site: *http://sunset.usc.edu/COCOMOII/cocomo.html*.

DoD Data & Analysis Center for Software, *http://www.dacs.dtic.mil*

Putnam, Lawrence & Ware Myers, *Industrial Strength Software: Effective Management using Measurement*, IEEE Computer Society 1997.

Putnam, Lawrence & Ware Myers, *Measures for Excellence: Reliable Software on Time, Within Budget*, Yourdon Press, 1992.

Other Estimation Tool Summaries and Discussions

Douglis, Charles, Cost Benefit Discussion for Knowledge-Based Estimation Tools, 1998, *http://www.spr.com/html/cost_benefit.htm*.

Giles, Alan E. & Dennis Barney, Metrics Tools: Software Cost Estimation, 1995, *http://www.stsc.hill.af.mil/CrossTalk/1995/jun/Metrics.html*.

Software Cost Estimation Web site (SCEW), *http://www.ecfc.u-net.com/cost/index.htm*.

Parametric Cost Estimating Reference Manual, *http://www.jsc.nasa.gov/bu2/resources.html*.

About the Author

Kathleen Peters is an independent software engineering consultant with an M.Sc. in Computing Science and 15+ years of industry experience developing software and managing projects. She is currently working with Software Productivity Centre Inc. (SPC) in Vancouver, British Columbia, Canada. She also teaches software engineering courses at Simon Fraser University. Contact her at kpeters@spc.ca or petersk@istar.ca.

Fundamentals of Function Point Analysis

DAVID LONGSTREET

Abstract

Systems continue to grow in size and complexity. They are becoming more and more difficult to understand. Improvement of coding tools allows software developers to produce large amounts of software to meet an ever-expanding need from users. As systems grow, a method to understand and communicate size needs to be used. Function Point Analysis is a structured technique of problem solving. It is a method to break systems into smaller components so they can be better understood and analyzed.

Function points are a unit measure for software much like an hour is to measuring time, miles are to measuring distance, or Celsius is to measuring temperature. Function Points are an ordinal measure much like other measures such as kilometers, Fahrenheit, hours, so on and so forth.

Introduction

Human beings solve problems by breaking them into smaller understandable pieces. Problems that may appear to be difficult are simple once they are broken into smaller parts—dissected into classes. Classifying things, placing them in this or that category, is a familiar process. Everyone does it at one time or another—shopkeepers when they take stock of what is on their shelves, librarians when they catalog books, and secretaries when they file letters or documents. When objects to be classified are the contents of systems, a set of definitions and rules must be used to place these objects into the appropriate category, a scheme of classification. Function Point Analysis is a structured technique of classifying components of a system. It is a method to break systems into smaller components, so they can be better understood and analyzed. It provides a structured technique for problem solving.

In the world of Function Point Analysis, systems are divided into five large classes and general system characteristics. The first three classes or components are External Inputs, External Outputs, and External Inquires. Each of these components transacts against files, therefore, they are called transactions. The next two Internal Logical Files and External Interface

Files are where data is stored that is combined to form logical information. The general system characteristics assess the general functionality of the system.

Brief History

Function Point Analysis was developed first by Allan J. Albrecht in the mid 1970s. It was an attempt to overcome difficulties associated with lines of code as a measure of software size, and to assist in developing a mechanism to predict effort associated with software development. The method was first published in 1979, then later in 1983. In 1984, Albrecht refined the method, and since 1986, when the International Function Point User Group (IFPUG) was set up, several versions of the *Function Point Counting Practices Manual* have been published by IFPUG. The current version of the *IFPUG Manual* is 4.1. A full-function point training manual can be downloaded from this Web site.

Objectives of Function Point Analysis

Frequently the term end user or user is used without specifying what is meant. In this case, the user is a sophisticated user. The user is someone who would understand the system from a functional perspective—more than likely someone who would provide requirements or do acceptance testing.

Since Function Points measure systems from a functional perspective, they are independent of technology. Regardless of language, development method, or hardware platform used, the number of function points for a system will remain constant. The only variable is the amount of effort needed to deliver a given set of function points; therefore, Function Point Analysis can be used to determine whether a tool, an environment, or a language is more productive compared with others within an organization or among organizations. This is a critical point and one of the greatest values of Function Point Analysis.

Function Point Analysis can provide a mechanism to track and monitor scope creep. Function Point Counts at the end of requirements, analysis, design, code, testing, and implementation can be compared. The function point count at the end of requirements and/or designs can be compared to function points actually delivered. If the project has grown, there has been scope creep. The amount of growth is an indication of how well requirements were gathered by and/or communicated to the project team. If the amount of growth of projects declines over time, it is a natural assumption that communication with the user has improved.

Characteristic of Quality Function Point Analysis

Function Point Analysis should be performed by trained and experienced personnel. If Function Point Analysis is conducted by untrained personnel, it is reasonable to assume the analysis will done incorrectly. The personnel counting function points should utilize the most current version of the *Function Point Counting Practices Manual* (at the moment version 4.1).

Current application documentation should be utilized to complete a function point count. For example, screen formats, report layouts, listing of interfaces with other systems and between systems, logical and/or preliminary physical data models will all assist in Function Points Analysis.

The task of counting function points should be included as part of the overall project plan. That is, counting function points should be scheduled and planned. The first function point count should be developed to provide sizing used for estimating.

The Five Major Components

Since it is common for computer systems to interact with other computer systems, a boundary must be drawn around each system to be measured prior to classifying components. This boundary must be drawn according to the user's point of view. In short, the boundary indicates the border between the project or application being measured and the external applications or user domain. Once the border has been established, components can be classified, ranked, and tallied.

External Inputs (EI)—is an elementary process in which data crosses the boundary from outside to inside. This data may come from a data input screen or another application. The data may be used to maintain one or more internal logical files. The data can be either control information or business information. If the data is control information it does not have to update an internal logical file. The graphic represents a simple EI that updates 2 ILF's (FTR's) (Figure 1 [12-10]).

External Outputs (EO)—an elementary process in which derived data passes across the boundary from inside to outside. Additionally, an EO may update an ILF. The data creates reports or output files sent to other applications. These reports and files are created from one or more internal logical files and external interface file. The following graphic represents that on an EO with 2 FTR's there is derived information (green) that has been derived from the ILF's (Figure 2 [12-11]).

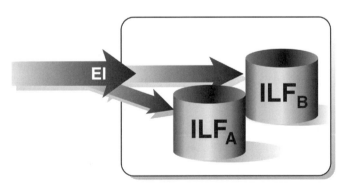

12-10 Figure 1.

External Inquiry (EQ)—an elementary process with both input and output components that result in data retrieval from one or more internal logical files and external interface files. The input process does not update any Internal Logical Files, and the output side does not contain derived data. The graphic below represents an EQ with two ILF's and no derived data (Figure 3 [12-12]).

Internal Logical Files (ILF's)—a user identifiable group of logically related data that resides entirely within the applications boundary and is maintained through external inputs.

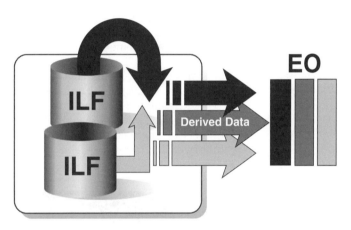

12-11 Figure 2.

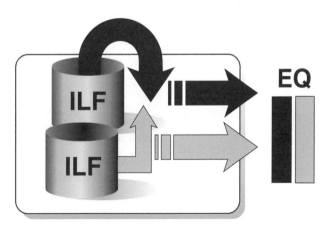

12-12 Figure 3.

External Interface Files (EIF's)—a user identifiable group of logically related data that is used for reference purposes only. The data resides entirely outside the application and is maintained by another application. The external interface file is an internal logical file for another application.

All Components Are Rated as Low, Average, or High

After the components have been classified as one of the five major components (EI's, EO's, EQ's, ILF's, or EIF's), a ranking of low, average, or high is assigned. For transactions (EI's, EO's, EQ's), the ranking is based upon the number of files updated or referenced (FTR's) and the number of data element types (DET's). For both ILF's and EIF's files the ranking is based upon record element types (RET's) and data element types (DET's). A record element type is a user recognizable subgroup of data elements within an ILF or EIF. A data element type is a unique user-recognizable, nonrecursive, field.

Each of the following tables assists in the ranking process (the numerical rating is in parentheses). For example, an EI that references or updates 2 File Types Referenced (FTR's) and has 7 data elements would be assigned a ranking of average and associated rating of 4. Where FTR's are the combined number of Internal Logical Files (ILF's) referenced or updated and External Interface Files referenced (Tables 1 through 3 [12-13, 12-14, 12-15]).

FTR's	Data Elements		
	1-4	**5-15**	**>15**
0-1	Low	Low	Average
2	Low	Average	High
3 or more	Average	High	High

12-13 Table 1. E1 Table

FTR's	Data Elements		
	1-5	**6-19**	**>19**
0-1	Low	Low	Average
2-3	Low	Average	High
>3	Average	High	High

12-14 Table 2. Shared EO and EQ Table

Like all components, EQ's are rated and scored. Basically, an EQ is rated (Low, Average, or High) like an EO, but assigned a value like an EI. The rating is based upon the total number of unique (combined unique input and output sides) data elements (DET's) and the file types referenced (FTR's) (combined unique input and output sides). If the same FTR is used on both the input and output side, then it is counted only one time. If the same DET is used on both the input and output side, then it is only counted one time.

For both ILF's and EIF's the number of record element types and the number of data elements types are used to determine a ranking of low, average, or high. A Record Element Type is a user-recognizable subgroup of data elements within an ILF or EIF. A Data Element Type (DET) is a unique user-recognizable, no-recursive field on an ILF or EIF (Table 4 [12-16]).

Rating	Values		
	EO	EQ	EI
Low	4	3	3
Average	5	4	4
High	7	6	6

12-15 Table 3. Values for transactions

RET's	Data Elements		
	1-19	20-50	>50
1	Low	Low	Average
2-5	Low	Average	High
>5	Average	High	High

Rating	Values	
	ILF	EIF
Low	7	5
Average	10	7
High	15	10

12-16 Table 4.

The counts for each level of complexity for each type of component can be entered into a table such as the following one. Each count is multiplied by the numerical rating shown to determine the rated value. The rated values on each row are summed across the table, giving a total value for each type of component. These totals are then summed across the table, giving a total value for each type of component. These totals are then summed down to arrive at the Total Number of Unadjusted Function Points (Table 5 [12-17]).

Type of Component	Complexity of Components			Total
	Low	Average	High	
External inputs	___ × 3 = ___	___ × 4 = ___	___ × 6 = ___	
External outputs	___ × 4 = ___	___ × 5 = ___	___ × 7 = ___	
External inquiries	___ × 3 = ___	___ × 4 = ___	___ × 6 = ___	
Internal logical files	___ × 7 = ___	___ × 10 = ___	___ × 15 = ___	
External interface files	___ × 5 = ___	___ × 7 = ___	___ × 10 = ___	
Total number of unadjusted Function points				_____
Multiplied value adjustment factor				_____
Total adjusted function points				_____

12-17 Table 5.

Value Adjustment Factor (General System Characteristics)

The value adjustment factor (VAF) is based on 14 general system characteristics (GSC's) that rate the general functionality of the application being counted (Table 6 [12-18]). Each characteristic has associated descriptions that help determine the degrees of influence of the characteristics. The degrees of influence range on a scale of zero to five. The ratings are:

0 Not present, or no influence

1 Incidental influence

2 Moderate influence

3 Average influence

4 Significant influence

5 Strong influence throughout (Table 6 [12-18])

GSC's at a Glance

General System Characteristic	Brief Description
1. Data communications	How many communication facilities are there to aid in the transfer or exchange of information with the application or system?
2. Distributed data processing	How are distributed data and processing functions handled?
3. Performance	Did the user require response time or throughput?
4. Heavily used configuration	How heavily used is the current hardware platform where the application will be executed?
5.Transactionrate	How frequently are transactions executed: daily, weekly, monthly, etc.?
6. On-Line data entry	What percentage of the information is entered On-Line?
7. End-user efficiency	Was the application designed for end-user efficiency?
8. On-Line update	How many ILF's are updated by On-Line transaction?
9. Complex processing	Does the application have extensive logical or mathematical processing?
10. Reusability	Was the application developed to meet one user's or many users' needs?
11. Installation ease	How difficult is conversion and installation?
12. Operational ease	How effective and/or automated are start-up, backup, and recovery procedures?
13. Multiple sites	Was the application specifically designed, developed, and supported to be installed at multiple sites for multiple organizations?
14. Facilitate change	Was the application specifically designed, developed, and supported to facilitate change?

12-18 Table 6. GSC's at a Glance

Considerations for GUI Applications

GSC items such as Transaction Rates, End User Efficiency, On Line Update, and Reusability usually score higher for GUI applications than on traditional applications. On the other hand, performance, heavily used configuration, and multiple sites, will score lower for GUI applications than traditional applications.

Once all the 14 GSC's have been answered, they should be tabulated using the IFPUG Value Adjustment Equation (VAF):

$$VAF = 0.65 + \left[\left(\sum_{i=1}^{14} Ci \right) / 100 \right]$$

where:

Ci = degree of influence for each General System Characteristic

i = is from 1 to 14 representing each GSC

$\sum$ = is summation of all 14 GSC's

Another way to understand the formula is: VAF = (65 + TDI)/100, where TDI is the sum of the results from each question.

Summary of Benefits of Function Point Analysis

- Can be used to size software applications accurately. Sizing is an important component in determining productivity (outputs/inputs).

- Can be an essential ingredient to measuring and managing scope creep.

- Can be the basis of creating estimating models, which can be explained, revised, and accurate.

- Can be used with other metrics to help pinpoint opportunities for improvement.

- Can help improve communications with senior management.

- Can be counted by different people, at different times, to obtain the same measure within a reasonable margin of error.

- Are easily understood by the non-technical user. This helps communicate sizing information to a user or customer.

- Can be used to determine whether a tool, a language, or an environment, is more productive when compared with others.

Conclusions

Accurately predicting the size of software has plagued the software industry for over 45 years. Function Points are becoming widely accepted as the standard metric for measuring software size. Now that Function Points have made adequate sizing possible, it can now be anticipated that the overall rate of progress in software productivity and software quality will improve. Understanding software size is the key to understanding both productivity and quality. Without a reliable sizing metric relative changes in productivity (Function Points per Work Month) or relative changes in quality (Defects per Function Point) cannot be calculated. If relative changes in productivity and quality can be calculated and plotted over time, then focus can be put upon an organization's strengths and weaknesses. Most important, any attempt to correct weaknesses can be measured for effectiveness.

Tool Based Estimating Tutorial

EBERHARD E. RUDOLPH

For this estimating exercise, we use the Project Historic Information System introduced in last week's exercise (Figure 1 [12-19]). (The counting example is loosely based on the exercise A-3: Project Tracking Database. See K. Schwalbe, *Information Technology Project Management, 2nd Edition*, Course Technology, 2002, pp. 522–524.) We now want to apply the function point count derived last week in order to estimate the effort required to develop the planned system. To do so, we will use the COSMOS estimating tool (Figure 2 [12-20]).

We assume that the system will be developed mainly using the development tools offered by database environments such as Oracle, Informix, or Access. The development environment is small (15 development staff), so the development is relative informal. The system will be developed by two new staff members who have good database language skills, but are still familiarizing themselves with the IT environment of the company.

Using the COSMOS estimating tool five major steps have to be completed to obtain a first estimation. We will go through these steps in order to derive the estimation report. The steps are:

- Set up the project.
- Enter the function point model.
- Enter the COCOMO model.
- Enter the Rayleigh model.
- Enter the display options.

Some of these steps will require more than one input screen to be filled.

To start the COSMOS estimating process we set up our project (Figure 3 [12-21]). This just requires to enter a project name, author, and a brief description. Having done that, we can start to enter the Function Point model (to enter the system size in Function Points) and the COCOMO model (to enter the productivity-relevant parameters).

Using the Function Point results derived in the previous exercise, we can enter the Function Point model screens in the COSMOS tool. Together with the Function Point count, we also record that the programming environment will be Database Language (Figure 4 [12-22]).

Note that the Adjustment Factor (VAF) was not discussed in the previous Function Point exercise. This factor will no longer be used in future versions of the IFPUG rules. The values suggested here reflect the character of the Project History system and are shown to be used in the COSMOS tool. The value of 1.0 for the VAF ensures that the originally counted 140 Function Points for the Project History system remain unchanged.

Using the first Function Point option, we enter the unadjusted Function Point values and select Database Language as programming language (Figure 5 [12-23]).

The programming language selection will be used to translate ("back-fire") the Function Point values into Lines Of Code used by the COCOMO model on which the COSMOS tool is based. In this case, each Function

Estimate: Project History System

☑ Case from function point exercise

☑ Spreadsheet implementation

☑ Relational database

☑ Small development environment

☑ Team of two new staff members

☑ Use of tools

☑ No pressure for early completion

☑ Informal development

© E. Rudolph 2002   Estimating case-1

12-19 Figure 1. Estimate: Project History System

COSMOS Tool

☑ Set up project

☑ FP size
  • FP size
  • Programming language

☑ COCOMO
  • Attributes
  • Cost drivers

☑ Rayleigh
  • Attributes

☑ Set display options

© E. Rudolph 2002   Estimating case-2

12-20 Figure 2. COSMOS Tool

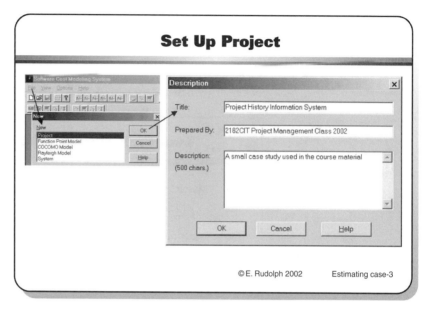

12-21 Figure 3. Set up Project

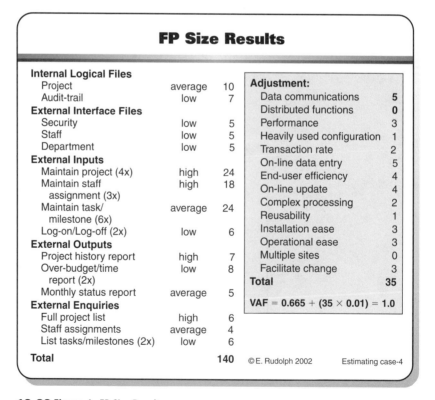

12-22 Figure 4. FP Size Results

Point is assumed to produce 40 lines of code. The system is therefore estimated to have 5600 LOC (Figure 5 [12-23]).

The Adjustment Factor reflects the quality constraints of the system. It can range from 0.65 to 1.35. In the latest (ISO-compliant) version of the IFPUG counting rules, the Adjustment factor is dropped. Most tools (such as COSMOS 4.1) still use it, but you can set it to 1.0 (meaning no change to the original derived Function Points). That is what we do here by entering the suggested selections from the previous slide (Figure 6 [12-24]).

The mode of the development addresses the character of the software development. For our project an "organic" project mode would be appropriate. The environment is stable and the project itself is small and would be developed quite informally (Figure 7 [12-25]).

The product does have to be very reliable since quotes for future projects will be based on project history, so reliability is "very high."

The database is not very large. It has to hold a maximum of 100 projects and all the changes to those projects. The size of the database is "nominal."

With an adjustment factor of 1, the product is of average complexity. The complexity is "nominal" (Figure 8 [12-26]).

Response time requirement is "nominal" since at any given time there will be only very few users seeking historical project details. There are also no stated response time requirements.

There are no stated memory requirements; the memory constraints are therefore "nominal" (Figure 9 [12-27]).

The system, however, is very stable, hence a "low" volatility.

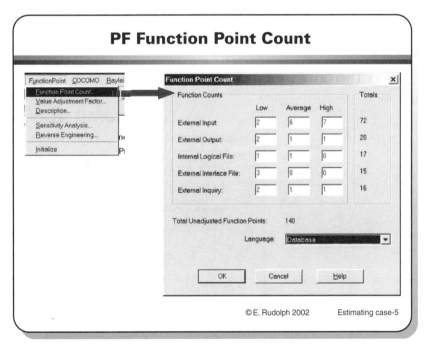

12-23 Figure 5. FP Function Point Count

Turnaround time is "low" since there are only few staff involved in the development, and communication is very informal.

The capability of the staff is "high" (since the company only hires top staff). Their experience with the application is "low" since they never had been involved with a similar project (Figure 10 [12-28]).

They have a "nominal" software engineering experience from some course work but without practical experience. They do have a "nominal"

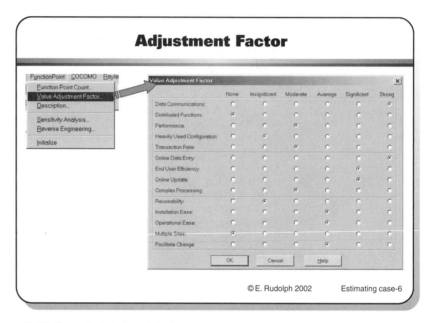

12-24 Figure 6. Adjustment Factor

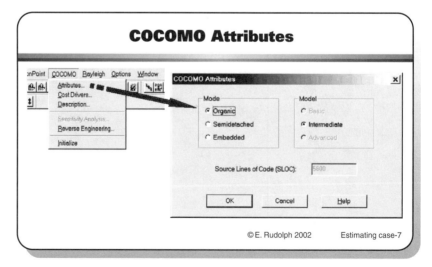

12-25 Figure 7. COCOMO Attributes

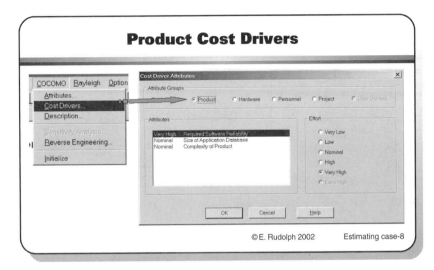

12-26 Figure 8. Product Cost Drivers

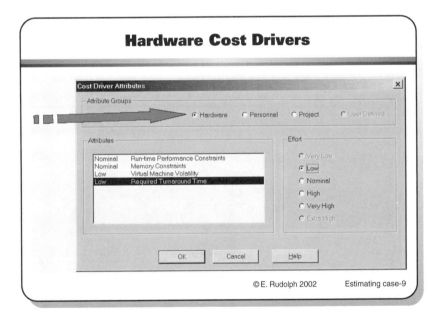

12-27 Figure 9. Hardware Cost Drivers

knowledge of the company's computer environment. Their experience with the database language, however, is "high."

Software engineering methods are only starting to be used, therefore a rating of "nominal" would be justified. Tools are very much used by the organization so this parameter is rated as "high." There is no pressure to complete the project ahead of time (or stretch it). The required development schedule is "nominal" (Figure 11 [12-29]).

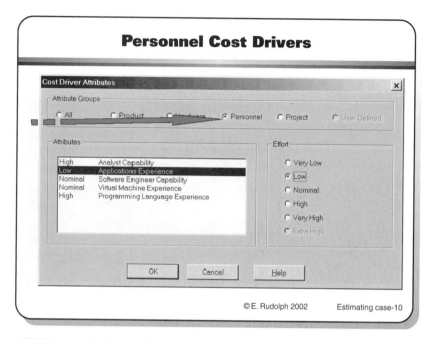

12-28 Figure 10. Personnel Cost Drivers

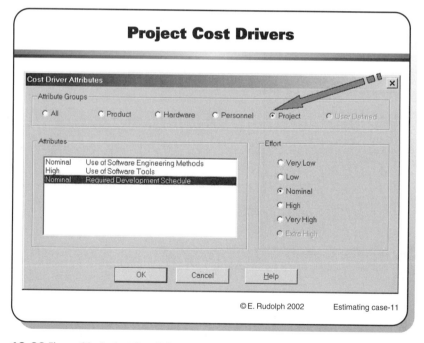

12-29 Figure 11. Project Cost Drivers

Select Attributes in the Rayleigh tab to define the application type of the Project History Information System. From the choices offered, Business Systems would be the most appropriate.

You could also change the preset value of 75% for the Main Build Phase percentage. This is the time defined in the Rayleigh model from detailed design to system completion. The suggested value seems realistic, so we do not alter it (Figure 12 [12-30]). The result obtained from the Rayleigh attributes is the Manpower Buildup Index Level, which is used to determine the development time.

Make sure that you select the COCOMO phase distribution. This will provide a breakdown of the effort into the main phases (assuming a waterfall model, which is suitable for our car manufacturing organization) (Figure 13 [12-31]).

Overall and based on 5600 lines of code, the COSMIC estimation is 17.4 person months of effort to develop the Project history system. With several team members this should be achieved and implemented in just over half a year (7.4 months). If that is too much or does not meet the deadline, then you can try to:

- Get more experienced development staff.
- Reduce the system size (functionality).
- Use a different programming environment (spreadsheet) (Figure 14 [12-32]).

You will be pleased to see that most of the development is optimally done by the two staff available (FSP). During the programming phase

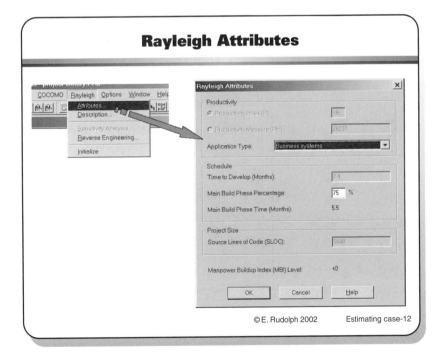

12-30 Figure 12. Rayleigh Attributes

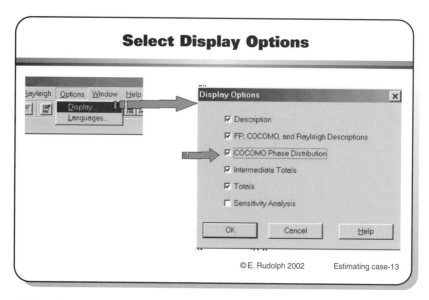

12-31 Figure 13. Select Display Options

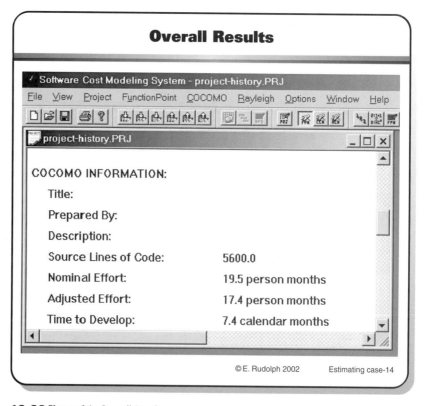

12-32 Figure 14. Overall Results

(which is usually the most labor-intensive phase), an additional part-time programmer is needed to stay within the scheduled project duration of 7.4 months.

The phase distribution effort is based on the waterfall model used by COCOMO (and therefore also by COSMOS). For applications using rapid prototyping or incremental development, the new (1998) COCOMO II technique and tool would be more appropriate.

Note: To get the phase distribution, you will have to select it in the display options. It is not selected in the default setting (Figure 15 [12-33]).

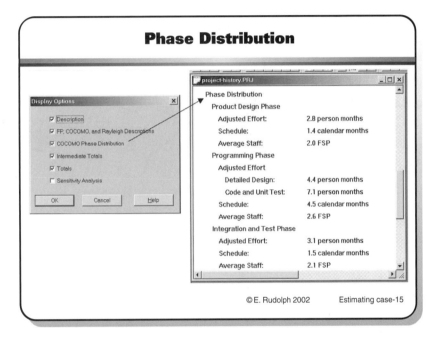

12-33 Figure 15. Phase Distribution

PERT Practice

MARK KELLY

McKinnon Secondary College

Below (Figure 1 [12-34]) is a PERT chart drawn to show the development of a system.

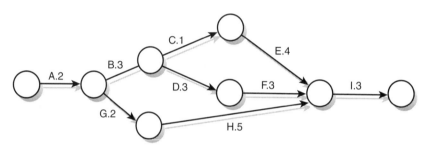

12-34 Figure 1.

Yes—it was not drawn very well, but it's late and I'm tired.

Here are the questions to ponder before we discuss the answers:

EXAM QUESTION 1: Which tasks are on the critical path of the PERT chart above? (1 mark)

EXAM QUESTION 2: What is the slack time for tasks C, D, and G? (1 mark)

EXAM QUESTION 3: The person working on task C tells the project manager he can't start work until one day after the scheduled starting date. What impact would this have on the completion date of the project? Why? (2 marks)

EXAM QUESTION 4: Task A will be delayed by 2 days because some equipment has arrived late. If the project manager still wants to finish the project within the original time frame, he will need to shorten the time for one or more of the tasks. What steps can he take to reduce the number of days allocated to a task? (2 marks)

EXAM QUESTION 5: The project manager decides to reduce the time needed for tasks D and F by one day each. How effective will this reduction be in achieving his aim of maintaining the original finish time for the project? (2 marks)

The CIRCLES mark the beginnings and ends of TASKS to be done in the project. They are also called NODES.

The ARROWS are the tasks themselves. They are identified by letters A to I. In a real PERT chart, the actual names of tasks would be used instead of letters. The length of the arrows does not relate to their length in time.

The NUMBERS after the task names are the DURATIONS of the task. The time interval may be anything from picoseconds to years. Let's assume these timings are in days.

Important point to remember: the ARROWS are tasks, not the circles (nodes).

When a node has two or more tasks branching from it, it means those tasks can be done concurrently (at the same time).

When a node has incoming arrows, it means the incoming task must be completed before progress may continue to any arrows heading away from the node. For example, Task A must be completed before tasks B or G may begin.

You need to be able to examine and interpret charts like this PERT. Let's examine it in English.

Task A is the first task and takes 2 days. When it is done, tasks B and G can begin. If we follow the task G line, it takes 2 days to reach task H, which takes 5 days. Task H leads to the final task, I. The total time for following this path is $2 + 2 + 5 + 3 = 12$ days. The path would be described as A, B, G, H, I.

When task G began, so did task B (with another team of workers). When task B finished, after 3 days, there is another opportunity to run some tasks concurrently. So after B, tasks C and D began at the same time.

If we follow task C, it takes 1 day to reach task E, which leads to the final task, I. Total time for this path was $2 + 3 + 1 + 4 + 3 = 13$ days.

If we followed task D, which takes 3 days, it leads to task F (also 3 days) before reaching the final task, I. Total time for this path is $2 + 3 + 3 + 3 + 3 = 14$ days.

Note that tasks E, F, and H must all be finished before task I can begin.

You will have noticed that there are several paths from task A to task I. Each of these paths takes a different amount of time.

What is the shortest possible time for the project to take (without leaving any tasks out)?

14 days (the longest possible path). Yeah, it sounds odd that the shortest time is the longest path, but consider another example. You are getting ready for school. At the kitchen table, you have to have breakfast while you finish your math homework. You have to finish both before you can leave. Breakfast takes 12 minutes. Math takes 20 minutes. What's the shortest time you would need to leave? Twenty minutes, because both tasks must be finished. Just because one task finishes before the other, you can't leave yet. So in the chart above, the shortest project time would be 14 days.

That is the CRITICAL PATH of the project: the sequence of tasks from beginning to end that takes the longest time. No task on the critical path can take more time without affecting the end date of the project. In other words, none of the tasks on the critical path has any SLACK.

SLACK is the amount of extra time a task can take before it affects a following task. In the breakfast example above, the breakfast could take another eight minutes before it affected the leaving time, so it has eight minutes' slack.

Tasks on the critical path are called CRITICAL TASKS. No critical task can have any slack (by definition).

EXAM QUESTION 1: Which tasks are on the critical path of the PERT chart above? (1 mark)

ANSWER: A, B, D, F, I

EXAM QUESTION 2: What is the slack time for tasks C, D, and G? (1 mark)

a. Slack time for task C: Let's isolate that bit of the PERT chart (Figure 2 [12-35]).

To work out the slack time for a task, backtrack from the task to the node where the task split off from other concurrent tasks. In our case, it is the node directly before task C. Also look forward to the node where task C and the other concurrent tasks (D, F) join up again with C.

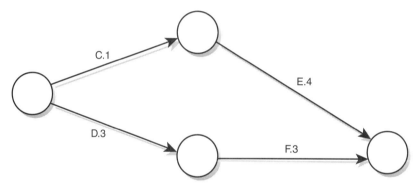

12-35 Figure 2.

In the picture below, the beginning node is marked [in light gray] and the ending node is marked [in dark gray] (Figure 3 [12-36]).

The top pair of tasks (C and E) is being done at the same time as the bottom pair of tasks (D and F). Together, C and E take $1 + 4 = 5$ days. Together, D and F take $3 + 3 = 6$ days, so tasks C and E will finish 1 day before D and

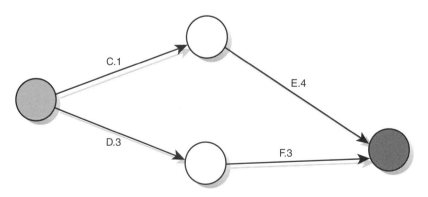

12-36 Figure 3.

F finish. Therefore, either task C or task E could take one extra day to finish without disturbing the task that comes after the [dark gray] node.

That is the SLACK time for task C. (It equally applies to task E, but remember the slack time is shared between them. They can't both take another day without causing delays.)

So, the slack time available to task C is ONE DAY.

b. Good. Let's try the next question: What is the slack time for task D? This is easy, when you remember that task D is on the critical path. By definition, critical tasks HAVE NO SLACK: they cannot run overtime without affecting the ending date of the project. So, the easy answer for this is THERE IS NO SLACK for task D.

c. Finally, what is the slack time for task G? Let's isolate the relevant bits of the chart again (Figure 4 [12-37]).

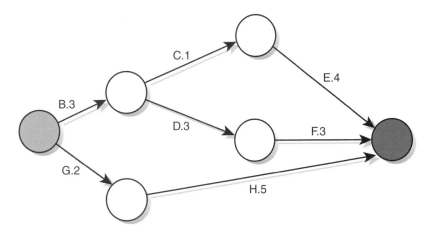

12-37 Figure 4.

Once again, I have gone back from task G to the [light gray] node where it branches off from a concurrent task. We look ahead to where task G's path rejoins its concurrent brothers (the [dark gray] node).

Tasks G and H take a total of 7 days. Meanwhile, tasks B, C, and E take $3 + 1 + 4 = 8$ days, and tasks B, D, and F take $3 + 3 + 3 = 9$ days. So, task G could run an extra 2 days before it caused delays, since it had to wait for tasks B, D, and F to finish anyway.

So the answer would be: The slack time for task G is 2 days.

EXAM QUESTION 3: The person working on task C tells the project manager he can't start work until one day after the scheduled starting date. What impact would this have on the completion date of the project? Why? (2 marks)

Let's look at the whole PERT chart again (Figure 5 [12-38]).

Task C starting one day late is not significant to the ending date of the project. It would cause task E to start a day late (because task E is dependent on task C finishing first), but remember earlier we found that task C had ONE DAY OF SLACK. Therefore, if task C started a day late, it would merely use up its day of slack and no disruption would be felt by the time

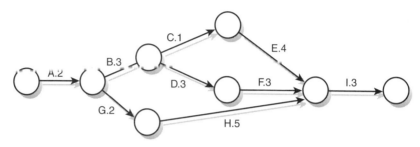

12-38 Figure 5.

task E finished and the other concurrent tasks joined up to begin task I. So the answer is: Task C finishing one day late would have no impact on the completion date of the project because it has one day of slack it could use.

EXAM QUESTION 4: Task A will be delayed by 2 days because some equipment has arrived late. If the project manager still wants to finish the project within the original time frame, he will need to shorten the time for one or more of the tasks. What steps can he take to reduce the number of days allocated to a task? (2 marks)

This is not really a PERT question at all. It is a common sense question. How can you finish a job more quickly? You could put more people to work on it, you could work more hours in a day, or you could increase the efficiency of work (e.g. automating a manual task). Always remember that common sense is your most valuable tool in an exam!

EXAM QUESTION 5: The project manager decides to reduce the time needed for tasks D and F by one day each. How effective will this reduction be in achieving his aim of maintaining the original finish time for the project? (2 marks)

Keep in mind that tasks D and F were chosen because they were on the critical path, and the only way to affect the finishing date is to affect critical tasks. Let's modify the PERT chart to show the new timeline if the manager shortened the time needed for tasks D and F (Figure 6 [12-39]).

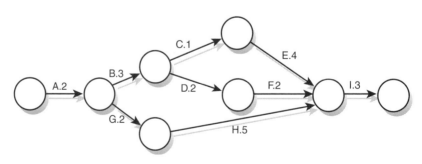

12-39 Figure 6.

Have a think: What has changed?

YES! Reducing tasks A, B, D, F, and I by a total of 2 days (to 12 days) means it is no longer the critical path! It is no longer the longest route from start to finish. In other words, it has been demoted.

What is the new critical path?

Right: Path A, B, C, E, and I is now the longest at 13 days, so it becomes the new critical path.

So the project manager has reduced the old critical path from 14 to 12 days, but the new critical path still takes 13 days. So, the project will now finish ONE day earlier than originally planned.

Reducing both tasks D and F by one day each was unnecessary because after a 1-day reduction, the tasks were no longer critical. To reduce the overall project time further, the manager would have had to shift his attention to the new critical path, and try to reduce the times of the new critical tasks.

So, an answer could be: Reducing tasks D and F each by one day would only shorten the project by one day since after a 2-day reduction, tasks D and F are no longer on the critical path. To further shorten the project time, the project manager would have to shorten tasks on the new critical path of A, B, C, E, and I.

There are a couple of different flavours of PERT charts: Activity on Arrow and Activity on Node (Table 1 [12-40]).

Task	Predecessors' Tasks (Dependencies)	Time (Weeks)
A	—	3
B	—	5
C	—	7
D	A	8
E	B	5
F	C	5
G	E	4
H	F	5
I	D	6
J	G - H	4

12-40 Table 1.

The critical path is through activities C, F, H, and J. (Can you prove it?) The expected project duration is 21 weeks $(7 + 5 + 5 + 4)$ (Figures 7 and 8 [12-41, 12-42]).

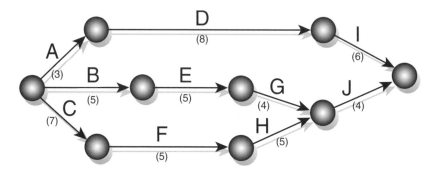

12-41 Figure 7. PERT Diagram Using Activity on Arrow (AOA) Convention

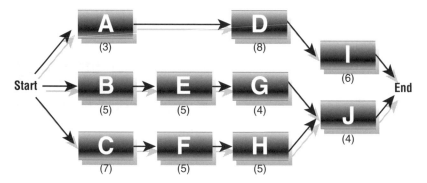

12-42 Figure 8. PERT Diagram Using Activity on Node (AON) Convention

Cost Management

Chapter 13 Contents

READING 1: Earned Value, Clear and Simple

READING 2: Cost Management

Chapter Overview

If time management is the most visible aspect of project management, then cost management is the favorite topic for senior management. Historically, projects have done poorly in both of these visible categories, and they currently lie at the core of many project management tools. When project status is described, these two topics are likely the first ones mentioned. Also, because most IT projects are labor intensive, the major part of the budget will be determined by the translation of labor hours into cost. For this reason, we describe cost and time as the linked pair of project management.

The *PMBOK® Guide* describes cost management as the processes required to ensure that the project is completed within the approved budget. [PMI, 121] The planning components of cost management are:

- Cost estimating: Defining costs for the resources defined
- Cost budgeting: Allocating the defined costs to project activities

Much of the cost estimating activity is based on cost parameters associated with the planning resource pool. In the resource pool, it is necessary to have forecasting data related to both skill and individual billing rates. In addition to this material, cost data will be required. Much of the basic cost estimating activity is linked to the task definition phase described in the previous Time Management section. Once a task is defined, it is possible to make an initial cost estimate based on pooled resource data. In similar fashion, once the activity (task) sequence is established, it is possible to turn this data into a time-phased budget. For the initial planning pass, resource costs are derived from the generic skill estimates related to the tasks. Likewise, material requirements for each task are translated into dollars to complete the time-phased view. As described previously in the Time Management section, the initial planned budget is often not accepted by management or the sponsor because of their own schedule or budget expectations. When support is lacking, it is necessary for the project manager to adjust the plan accordingly. A replanning process requires that a trade-off be made in another project attribute for cost. The most typical tradeoff option for optimizing time is to cut cost or decrease scope. Depending on the nature of the project, other potential strategies could improve the cost estimate.

One of the universal rules of projects is that they grow over time. Better understanding of the problem causes part of this growth. In this category, the change management process might approve a new slate of requirements. From a theoretical standpoint, such approved changes would correspondingly change the project. However, there are two other forms of change that fall outside of the approved scope change. First, estimates can prove to be wrong and the corresponding task cost can escalate. Left alone, a budget overrun occurs. In the same manner, there are other external factors that can erode the budget that are essentially outside the control of the team. One such example is a risk event that occurs. The approach to handling these two types of cost increases falls into the category of a reserve fund. Basically, the strategy is to augment the planned budget with funds that can be allocated. So, when a budget is approved, it should contain both the base-defined requirements and a reserve amount to handle the project's vagaries. There are three types of reserves that might be used:

- Project reserve authorized to handle minor changes and some estimating errors.
- Contingency reserve based on a set of potential risk events that have been examined and quantified in regard to probability of occurrence and level of cost.
- Management reserve set aside to handle unknown and undefined events.

These reserve groups should be viewed as expected values, meaning they are not the sum of all the bad things one can potentially identify, but are the event probability times the magnitude of those events. Ideally, the project manager would have control over the approval to use the first two reserve types, but the management reserve would normally be under the control of an external management entity. The larger the reserve, the higher the level of approval required to release it. Each of the reserve types should be included in the project budget from an organizational view because they represent the total financial exposure represented by the project.

When a project is approved, there is a baseline established for all reporting items, particularly time, cost, and scope. As the project unfolds, status reporting and comparisons are based on this baseline value. It is possible to have a floating baseline as changes are introduced, but the normal approach is to hold the original baseline as a point of future comparison. Obviously, if you let the baseline drift too easily, the comparisons of plan versus actual would not mean much. The purpose of baselining is to be able to track the project versus the initial vision.

One more aspect of budgeting is the funding approval. Some projects are "funded" from the beginning, while others might only be funded for one phase at a time, subject to the results of that phase. In any case, it is the prerogative of management to stop funding at any point. Project cancellation can occur because of poor project results or changes in organizational goals. The project manager needs to understand the funding status as resource commitment decisions are made. For example, contract terms with outside vendors should fit the funding profile.

One of the contemporary techniques for tracking project status is the use of earned value. Basically, earned value operates off of the concept of a planned cost for executing each task or work package. As work is completed, earning value is based on the budget for that task. It is only possible to earn what the task was estimated to earn regardless of how much is spent to complete the task. The traditional status tracking approach was to compare plan versus actual amounts and ignore accomplishment. This approach often gives a false measurement of project status in that resources were consumed **but fewer were completed than planned**. By computing the earned value metrics, it is possible to evaluate cost, budget, and functional progress in an integrated fashion. The key process to earned value is a work package plan that is measured through the life cycle. More can be learned on this topic from the Tammo Wilkens article.

Readings

"Earned Value, Clear and Simple," by Tammo Wilkens, offers an important introduction to earned value (EV), which is now recognized as the contemporary standard for defining cost, schedule, and functional project status. This tutorial-like overview and the rationale behind earned value use in progress reporting will provide the reader with a solid foundation for using the technique.

The second reading for this section, "Cost Management," is provided by Hill Air Force Base from Chapter Six of their development guidelines. This material offers very pragmatic examples of cost management designed for working developers. Included with this is a cost management checklist that is designed to ensure that all of the major items related to this process have been considered.

Earned Value, Clear and Simple

TAMMO T. WILKENS

Los Angeles County Metropolitan Transportation Authority (Currently with Primavera Systems, Inc.) April 1, 1999

Introduction

The term "Earned Value" is gaining in popularity around project management circles as if it is some wonderful new concept to be embraced. Yet, it has been in use since the 1960s when the Department of Defense adopted it as a standard method of measuring project performance. The concept was actually developed as early as the 1800s when it became desirable to measure performance on the factory floor. Today, it is both embraced and shunned, often in response to prior experience or stories told "in the hallway." The opponents will generally cite the cost and effort to make it work, and the limited benefit derived from its implementation. The proponents will cite the cost savings to the project overall, the improved analysis, communication, and control derived from its implementation. No doubt, the two camps have vastly different experiences to formulate their perceptions.

This paper will explore the three major questions regarding this topic: What, Why, and How? The purpose is to allay any fears the reader might have about applying this useful project management tool and to point the way to making it work. It is expected that the reader will gain a thorough understanding of the concept as well as a recipe for implementing Earned Value on his/her project.

What Is Earned Value?

When we speak of Earned Value, we generally are speaking of a methodology. While Earned Value is just one element of this methodology, it is the key element. The simplest way to think of Earned Value is to equate it with physical progress. As the name implies, it is something that is gained through some effort. In project management, this value is earned as activities are completed.

Consequently, Earned Value is also a measure of progress. As we shall see later, there is a direct relationship between Earned Value and percent complete. The attributes of Earned Value are threefold. First, it is a uniform unit of measure for total project progress or for any subelement of the project. Second, it is a consistent method for analysis of project progress and performance. Third, it is a basis for cost performance analysis of a project.

If set up properly, Earned Value provides a uniform unit of measure for reporting progress of a project. The traditional units that are used include workhours and dollars. For labor-intensive efforts, workhours are often considered adequate. In such instances, the financial details of the remaining project cost are controlled by the accounting system. These costs include subcontractors, overheads, and other direct costs. When the entire project cost is to be controlled from the project control system, then it is more effective to use dollars as the unit of measure for Earned Value. Since each labor hour has a price, dollars can be used to control labor as well. However, when using dollars, additional factors enter into the performance evaluation. This includes salary rate differences, escalation, overhead adjustments, and differences, for example. Consider the effect if the plan calls for Tom, Dick, and Harriet to do the work, but the actual work is performed by Lucy, Bill, and Mary, who have different salaries. The dollar measure will include the effect of the salaries. For project financial control, this is good information. However, for project performance control, this information muddies up the waters.

Earned Value also is a consistent method for analysis of project performance. Suppose you ask the bricklayers and the carpenters how they're doing. You are likely to get different answers, influenced not only by how they are actually doing, but also by how they calculate their plan and their progress. As we shall see below in the discussion of "How," using Earned Value establishes a particular method for determining what the plan to date is and what the progress actually achieved is.

Earned Value provides the basis for cost performance analysis. If you want to know what's happening to the cost of your project BEFORE it is completed, you need to know what the planned cost at any time was and also what the cost of the completed work is. Referring to Figure 1 [13-1], should this project manager be happy or concerned? It seems that the actual costs are considerably below the planned cost. This appears to be good news. However, unless you look at the planned cost of the completed

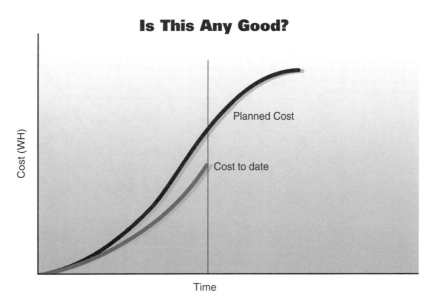

Is This Any Good?

Planned Cost

Cost to date

Cost (WH)

Time

13-1 Figure 1. Traditional Cost Analysis

work, you don't really know if this is good news or not. That is exactly the missing information that Earned Value provides.

In order to understand Earned Value thoroughly, we must become familiar with all the elements of the Earned Value method. Figure 2 [13-2] provides an overview of these elements. While many people shy away from the acronyms used to label the elements, they quite accurately describe the elements. The project management practitioner should be familiar with the "alphabet soup." In this paper, we will use both the formal acronyms and more familiar terms to describe the elements.

BCWS is the Budgeted Cost of Work Scheduled. Quite literally, it represents the budgets of the activities that are planned or scheduled to be completed. In the discussion of how to apply Earned Value, we shall see how this is developed and why the BCWS curve has the traditional S-curve shape.

The ACWP is the Actual Cost of Work Performed. Again, quite literally, it represents the actual cost charged against the activities that were completed. Later we shall see how we deal with activities that are in progress but not yet completed.

The BCWP is the Budgeted Cost of Work Performed. This is the traditional Earned Value that we speak of. It represents the planned or scheduled cost of the activities that are completed. The distinction between the BCWS and the BCWP is that the former represents the budget of the activities that were planned to be completed and the latter represents the budget of the activities that actually were completed.

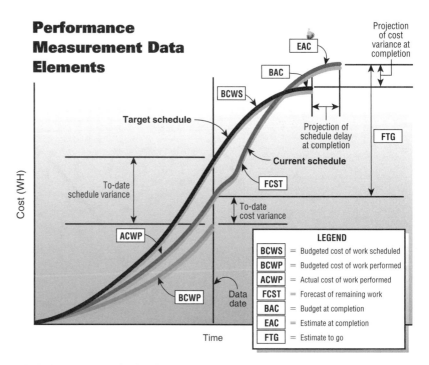

13-2 Figure 2. Earned Value Elements

These are the three major components of Earned Value. At any point in time, we have the planned work, the actual work, and the cost of the actual work. This allows us to make the full analysis of our project progress and performance. Some of the other, related terms shown in Figure 2 include the Budget At Completion (BAC), the Estimate At Completion (EAC), the Schedule Variance (SV), and the Cost Variance (CV). We will learn more about these in the discussion on how to apply Earned Value.

Why Use Earned Value?

Before we consider the mechanics of Earned Value, let us examine the reasons for using it. After all, it does cost something to put it into operation. And, to do it right, it requires some effort on the part of the project team. If we review the discussion above on what Earned Value is, we have the main reasons for using it. Recall that Earned Value is a uniform unit of measure, a consistent methodology, and a basis for cost performance analysis.

You might ask "What's so great about a uniform unit of measure?" Suppose that you are the project manager of a software development project. You're partway through your project and you wonder how things are. First, you want to know what percent complete the project is. At a summary level, let's say that the project includes conceptual design, program specification, coding, documentation, user manual production, and debugging. Further, let's say that conceptual design and program specification are complete, coding and documentation are in process, and manual production and debugging haven't started yet. So, how complete is the project? We've completed two out of six parts and are in process with two more. Does that mean we are 50% complete? Maybe, but we don't know. What is each part worth? Does writing one line of program specification equal one line of code and they, in turn, equal one line in the documentation? How is one to equate the various parts?

Now suppose we determine that conceptual design is expected to take 200 workhours, program specification writing 300 hours, coding 600 hours, documentation 100 hours, user manual 400 hours, and debugging 500 hours. These labor "budgets" can easily be used as a weighting factor in establishing the worth of the various parts. That is exactly what Earned Value does. Since conceptual design and spec writing are done, we have "earned" 500 hours of value. For the in-process activities, we need to decide how we will earn the value. More on earning rules later. For now, let's just say we are one quarter done with the coding and 10% with the documentation. We could then claim 150 hours for the coding and 10 hours for the documentation. The total earnings are then 660 hours. So, how complete is the project? Using Earned Value methodology, we would determine that the project is 31.4% complete (660 earned hours divided by 2100 hours of total project budget). Earned Value has allowed us to combine the progress of vastly different work efforts. The same thing works with any kind of project. Earned Value lets us combine cubic yards of concrete with square feet of forms, tons of rebar, feet of pipe, feet of conduit and cabling, etc. If we're in the banking business, Earned Value allows us to combine product development with market research, systems design, marketing, and product introduction. In Hollywood, we can combine writing the screenplay with scouting for locations, set production, filming, editing, and marketing. By now you probably get the idea that Earned Value can be employed whenever your project involves defined tasks.

So much for a uniform unit of measure. What does consistent methodology do for me? Remember the bricklayers and carpenters? If you ask the carpenters how they are doing, you might get an answer such as: "We're doing fine, we've already used half the lumber you sent us at the beginning of the project. We'll have the rest used up by next week." The bricklayer might say: "We're doing great. Ninety percent of the budgeted labor hours are spent, therefore we're 90% complete." Both parties might be correct, but what can you as the project manager do with that information? You can pass it along, but chances are that your management is not interested in the nitty gritty details, they want summary information. Using Earned Value, the bricklayers and the carpenters would measure the total quantities of bricks and lumber installed and compare that against the budgeted quantities to determine the percent complete. Similarly, they would compare the installed quantities against the quantities planned to be installed up to this point in time to determine if they are ahead or behind schedule. You can see that Earned Value has provided a method that both the bricklayers and the carpenters can use to report progress.

Now let us consider the third reason. Using Earned Value enhances the cost performance analysis of a project. Traditional cost analysis centers around the actual cost of the work that was completed. Therefore, much progress has been done to collect the actual costs through the time charge and accounting systems that exist on practically all projects. What Earned Value brings to the process is a measure of the amount of work that has been done in a unit of measure that is consistent and comparable with costs. In other words, it allows us to compare "apples and apples" by using the same unit of measure for physical progress as for cost. Now we can more meaningfully assess whether the costs spent to date (see Figure 1 [13-1]) are higher or lower than was planned.

How Do We Use Earned Value?

At this point we come to the practical part of actually seeing how Earned Value is applied on any project. There are 5 steps in setting up the Earned Value system on a project, and 4 steps in using it. These steps are described generically but they are the same for all projects. Each of these steps will be discussed in detail. To set up the Earned Value system:
1. Establish the Work Breakdown Structure (WBS) to divide the project into manageable portions.
2. Identify the activities to be scheduled that represent the entire project.
3. Allocate the costs to be expended on each activity.
4. Schedule the activities over time.
5. Tabulate, plot, and analyze the data to confirm that the plan is acceptable.

To use the information generated by the Earned Value calculations:
6. Update the schedule by reporting activity progress.
7. Enter the actual costs on the activities.
8. Execute the Earned Value calculations, print and plot the reports and charts.
9. Analyze the data and write the performance narrative.

STEP 1: ESTABLISH THE WBS

The WBS is the roadmap for analyzing the project progress and performance. It provides a multilevel structure for analyzing the project at varying degrees of detail. A properly defined WBS also provides that each element of the structure at each level is the responsibility of an individual who has management authority over that element and all the elements that roll up into that element. Furthermore, the WBS must contain the full scope of the project. Otherwise, the information generated will not represent the total project. The WBS is generally a hierarchical structure in which each lower level element rolls into one and only one element at the level above it. The bottom level of the WBS should be the activities of the project. Figure 3 [13-3] illustrates this. The key here is that each element has a responsible individual identified with it and each element represents a part of the project that someone or more people are interested in monitoring.

While this personal responsibility might bring to mind an Organizational Breakdown Structure (OBS), the WBS should not be confused with

13-3 Figure 3. Work Breakdown Structure

an OBS. Either structure can function as the framework for analyzing the project performance. However, an OBS is generally employed in a matrix organization where the functional management of the organization wants to analyze the performance of their functional unit on the project. The WBS is organized along the component lines of the project. For example, the project team member who is responsible for the Fan Assembly in Figure 3 [13-3] has components (cost accounts and activities) in several engineering disciplines within the OBS. On the other hand, the Mechanical Design Manager in the OBS is interested in all the mechanical elements of all project components.

STEP 2: IDENTIFY THE ACTIVITIES

The second step is to identify the activities of the project. The WBS provides the framework for identifying the project components. As illustrated in Figure 3, each activity should be assigned to one element in the WBS. The completion of this step will produce the project schedule of activities, typically in a CPM network.

STEP 3: ALLOCATE THE COSTS

The third step is to identify and allocate the costs to be expended for each activity. Since an activity represents a finite effort within the project, it has a time duration and it requires the expenditure of some resources. The practitioner needs to decide whether to use labor resources only, such as work hours, or to use dollars and load all project costs into the schedule. The allocation of resources (costs) requires a choice of the degree of detail with which one will allocate the resources. These options include linear spread across the duration of the activity, or use of a curve to approximate the expected expenditure during the activity's execution. These curves have an unlimited variety of shapes, the most common ones being symmetrical bell shape, front-loaded triangle, back-loaded triangle, equal triangle, and lump sum at the beginning or end of the activity. However, detailed discussion of the application of resource curves is beyond the scope of this paper.

STEP 4: SCHEDULE THE ACTIVITIES

The fourth step is to calculate the schedule of the activities. This step generally provides the spread of the resources over the entire time duration of the project. It generates the traditional S-curve of the project plan or baseline, also called the BCWS Curve.

STEP 5: TABULATE, PLOT AND ANALYZE

The final step is to tabulate and plot the information that was loaded and then to analyze this information. The purpose is to assure that the allocation of resources is properly planned. This includes analysis of individual resources to see if the maximum requirement during any time period is available. It also includes review of cash flows, if dollars are entered, to see if the financing plan for the project supports the schedule. Third, it provides a review to see that all project resources and costs that are budgeted are entered into the program. Of course, correction of any anomalies discovered during this step is implied to be a part of this step. Figure 4 [13-4]

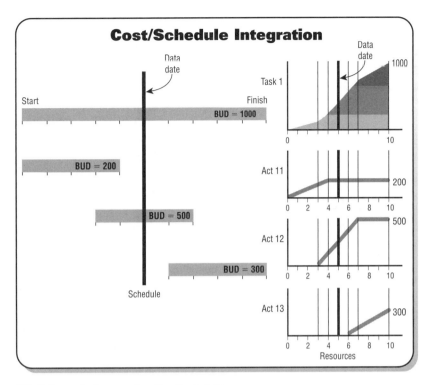

13-4 Figure 4. Resource Loading the Activities

represents a very simple illustration of this process. It also illustrates with this very simple example that the result is the traditional S-curve.

Once these five steps are completed, the project team will have the basis for conducting periodic analysis of the project progress and performance. That process is explained in the next four steps.

STEP 6: UPDATE THE SCHEDULE

The first step in the periodic process is to update the schedule with the period progress. This is generally done whether Earned Value is used or not. The project schedule activities are reported as started, completed or with a remaining duration, as appropriate. The percent complete of unfinished activities should also be reported. Here is where the practitioner should avoid subjectivity. For physical work, it may be easy to determine the percent complete. If 1000 cubic yards of concrete are planned to be poured and 300 yards have been done to date, then the activity is 30% complete. For efforts that are not so easily measured, special earning rules might have to be employed. Full discussion of earning rules is also beyond the scope of this paper. Two examples are presented to illustrate the point. One common rule is to report percent complete according to completed milestones within the activity. For example, if the activity is the creation of a design drawing, progress might be reported as follows: 10% when the preliminary research and background study are completed, 20% when the drawing draft is completed and passed on to drafting, 40% when the first draft is printed, 50% when the first draft is reviewed, 60% when the second draft is completed, 75% when the client review is completed, 90% when the final draft is completed, and 100% when the drawing is issued for construction. The key in defining this kind of rule is that each "milestone" is discrete, and its achievement is easily recognized by such evidence as transmittal memos.

A second common rule that is quite effective when the project has several thousand activities is to use the 50-50 rule. In this rule, each activity is considered 50% complete when its start date is reported, and it is 100% complete when the activity finish date is reported. Reporting progress provides the basis for the Earned Value calculations.

STEP 7: ENTER THE ACTUAL COSTS

The second step in the periodic process is to enter the actual costs into the schedule. This information comes from the time sheets and invoices to the project. Whether the data is entered manually or electronically is a matter of choice, depending on the degree of integration between the company's financial accounting system and the project control systems. In any case, it is necessary to determine which costs are to be allocated to which activity. By proper integration of the financial and project accounting systems, this process is facilitated to the point of total automation. However, human analysis of the actual data is recommended to assure that improper data doesn't inadvertently enter the system.

STEP 8: CALCULATE, PRINT AND PLOT

The next step in the periodic process is to calculate the Earned Value and to print reports and plot charts for analysis. The Earned Value is simply the percent complete of an activity times its budget. This provides the key value in the Earned Value process. Other calculations include the schedule and cost variances, performance indices, estimates at completion, and percent complete of the upper elements of the WBS. Referring to Figure 2 [13-2] will aid in understanding the following calculation discussion:

- Schedule Variance (SV) is the Earned Value minus the planned budget for the completed work (BCWP – BCWS).
- Cost Variance (CV) is the Earned Value minus the actual cost (BCWP – ACWP.)
- Performance indices are merely ratio expressions of the SV and CV.
- Schedule Performance Index (SPI) is the Earned Value divided by the planned value (BCWP/BCWS).
- Cost Performance Index (CPI) is the Earned Value divided by the actual cost (BCWP/ACWP).

The Estimate At Completion (EAC) is a number of great interest each update cycle. It indicates where the project cost is heading. Calculating a new EAC is one of the great benefits of Earned Value. However, the actual formula to use for this calculation is a matter of much discussion. For the purpose of this paper, we will look at the basic impact of cost performance on the EAC. The intent is to show that Earned Value is a key forecasting tool for managing a project. Refer to Figure 5 [13-5]. Let us assume a project is having some trouble meeting its cost goals. At the data date, the actual cost is greater than the planned cost for the completed work (ACWP > BCWP).

EAC as a Function of CPI

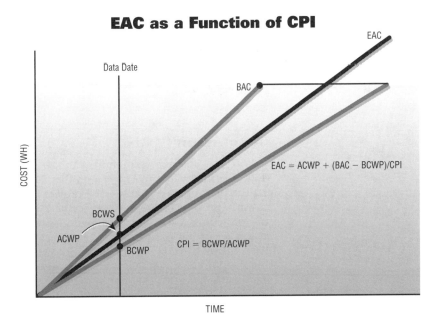

13-5 Figure 5. Forecasting the Estimate at Completion

If performance continues at the same trend, we can easily see that at completion, the actual cost (EAC) far exceeds the budget (BAC). The simplest formula for arriving at the EAC at the time of the data date is:

$$EAC = (BAC - BCWP)/CPI + ACWP$$

This formula determines the unfinished or unearned work (BAC – BCWP) and divides it by the CPI. To that is added the sunk cost, or the cost of the completed work (ACWP). From this we can see that poor cost performance, a CPI less than 1, would result in an EAC that is greater than the BAC. More complex formulas are used which factor the CPI to give it more or less influence on the EAC.

One more calculation is noteworthy since it is specifically made possible by the use of Earned Value. That is the percent complete at the upper levels of the WBS. While progress is typically recorded at the activity level of detail (the bottom of the WBS), those responsible for the project at higher levels of the WBS want to know the same kind of information as the "activity managers." The process involves rolling up the data through the WBS. Budgets and actual costs are easy to roll up; simply add the values of the lower elements to get the value of the parent element. However, how does one roll up percent complete? The answer is, of course, Earned Value. Since Earned Value is directly related to percent complete, one can simply add the Earned Value of the lower elements to get the value of the parent element. Then, one can use this information at the upper levels to back calculate the percent complete of the upper elements. Just as Earned Value equals the BAC times the percent complete at the lower levels, so does percent complete equal BAC divided by Earned Value for any element in the WBS.

STEP 9: ANALYZE AND REPORT

The final step in the Earned Value process is to analyze the data and then report the result of that analysis. The scope of this paper does not allow detailed discussion of the analysis process. However, from the preceding, the reader can recognize the significance of the various calculations discussed. How he or she interprets that information is left to his or her common sense.

Conclusion

With the above presentation, we have explored the What, Why, and How of Earned Value. We have seen that Earned Value is a tool for improving the performance analysis of a project by: providing a uniform unit of measure for project progress; enforcing a consistent method for analysis; and providing a basis for cost performance analysis of the project. The reason for using Earned Value is tied closely to what Earned Value is. The process of implementing Earned Value is organized into five steps and the process of periodic analysis consists of four additional steps. While the manipulation of the vast amount of data that is involved may seem daunting, the use of available computer tools designed for the purpose makes the implementation a relatively simple "cookbook" procedure. If the reader takes one thing away from this paper, it should be that Earned Value simply represents the budgeted value of the completed work and is directly related to the percent complete of the activity or WBS element under consideration.

Cost Management

This article is adapted from the U.S. Air Force's Software Technology Support Center's Guidelines for Successful Acquisition and Management Checklist, Version 3.0, May 2000. The full edition can be found at http://www.stsc.hill.af.mil/resources/tech_docs/.

6.1 Introduction

Cost is one of the three pillars supporting project success or failure, the other two being schedule and performance. Projects that go significantly "over budget" are often terminated without achieving the project goals because stakeholders simply run out of money or perceive additional expenditures as "throwing good money after bad." Projects that stay within budget are the exception, not the rule. A project manager who can control costs while achieving performance and schedule goals should be viewed as somewhat of a hero, especially when we consider that cost, performance, and schedule are closely interrelated.

The level of effort and expertise needed to perform good cost management is seldom appreciated. Too often, there is the pressure to come up with estimates within too short a period of time. When this happens, there is not enough time to gather adequate historical data, select appropriate estimating methods, consider alternatives, or carefully apply proper methods. The result is estimates that lean heavily toward guesswork. The problem is exacerbated by the fact that estimates are often not viewed as estimates but more as actual measurements made by some time traveler from the future. Estimates, once stated, have a tendency to be considered facts. Project managers must remember that estimates are the best guesses by estimators under various forms of pressure and with personal biases. They must also be aware of how others perceive these estimates.

Cost management consists of processes shown in Figure 1 [13-6]. It requires an understanding of costs far beyond the concepts of money and numbers. Cost of itself can be only measured, not controlled. Costs are one-dimensional representations of three-dimensional objects traveling through a fourth dimension—time. The real-world things that cost represents are people, materials, equipment, facilities, transportation, etc. Cost is used to monitor performance or use of real things, but it must be remembered that management of those real things determines cost, and not vice versa.

Project Cost Management

| Resource Planning | → | Cost Estimating | → | Budgeting | → | Cost Control |

13-6 Figure 1. Cost Management Processes

6.2 Process Description

The first three cost management processes are completed, with the exception of updates, during the project planning phase. The final process, controlling costs, is ongoing throughout the remainder of the project. Each of these processes is summarized below.

6.2.1 RESOURCE PLANNING

Cost management is begun by planning the resources that will be used to execute the project. Figure 2 [13-7] shows the inputs, tools, and product of this process. All the tasks needed to achieve the project goals are identified by analyzing the deliverables described in the Work Breakdown Structure (WBS). The planners use this, along with historical information from previous similar projects, available resources, and activity duration estimates, to develop resource requirements. It is important to get experienced people involved with this activity, as noted by the "expert judgment" listed under Tools. They will know what works and what doesn't work.

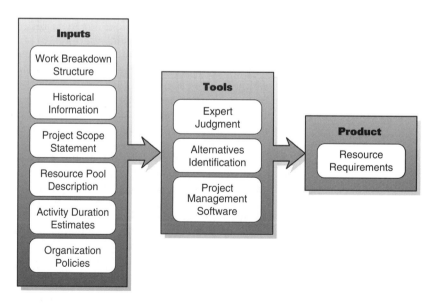

13-7 Figure 2. Resource Planning Elements [1]

In trying to match up resources with tasks and keep costs in line, the planners will need to look at alternatives in timing and choosing resources. They will need to refer back to project scope and organizational policies to ensure plans meet with these two guidelines.

Except for very small projects, trying to plan without good project management software is tedious and subject to errors, both in forgetting to cover all tasks and in resource and cost calculations.

The output of this process is a description of the resources needed, when they are needed, and for how long. This will include all types of resources, people, facilities, equipment, and materials. Once there is a resource plan, the process of estimating begins.

6.2.2 ESTIMATING COSTS

Estimating is the process of determining the expected costs of the project. It is a broad science with many branches and several popular, and sometimes disparate, methods. There are overall strategies to determining the cost of the overall project, as well as individual methods of estimating costs of specific types of activity. Several of these can be found in the resources listed at the end of the chapter. In most software development projects, the majority of the cost pertains to staffing. In this case, knowledge of the pay rates (including overhead) of the people working on the project, and being able to accurately estimate the number of people needed and the time necessary to complete their work will produce a fairly accurate project cost estimate. Unfortunately, this is not as simple as it sounds. Most project estimates are derived by summing the estimates for individual project elements. Several general approaches to estimating costs for project elements are presented here.[3] Your choice of approach will depend on the time, resources, and historical project data available to you. The cost estimating process elements are shown in Figure 3 [13-8].

Cost estimating uses the resource requirements, resource cost rates, and the activity duration estimates to calculate cost estimates for each activity. Estimating publications, historical information, and risk information are used to help determine which strategies and methods would yield the most accurate estimates. A chart of accounts may be needed to assign costs to different accounting categories. A final, but very important, input to the estimating process is the WBS. Carefully comparing activity estimates to the activities listed in the WBS will serve as a reality check and discover tasks that may have been overlooked or forgotten.

The tools used to perform the actual estimating can be one or more of several types. The major estimating approaches shown in Figure 3 [13-8] are discussed here. While other approaches are used, they can usually be classed as variations of these. One caution that applies to all estimating approaches: If the assumptions used in developing the estimates are not correct, any conclusions based on the assumptions will not be correct either.

6.2.2.1 Bottom-Up Estimating

Bottom-up estimating consists of examining each individual work package or activity and estimating its costs for labor, materials, facilities, equipment, etc. This method is usually time consuming and laborious but

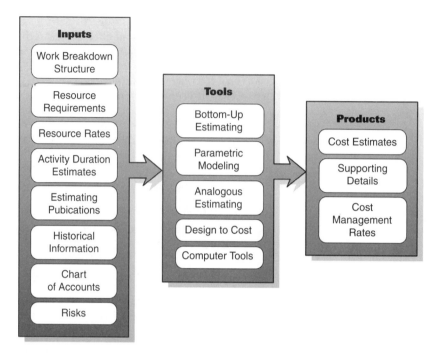

13-8 Figure 3. Cost Estimating Elements [1]

usually results in accurate estimates if well prepared, detailed input documents are used. [3]

6.2.2.2 Analogous Estimating

Analogous estimating, also known as top-down estimating, uses historical cost data from a similar project or activities to estimate the overall project cost. It is often used where information about the project is limited, especially in the early phases. Analogous estimating is less costly than other methods but it requires expert judgment and true similarity between the current and previous projects to obtain acceptable accuracy. [1]

6.2.2.3 Parametric Estimating

Parametric estimating uses mathematical models, rules of thumb, or Cost Estimating Relationships (CERs) to estimate project element costs. CERs are relationships between cost and measurements of work, such as the cost per line of code. [3] Parametric estimating is usually faster and easier to perform than bottom-up methods but it is only accurate if the correct model or CER is used in the appropriate manner.

6.2.2.4 Design-to-Cost Estimating

Design-to-cost methods are based on cost unit goals as an input to the estimating process. Tradeoffs are made in performance and other systems design parameters to achieve lower overall system costs. A variation of this method is **cost-as-the-independent-variable**, where the estimators start with a fixed system-level budget and work backward, prioritizing and selecting requirements to bring the project scope within budget constraints. [3]

6.2.2.5 Computer Tools

Computer tools are used extensively to assist in cost estimation. These range from spreadsheets and project management software to specialized simulation and estimating tools. Computer tools reduce the incidence of calculation errors, speed up the estimation process, and allow consideration of multiple costing alternatives. [1] One of the more widely used computer tools for estimating software development costs is the Constructive Cost Model (COCOMO). The software and users manual are available for download without cost. (See COCOMO in the Resources.) However, please note that most computer tools for developing estimates for software development use either lines of code or function points as input data. If the number of lines of code or function points cannot be accurately estimated, the output of the tools will not be accurate. The best use of tools is to derive ranges of estimates and gain understanding of the sensitivities of those ranges to changes in various input parameters.

The outputs of the estimating process include the project cost estimates, along with the details used to derive those estimates. The details usually define the tasks by references to the WBS. They also include a description of how the cost was derived, any assumptions made, and a range for estimate (e.g. $20,000 +/− $2000). Another output of the estimating process is the Cost Management Plan. This plan describes how cost variances will be managed, and may be formal or informal. [1] The following information may be considered for inclusion in the plan:

- Cost and cost-related data to be collected and analyzed.
- Frequency of data collection and analysis.
- Sources of cost-related data.
- Methods of analysis.
- Individuals and organizations involved in the process, along with their responsibilities and duties.
- Limits of acceptable variance between actual costs and the baseline.
- The authority and interaction of the cost control process with the change control process.
- Procedures and responsibilities for dealing with unacceptable cost variances.

6.2.3 COST BUDGETING

Once the costs have been estimated for each WBS task, and all these put together for an overall project cost, a project budget or cost baseline must be constructed. The budget is a spending plan, detailing how and at what rate the project funding will be spent. The budgeting process elements are shown in Figure 4 [13-9]. All project activities are not performed at once, resources are finite, and funding will probably be spread out over time. Cost estimates, WBS tasks, resource availability, and expected funding must all be integrated with the project schedule in a plan to apply funds to resources and tasks. Budgeting is a balancing act to ensure the rate of spending closely parallels the resource availability and funding, while not exceeding either. At the same time, task performance schedules must be

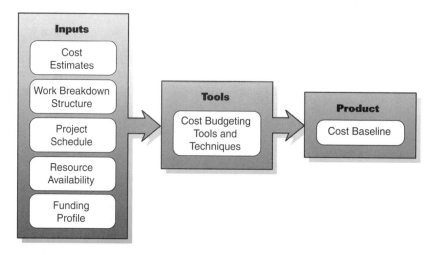

13-9 Figure 4. Cost Budgeting Elements [1]

followed so that all tasks are funded and completed before or by the end of the project schedule.

The spending plan forms the cost baseline, which will be one of the primary measures of project health and performance. Deviations from this cost baseline are major warning signs requiring management intervention to bring the project back on track.

Various tools and techniques are available to assist in the budgeting process. Most of these are implemented in some form of computer software. Budgeting is usually a major part of project management software.

6.2.4 COST CONTROL

Cost control is the final step of the cost management process but it continues through the end of the project. It is a major element of project success and consists of efforts to track spending and ensure it stays within the limits of the cost baseline. The following activities make up the cost control process: [1]

- Monitor project spending to ensure it stays within the baseline plan for spending rates and totals.
- When spending varies from the plan, determine the cause of variance, remembering that the variance may be a result of incorrect assumptions made when the original cost estimate was developed.
- Change the execution of the project to bring the spending back in line within acceptable limits, or recognize that the original estimate was incorrect, and either obtain additional funding or reduce the scope of the project.
- Prevent unapproved changes to the project and cost baseline.

When it is not possible to maintain the current cost baseline, the cost control process expands to include these activities: [2]

- Manage the process to change the baseline to allow for the new realities of the project (or incorrectly estimated original realities).
- Accurately record authorized changes in the cost baseline.
- Inform stakeholders of changes.

The input, tool, and product elements of the cost control process are shown in Figure 5 [13-10].

The cost control process compares cost performance reports with the cost baseline to detect variances. Guidance on what constitutes unacceptable variance and how to deal with variance can be found in the cost management plan, developed during the estimation activities. Few projects are completed without changes being suggested or requested. All change requests should run the gauntlet of cost control to weigh their advantages against their impact to project costs.

Cost control tools include performance measurement techniques, a working cost change control system, and computer-based tools. A powerful technique used with considerable success in projects is Earned Value Management, if used appropriately. It requires a fully defined project up front and bottom-up cost estimates, but it can provide an accurate and reliable indication of cost performance as early as 15% into the project. [4]

The outputs of cost control include products which are ongoing throughout the life of the project: revised cost estimates, budget updates, corrective actions, and estimates of what the total project cost will be at completion. Corrective actions can involve anything that incurs cost, or even updating the cost baseline to realign with project realities or changes in scope. Cost data necessary to project closeout are also collected throughout the life of the project and summarized at the end. A final product, extremely important to future efforts, is a compilation of lessons learned during the execution of the project. [1]

6.3 Cost Management Checklist

This checklist is provided to assist you in cost management. Consider your answers carefully to determine whether you need to examine the situation and take action.

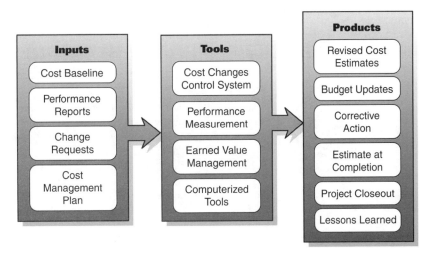

13-10 Figure 5. Cost Control Elements [1]

☐ 1. Is cost management planning part of your project planning process?

☐ 2. Have you established a formal, documented cost management process?

☐ 3. Do you have a complete and detailed WBS, including management areas (see Mil-HDBK-881, Appendix H)?

☐ 4. Do you have historical information, including costs, from previous similar projects?

☐ 5. Have you identified all sources of costs to your project (that is, different types of labor, materials, supplies, equipment, etc.)?

☐ 6. Have you identified proven and applicable estimating methods, models, and/or guides?

☐ 7. Have you selected computer software to assist you in estimating, budgeting, tracking, and controlling costs?

☐ 8. Do you have justifiable reasons for selecting your methods, models, guides, and software?

☐ 9. Are cost issues adequately addressed in your risk management plan?

☐ 10. Do you have a working change control process in place?

☐ 11. Does the change control process adequately address cost impact?

☐ 12. Do your estimates cover all tasks in the WBS?

☐ 13. Do you understand your project's funding profile, that is, how much funding will be provided? At what intervals? How sure is the funding?

☐ 14. Have you developed a viable cost baseline that is synchronized with the project schedule and funding profile?

☐ 15. Do you have adequate flexibility in the cost baseline?

☐ 16. Do you have a plan/process for dealing with variances between cost performance and the baseline?

☐ 17. Have you considered incorporating earned value management into your cost management efforts?

☐ 18. Are you keeping records of your cost management activity for future efforts?

References

[1]*Guide to the Project Management Body of Knowledge*, A, Chapter 7, Project Management Institute, 2000.

[2]Baker, Sunny and Kim, *Complete Idiot's Guide to Project Management*, 2 ed., Chapter 15, Alpha Books, 2000.

[3]Chapman, James R., "Cost Estimating, 1997, Principle Based Project Management" Web site: *www.hyperthot.com/project.htm.*

[4]Flemming and Koppelman, "Earned Value Project Management, A Powerful Tool For Software Projects," *Crosstalk*, July 1998: *www.stsc.hill.af.mil/crosstalk/1998/jul/value.asp.*

Resources

Air Force Cost Analysis Agency (AFCAA): *www.saffm.hq.af.mil/afcaa/*
   Air Force Cost Reference Documents: www.saffm.hq.af.mil/afcaa/reference.html.
   Cost Tools: *www.saffm.hq.af.mil/afcaa/models/models.html.*

Chapman, James R., Principle Based Project Management Web site:
   www.hyperthot.com/project.htm.

Constructive Cost Model (COCOMO), information and software, University of
   Southern California, Center for Software Engineering: *http://sunset.usc.edu/*
   research/COCOMOII/index.html.

Crosstalk Magazine: www.stsc.hill.af.mil/crosstalk/.

   – "Metrics Tools: Software Cost Estimation": *www.stsc.hill.af.mil/crosstalk/1995/*
     jun/metrics.asp.

   – "Cost Realism Methodology for Software-Intensive Source Selection Activities":
     www.stsc.hill.af.mil/crosstalk/1995/jun/cost.asp.

   – "Earned Value Project Management": *www.stsc.hill.af.mil/crosstalk/1998/jul/*
     value.asp.

   – "Pattern-Based Architecture: Bridging Software Reuse and Cost Management":
     www.stsc.hill.af.mil/crosstalk/1995/mar/pattern.asp–

"Does Calibration Improve Predictive Accuracy": *www.stsc.hill.af.mil/crosstalk/2000/*
   apr/ferens.asp.

   – "Project Recovery... It Can be Done": *www.stsc.hill.af.mil/crosstalk/2002/jan/*
     lipke.asp.

   – "Driving Quality Through Parametrics": *www.stsc.hill.af.mil/crosstalk/1998/nov/*
     galorath.asp.

   – "Future Trends, Implications in Cost Estimation Models": *www.stsc.hill.af.mil/*
     crosstalk/2000/apr/boehm.asp.

   – "Practical Software Measurement, Performance-Based Earned Value": *www.stsc.*
     hill.af.mil/crosstalk/2001/sep/solomon.asp.

   – "New Air Force Software Metrics Policy": *www.stsc.hill.af.mil/crosstalk/1994/apr/*
     xt94d04a.asp.

   – "Statistical Process Control Meets Earned Value": *www.stsc.hill.af.mil/crosstalk/*
     2000/jun/lipke.asp.

Guidelines for the Successful Acquisition and Management of Software-Intensive
   Systems (GSAM), Version 3.0, Chapter 13, OO-ALC/TISE, May 2000. Download at:
   www.stsc.hill.af.mil/gsam/guid.asp.

MIL-HDBK-881, Work Breakdown Structure: *www.acq.osd.mil/pm/newpolicy/wbs/*
   mil_hdbk_881/mil_hdbk_881.htm.

http://web2.deskbook.osd.mil/reflib/DDOD/003EH/001/003EH001DOC.HTM.

NASA, *Parametric Cost Estimating Handbook, 2 ed.* Online version: *www.jsc.nasa.gov/*
   bu2/PCEHHTML/pceh.htm.

Download and print version: *www.jsc.nasa.gov/bu2/NCEH/index.htm.*

Parametric Estimating Handbook: *http://web2.deskbook.osd.mil/reflib/DDOD/005EV/001/*
   005EV001DOC.HTM#T2.

Practical Software and Systems Measurement Support Center: *www. psmsc.com.*

Software Cost Estimation Web site: *www.ecfc.u-net.com/cost/index.htm.*

Software Technology Support Center Course: Life Cycle Software Project Management, Estimation, earned value, etc., 9 October 2001.

Xanadu, Slides on software project estimation: *http://xanadu.bmth.ac.uk/staff/kphalp/*
   students/bsi/predict/tsld002.htm.

Communications Management

Chapter 14 Contents

Chapter Overview

On a daily basis, project managers face the challenge of communicating information about their projects to stakeholders in order to keep them informed and gain or maintain their support. Communication can be difficult when stakeholders have different perspectives and, in some sense, "speak a different language" than the internal language of the team. The basic theme of project communication is to make visible to all stakeholders appropriate status information of a proposed or current project.

The *PMBOK® Guide* defines this knowledge area to include the processes required to "ensure timely and appropriate generation, collection, distribution, storage, retrieval, and ultimate disposition of project information." [PMI, 117] Project communications are often handled in an ad hoc manner that does not meet the expectations of the various stakeholders. In recent periods there has been an increased recognition that this process needs to be just as rigorous as other knowledge areas and that proper communication is a critical element in project success. Sometimes a stakeholder would define failure as, "I didn't know that was what you were going to deliver." PMI literature states that the project manager spends up to 90% of his or her time communicating.[F] Given this time allocation, the goal should be to do this effectively.

Schwalbe offers an excellent overview of this topic area. [Schwalbe] The important message to deliver is that communication is vital to project success, and it is often performed inadequately (at least from a user perception). The project team should seek ways to satisfy the communication needs of the various stakeholders effectively and efficiently.

The *PMBOK® Guide* Communications Management processes include the following:

- 10.1 Communications Planning
- 10.2 Information Distribution
- 10.3 Performance Reporting
- 10.4 Managing Stakeholders

The 10.X reference numbers above relate to the *PMBOK® Guide* chapter sections that describe these processes.

Communications Planning

The goal of this process is to integrate the project scope definition, technology to be utilized for communications, and the underlying development process with the organizational culture. Each stakeholder segment has unique communication needs, and these are identified in this phase. Upon completion, a Communications Management Plan is formulated and approved outlining such factors as frequency, format, technology media, and other stakeholder communication triggers including scope changes, budget information, and schedule implications.

Information Distribution

There are many media options for distributing planned communications items. Options such as face-to-face, telephone, paper (snail mail), e-mail, and intranet are typical delivery options. Each major stakeholder group has a preferred communication medium that must be considered. Secondly, the delivery issue of "push" versus "pull" needs resolution. A push format would mean that the project team pushes the information to the target source, while the pull option indicates that the project team will place the information in a known location and let the stakeholders fetch it at their will from a filing cabinet, a Web server, or a bulletin board. A third definitional consideration is the way in which the information can be seen. It is one thing to send a detailed status report and expect everyone to wade through the details to find what they are looking for. It is quite another to send a summary that has color coding to highlight significant areas, and then allow the stakeholder to drill down into detail as they see fit. There is an art to modern communication, and large stacks of data-intensive paper reports are no longer considered appropriate communication. One common presentation approach is to present a "dashboard" showing major project variables. This type of presentation is becoming the most popular way to deliver high content in the most pleasing human format. A hypothetical dashboard is shown in Figure 1 [14-1].

A graphically designed project portal (see Figure 1 [14-1]) is more pleasing to the typical user than stacks of raw data through which the user must sift to obtain information, especially when project data includes information regarding productivity, percentage completion, staffing data, quality indicators, and risk assessment monitoring. Additional data such as earned value can also be provided.

Another important process embedded in the information distribution activity is that of collecting and distributing lessons learned as the project

14-1 Figure 1. Project Status Dashboard

unfolds. Technical, managerial, and process aspects of the project performance can be analyzed. In order to do this effectively, there must be a disciplined collection, storage, and distribution system for the lessons learned process. The goal of this process is to recognize activities that improve project processes and those that degrade those activities. Most projects often fall short in analyzing lessons learned. The value of the activity is somewhat external to the producer, because the lessons learned will primarily benefit subsequent efforts by others. Nevertheless, this activity provides the base information for the enterprise to improve, and for that reason should be considered a mandatory activity.

Performance Reporting

Closely related to the distribution process is the question of what information to distribute. Typical project reporting metrics would focus on tracking budget, schedule, and functionality. However, there are other considerations that might be of interest to other stakeholder groups. For example, status in many of the knowledge areas could also have interest to special groups including quality, risk, procurement, and HR. Here again, we see some of the hidden complexity of the communications activity. Beyond reporting basic status metrics, there is increased interest in reporting project performance through earned value metrics that aggregate the individual metrics into a single, consistent status set of performance variables. Earned value should be considered one of the base metrics for all projects.

Basic reporting would often be accomplished via a predefined status report outlining where the project stands versus current plan parameters, or a set baseline comparison. A second form of report could be focused more on the project team in the form of individual accomplishment, or a consolidated view of total team accomplishment in the current period. A third reporting view shows forecast status of specific parameters at project completion. When is the project going to finish? What is the forecast final budget? What level of functionality will be in the final result? These are valuable views for expectation setting.

Managing Stakeholders

Although somewhat vague in its task definition, this process relates to the overall actions of the project manager and team to resolve stakeholder issues. Few projects run according to the original plan. Therefore, project life is more than executing the planned tasks as originally defined. Rather, unplanned issues, disagreements, miscommunication, deviations, conflicting objectives, and other human events upset the orderly life of the project team. It is one thing to have a process for handling change, but quite another to make this process work smoothly. In all of these cases, the events have to be executed dynamically and they require considerable behavioral skills on the part of the project team and especially the team leader.

Readings

The three readings in this section offer insights into concepts and techniques to make the communication process more effective. In the first reading, "Communications as a Strategic PM Function" (delivered in two parts), Patricia Davis-Muffett advises project managers on how to communicate information effectively to diverse stakeholder groups in order to gain and maintain their support. The second reading, by Jamie Barber, focuses on the importance of collecting and effectively using HR information to support business objectives in his discourse on "The Numbers Game: Nine Steps to Making the Most of your HR Metrics."

In the third reading, titled "The Post-Internet Organization: The *Real* Virtual Organization," Brad Jackson examines the characteristics of a contemporary networked organization. This reading advises managers how to effectively direct informational interactions of those they supervise and others elsewhere in the organization.

Reference

Schwalbe, K. *Information Technology Project Management, 3rd Edition*, Course Technology, 2002.

Communications as a Strategic PM Function— Part I

PATRICIA DAVIS-MUFFETT

Posted: August 1, 2004. Copyright © 2004, Patricia Davis-Muffett. All rights reserved. Originally published as a part of 2004 PMI Global Congress Proceedings, Prague.

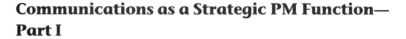

Patricia Davis-Muffett is Vice President of Marketing at Robbins-Gioia, LLC.

Abstract

As information technology becomes more and more enmeshed in every aspect of global business, we increasingly hear about the need for chief information officers and their teams to gain a better understanding of the needs of business executives and to understand how best to communicate with them. This poses a major challenge. And since project management is a profession that emerged primarily from the technical disciplines of engineering and technology, it poses a major challenge for the project manager as well. Project managers have typically been highly technically proficient and very good at motivating a team. The disciplines associated with communications and marketing, however, are quite foreign. As more and more project managers gain a place at the table with business executives, these skills become increasingly critical. It is no longer sufficient to have a communications plan built around providing the appropriate status reviews at the right point in the governance process. Instead, project management offices must take a proactive approach to actively marketing their project goals to the wider organization and to other stakeholders beyond their organization if they want to keep their funding, maintain focus on their efforts, and ultimately, ensure success.

Introduction

Browse the technology press from the past few years and one theme will emerge loud and clear—it is essential to earn a seat at the table. As technology executives have struggled for relevancy in the wake of Internet hype, they have increasingly realized the need to learn the language of business and to create connections to business executives through more and higher quality communication. In fact, according to the Meta Group (Rubenstrunk, 2002), communications as a discipline has become so important that it should be part of every CIO organization.

Project management is ripe for a similar transformation. While project managers have always practiced their own brand of communication, it has been a very precise form of responsive communications, following the pre-scriptions of project management methodology and nearly always subser-vient to other project management disciplines. The communication environment, however, has become much more complex—between e-mail, intranets, extranets, increasingly targeted and aggressive direct marketing, and a proliferation of magazines, online content, and newsletters—creating more and more demands for stakeholder attention. Given this reality, new perspectives, skills and methods are called for that reach beyond the tradi-tional boundaries of project management discipline.

From Active to Proactive

THE STATE OF PROJECT COMMUNICATIONS

Frequent communication has always been a critical component of the project manager's role—but the question is, what form should that com-munication take? The Project Management Body of Knowledge (PMBOK) asserts that communications management consists of:

- Communications Planning
- Information Distribution
- Performance Reporting; and
- Administrative Closure (2001, PMI)

While these disciplines are perfectly adequate for coordinating activity and informing team members of project status, they belie a myopic focus on the immediate project team and its most obvious stakeholders.

Let's look at an example communications model from one project's toolkit (2000, *PMBoulevard.com*) (Figure 2 [14-2]).

The sample toolkit includes the following artifacts: Progress Turnaround Report; Work Plan Update; Weekly Status Meetings; Summary Status Reports; Enterprise Level Program Performance Summaries; and War Room Contents (2000, Robbins-Gioia). In terms of communicating with execu-tives and workers directly connected to a project, it's comprehensive. The model even includes the structure for weekly meetings and the communi-cation outputs from those meetings:

Impressive. Especially if your questions center around what is getting done, who is doing it, and when it's going to happen. But what if you have other questions?

I am not suggesting that the kinds of project communications contained in status reports and executive briefings are irrelevant. Quite the opposite. They need to be well done so that they can create a strong platform on which more sophisticated and proactive communications can be built. But the goal of project communications in general must be questioned. Many project managers would probably agree that "the goal of project communi-cations management is the accurate and timely collection, dissemination, and storage of information" which helps "all people in the project commu-nicate in the same project language." (2004, Polar Bear Corporate Educa-tion Solutions) But what about the people outside of the project? Couldn't they be relevant? And what about the effect of external communications on the project team?

Weekly Meeting and Output Cycle

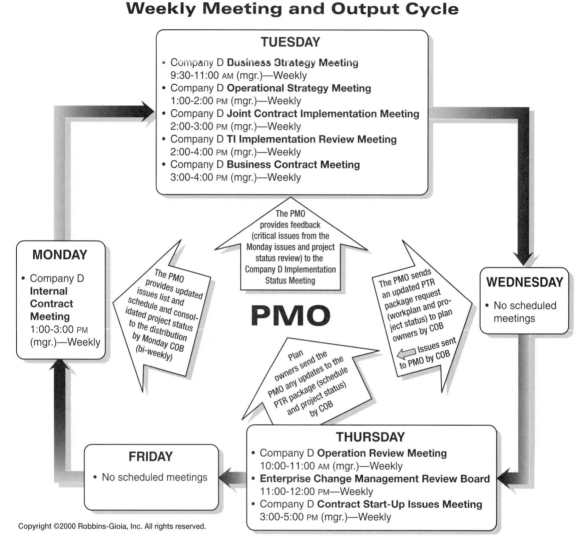

TUESDAY
- Company D **Business Strategy Meeting**
  9:30-11:00 AM (mgr.)—Weekly
- Company D **Operational Strategy Meeting**
  1:00-2:00 PM (mgr.)—Weekly
- Company D **Joint Contract Implementation Meeting**
  2:00-3:00 PM (mgr.)—Weekly
- Company D **TI Implementation Review Meeting**
  2:00-4:00 PM (mgr.)—Weekly
- Company D **Business Contract Meeting**
  3:00-4:00 PM (mgr.)—Weekly

The PMO provides feedback (critical issues from the Monday issues and project status review) to the Company D Implementation Status Meeting

PMO

MONDAY
- Company D **Internal Contract Meeting**
  1:00-3:00 PM (mgr.)—Weekly

The PMO provides updated issues list and schedule and consolidated project status to the distribution by Monday COB (bi-weekly)

WEDNESDAY
- No scheduled meetings

The PMO sends an updated PTR package request (workplan and project status) to plan owners by COB

Issues sent to PMO by COB

Plan owners send the PMO any updates to the PTR package (schedule and project status) by COB

FRIDAY
- No scheduled meetings

THURSDAY
- Company D **Operation Review Meeting**
  10:00-11:00 AM (mgr.)—Weekly
- **Enterprise Change Management Review Board**
  11:00-12:00 PM—Weekly
- Company D **Contract Start-Up Issues Meeting**
  3:00-5:00 PM (mgr.)—Weekly

14-2 Figure 2.

REDEFINING THE STAKEHOLDER

We all know that poor communications can kill a project. According to one survey, it is the third most common cause of project failure (Matteucci, 2001). But what about those projects that create their own self-contained world? Inside of the project's bubble, everyone is very clear about project goals, status, its relevance to the organization's strategy, and its potential impact on world events. Outside of the bubble, no one even knows what the acronyms mean.

In order for a project to get funding and be initiated, it probably has an established link to the organization's strategic objectives. Unfortunately, once the project is started, that link to strategy is often forgotten. One management tool that has gained increasing acceptance over the past several years can prove helpful in sustaining that strategic focus—the balanced scorecard. The balanced scorecard approach is important in defining links to strategy, but it also helps by identifying the long list of possible stakeholders for an organization's strategic initiatives.

Let's consider an example. If your project is the implementation of a new financial system, you would certainly think of stakeholders such as the executive who funded the project, the accounting department, and other users of the system. It's important, however, to consider why the project was funded and what its broader impacts might be. Perhaps the reason for the new financial system was concern among the stockholders and potential investors that the company's financial information was inaccurate. Maybe they had received bad press or customer complaints because of inaccurate bills. It could be that they were trying to streamline internal processes to increase profitability and make their employees' salaries more competitive.

Each of these possible scenarios calls for a different communications strategy—one that stretches beyond basic project communications. These messages that will reach broader audiences, such as stockholders, potential investors, customers, prospects, and employees, will also be helpful in gaining increased buy-in with senior executives. There has been some recognition of this need in the business press, but it still hasn't gone far enough. According to GartnerGroup's Tech Republic, "[Project Communications Management] is another area that often gets short shrift in compressed projects, to the detriment of the end result. Experienced project managers understand that creating a compelling marketing message for the project, preparing the user community to accept and embrace the new technology, and keeping stakeholders and sponsors informed and involved throughout the life of the project are key success factors." (Freedman, 2002) This is a good start, but again, it addresses primarily the first ring of stakeholders around the project bubble (users and sponsors), not the broader potential stakeholder community.

OVERCOMING INFORMATION OVERLOAD

One of the basic realities of the current work environment is a tremendous inflow of information. We all have so many information sources, and we're bombarded with e-mails, marketing messages, and other demands on our attention. Over the last decade or so, it has become increasingly difficult to capture attention—the rule of thumb in marketing used to be that a prospect needed to see or hear a message three times before they paid attention, now it is between five and seven (MarketingProfs.com, 2004).

In this environment, it is essential to be very clear about what message you want to send and to reinforce it consistently. This is one place where typical project communications fall down. While the full details of project status are useful for those intimately involved in a project, the details are likely to confuse the message for executives and the larger stakeholder community. The keys to reaching those audiences are a focused message and delivering the communication at the right time.

It is essential to remember that perception is often more powerful than reality as well. To prove this point, let's consider the differences between the Standish Group study of project failure, and Tarnow and Frame's more recent validation of study. The Standish study found that only 16% of projects were technically successes—defining success as meeting cost, time, and requirements targets. When Tarnow and Frame replicated the study, they found that this was accurate—only 12% met those three targets. However, when the question was, "was your project successful?" over 75% of respondents from that same group of projects responded in the positive. The important thing here is that the stakeholder perceptions of project success often outstripped the actual data about the project. (Frame, 2003)

The PR and marketing effort around a project must recognize this reality of information overload and try to move the perception needle in a positive direction. To break through the information clutter, the message to stakeholders must be simple and consistent, and it must also use the channels that will have the greatest impact on the intended audience.

Sean Gorman has put forth an excellent theory of information networks as they related to communication inside the project bubble. He relies on the concept of "six degrees of separation" to show how a few "well-connected nodes" can create an ideal information flow: "When we look at a project as a network, the obvious well-connected node is the project manager. The project manager needs to be linked to all the nodes in their network, but all the nodes in the network do not need to be connected to each other for the network to communicate efficiently.... The project management nodes need to be linked to everyone in order for the network to efficiently distribute communications throughout the team." (Gorman, 2001)

Gorman extends this concept somewhat by noting: "Your project network does not act alone. Your firm, project stakeholders, partners, collaborators, and competitors all form networks that interconnect with yours at different levels. Understanding how your network interconnects with your neighboring networks can be a crucial insight... Networks, by their nature, initiate communications. Only by initiating your own messages to fill the bandwidth can you control them." (Gorman, 2001) What he does not consider, however, is where those messages should be directed. Selecting the message and sticking with it is absolutely the first step. But finding those external "well-connected nodes" is also critical. Volume of communication is not the answer here; the project communicator must find the most efficient and influential communication mode to create positive perceptions. This may lead to unconventional modes of communication, but if stakeholders are more likely to listen to, say, Gartner analysts or CIO magazine journalists than to their own company newsletter, that may be the more efficient communication node.

Editor's Note: Next week *PM Boulevard* will feature part two, Communications as a Strategic PM Function: Creating the PR and Marketing Infrastructure.

References

A Guide to The Project Management Body of Knowledge [electronic version 1.3], (2000). Newtown Square, PA: The Project Management Institute.

Company D Toolkit. (2000). Robbins-Gioia, 2000, posted on *PMBoulevard.com*.

Frame, Davidson. (2003). "Breaking Murphy's Law: Building Project Management Competence." Paper presented at the e-gov Program Management Summit, Washington, DC.

Freedman, Rick. (2002, August 7). Encourage success by following PMI's knowledge areas. Tech Republic. Retrieved March 3, 2004, from *http://techrepublic.com.com/5100-6330-1051548-1-1.html?tag=search*.

Gorman, Sean P. (2001) It's a Small World After All. PM Boulevard. Retrieved March 3, 2004, from *http://www.pmboulevard.com/expert_column/archives/reg/small_world_gorman.pdf*.

How many times must a customer see advertising … ? (2004, February 11+). MarketingProfs.com. Messages posted to Customer Behavior Know-How Exchange, archived at *https://www.marketingprofs.com/ea/qst_question.asp?qstID=291*.

Matteucci, Nick. (2001). Virtual Program Management. Paper presented at Project World, Chicago, IL.

Polar Bear Corporate Education Solutions. (2004). *Preparation Program 'PM-Blazer*™*' for PMI®'s Project Management Professional (PMP®)* Certification Exam. Retrieved March 3, 2004, from *www.polarbear.com/outline_storage/SPM800A.pdf*.

Rubenstrunk, Karen & Michael Pedersen. (2002, February). "Executing on IT's Promise: Leadership, Culture, and Relationships." Paper presented at the MetaGroup/DCI MetaMorphosis Conference, San Diego, CA.

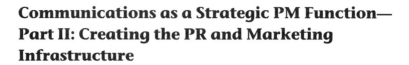

Communications as a Strategic PM Function—Part II: Creating the PR and Marketing Infrastructure

PATRICIA DAVIS-MUFFETT

Posted: August 10, 2004. Copyright © 2004, Patricia Davis-Muffett. All rights reserved. Originally published as a part of 2004 PMI Global Congress Proceedings, Prague.

Patricia Davis-Muffett is Vice President of Marketing at Robbins-Gioia, LLC.

Situation Analysis

Before creating a strategic communications plan for a project, it is essential to analyze the situation. As discussed in Part I last week, ideally the links with the organization's strategy and key stakeholders for the organization have already been established, either through a generic strategic planning process or a balanced scorecard approach. These items should establish major goals, key audiences to influence, and current perceptions of those audiences.

Whether these artifacts pre-exist the project or not, it is smart to identify layers of stakeholders (employees, executives, customers, investors, the general public, etc.) and check them against the project goals. Useful questions to ask at the outset are:

- What are the stakeholder groups that interact with my organization? (Think broadly.)
- What are the organization's key strategic goals?
- How does my project connect with those goals?
- What is the relationship of each stakeholder group to the strategic goals connected with my project?
- What do we want those stakeholder groups to know about this project?
- When should we tell them? (What are the triggers/milestones in the project that would warrant a communication to each of them? You want to think through this one for each stakeholder group.)
- What are the current perceptions of each stakeholder group related to the key goals?
- How do we want their perceptions to change?
- What communication vehicles do those stakeholder groups value, and what tactics have worked to influence them in the past?

This assessment may seem daunting, but it is likely that most of this information is available in strategic planning or market research artifacts within the organization. It would be very easy to get too focused on this step and stretch it out beyond its usefulness. Broad-based, highly scientific market research studies are probably not called for here. Talk to people inside of your organization and work through these issues. If it becomes clear that something is truly an unknown, conduct some informal interviews to gain a better understanding. The important point is to work through the process and to be clear about who you want to influence and why before you begin crafting communication tactics.

Planning

Once this "as-is" analysis has been established, the project communicator must create a campaign to influence perceptions by developing specific tactics for each stakeholder group that are designed to move them closer to the desired mindset. Armed with an understanding of the relationships between the project, the project stakeholders, the corporate goals, and the corporate stakeholders, it becomes possible to prioritize those stakeholder groups and develop distinct, yet interrelated, tactical plans for each audience.

Using the prioritized stakeholder groups, the project communicator should develop "key messages" for the project that convey critical information—what it is, why it is important, and how it will be/has been implemented. These should be straightforward, non-technical, based on reality, and short. It may be necessary to also develop subgroupings of key messages that are specifically designed for certain stakeholder audiences, but they should be clearly aligned with the overall key messages for the project.

Next, the project communicator should develop a comprehensive marketing and communications execution strategy, incorporating the key messages into a full range of marketing tactics that are appropriate to each audience, such as conferences, tradeshows, electronic communications, collateral, direct marketing, in-person "road shows" and Q&A opportunities, and public relations strategies. It is critical at this point to maintain a focus outside of the project bubble, identifying external trends and activities that may be related to project goals, and considering the real "hooks" that will capture the attention of stakeholders.

Timing is also essential, and here's where traditional project management comes back into the process. It may be that certain milestones deserve strategic communications. For instance, the first successful pilot of a new technology implementation might be a great opportunity for a case study, which can then be used immediately for internal PR (perhaps a celebration where the new users share their experiences with future users), and then employed for external PR to gain critical momentum (submission for technology best practice awards, pitching to the technology press, capturing speaking engagements about the success, etc.) that will build confidence among stakeholders outside of the project bubble. These communications must be a key component of the project plan, so that they can occur at strategic points in the project and ensure that they further the project's goals rather than becoming obstacles.

Regardless of the specific communication activity, each tactic should focus on one or more of the target stakeholder audiences, send a clear message, communicate in a way that stakeholders will understand and appreciate, and be consistent with all other communications. The ultimate goal is to use this consistent strategic communication to establish a positive relationship with all stakeholder audiences and build confidence and credibility for the project team.

Of course, no program is successful if that success cannot be measured. The development of metrics at the outset that establish a baseline and track progress is key. Some of the typical measures of effectiveness for strategic communication around projects are:

- Comparison of "as is" awareness with current state at various points in the program.
- Awareness surveys to measure recognition before and after milestones.
- If the project attempts to influence employee or customer satisfaction, satisfaction surveys to determine how happy those groups are with the project's progress and/or outcomes.
- Number of stakeholder contacts or "touches."
- Changes in Internet/intranet traffic on the topic, if applicable.
- Reduction in complaints and/or help inquiries, if applicable.
- Number of speaking engagements captured, media pick-ups.
- Response level to internal/external marketing programs.

Throughout the project lifecycle, these metrics should be used to evaluate the effectiveness of the communications program—and to make changes to tactics, when appropriate.

Staffing

While this process may seem daunting to many project management professionals, the reality is that most organizations probably have a wealth of resources at their disposal already. Ideally, the project office will have at least one member who is charged with project marketing/PR and has a professional background in those areas, but even without that, there is probably a group in your organization who would be thrilled to be involved with the project as intimately as this approach suggests. Again, the key is to look outside of the project bubble.

In your organization, regardless of its mission, someone is charged with "getting the word out." That may be Marketing, Public Relations, Public Affairs, Investor Relations—even Strategic Planning, Sales, or Customer Service. The professionals in that department probably have the contacts, the professional experience, and the knowledge to strategize about how to communicate with various stakeholder groups. It is essential to value those skills as unique and important to your project's success.

Too often, project managers take the weight of the world on their shoulders in this area when there are abundant resources to help them out. You may even have resources standing ready outside your organization. If you're deploying a technology, the vendor may have resources to help you. If you're creating a product that will be marketed through another organization, that channel may have resources. Ask for help and engage the skills and resources of your entire organization, and the entire network of partners, customers, vendors, and others as you build and execute on a strategic communications program to further your project's success.

Conclusion

The world has changed dramatically in recent years, and project management can't afford to remain static in any area—especially one that has been so radically transformed as communications. It is no longer enough to adequately communicate within the project bubble. Project managers must become strategic evangelists for their projects in the greater stakeholder community and take on the often frightening task of marketing and public relations for their projects.

The reality that these skills are typically foreign to project management professionals doesn't negate the necessity of their implementation. The Dilbertesque environment in which the ivory tower of Marketing is constantly at odds with technical project teams can be alleviated by building strategic communications into the project management process and harnessing the value of marketing and public relations skills as a strategic asset that will build momentum, increase visibility, and ensure that projects are clearly linked with strategic goals in the minds of critical stakeholders.

References

A Guide to The Project Management Body of Knowledge [electronic version 1.3], (2000). Newtown Square, PA: The Project Management Institute.

Company D Toolkit. (2000). Robbins-Gioia, 2000., posted on *PMBoulevard.com.*

Frame, Davidson. (2003). *Breaking Murphy's Law: Building Project Management Competence.* Paper presented at the e-gov Program Management Summit, Washington, DC.

Freedman, Rick. (2002, August 7). Encourage success by following PMI's knowledge areas. *Tech Republic.* Retrieved March 3, 2004, from *http://techrepublic.com.com/ 5100-6330-1051548-1-1.html?tag=search.*

Gorman, Sean P. (2001) It's a Small World After All. *PM Boulevard.* Retrieved March 3, 2004, from *http://www.pmboulevard.com/expert_column/archives/reg/small_world_gorman.pdf.*

How many times must a customer see advertising . . . ? (2004, February 11+). Marketing Profs.com. Messages posted to Customer Behavior Know-How Exchange, archived at *https://www.marketingprofs.com/ea/qst_question.asp?qstID=291.*

Matteucci, Nick. (2001). *Virtual Program Management.* Paper presented at Project World, Chicago, IL.

Polar Bear Corporate Education Solutions. (2004). *Preparation Program 'PM-Blazer™' for PMI®'s Project Management Professional (PMP®)* Certification Exam. Retrieved March 3, 2004, from *www.polarbear.com/outline_storage/SPM800A.pdf.*

Rubenstrunk, Karen & Michael Pedersen. (2002, February). *Executing on IT's Promise: Leadership, Culture, and Relationships.* Paper presented at the MetaGroup/DCI MetaMorphosis Conference, San Diego, CA.

The Numbers Game: Nine Steps to Making the Most of your HR Metrics

JAMIE BARBER

June 2004

Jamie Barber is a Consultant for IntroNet, the providers of Total Resourcing Solutions. In addition to analysing client requirements in relation to market trends for a number of blue-chip organisations within the UK and Europe, Jamie also has extensive hands-on and managerial experience gained with the UK's largest specialist finance recruitment consultancy. He holds an MSc in Information SystemsManagement from the University of Stirling. He can be contacted at Jamie.Barber@IntroNet.com.

Reading Overview

If you've taken part in HR strategy meetings or attended any industry conferences in the last few years, chances are you will have noticed the amount of time devoted to the topic of metrics. The collection and analysis of data have evolved from the preserve of a small number of dedicated number crunchers into a tangible and highly visible tool, able to play a crucial role in strategic decision making.

However, the collection of meaningful and valuable data can still seem daunting and shrouded in mystery. So, by way of an introduction, it's worth looking at why metrics are captured in the first place.

Why Bother?

Perhaps the most crucial advantage of a sound HR metrics programme is that it enables HR to converse with senior management in the language of business.[1] Operational decisions taken by HR are then based on cold, hard facts rather than gut feeling, the figures being used to back up business cases and requests for resource. The HR function is transformed from a bastion of 'soft' intangibles into something more 'scientific,' better able to punch its weight in the organisation. In addition, the value added by HR becomes more visible. This will become increasingly important as more and more functions attempt to justify their status as strategic business partners rather than merely cost centres.

The capture of metrics also underpins the old adage of 'what you can't measure, you can't improve.' The five key practices of the Human Capital Index (recruiting excellence, clear rewards and accountability, prudent use of resources, communications integrity, and collegial flexible workplace) require the capture of metrics for their very definition. A study conducted by the HR consulting firm Watson Wyatt has shown a strong correlation between these five practices and a 30% increase in shareholder value.[2]

Furthermore, a survey of 200 Managing Directors and HR Directors showed that 82% believed Human Capital Management (HCM) to be critical to the fundamental success of a business, while 80% thought that effective measurement is crucial to deliver effective HCM.[3] Another study shows 82% of HR practitioners citing metrics as either 'very important' or at least 'important' to the ultimate success of internal redeployment initiatives.[4] An ever-present factor among companies with widely acclaimed HR procedures and practices—the likes of Microsoft, Intel, and Cisco, among others— seems to be their extensive use of metrics to drive strategic decisions.[5]

So, given the benefits of establishing a new metrics initiative or overhauling an existing process of data collection, how do you actually go about it?

Nine Steps to Metrics Excellence

The steps outlined here are not intended to be fully comprehensive or applicable in every circumstance, but they should give you some idea as to where and how to start.

1. Re-examine your business objectives.

Before doing anything else, revisit your organisation's strategic business objectives. While there is some value in each function measuring it's own performance, the overriding priority should be the satisfaction of the end customer (either internal or external). As customer satisfaction is more 'process-oriented,' your chosen metrics suite will likely straddle departmental boundaries.

As overall business objectives take precedence over functional 'silos,' processes tend to become more effective and focused, and the beginnings of a real team culture are fostered. This is particularly important as organisations become more geographically spread and the number of staff working remotely increases. The move towards a more 'process-oriented' culture also creates ideal conditions for the propagation of continuous improvement initiatives such as Six Sigma.[6]

2. Take the 'CUP' test.

It is surprising how many organisations are busily accumulating reams of data from which no one seems to be able to extrapolate much useful information. If you already collect metrics, take this opportunity to rifle through the reporting archives. Give each set of data the 'CUP' test. Does it make a contribution to overall organisational business objectives? Does it provide an insight into whether organisational resources are being utilized at their optimum level? Does it make any assessment of productivity that could lead to efficiency gains and therefore a better customer experience? If each set of data does not address at least one of these three criteria, then question the usefulness of continuing to collect it.[7]

3. Keep it simple.

For all the potential of HR Information Systems (HRIS) to 'slice and dice' data in a myriad of ways, it has been suggested that 'information overload' is a greater threat to the effectiveness of HR than a complete lack of measurement.[8] Measuring everything that moves also results in lengthy reports which may be off-putting to others. One Chief Executive complained in a recent interview that he 'didn't look at the report anymore; it's too long.' The report in question weighed in at three pages.[9] Research has suggested that in order to focus on the priority areas, around five key metrics are a good place to start,[10] although the exact number will vary depending on strategic business objectives.

4. Decide what types of metrics to capture.

Metrics fall into three principal categories: historical, real-time, and forward-looking.[11] Historical metrics give a good general indication of an organisation's health, but reliance on them has been compared to trying to drive a car while looking only in the rear-view mirror.[12] Real-time metrics are the 'snapshots' which can act as warning signs that a process may be about to go horribly wrong (for example, a sudden drop in incoming applicants), while forward-looking metrics extend current and historical trends into the future to enable contingency planning.

5. Establish a benchmark.

The current state of affairs should be measured so that the future impact of any changes can be assessed. You may have some idea where you're heading, but if you don't know your starting point on the map, you're still very likely to get lost. You could also look at benchmarking your organisation against other similarly sized organisations or industry 'best of breeds.' For more information on industry benchmarking, try the Saratoga Institute (*www.saratogainstitute.com*) or, for a more UK-centric perspective, The Benchmarking Centre (*www.benchmarking.co.uk*).

6. Integrate data collection into existing workflows.

Avoid burdening staff with extra workloads. Data should be collected automatically without the need for manual maintenance of parallel systems; otherwise you will decrease the chances of collecting a comprehensive set of data.[13] This is the arena in which Enterprise Resource Planning (ERP) and Applicant Tracking Systems (ATS) have a key role to play, especially when the organisation has departments scattered across the globe. The latest HRIS make it possible to data-mine in a way that would have been inconceivable as little as 15 years ago.

7. Allocate resource for analysis.

Only by undertaking rigorous analysis will HR be able to transform data into meaningful and valuable strategic information. However, avoid 'paralysis by analysis:' make the results too complex and they may be dismissed out of hand as being too scientific or too academic.[14] Graphical representations with short textual summaries make for greater accessibility and readability.

8. Have the power to act.

The gathering of metrics is a futile exercise in administration if HR lacks the teeth to act promptly on the findings. For example, if the metrics indicate that retention rates would be dramatically improved by increasing performance-related bonuses, but HR has no means of prompting this remedial action, then a potentially valuable tool has been wasted.

9. Close the loop.

Good business practice stipulates that all business processes and procedures should be subject to periodical review. The gathering of metrics should be no exception. When initially defining the metrics suite, ensure that a review date is built in. For seasonal cycles (for example, graduate recruitment), it would be advisable to build up statistics over a number of years. If a metric is enhanced following a review, make this clear in all future reports so that readers analysing historical trends are under no illusion as to what they are comparing.

So, you've followed the nine steps outlined in the preceding and, let's face it, none of the suggestions needs a degree in Statistics to implement. Surely every organisation worth its salt will have been rushing to implement metrics initiatives based on such sound common sense, right?

Wrong.

While a number of organisations have come to concede that metrics have a role to play in the basic operational arena, many are missing the strategic potential. A recent survey of HR practitioners found that: while 76% of respondents stated the goal of improving retention rates, only 39% actually tracked turnover; 56% had a strategic business objective of lowering staffing costs; and yet only 29% actually tracked the cost of each hire.[15]

The prospect of taking real competitive advantage is very much alive and should be extremely enticing. Once you've seen the effect on your bottom line and you've had other organisations approaching you in order to benchmark against your HR practices and procedures, then you can feel justifiably satisfied that you've used metrics to take the strategic initiative.

References

1. Sullivan, J., February 2003, 'Why Metrics Are Essential For Success in Recruiting.' *erdaily*, retrieved April 2004.
2. 'Value at Work: The Risks and Opportunities of Human Capital Measurement and Reporting,' The Conference Board (*www.conference-board.org*), 2002.
3. Finn, R., January/February 2004, 'Five steps to effective human capital measurement,' *Strategic HR Review.*
4. 'Internal Mobility,' iLogos Research, 2003.
5. Sullivan, J., February 2003, 'Why Metrics Are Essential For Success in Recruiting,' *erdaily*, retrieved April 2004.
6. Ibid.
7. Bedore, K., March 2003, 'Analysis Paralysis,' *erdaily*, retrieved May 2004.
8. Boudreau, J. W. & P. M. Ramstad, January/February 2004, 'Talentship: a decision science for HR,' *Strategic HR Review.*
9. Sullivan, J., November 2003, 'The Status of Metrics: A Look at Top Issues Facing Retail Organizations,' *erdaily*, retrieved April 2004.
10. Ibid.
11. Adler, L., June 2003, 'Using Metrics to Create a Six Sigma Hiring Process,' *erdaily*, retrieved April 2004.
12. Adler, L., November 2003, 'Why Forward-Looking Metrics are Needed in a Changing Economy,' *erdaily*, retrieved April 2004.
13. In order to present a comprehensive picture, your chosen metrics suite should ideally contain all three types of figures, though the exact proportions will depend on your industry type and strategic business objectives.
14. Lermusiaux, Y., November 2003, 'Metrics in Centralized and Decentralized Staffing Functions,' *erdaily*, retrieved May 2004.

15. Szary, D., June 2003, 'Metrics for Dummies,' *erdaily*, retrieved April 2004.
'Internal Mobility', iLogos Research, 2003.
The following sources are suggested for further reading:
Deploy Solutions White Papers
Electronic Recruiting Exchange (*www.erexchange.com*)
HR.com (*www.hr.com*)
iLogos Research (*www.ilogosresearch.com*)
Saratoga Institute (*www.saratogainstitute.com*)
Strategic HR Review (*www.researchandmarkets.com*)
The Benchmarking Centre (*www.benchmarking.co.uk*)
The Conference Board (*www.conference-board.org*)

The Post-Internet Organization: The *Real* Virtual Organization

BRAD M. JACKSON

August 2004

Brad Jackson in an independent consultant in the area of knowledge and collaborative management. He has consulted internationally on these topics and was a pioneer in the development of early collaborative software systems.

"To make knowledge work productive will be the great management task of this century, just as to make manual work productive was the great management task of the last century."

— Peter Drucker, *1978*

Reading Overview

The Post-Internet Organization is truly the Networked Organization whose beginning can be traced back to the late 1970s. As depicted in the timeline shown in Figure 1 [14-3], companies began to broaden access to enterprise information in the late 1970s with the formation of the "Information Center" concept. This approach was designed to provide easy access for "end-users" in near real time. Shortly after this, PCs were added to the mix, along with some simple software programs, such as a spreadsheet package, that the "end-user" could "program" without the assistance of the information technology (IT) staff. Subsequently, local area networks (LANs) were added to interconnect the PCs, and enterprise e-mail followed closely behind, though e-mail messages could only be routed internally and not company-to-company. In fact, even within the same company, many people could not send messages to each other because of the multiple, incompatible e-mail systems implemented by different divisions. While the accessibility of transaction data, PCs, spreadsheet software, and e-mail together laid the early groundwork for the transformation to the Networked Organization, it was the universal acceptance of the Internet, in the mid-1990s, that completed the foundation that set the stage for revolutionary change in organizational design and performance.

Thus far, implementation of these communication technologies, have not led to substantial change in how knowledge work is performed. This paper identifies the problems that have arisen from current practices of existing technology and then defines new structures that build upon the foundation which will in turn facilitate substantive change in knowledge work.

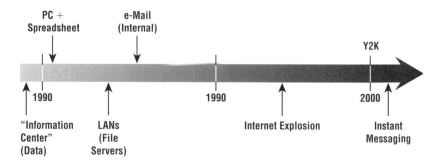

14-3 Figure 1. Progression of technology platform for knowledge work

The Current State: E-Mail, Conf Calls, Instant Messaging, File Servers, and Meetings!

The most common way of moving ideas, thoughts, decisions, and documents (or files) around in today's organization is through e-mail, though many are beginning to realize that they have pushed this medium to the point of creating an 'e-mail hell.' It is not usual today for an individual to receive 50, 100, 120 or more e-mail messages a day. In addition to e-mail, team members store documents on file servers (or document management systems), hold interminable meetings, send faxes, and play telephone tag. Meetings are most frequently in person or via audio-conferencing. More recently, there has been an increase in the use of instant messaging often as a substitute for a phone call or to set one up ("Are you there? Can I give you a call?").

As organizations begin to heavily use these technologies, they soon begin to realize some of the pitfalls. The following are three issues identified regarding e-mail use from a study of a cross-functional team in a multinational energy company:

1. **E-mail overload**
   - "Too many messages are sent to the whole team that only involve a few people."
   - "This results in a lot of 'noise' that prevents people from focusing on their core tasks."
   - "I'm not interested in talking back and forth on a technical issue. I see a lot of people sending out [e-mail messages] to 20 people, when in fact there should only be 2–3 people concerned with that issue ... you may get 20 to 70 pieces of [e-mail] a day."

2. **E-mail 'ping-pong'**
   - "Messages go back and forth and back again, making it difficult to get resolution on certain issues."
   - Projects that should be completed in a 'parallel fashion' are instead done 'sequentially.'
   - This is even more frustrating with the time delay from different sites; it is difficult to avoid sequential work since it is more difficult to have 'real-time' communication from those members.

3. Fragmented threaded conversations

- "People send messages to the whole team. Several will then respond to the whole team, then I end up with many different versions of an e-mail thread."

The increasing volume of spam further adds to the problems of e-mail. In managing the team's work, many team leaders use a work breakdown structure to outline the major work to be done, by whom, and when. Many will use pencil and paper for this task. Others use a spreadsheet program, while yet others use a more sophisticated project management tool. In any case, how the team leader receives updates regarding the status of the work is most probably to schedule group "status meetings." Typically, in these meetings, each member provides a status on his or her project tasks. These meetings, often weekly, tend to be individual meetings between the team leader and each individual team member with all of the team members present awaiting their turn "in the barrel." If there are multiple teams involved, then the team leader will meet with the next higher-level team to do the same thing. Following these meetings, the team leader will consolidate all of the information to produce the weekly status report and prepare for a meeting with the high-level project board.

To store the team's documents, teams commonly use a file server, a virtual drive (e.g., the "Z:/" drive), or a document management system. These repository systems allow team members to store documents and presentations that other team members can access at their discretion. One of the problems with just using a file server or document management system is that there is very little context about the document or presentation to help users to define which ones are relevant to their work. Usually, the only context is a folder name and the cryptic filename. There is no context for the purpose of the document, others' feedback, or how it relates to the rest of the team's work products.

At the beginning of a recent merger integration project, the group working on the migration of the financial systems and data looked at the artifacts from the previous merger integration project at their company. All of the documents were stored on the file server. The project manager commented that "the files were there, but there was no story around the files to help me understand the files." In other words, the files were out of context. While there was a folder structure and filenames, which is admittedly some context, there was no association of the file to the objectives and conversations surrounding them.

The Networked Organization: Structured Workspaces, Clusters

Whether a sales team, a marketing team, a drug development team, an information technology support team, a legal team, an upstream asset team, or a software development team, the common need is for all team members and team leaders to know:

- What are our objectives?
- Who is doing what to achieve them?
- What has been done so far?
- What's coming up?

- What are the dependencies?
- What are the issues or risks that prevent us from achieving our objectives?
- How do we resolve them?

Additionally, team members collaborate around work products, or deliverables, such as a report, presentation, or software modules. Team members often work in a give-and-take fashion where one member works on a portion of the work product and then another adds to it. The development of the work product continues through this iterative process until it is deemed acceptable by a "customer," or a deadline is reached.

STRUCTURED WORKSPACES

A structured workspace is the combination of language, relationships, and processes in a secure repository through which users communicate, coordinate, and collaborate. There are four basic types: project, service request, management, and community.

Project. Projects are often described as a defined work objective with a start date and an end date. Some projects are multi-year, multi-million dollar initiatives, while others are short in duration, lasting only a few weeks or months and costing in the hundreds or thousands of dollars. A workspace for a project comprises one or more sections that organize the team's work at a high level. A common configuration of workspace for a project will include:

1. *Project Plan*—to schedule and track objectives and activities that will achieve the project's goal.
2. *Issues/Risks/Scope Change*—to raise and resolve issues or mitigate risks that have an impact on the project plan.
3. *Events*—to schedule events, such as meetings, conferences, and store support information (e.g., agendas, minutes, notes).
4. *Discussion*—to share information or explore ideas not directly related to items on the project plan.
5. *Library*—to store reference materials (e.g., report templates) used by the team.
6. *Contacts*—to store/retrieve contact information of people outside the team.

As illustrated in Figure 2 [14-4], using a structured workspace removes the communication bottleneck that is created by traditional, individual productivity technologies alone because it facilitates a "many-to-many" relationship rather than a "one-to-many." In the structured workspace concept team members update the workspace by making status changes (e.g., marking an activity as 'complete'), adding commentary about an activity, or linking a work product file to an activity, as part of the process of doing the work. In this model, all team members, including the team leader, have the latest information available to them at any time. As mentioned previously, these updates occur today through e-mail, instant messaging, hallway conversations, and conference calls. The difference is that instead of team members using those media for the purpose of communicating information about the team's work to the team leader who then updates his personal file, the whole group deals with a single structured workspace which facilitates

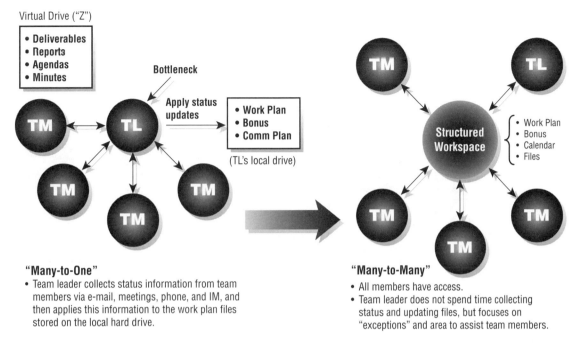

Virtual Drive ("Z")

- **Deliverables**
- **Reports**
- **Agendas**
- **Minutes**

Bottleneck

Apply status updates

- **Work Plan**
- **Bonus**
- **Comm Plan**

(TL's local drive)

Structured Workspace

- Work Plan
- Bonus
- Calendar
- Files

"Many-to-One"
- Team leader collects status information from team members via e-mail, meetings, phone, and IM, and then applies this information to the work plan files stored on the local hard drive.

"Many-to-Many"
- All members have access.
- Team leader does not spend time collecting status and updating files, but focuses on "exceptions" and area to assist team members.

14-4 Figure 2. Shift from Traditional Tools for teamwork to Structured Workspace removes the communication bottleneck.

other members being informed and involved as appropriate without the team leader having to be an administrator and a bottleneck.

Service Request. For many groups, the origination of work comes in the form of a request for service. The group processes the request through a series of stages. It is not uncommon for there to be multiple entry points and closing states. Examples of service requests groups can be found in the information technology and legal functions. Business users will request enhancements to an application or upgrading of the network infrastructure to accommodate a new facility, or a client will request assistance on a particular legal matter. Decisions regarding which requests to do and in what are order have to be made and then are managed to completion.

The difference between a project group and a service request group is that the former has a start and end date, while the latter is continuous. One of the challenges for the service request groups is to manage a volume and frequency of requests that varies week-to-week. While some requests can be handled in a short timeframe with few resources, others become projects in their own right.

The service request workspace will be customized to the particular type of work process involved, such as information technology, finance, human resources, or legal.

Management. A management, or decision-making, team comprises members from across different disciplines or functional areas. The individual members spend much of their time focused within their area or discipline with a much smaller portion of their time devoted to coordination and communication efforts of the management team. A management workspace helps the management team with organization of its work, predominately in the form of meetings, and its outputs and decisions. A management workspace is organized around the meeting flow. It will contain the following types of objects: agenda, minutes, action items, decisions, and presentation materials.

Community. Formal and informal communities exist within and across enterprises as knowledge-sharing mechanisms where there is a compelling area of interest among a group of people. A workspace for a community often contains:

- Discussion area—to share information, raise issues, explore problems, and ask and answer questions.
- Library—to share files (e.g., spreadsheet templates, presentations).
- Calendar—to post dates and information of professional interest, such as seminars, classes, and presentations.

More formal communities will have subteams (or 'subcommittees') and will require additional sections, or new workspaces, for managing a project plan and issues for them, for example, a subteam to plan for an annual conference.

Participation in communities is voluntary and part-time. A person may be part of a project team full-time, but he can contribute to and pull-down information from a community space as appropriate. He may be working on a project that requires some of the latest knowledge about wireless technology. In this case, the community space for wireless is easily available to find documentation or ask for assistance. As the knowledge worker applies what he has learned from the community to his project work, he may discover some additional knowledge that he can contribute back to the community. Once stored, it can be fully shared with others across the enterprise.

Networked Organization

In an enterprise, there are multiple teams that work together to achieve a goal. Linking related workspaces together forms a cluster which facilitates all members in viewing the complex structure and tracking dependencies between teams. There are three fundamental cluster structures in the enterprise:

1. *Service Request Network*—one or more "service request" teams interconnected. An example of a service request network is the support function within a company's information technology department where a customer makes a request (e.g., "enhancement" to an existing application a new router installed in the physical network) and it is processed by a series of groups (demand management, release management, change control, and production). Each of these groups will have a structured workspace that reflects their process as it relates to working on the 'request.' The spaces are linked in a way that allows one group to forward it to another.

2. *Project Organization*—multiple, inter-related project teams aimed at a collective goal. An example of a project organization is a merger integration project. The sole purpose of the integration effort is to integrate

two companies into one following a merger or acquisition. The project organization for such an effort typically has a 'Steering Team'' or group of executives who have overall decision-making responsibility. The teams are most commonly organized along the major business functions or processes, such as finance, IT, marketing, sales, etc. Each of these areas might be further broken down into subteams. For example, in the IT subgroup, there might be three subteams organized around applications, data, and infrastructure tasks. Each subteam is in itself a project team, but there are dependencies between the three subteams that relate to decision making and managing cross-team issues. All of the teams in the project organization are collectively working to achieve a successful integration.

3. *Portfolio of Projects*—a pipeline of multiple projects. An example is a portfolio of drug teams in a biotechnology or pharmaceutical company. At the high level, the portfolio is organized as a pipeline of drug teams that move through a set of stages, such as preclinical trial, clinical trial-phase 1, clinical trail-phase 2, clinical trail-phase 3, and drug application. Each drug team is a project team that works to accomplish a set of milestones in order to proceed to the next stage with the ultimate goal of getting approval from a governmental approval agency in order to market the new drug.

Interlinking clusters creates the Networked Organization. Figure 3 [14-5] illustrates the relationship of an asset team in the Exploration and Production industry with different communities. Knowledge is shared across the enterprise when team members contribute their insights from their day-to-day work on either a project team or a service request team into the community space.

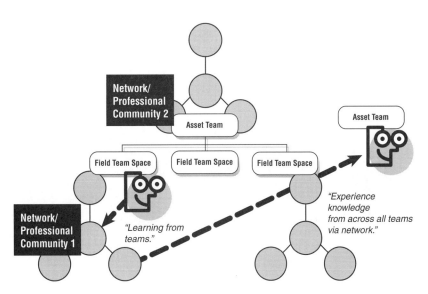

14-5 Figure 3. The Networked Organization is the combination of network clusters, such as Asset Team of Field Teams, and communities that collectively form powerful knowledge-sharing capabilities across the enterprise.

Conclusion

The Internet completed the foundation upon which the next generation organization, the Networked Organization, is being built. While e-mail, file servers (or document management systems), conference calls, and meetings have served to support the team's coordination needs in the past, structured workspaces streamline communication processes because of their multi-user access, and have the potential to remove the team leader as a communication bottleneck. These structures create a living storybook for the team that facilitates learning for newer members. Linking workspaces together into clusters creates a unique management structure that provides transparency and visibility in a way not previously possible. Juxtaposing communities against these traditional hierarchical team structures creates a powerful way to share specific project and process knowledge across the enterprise.

Human Resource Management

Chapter 15 Contents

Chapter Overview

Given the technical complexity of IT projects, it is easy to see how the proper management of this knowledge area is critical to success. Fundamentally, the key elements in project HR management are organizational structure, proper acquisition of the team members, and ongoing development of the team's skills.

Organizational Structure

There are many considerations regarding how to set up an organizational structure for a project. Ideally, a small project team consisting of dedicated full-time members (IT and subject matter experts) all co-located in one place is the optimum arrangement, but not always feasible. One of the readings in this section describes the productivity implications related to team size. If team groupings of five to seven can be organized around a single goal, then communication and productivity will improve. Larger team sizes increase the complexity of the communication processes, and evidence shows a decrease in the project success rate.

As project scope grows in size and complexity, the organizational structure issues grow correspondingly. Larger projects must deal more with formalization of their internal processes. As an example, processes for change management, issue resolution, task assignment, and time and progress reporting must be more consistent than for the small team where the overall scope and status can be more easily observed. Related to size is the permanence of the team members, meaning whether they work full- or part-time on the project. Experience shows that full-time participants work with more flexibility and fewer communication needs than can the worker who is only available on a partial schedule and is not so in tune with the project needs. A third structuring issue arises with the inclusion of third-party resource providers, especially if those providers are offshore with many time zones to cross. In this case, the partitioning of roles has to be more carefully defined and communications are obviously more cumbersome.

Regardless of the physical organizational topology in place for the project, it is important to recognize that formal definition of roles and responsibilities is a management requirement. There are three basic mechanisms that aid in this activity. First, a team organization chart with skill or functional role definition should be formalized. Second, a work breakdown structure showing some level of partitioned task definition should be the common tool for task management and assignment. Third, a responsibility assignment matrix (RAM) should be used to map work tasks to organization, group, or individual team elements.

Staff Acquisition

The recognition that a high performer will produce ten times that of a low performer highlights the fact that the selection of team staff is not a "pick out who is available" process. Just as in sports, teams need the proper combination of star and solid role performers. The bad news is that individuals with these traits are highly sought. So, the project manager will generally have to compromise on selection options. A team of all star performers is probably not the best choice in any case. The resource acquisition chore becomes finding a team that will work together productively, it is hoped with sufficient stars (technical and subject area knowledge) to accomplish the desired output. In high technology projects there must be sufficient skilled technical resources to handle those tasks that only they can do. Lacking that skill level will doom the project or, at least, result in suboptimum decisions that create time and cost overruns. Similarly, lack of proper subject area knowledge will result in a system that may be technically great but will not meet the business needs.

In the case of the matrix team organization, the various functional departments would supply members according to some agreed-upon staffing plan. This model makes the acquisition process more difficult in that the project manager will have to negotiate with the functional manager to obtain the skill levels, timing, and quantities. Too often, the functional manager will not match the planned staffing profile. When this occurs, the schedule is put at risk. Mismatches of skill, timing, or quantity potentially sabotage the project outcome. In addition, if a worker does not really want to work on the assigned project, there can be motivational issues. Resolving all of these resource-related events requires a high degree of behavioral skill for the project manager.

Team Development

Once a project team is in place, the question becomes whether they have the proper skills in place to execute the technical target. If not, a plan is needed to upgrade them to an appropriate level. Not quite so obvious is the situation where the team can execute the currently needed activities. At the same time, they are falling behind their peer group in terms of other skills. If a project lasts for three years, the erosion in skill base can be a significant issue. Too often, the project management attitude is to work the team hard to accomplish the short-term goal and ignore long-term personnel growth.

Readings

HR management practices have traditionally not been the strong suit of IT project managers. We believe that the concepts outlined in this section need to be better understood by working project managers.

The first reading in this section is "Project Managers as Politician: A Shift in Roles," by Andrew Anderson. This reading describes the evolution of project management from a technician view to a broader, political one. Traits of a successful project manager are mapped against similar traits of a politician.

Johanna Rothman provides a second reading, titled "Successful Software Management: 14 Lessons Learned." This prescriptive overview outlines a work managerial style format that is needed as you convert yourself from technician to manager.

The remaining three readings focus on organizational factors associated with HR management. First, Doug Putnam quantifies the impact of team size on productivity in his reading, titled "Team Size Can Be the Key to a Successful Project." This reading provides insight into how statistical data can be used to predict project outcomes. Following this, the next reading comes from the staff of the Software Engineering Institute (SEI) and is titled "Experiences Applying the People Capability Maturity Model." This work is basically an extension of the landmark work previously done at SEI. This version explores the notion that maturity concepts impact the organizational work force in much the same way as optimized processes work on system development. The final reading in this section is provided by Corey Ferengul of the META Group; it describes a contemporary approach to improving organizational productivity by creating Centers of Excellence. META describes this as the next step in IT organization evolution. This is a very thought-provoking approach to organization structure.

Understanding both the human and organizational elements is fundamental to project success, yet not easy to quantify. Issues such as organizational culture, morale, and skill have an often subtle yet significant impact on the project outcome.

READING 1

Project Managers as Politician:
A Shift in Roles

A. ANDREW ANDERSON

Originally presented at Project World, Boston, MA, 2002.

About the Author

A. Andrew Anderson, PMP, is the former vice president of civil and state/ local government for Robbins-Gioia, LLC. Mr. Anderson has over 20 years of program and project management experience. In those 20 years, Mr. Anderson has assisted forming, managing, and controlling programs and projects in the DOD, Federal, State, Local, and Commercial environments. In addition, he is a graduate and alumni of the Defense Systems Management College and is a certified business manager (CBM). Mr. Anderson is currently the Assistant Director for the Transportation Security Administration's Office of Information Technologies Solutions Delivery Directorate.

Historically, project managers (PMs) were more like technicians, oversee-ing the details of isolated pieces of a project. They worked with details more than they worked with people, and they held mid-level positions within the chain of command. The change we are seeing today is PMs moving toward upper management and executive roles. CEOs, CFOs, and COOs are looking to PMs to be their business managers for projects, and PMs are less involved in the details and more involved in managing all the parts and people related to a project.

Whatever PMs do in a project—whether it is large or small—they literally have to negotiate piece after piece to take a project down the path toward completion. This negotiation requires an ability to advocate, facilitate, motivate, communicate, and defend. In short, today's PMs are politicians, requiring each of those soft skills to move a project toward success.

PM as Politician

Some PM professionals may feel that "politician" doesn't describe what we do, or that it is a word that carries with it a negative tone. For a moment, disregard any offensive connotations you associate with the word "politician" and compare the following list of characteristics.

Characteristics of a Successful PM:
- Leader
- Communicator
- Facilitator
- Negotiator

322

- Marketer
- Advocate
- Motivator
- Visionary
- "Doer"

Characteristics of a Successful Politician:

- Leader
- Communicator
- Facilitator
- Negotiator
- Marketer
- Advocate
- Motivator
- Visionary
- "Doer"

You can see that the characteristics that make a politician successful among his or her constituency mirror those that make a PM a success with a project. Now compare their jobs: A politician's job is to advocate for his or her special interests, to be able to generate tax dollars to his constituency, and to get re-elected to office. Similarly, PMs will advocate for their projects, generate the resources they need (human and capital), and be successful so that they get the next project. PMs politely politic their projects to success.

As a relatively new field, at least in terms of formal recognition, most PMs come from a background outside of project management, and what's missing is that they are not well versed in the soft skills needed by politicians. They are experts at what they do, but they still need to develop the social skills to be able to manage people. A PM needs to be able to direct a team, while at the same time motivate and empower them. Few people want to be told what to do, which means that leading a team requires a certain amount of political savvy. That's where the soft skill side of project management comes into play.

Softer Side of Project Management

The first step to building the soft skills needed as a PM (and politician) is a self-assessment. Be honest and introspective. What are your strengths and weaknesses as a leader? As a communicator? A facilitator? A negotiator? A marketer? An advocate? A motivator? A visionary? A "doer"?

In my self-assessment, I found out that I had a shortcoming in the area of communication: I did not listen very well. Because it is essential for PMs to listen well and communicate well, I had to work on that skill. I needed to learn to truly listen to my team, to show compassion, to let them know they were heard, and to promise to see what I could do. Then I followed through. Like a politician, I needed to build credibility and trust, and ultimately be liked.

And when there's a soft skill in which you're lacking and you can't see a change on the near horizon, find someone who brings that skill to the table. Surround yourself with a team that compliments and completes what you as a PM (and a politician) have to offer.

Approaching the Project Successfully

In the PM's new role as politician, it's important to reevaluate the way you approach a project. Review the project and each of its stages from the five following angles, keeping in mind the soft skills mentioned above.

AWARENESS

- Assess your organizational and project environment.
- Note the politics in play.
- Understand what is expected.

FLEXIBILITY

- Develop tactics that are win-win.
- Look for options and middle ground.
- Be open to ideas and opportunities that serve the project.

INFORMATION

- Develop a structured approach to information.
- Check your data and information inputs and outputs.
- Use triangulation as a means to target information.
- Shape your response to the environment.

COMMUNICATIONS

- Be open and concise with how you communicate.
- Plan your communications.
- Communicate often.
- Communicate to the levels being served.

NEGOTIATION

- Look for win-win opportunities.
- Approach issues with "problem-solving" skills.
- Look for benefits and opportunities.

Accepting the Shift

The role of the PM is a changing one, and today's shift calls for the soft skills of a politician. PMI and other educational institutions are acknowledging the need for soft skill development, rather than leaving success just to those who seem to be "born with it." (I should note here that some people are born with it, and others just don't seem to have it.)

Today's PMs need to be aware and sensitive to organizational politics; they must assess the project environment and act accordingly within a given situation. PMs need to self assess in order to be successful in a political world, and with every project they need a strategy and a willingness to communicate openly and frequently. Finally, today's PMs need to accept their roles as politicians.

Successful Software Management:
14 Lessons Learned

JOHANNA ROTHMAN

Rothman Consulting Group, Inc.

About the Author

Johanna Rothman consults on managing high technology product development, which helps managers, teams, and organizations become more effective. Rothman uses pragmatic techniques for managing people, projects, and risks to create successful teams and projects. A frequent speaker and author on managing high technology product development, she has written numerous articles and is now a columnist for Software Development, Computerworld.com, *and* StickyMinds.com. *Rothman served as the program chair for the Software Management conference and is the author of* Hiring the Best Knowledge Workers, Techies & Nerds.

Successful managers realize that they need to balance the needs of the business, the employees, and the work environment to be effective. In this reading, the author summarizes her experiences in determining the work to accomplish and planning it, managing successful relationships with the group, and managing reactions to typical management mistakes

Shortly after I became a manager, I dragged myself home from work, flopped on the couch, and sighed to my husband, "This management stuff is hard. Nothing I learned in school prepared me for this people stuff. And that 'management training'—that was just form-filling-out nonsense. The soft skills—dealing with people—is the hardest." My husband chuckled and commiserated.

If you are like me, and you started your professional career as a technical person, this "management stuff" is hard to do. Not the forms, although the forms can be irritating, but knowing how to deal with people and completing the work your organization expects of you is difficult. I have now had over fifteen years of management experience and I have learned a number of lessons about managing people.

Define the Manager's Role

When you become a manager, your role is to organize purposefully [1]. For me, that means creating an environment in which people can perform their best work. As a software manager, that means I work to create business value by balancing the needs of the business, the employees, and the environment. There is no One Right Way to do this; every organization is different. However, these lessons have served me well in numerous organizations.

1. Know what they pay you to do.

I have been a manager of developers, testers, and support staff. You would think it would be easy to know what the company paid me to do. However, my mission as a test manager, to report on the state of the software, is sometimes different from what my organizations desired: find the Big Bad Bugs before the customer does; or bless this software. Even my mission as a development manager, develop the team members as much as the software, can be different from what one organization desired: create software just good enough that we can be bought out.

My mission does not have to be the same as yours, and you may modify your mission as your organization changes. However, delivering on your mission as a manager is what your organization pays you to do. What is important is to notice when your title, your mission, and what the company pays you to do are not synchronized.

One QA Manager said it this way, "My management only wants to me to manage the testing, not raise risks, look for process improvement opportunities, or even gather and report on what I think are standard metrics. My manager and I are both frustrated. Focusing on just the testing is wrong." This QA manager has at least one alternative—change his title so that he and the organization both know that he is not attempting to perform organization-wide process improvement, to clarify expectations in the organization.

Doing what the organization pays you to do, and not doing what they do not pay you to do makes a huge difference in how successfully you and your group can accomplish your mission. Make sure you clarify your mission at your organization, so you can create a to-do and not-to-do list. These lists help you plan the work—for you and your group.

One development manager who temporarily took over installations from the tech support people realized that he no longer had a development team, but an installation support team. The development manager put installations on his not-to-do list and developed a plan to move installations back to tech support.

When you align yourself with your manager's priorities, you do the work they pay you to do.

2. Plan the work: Portfolio management.

It is easy to be reactive at work, and feel buffeted by the requested changes of your group. It is harder and necessary to be proactive and plan your group's work, even if that work changes every week. For me, planning includes these activities: identifying the project portfolio (new work, ongoing work, periodic work, ad hoc work), developing strategies for managing the work for each project, and knowing what done means for each project. One of the questions I like to ask is "How little can we do?" I do not want to shortchange any project, so by asking about the minimum requirements, I can accommodate more projects successfully.

Part of planning the work is assigning the people to projects. I assign people to one important project, and allow them to take on little bits and pieces of much less important work when they need a break or are stuck on the important project. I avoid context switching (moving from one unrelated task to another) as much as possible.

3. Accept only one no. 1 priority at one time.

I have worked for many managers who demanded my staff and I work on several top-priority projects simultaneously.

Senior managers perform different work than first-line and middle managers. It is not possible for senior managers to work on more than one top-priority task at one time, but because they tend to have more wait states in their work, these senior managers are under the illusion they are working on several top-priority projects at the same time.

Middle and first-line managers can only work on one #1 priority task at one time. However, sometimes we confuse urgency and importance [2]. At one organization, I would arrive at work in the morning, check my voicemail, and respond to all the voicemail requests. That took me until noon. I would check my e-mail and voicemail after lunch, and run around responding to those urgent requests. After a week of this, I realized I wasn't performing any of the important work, such as planning for the group and lab, reviewing critical development plans, or planning my hiring strategy. And, I would notice that although people marked their e-mails and voicemails high priority, they didn't utilize the information I had given them at the time I responded.

I stopped immediate response to urgent requests, and replanned my days. I still checked voicemail and e-mail, but I tended to ask more questions about the deadlines for these requests. Prioritizing requests helped me manage my management time.

I still had the problem of too many high-priority projects coming into my group, so I asked my manager these questions:

- If you could have one project first, which one would it be?
- What are the consequences if we release any of these projects late?

We talked and negotiated which projects had to be completed when and why. When I understood the tradeoffs between projects, I was able to manage the work coming into my group.

4. Commit to projects after checking with your staff.

Business needs change, and sometimes your manager will grab you in the hall, and say, "Hey, can you do this project now, and finish it in two months?" Or, a senior management planning committee will call you into their meeting, and say, "We need this project now. Can you commit to it?"

It is very tempting to say yes. And saying yes is exactly the wrong thing to do. You can say, "Let me check to see if my previous estimate is still accurate, and I will get back to you before 5 p.m. today."

If you say yes, you are training your senior management to ask you for answers when you do not know the answers, and you have committed your staff to a project that may not be the same scope you originally estimated.

5. Hire the best people for the job.

Especially if you manage many projects, your greatest leverage point is in hiring appropriate staff for the jobs you need filled. Too often, we hire people who have similar technical skills and personalities as the people already in our groups. Hiring people who are just like the ones we have now does not always provide the best people for the job.

When you hire people your staff thinks are great, you increase morale in the group, and you increase your group's capacity over time. I recommend you develop a hiring strategy, so you know the kinds of technical and soft skills you are looking for, and that you choose a variety of techniques for interviewing.

I have found auditions [3,4,5] to be an essential technique for interviewing technical staff. I normally create auditions of 30–45 minutes duration, so I can see how a person works in a particular setting. Auditions help candidates show what they can do. If you organize a congruent audition, you do not trip people up on esoteric ideas or jargon; you create a simplified situation that the candidate could encounter at work. Watching the candidate, or having the candidate explain their answers/results, are powerful interview techniques.

You can create auditions for any position, including project managers, developers, testers, writers, support staff, analysts, systems engineers, product managers, program managers, and people managers. Define the behaviors you require in a position, and then create an audition, using your products or open source products to see the person at work. Create auditions that are 30 minutes long to start. If you are having trouble deciding between multiple candidates, define another audition that is one hour long, and invite the candidates back to see how they manage that audition. Auditions show you how the person works at work, priceless information.

I also recommend behavior-description interview questions [5,6], to understand how a candidate has performed in previous jobs. Behavior-description questions are open-ended, and ask the candidate to tell you the story of previous work. For example, if you would like to understand how a project manager deals with a project team who has not yet met a schedule, you could ask this series of questions: "Have you ever managed a project where the team had trouble meeting the schedule?" If the answer is no, you can decide if the project manager has enough experience to manage your team. If the answer is yes, ask, "What did you do? What actions did you take on that project to help the project team meet the schedule?" The answers you hear will help you assess that candidate's ability to work in your organization.

6. Preserve good teams.

Part of my hiring strategy is to hire people who fit into my already-existing team, but sometimes you inherit teams, or a project has completed and a team is ready to move on. When a team is successful, I try to keep the team together, so they can continue working well together. I may bring more people into the team, one at a time, especially if the team has been highly productive. But I do not scatter the productive team and hope they will form more productive teams. That just reduces the productive people's productivity.

Teams can overcome bad management and bad process, but they cannot overcome a team un-jeller. A team un-jeller is the person who walks into the lunchroom, and suddenly everyone else leaves. Or, the un-jeller creates an argument out of every conversation. If you have a team un-jeller, find another place for that person to work, preferably at your competitor.

7. Avoid micromanaging or inflicting help.

Many of us were software developers, testers, analysts, or had some other technical role before we became managers. When we were technical contributors, we knew how to perform the technical jobs. However, once you have been a manager for a while, you probably do not know precisely how to perform the employee's job.

I once had a boss who liked to creep into my office, stare over my shoulder, and say, "On line 16, shouldn't that be a ..." By the time he had reached the 16, I jumped out of my chair, flustered, with my concentration gone. Micromanagement neither gets the job done faster, nor does inflicting advice or help.

On the other hand, you and the employee both need to know that the employee is progressing. I ask my staff to decide when they have been stuck for too long (time-box the work). Some tasks require weeks of study, but most tasks require days or hours. If the employee spends more than the agreed-upon time on the task, their job is to ask for help. As the manager, your job is to find them help, not necessarily inflict your help.

8. Treat people individually and with respect.

Buckingham and Coffman [7] claim that each employee's relationship with their manager is key to that employee's success and long-term happiness in the organization. That means we need to treat people fairly, but uniquely, so that we build and maintain the best possible relationships with each employee.

Everyone has their own preferences, especially in their communications patterns, and how they organize their thoughts about their work. Some people prefer e-mail communications; some prefer in-person discussions. Some people want to understand all the reasons behind your requests, and others will take the requests at face value. Some people need to gather data to make decisions; others will develop a model about the situation and make a decision based on their model.

It does not matter if people work top-down or bottom-up, or if they want to talk in person or by e-mail. What matters is that you, within reason, accommodate everyone's uniqueness.

I once managed two very talented developers. They shared a large office. Begrudgingly, they allowed me to have 20-minute one-on-ones with each of them every two weeks. In between, if I wanted to talk to either of them, I had to e-mail them first—dropping in was not allowed. I treated them differently than the other people in my group, but fairly, taking their preferences into account.

They frequently worked on the same software. They never spoke to each other aloud, they only communicated via e-mail, even though they shared an office. Because they were so successful at their work together, and even mentoring others in the organization by e-mail, their communications preferences were a bit odd, but acceptable. If I had tried to change them, to meet my needs and work with them the same way I worked with the other people, none of us would have been happy.

9. Meet weekly with each person.

Even if you have hired stars, you still need to know each person's progress on their tasks, and how the project as a whole is progressing. I use one-on-ones weekly to meet with each person. We discuss the employee's progress on their tasks. Sometimes, tasks are amorphous and difficult to know when to stop or if the employee needs help. I ask each employee to show me visible progress on each task: drafts of plans, multiple designs, prototype test results, anything that shows me the employee is making progress and is not stuck. If the employee needs help to complete the task, we discuss which kinds of help are appropriate.

I receive many benefits from weekly one-on ones with my staff. I learn weekly what everyone is doing, and I can track that in my notebook, so it is easy to write up useful performance evaluations, including examples of successful and not-so-successful actions the employee has taken over the year. And, because we meet weekly, I can give feedback each week, not when we make time. I also reduce the number of staff interruptions, because everyone knows they can ask me non-urgent questions in the one-on-one. I can perform weekly career development and learn if my staff has personal issues affecting their ability to do their jobs.

If I am managing more than eight people, I meet biweekly with more senior staff, because they need less direct supervision.

Some of you are probably thinking you do not have time to meet with everyone once a week. However, if you do not set up specific times to meet with everyone, you tend to either not know what people are doing, or you are interrupted frequently by your staff with questions.

10. Plan training time each week.

Technical work is constantly changing, and most of the technical people I know enjoy learning new things. If you have a budget for formal training, that is great. Even if you do not have a budget, plan training time each week, in the form of brown-bag lunches, presentations from other groups in your organization, an internal user-group meeting of one of your tools, or presentations from people in your group about their successes or difficulties.

I use the weekly group meeting as a time to deliver the training. When I managed development groups, I organized this internal training: technical leads of other subprojects to explain their architecture and API to other groups, testers to explain patterns of defects they found, different techniques for peer review, or discussion of a particularly interesting article in one of the technical magazines someone had read.

11. Fire people who cannot perform the work.

Even when you meet regularly with your staff, encourage your staff, and acquire help when they need it, some people in your group may not be able to perform to the level that you require. First, make sure you have been specific and given feedback to the employee, with examples of inadequate behavior. If the employee understands the lack of performance, you can choose whether to coach the person, or perform a get-well plan, or in radical circumstances, escort the employee out the door.

Keeping nonproductive employees has direct and indirect costs. The direct costs are easier to define: you are paying a salary and benefits and not receiving the expected work. The indirect costs are much more subtle and more damaging.

When you continue employing an inadequate employee, the morale of the entire workgroup declines. If morale declines enough, your best people will leave. Not only do you have someone in your group who is not successful, that person has driven away the people who are the most successful.

In addition to low morale, you and your group accomplish less than you expected. You are not just accomplishing less because of the one employee who cannot work at the level you require; that person probably has handoffs to others in your group, and those other people will be delayed by the inadequate work.

I once inherited a group where the previous management had "spared" an employee from previous layoffs, because he was having personal problems. Those personal problems affected his work—he did not always come to work, he was late on every deliverable, and he was unable to perform most of his work. In my one-on-ones with the employee, I gave him examples of his work and asked if he was able to work. He said yes. (If he had said no, we would have put him on short-term or long-term disability.) We chose to perform a get-well plan, which the employee stopped after a week. After the employee left, the morale in the group jumped dramatically, and we were able to accomplish more work.

12. Emphasize results, not time.

I have worked for senior managers who rewarded individuals on the basis of their work hours—who started early and stayed late. Unfortunately, these managers had no ability to understand the results the long-working employees imposed on the rest of the organization: buggy code, inadequate designs, and tests that did not find obvious problems. When people work long hours, their productivity decreases, not increases [DeMarco, Peopleware]. In *Slack* [8], Tom DeMarco says, "Extended overtime is a productivity–reduction technique." The longer people stay at work, the less work they do. Instead they perform the life activities they are not performing outside of work.

Make it possible for people to only work 40 hours a week. The less overtime people put in, the better their work will be.

If people tell you they are working long hours because they cannot accomplish anything in their regular work weeks, ask your staff where they spend their time. Look for patterns such as multitasking, or meetings that do not have any productive output. Use your management power to discover and remove the obstacles preventing people from working a 40-hour week.

13. Admit your mistakes.

Sometimes, those obstacles to people completing their work successfully in 40 hours arise from your management mistakes. It is difficult, and sometimes embarrassing, to have to admit you have made a mistake. In my experience, when I have admitted mistakes to my staff, they've respected me more for it.

14. Recognize and reward good work.

Money is not an adequate reward for many technical people. If people think they are paid fairly, more money is not enough of a reward. Recognition of good work and the opportunity to perform meaningful work [Kohn] is much more important than monetary rewards. Lack of money can be a demotivator, but only money is not sufficient for a significant reward.

Kohn [9] says, "[Rewards] motivate people to get rewards." If your organization has trained employees to expect money as a reward, this appreciation technique may seem small. Try it anyway.

When I use appreciations as a recognition technique I say, "I appreciate you Jim, for your work on the blatz module and API definition. Your work made it possible for Joe to write great tests and for me to predict the project's progress." Appreciations between peers could mean even more than money from you. When you appreciate a person for good work and you explain what the work meant to you, you are motivating the person to continue performing similar work.

In addition, consider time off, group activities, movie tickets, or funny awards, such as best recursion of the week, as recognition techniques.

The most important part of rewards is to make sure the recognition and/or reward is congruent with each person's performance. Your staff knows who is performing well and who is coasting. If you recognize and reward evenly, you are not differentiating between outstanding performance and adequate performance. Make sure you reward a person's entire contribution (the entire work product, including how good the work product is, the timeliness of the deliverable, and the person's ability to work with others, and whatever else is important to you), not just the size or quality of the work.

Summary

Managers exist to help people do their best work to serve the business of the organization. Technical people can make great managers, as long as they understand people and want to succeed at working with them. Many successful technical managers took the time to learn about management, putting as much effort (if not more) than the effort they took to learn the necessary technical background for the technical jobs. Managers do not have to be perfect; they have to be good enough to create a working environment for their employees to deliver great work.

Acknowledgements

I thank Dwayne Phillips and the Crosstalk reviewers for their review of this article.

References

[1]Magretta, Joan. *What Management Is: How it Works and Why It is Everyone's Business*. The Free Press, New York. 2002.

[2]Covey, Stephen R. *The Seven Habits of Highly Effective People*. Simon & Schuster, New York. 1989.

[3]DeMarco, Tom, and Tim Lister. *Peopleware: Productive Projects and Teams, 2nd edition*. Dorset House, New York.1999.

[4]Weinberg, Gerald M. *Congruent Interviewing by Audition, in Amplifying Your Effectiveness, Collected Essays*. Dorset House. New York. 2000.

[5]Rothman, Johanna. *Hiring the Best Knowledge Workers, Techies & Nerds: The Secrets & Science of Hiring Technical People*, Dorset House, New York, 2004.

[6]Janz, Tom, et al. *Behavior Description Interviewing*, Prentice Hall, Englewood Cliffs, NJ. 1986.

[7]Buckingham, Marcus, and Curt Coffman. *First, Break All the Rules: What the World's Greatest Managers Do Differently*. Simon & Schuster. 1999.

[8]DeMarco, Tom. *Slack*. Broadway Books, New York, 2001.

[9]Kohn, Alfie. *Punished by Rewards*. Houghton-Mifflin, New York, 1993.

Team Size Can Be the Key to a Successful Project

DOUG PUTNAM

How Many People Should I Use on My Development Team?

People frequently ask if there is an optimum staffing level for a software development project? At one extreme, the number of people could be below a critical mass and the project is vulnerable to the loss of a key person. Very small teams are also highly dependent on the skills of the "individual." At the other extreme, large teams experience human communication complexities. Large teams quickly gravitate toward the average skill set of the group. Somewhere in the middle there should be an optimum situation. So, the quick and dirty answer to the question is; yes there is an optimum team size, but it is dependent on a number of variables. Some obvious variables are:

- The size of code to be developed and reused.
- The application complexity.
- The degree to which schedule or cost is the overriding schedule constraint.

The Research

In this research, we set out to find the optimum staffing for a specific application domain and size regime. In this work, we will define optimum staff size as the team size most likely to achieve the highest productivity, the shortest schedule, and the cheapest cost with the least amount of variation in the final outcome.

Our Method

To minimize the variables that could impact our results we decided to select a set of medium-sized information systems that were completed in the last three years. Medium sized was defined as products that contained 35,000 to 95,000 new or modified source lines of code. There were 491 projects that satisfied the conditions. The sample was then stratified into team size groupings, which is shown in Figure 1 [15-1]. Notice that all of the data sets are fairly well distributed across the entire size regime. The average size of all five data sets is 57,412 ESLOC. None of the data set averages are more that 3,000 SLOC away from the overall average size.

The Results

The average productivity, schedule, and effort were analyzed for each of the data sets along with the standard deviation. We plotted the averages

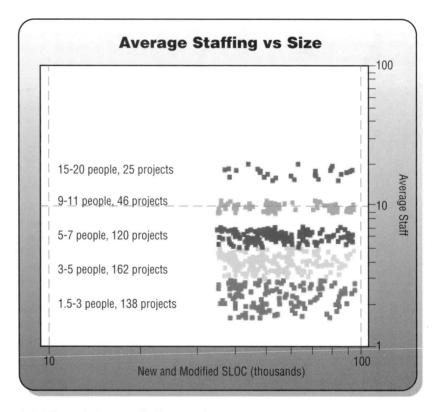

15-1 Figure 1. Data stratified by team sizes.

and compared them to see which had the best performance and observed overall trends if they were apparent.

Productivity Data

The average Productivity Index (a measure that uses size, schedule time, and development effort in it's calculation) was calculated for each of the five data sets. The Productivity Index for the one and one-half to three, three to five, and five to seven person data sets was very similar and had the highest level of efficiency. The "smaller teams" were two or more Productivity Indices higher than the "larger teams." The five to seven person data set had approximately nine percent less variation than the three to five person projects and 12 percent less variation compared to the one and one-half to three person projects. The variation is displayed using the high-low bars, which represent one standard deviation from the average (Figure 2 [15-2]).

Schedule Data

The schedule data shows that there is a decreasing trend in schedule performance as the team sizes get larger until the team sizes reach nine to

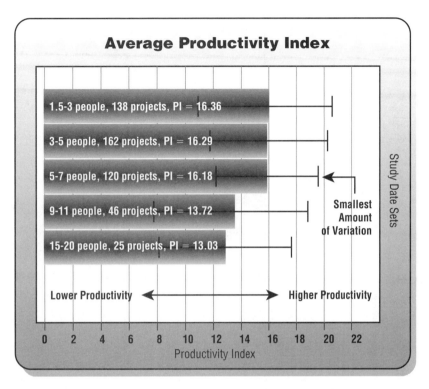

15-2 Figure 2. Average Productivity Index for each project staffing group with variation bounds.

11 people where the average time starts to increase. The schedule performance data show the five to seven person data set as having the best performance, however the three to five person data set is a very close second (Figure 3 [15-3]).

Effort Data

The development effort statistics show that larger teams translate into more effort and cost. The trend appears to have an exponential behavior. The most cost-effective strategy is the smallest team, however the extreme non-linear effort increase doesn't seem to kick in until the team size approaches nine or more people (Figure 4 [15-4]).

Conclusions

The goal of our research was to find optimum team size for building medium-sized information systems. From the 491 projects that were analyzed, we would conclude that a three to seven person team has the best performance (three to five would be the best, but five to seven people is a very close second). The three to five person data set was not the outright

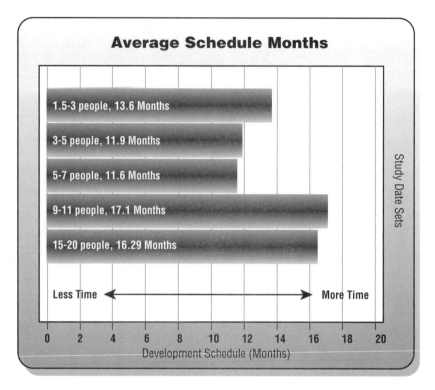

15-3 Figure 3. Average Schedule for each project staffing group.

winner in any of the assessment categories; however, it had very good performance in all areas. One can speculate on why we see this behavior on the moderately small teams, but common sense suggests the following reasons:

- This team size provides some protection against the loss of a key person.
- Individual performance is not overcome by group dynamics.
- Team size is probably close to optimum in building motivation and cohesion.
- There is minimum human communication complexity among team members.
- It doesn't require significant management overhead.

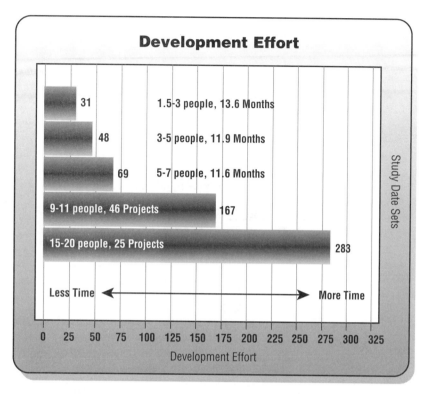

15-4 Figure 4. Average effort for each project staffing group.

Next time you are planning a project, think hard about the optimum staffing levels because it can clearly have a significant impact on the overall results. This study gives you some insights into an application and size domain where many systems are being built today. Coupled with good peopleware practices, you should be able to make a real impact on your organization's bottom line performance.

Experiences Applying the People Capability Maturity Model

DR. BILL CURTIS

TeraQuest

DR. WILLIAM E. HEFLEY

Carnegie Mellon University

SALLY A. MILLER

Software Engineering Institute

About the Authors

Bill Curtis, Ph.D., is co-founder and chief scientist of TeraQuest. He is a for-mer director of the Software Process Program at the Software Engineering Institute. He is co-author of the Capability Maturity Model® for Software (SW-CMM®), principle architect of the People CMM®, and a member of the CMM® Integration[SM] product team. Previously, Curtis directed research on user inter-face technologies and the software design process at MCC, developed software measurement systems at ITT's Programming Technology Center, evaluated software methods for the GE Space Division, and taught statistics at the University of Washington.

William E. Hefley, Ph.D., is a senior lecturer at Carnegie Mellon University. He is a lead assessor for the People Capability Maturity Model® (CMM®), CMM-Based Appraisal for Internal Process Improvement, and Standard Capability Maturity Model Integration[SM] Assessment Method for Process Improvement. He is co-author of "The People CMM" and its assessment method, and a mem-ber of the CMM® Integration[SM] product team. He was instrumental in launch-ing the Software Engineering Institute's software process improvement efforts. In prior industry roles, he participated in and managed systems devel-opment and user interface projects in areas such as space system; Command, Control, Communications, and Intelligence; and manufacturing systems.

Sally A. Miller is coauthor of the People Capability Maturity Model® (CMM®) Versions 1 and 2, and is a senior member of the Technical Staff, Software Engineering Institute (SEI). She is the SEI's lead instructor for the Introduction to the People Capability Maturity Model® course and coordinator of the People CMM Lead Assessor Track of the SEI's Lead Appraiser Program as well as an SEI-authorized People CMM lead assessor. Miller manages the SEI's People CMM efforts. She is a guest lecturer at Carnegie Mellon University and a graduate of Grove City College.

This reading introduces the People Capability Maturity Model® (People CMM®), describes key contributions of the People CMM[1], and provides a summary of benefits and lessons learned from its use. The People CMM was first published in 1995 [1]. Anticipating the emergence of human capital, information technology work force, and work force aging issues [2, 3], senior leaders in the Army's Chief Information Office and Office of the Assistant Secretary of Defense for Command, Control, Communications, and Intelligence sponsored development of the People CMM. In the seven years since its first release, the People CMM has successfully guided work force improvement programs in many organizations, such as The Boeing Company, Lockheed Martin Corporation, Computer Sciences Corporation, Intel Corporation, Novo Nordisk A/S, Tata Consultancy Services, Infosys Technologies Ltd., Wipro Technologies, the U.S. Army, and the Federal Emergency Management Agency [4, 5, 6].

The People Capability Maturity Model® (People CMM®) is a road map for implementing work-force practices that continually improve the capability of an organization's work force. The People CMM1 is a process-based model that assumes work-force practices are organizational processes that can be continuously improved through the same methods used to improve other business processes.

In particular, the People CMM assumes that work-force practices can be improved through the staged process transformations that underpin Humphrey's Process Maturity Framework [7]. The People CMM applies the Process Maturity Framework to develop the work-force capability of an organization. Each successive level of the People CMM produces a unique transformation of the organization's culture by equipping it with more powerful practices for attracting, developing, organizing, motivating, and retaining its work force.

The People CMM establishes an integrated system of work-force practices that mature through increasing alignment with the organization's business objectives, performance, and changing needs. Although the People CMM was designed primarily for application in knowledge-intense organizations, it can be applied in almost any organizational setting with appropriate tailoring.

The practices at Level 3 of any well-formed capability maturity model produce an architecture for a critical aspect of an organization's strategic infrastructure. For instance, Level 3 practices in the Capability Maturity Model® for Software (SW-CMM®) and CMM Integration^SM (CMMI®) produce the architectures of standardized processes that support an organization's software and systems business.

Likewise, the People CMM produces the architecture of work-force competencies an organization requires for executing its business. Achieving Level 3 of the People CMM and either SW-CMM or CMMI will enable an organization to have a standardized architecture for its development processes and a strategically designed work force strong in the domain specialties required to perform them.

The People CMM was designed to achieve four objectives in developing an organization's work force: develop individual capability, build work groups and culture, motivate and manage performance, and shape the work force. Figure 1 [15-5] depicts how the process areas at each maturity

People CMM Objectives and Their Supporting Process Areas				
Levels	Development Competency	Building Workgroups and Culture	Navigating and Managing Performance	Shaping the Workforce
5 **Optimizing**	Continuous Capability Improvement		Organizational Performance Alignment	Continuous Workforce Innovation
4 **Predictable**	Competency-Based Assets Mentoring	Competency Integration Empowered Workgroups	Quantitative Performance Management	Organizational Capability Management
3 **Defined**	Competency Development Competency Analysis	Workgroup Development Participatory Culture	Competency-Based Practices Career Development	Workforce Planning
2 **Managed**	Training and Development	Communication and Coordination	Compensation Performance Management Work Environment	Staffing

15-5 Figure 1. Objectives Pursued Across Levels in the People CMM

level are organized to support the four primary objectives (represented in the columns) of the People CMM.

Although the People CMM can be represented in the appearance of a continuous model, failure to implement a cohesive system (or bundle) of integrated practices at each level can have harmful consequences. One example of these consequences is often seen in organizations that encourage people to work as teams, while still rewarding them as individuals. Thus, practices in the People CMM should be implemented using a staged, rather than continuous, strategy.

Guidance for Improving Work-Force Capability

The Process Maturity Framework was designed to apply to practices that contribute directly to the business performance of an organization, that is, to the organization's capability for providing high-quality products and services. Since the capability of an organization's work force is critical to its performance, the practices for managing and developing them are excellent candidates for improvement using the Process Maturity Framework. Thus, the People CMM has been designed to increase the capability of the work force just as the SW-CMM is designed to increase the capability of the organization's software development processes.

The People CMM's primary goal is to guide organizations in improving the capability of the work force. Work-force capability can be defined as the level of knowledge, skills, and process abilities available for performing an organization's business activities. Work-force capability indicates an organization's readiness for performing its critical business activities, its likely results from performing these business activities, and its potential for benefiting from investments in process improvement or advanced technology.

The following paragraphs describe how the People CMM supports growth in workforce capability as the organization matures. At the Initial Maturity Level (Level 1), work-force practices are performed inconsistently or ritualistically and frequently fail to achieve their intended purpose. Managers usually rely on their intuition for managing their people and may not receive guidance on practices unless they are legally mandated.

To achieve the Managed Maturity Level (Level 2), managers begin performing basic people-management practices such as staffing, managing performance, and making adjustments to compensation as a repeatable management discipline. The organization establishes a culture focused at the unit level for ensuring that people have the skills and resources needed to meet their work commitments. The fundamental objective of all capability maturity models at Level 2 is to stabilize the local work environment, whether it is a project or some other form of work unit.

By applying the concept of committed work at Level 2, both staffing and performance-management activities are integrated into a framework that balances workload and objectives with the resources available for performing the work. These practices control commitments in the same way achieved in other capability maturity models through project planning. Managers ensure that people have the skills needed to perform their work, that they have the information and coordination skills needed to work effectively with others, and that the work environment provides the needed resources and minimizes distractions. At Level 2, units are able to manage the skills and performance needed to accomplish their committed work.

To achieve the Defined Maturity Level (Level 3), the organization identifies and develops the knowledge, skills, and process abilities that constitute the work-force competencies required to perform its business activities. The organization develops a culture of professionalism based on well-understood work-force competencies. A work-force competency is a cluster of knowledge (what must be known to perform skills), skills (what must be done to accomplish work tasks), and process abilities (how skills are to be performed using the organization's standardized processes).

An organization's strategic work-force competencies might include software engineering, systems engineering, manufacturing, and field service, among others. It is the process abilities within a work-force competency that enable the organization to integrate its architecture of competencies with its standardized process architectures. These process abilities also provide a formal structure for developing work groups through roles and standard processes that can be tailored. In achieving Level 3, the organization develops the capability to manage its work force as a strategic asset.

To achieve the Predictable Maturity Level (Level 4), the organization quantifies and manages the capability of its work force and their competency-based processes, in addition to exploiting the opportunities afforded by defined work-force competencies. Level 4 of the Process Maturity Framework has traditionally been limited to quantitative management of the organization's standard processes. Results and observations of high-maturity organizations during the past decade indicated that they were implementing more than just quantitative management. Level 4 software organizations were implementing a range of practices such as software reuse and structured mentoring that were enabled by having a defined Level 3 process, and that had the effect of reducing variation through means other than quantitative management.

The People CMM incorporates process areas at Level 4 that extend beyond the traditional quantitative management focus, but remain within the philosophy of reducing variation and performing predictably. The organization creates a culture of measurement and exploits shared experience. At Level 4, the organization has the capability to predict its performance and capacity for work.

To achieve the Optimizing Maturity Level (Level 5), everyone in the organization is focused on continuously improving their capability and the organization's workforce practices. The organization creates a culture of product and service excellence. At Level 5, the organization continuously improves its capability and deploys rapid changes for managing its work force.

Where Has the People CMM Been Adopted?

Early adoption of the People CMM has occurred primarily in organizations that have already adopted the SW-CMM. Not surprisingly, among the earliest adopters were aerospace companies such as The Boeing Company, Lockheed Martin Corporation, and GDE Systems (now BAE Systems). Government agencies such as the Federal Emergency Management Agency are adopting the People CMM to address the government's objective of raising the performance and capability of the federal work force. The strongest adoption has occurred in many Indian software companies. The maturity profile of reported People CMM assessments during the last seven years is displayed in Figure 2 [15-6].

Although many companies were using the People CMM to reduce the high employee turnover rates endemic during the late 1990s, the three main reasons for adoption in the Indian software industry were more complex. First, India's interest is a natural outgrowth of their belief that their highly skilled work force is their greatest natural asset. As Narayana Murthy, chairman of Infosys Technologies Ltd., said, "Every night all my assets walk out the gate."

Thus, the People CMM provides Indian software companies with a road map for investing in their most valuable asset. Based on software companies' success using the People CMM, the Confederation of Indian Industries is now engaged in a vigorous campaign to extend the adoption of the People CMM to all industries in India.

Second, the People CMM allows Indian software companies, especially those in the outsourcing business, to address one of their customers' most important concerns. The outsourcing business has been plagued by deals that transferred all of one company's software people to another company, only to see decades of application knowledge disappear as many of these people leave the outsourcer within a few years. Even if no developers are transferred to an outsourcer, which is often the case with

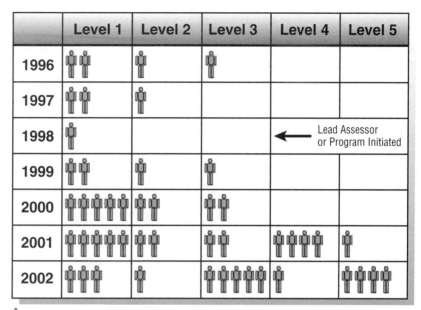

	Level 1	Level 2	Level 3	Level 4	Level 5
1996	👤👤	👤	👤		
1997	👤👤	👤			
1998	👤			← Lead Assessor or Program Initiated	
1999	👤👤	👤	👤		
2000	👤👤👤👤👤	👤👤	👤👤		
2001	👤👤👤👤👤	👤👤	👤👤	👤👤👤👤	👤
2002	👤👤👤	👤	👤👤👤👤👤	👤	👤👤👤👤

👤 = 1 Organizational Assessment Reported by an SEI-Authorized People CMM Lead Assessor

15-6 Figure 2. People CMM Maturity Profile of 49 Organizations Assessed Through November 2002

outsourcing arrangements between U.S. firms and India-based service providers, the clients consider their business with the outsourcer to be an investment in the outsourcer's employees who are learning the client's applications.

Thus, many Indian companies are using the People CMM to demonstrate that they have implemented work-force practices that maximize their ability to retain the staff serving their clients. Since the client sees the outsourcer's staff as a critical resource in which they have invested heavily, the People CMM provides an assurance that their investment in application knowledge will be retained. Otherwise, the client may pay for the development of the outsourcer's application knowledge many times over.

Third, the People CMM has been used as a means for sustaining the capability achieved in a high-maturity environment. By the late 1990s, excessive turnover among many Indian software companies was threatening their ability to sustain the performance and capability of their highmaturity practices and their achieved capabilities. The People CMM not only addressed turnover, but also implemented a system of practices that builds a workforce capable of achieving the performance levels that most benefit from quantitative management. These practices supplement and are complementary with those of other CMMs [8].

Not surprisingly, the recent People CMM assessments reporting attainment of Level 4 and Level 5 capabilities all emerged from India. The implementation of structured mentoring, reusable assets and experiences, empowered work groups, and quantitative analysis of the effect of work-force practices on process performance reinforced and supported the practices implemented through SW-CMM and CMMI. Comments from students in the "Introduction to the People CMM" course indicate that they better under stand and appreciate the intent of SW-CMM and CMMI at higher maturity levels when they understand how high-maturity workforce practices contribute to the organization's capability.

What Benefits Have Been Achieved?

The benefits of implementing the People CMM differ by the maturity level attained. Organizations achieving the People CMM Level 2 uniformly report increases in workforce morale and reductions in voluntary turnover. Table 1 [15-7] presents a sample of the voluntary turnover reductions for companies that reported achieving Level 2. These results are not surprising since years of research have shown that one of the best predictors of voluntary turnover is employees' relationships with their supervisors. The primary change at Level 2 is to get unit managers to develop repeatable practices for managing the people who report to them and to ensure the skill needs of their units are met.

Organizations that achieve Level 3 experience productivity gains associated with developing the work-force competencies required to conduct their business activities. For instance, Figure 3 [15-8] compares the level of competency among the members of a software development project at Infosys (shown as the overall competency index) with the project's cost of quality (rework). Infosys reports a significant correlation of 0.45 ($p < 0.05$) between these variables, indicating that 21 percent of the variation in the cost of quality can be accounted for by the collective competency of the team. That is, the more competent that the members of a development team are in the knowledge and skills related to the technology and application on a project, the less rework the project will experience.

These results are consistent with results obtained by Boehm and his colleagues in calibrating the productivity factors in COCOMO [9, 10]. These

Company	Initial Turnover	Level 2 Turnover
Boeing BRS	1998	1999
	7%	5%
Novo Nordisk	1996	2000
	12%	8%
GDE System	1996	1998
	7.8%	7.1%

15-7 Table 1. Annualized Voluntary Turnover

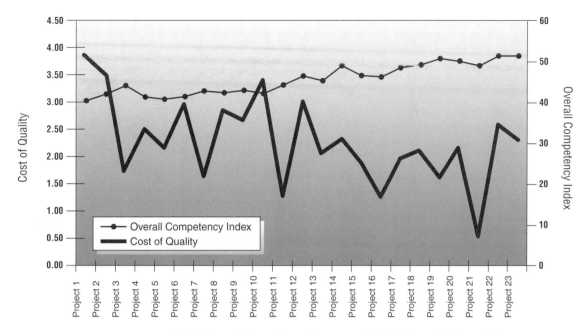

15-8 Figure 3. Correlation of Competencies With Cost of Quality at Infosys

data are an example of the quantitative analyses of workforce capability implemented at Level 4 from an Infosys site that has recently reported attaining People CMM Level 5. Infosys was recently assessed at the People CMM Level 5 and uses data such as these for evaluating the effectiveness of its workforce management practices.

At Level 4, an organization begins to achieve what Deming [11] referred to as profound knowledge about the impact of its work-force practices on its work-force capability and on the performance of its business processes. This knowledge enables management to make trade-off decisions regarding investments in work-force practices. For instance, Figure 4 [15-9] presents a comparison developed by Tata Consultancy Services regarding the percent of time spent in training and its correlation with criteria such as defects per person-hour, review efficiency, effort, and rework.

The trends in Figure 4 [15-9] are all in a favorable direction with various measures of effort and quality decreasing, and review efficiency increasing as training time increases; however, data are needed through more quarters to determine the absolute strength of these relationships. Once the strength of these relationships is understood, and asymptotes or other important trends have been determined, then management is armed with a powerful quantitative tool to make decisions regarding the optimal investment in training. Similar mentoring data identified trade-offs regarding sending senior people on overseas assignments versus using them as mentors at sites in India. High-maturity organizations are able to adjust their workforce practices to achieve targeted performance objectives using their workforce.

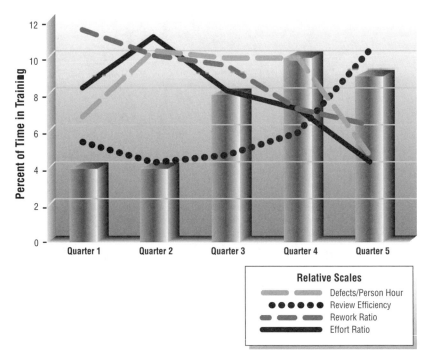

15-9 Figure 4. Relationship of Percent Time in Training to Various Performance Baselines at TCS

Lessons Learned in Applying the People CMM

People CMM-based improvement programs should be conducted as part of an overall organizational improvement strategy. Human resources professionals have stressed that a program based on the People CMM model should not be treated as just a human resources initiative. Rather, it should be presented as a program for operational management to improve the capability of its workforce. Professionals in human resources, training, organizational development, and related disciplines have unique expertise that can assist operational managers in improving their workforce practices. Nevertheless, the responsibility for ensuring that an organization has a workforce capable of performing current and future work lies primarily with operational management.

When introducing multiple improvement programs, the organization needs to assess the amount of change it can reasonably absorb and adjust expectations and schedules accordingly. This is especially acute at Level 2, where the individuals absorbing the majority of the changes are project- and unit-level managers. In order not to overload these managers with change, the organization should stage the introduction of improvement programs. Under many circumstances, project managers should first master project-management skills (SW-CMM or CMMI). After acquiring these skills, managers can then undertake improvements guided by the People CMM to supplement their project-management activities.

Many People CMM improvement programs start with performance management. While some managers may not have open positions requiring staffing activities, and others may not be involved in compensation decisions, all are involved in managing performance. Implementing improvements guided by the performance management process area has the added advantage of focusing on the relationship between managers and those who report to them, which is critical for retaining employees.

Performance management is also the process area at Level 2 most likely to have near-term effects on productivity, quality, and efficiency, at least at the unit level. Performance management, and especially handling unsatisfactory performance, is typically one of the weakest areas in low-maturity organizations. Therefore, improvements in conducting performance-management activities often yield benefits for the organization, while getting the entire management team engaged in the launch of a People CMM-based improvement effort.

When an organization achieves Level 3 or higher on SW-CMM or CMMI, it is easier to integrate the People CMM activities simultaneously with process improvements, since many of the higher level process issues have been incorporated into People CMM practices. As organizations progress with multiple capability maturity models, they find that they are able to develop interlinked architectures for both their business processes and the workforce competencies required to perform these processes. When implemented effectively, these architectures enable effective execution of the organization's business strategy.

References

[1]Curtis, B., W. E. Hefley, and S. Miller. People Capability Maturity Model®. Pittsburgh, PA: Software Engineering Institute, Carnegie Mellon University, 1995.

[2]Walker, David M. "Human Capital: Building the Information Technology Work Force to Achieve Results." Testimony before the Subcommittee on Technology and Procurement Policy, Committee on Government Reform, U.S. House of Representatives. Washington: GAO, 2001. GAO-01-1007T.

[3]McClure, David L. "Human Capital: Attracting and Retaining a High-Quality Information Technology Work Force." Testimony Before the Subcommittee on Technology and Procurement Policy, Committee on Government Reform, U.S. House of Representatives. Washington: GAO, 2002. GAO-02-113T.

[4]Curtis, B., W. E. Hefley, and S. A. Miller. *People Capability Maturity Model: Guidelines for Improving the Work Force.* Reading, MA: Addison Wesley Longman, 2002.

[5]Gray, R. People CMM Panel Session: Practical Approaches to Initiating and Sustaining a Successful People CMM Effort. Proc. of Software Engineering Process Group Conf., Phoenix, AZ, 2002.

[6]Snyder, C. Initiating and Deploying the People CMM Across Intel's Information Technology Department. Proc. of Software Engineering Process Group Conf., Boston, MA, 2003.

[7]Humphrey, Watts S. *Managing the Software Process.* Reading, MA: Addison Wesley Longman, 1984.

[8]Hefley, W. E., and S. A. Miller. Software CMM® or CMMSM? The People CMM® Supports Them Both. Proc. of Software Engineering Process Group Conf. Boston, MA, 2003.

[9]Boehm, B., et al. *Software Cost Estimation with COCOMO II.* Upper Saddle River, NJ: Prentice Hall, 2000.

[10]Clark, B. "Quantifying the Effects of Process Improvement on Effort." IEEE Software Nov./Dec. 2000: 65–70.

[11]Deming, W. Edwards. *Out of Crisis.* Cambridge, MA: MIT Press, 1986.

Notes

1. The *People CMM* is available as both a technical report from the Software Engineering Institute and as an Addison-Wesley book. For more information, see *www.sei.cmu.edu/publications/documents/01.reports/01mm001.html* and *www.awprofessional.com/catalog/product.asp?product_id={2699E666-10C7-4865-B5DA-01C6 78D54988}.*

2. Capability Maturity Model, CMM, and CMMI are registered in the U.S. Patent and Trademark Office by Carnegie Mellon University.

3. CMM Integration, SEI, and SEPG are service marks of Carnegie Mellon University.

Maturing to Centers of Excellence:
The Next Step in IT Organizations

COREY FERENGUL

A META Group White Paper

About the Author

Corey Ferengul is vice president and principal analyst with Operations Strategies, an advisory service of META Group, Inc. For additional information on this topic or other services, contact info@metagroup.com.

Executive Summary

The change currently facing IT organizations (ITOs) is how to improve their delivery of value to the business and their alignment with overall business goals, as well as offer business units more value and technology options. All of this is expected, while not killing profit margins. ITOs are adopting several new approaches and embracing change to achieve these goals. One of these new approaches is creation of centers of excellence (COEs). The COE concept is not a new one—it is used widely in many industries—but it is a new approach for many ITOs.

ITOs leverage COEs to bring together similar processes (e.g., application quality, application performance, and availability management). This ensures that the processes are consistent across the organization, everyone is well versed in the best practices, and knowledge is shared across the company. Fragmentation and wasted effort within ITOs can often be attributed to an excessive number of people doing the same thing, just doing it in different ways. This is caused by siloed decision making. COEs provide a way to physically reorganize or virtually realign the organizational structure, the organizational processes, and even the technology used, under a single cohesive structure.

For COEs to be successful, they must be defined and executed in a consistent manner. This starts with management support as the shift to a COE is executed. Also, each COE must be outlined in the same way—with each COE having a clear definition as well as clearly established goals, key performance indicators, processes and process linkages, skills, and, especially, common tools and technology.

COEs will impact the organization through either full reorganization of staff or creation of "virtual" organizations (i.e., a matrix structure). Technology will also be affected by a COE structure. META Group recommends that some COEs share the same tools to accomplish their goals.

The benefits of COE efforts will include gains in efficiencies and flexibility, facilitation of vendor and process consolidation, increased knowledge sharing and collaboration across the organization, facilitation of stronger business alignment, and reduction in overall costs.

Leading companies will drive toward some leverage of COE structures during the next two to three years. Examples of centers of excellence include an application performance COE, an asset management COE, a business availability/command center COE, a customer advocacy COE, a governance COE, a security COE, and a quality/testing COE.

Introduction

Change is always difficult. A company's success will be determined by how it handles change, how change is embraced, and what new opportunities are recognized and exploited during change [1]. Successful companies embrace change and leverage it to create competitive advantage.

Currently, there are several changes underway within businesses. In particular, the business is changing what it expects from and how it leverages its information technology. Although the fundamentals remain the same, business itself is not only more dependent on technology, it also requires technology to remain competitive, retain clients, and even to achieve competitive advantage. For their part, IT organizations are being asked to contribute to the company, and like any other business unit, the ITO is being measured based on the value [2] it contributes to the organization. One side of the IT value equation includes the capability the ITO can provide, how it can apply technology to a business problem, and the utility. The other side of the equation is the cost of delivery.

As ITOs face the current change of improving delivery of value to the business and alignment with overall business goals, they are working to improve the overall IT product delivered and reduce the cost and complexity of delivery. This means offering business units more technology options, while not killing the margins. By evolving the organization to be adaptive through leveraging new organizational constructs such as centers of excellence, successful ITOs are leveraging change to take the next step in maturity.

Evolving to the Adaptive Organization

ITO internal analysis is uncovering the unfortunate reality that most IT organizations exist in a non-optimized state, which can translate to extra cost and inefficiency. Although the business itself tends to adapt to the ever-changing demands of the markets, the ITO is typically slower to change and cannot easily shift to meet new demands. Projects are long, expensive, and complex, with a high risk of failure, or are coming in over budget for large projects. The goal of any ITO must be to become an adaptive organization, which provides the following benefits:

- Increased efficiency
- Optimized utilization
- More efficient use of all IT resources (human capital, financial, and physical)
- Reduced waste
- Increased flexibility

- Timeliness
- Faster delivery
- Enhanced value

Achieving this goal will require maturity of the organization through several organizational states (Figure 1 [15-10]):

- **Reactive state**: Companies that take action based on stimulus. There is a desire to plan, but execution is disorganized, with an overall lack of planning and poor internal coordination.
- **Managed state**: Companies that are reactive, but have a set of processes and procedures that are used to react. The planning is focused on how to react better and on optimizing that process.
- **Proactive state**: Companies that anticipate needs and spend extensive effort in planning, with processes that are triggered having a degree of automation (though occasionally the organization still has to react). These companies are rarely caught off guard and able to cite long-term plans, well-documented processes, and extensive organizational coordination.
- **Adaptive state**: Companies that are not only proactive, but also have ITOs that are able to trigger change automatically based on automated metric analysis. For example, an organization's analytics might identify that business demand has increased for a certain product and automatically divert resources to the systems supporting that specific business process.

No IT organization can become fully business aligned without at a minimum becoming proactive and striving to become adaptive. A key element of attaining a proactive and adaptive state is the leveraging of well-designed processes, complete with automation.

The past several years have brought investment in technology and development of processes, but now organizational and governance issues

Goal—Adaptive

Source: META Group

15-10 Figure 1. Becoming an Adaptive Organization.

must be attacked. Technology and process investments have resulted in highly fragmented and disconnected organizations that are cumbersome to deal with. These organizations have no chance of becoming adaptive and will not deliver optimal value to the business.

Building centers of excellence is a best practice for realigning the IT organization more closely with business goals and enabling it to mature toward becoming an adaptive organization.

What Is a Center of Excellence?

DEFINING A COE

The COE concept is not a new one. Academia and public-sector organizations make extensive use of COEs, as do several commercial industries, especially pharmaceuticals. The COE concept is credited with technological breakthroughs [3] and kick-starting new efforts [4]. Organizations as diverse as the U.S. Department of Health and Human Services [5], Microsoft, numerous hospitals worldwide, and even the European Union [6] have all leveraged or funded use of the COE structure to their advantage.

The U.S. Joint Forces Command defines a center of excellence as follows:

Institutions possessing special knowledge or expertise in a particular area of concern and incorporated into the collaborative environment to facilitate development of the products supporting (key) functions and operations

Why have such diverse groups, many with life or death implications, leveraged COEs? It is because the COE concept can bring diverse people and groups together to solve difficult problems. When the knowledge of individuals is combined, the result is a stronger whole. All of these groups are seeking new ways to look at the same problems, and new approaches for others to learn from. A faster result is attained through leveraging the best practices each person brings to the situation, thereby producing a more mature set of best practices, tested the world over. A center of excellence is about sharing information, sharing workload, and producing a result that the individuals themselves would not have been able to accomplish within a reasonable time or for a reasonable cost.

Not only does a COE deliver higher-level benefits, but it does so at a reduced cost. By leveraging broad knowledge from numerous organizations, a COE saves everyone from having to learn it the first time on their own. The experiences of the collective are expected to act as a training mechanism for others. Results are achieved faster as well as cheaper.

Applying COEs to IT

It is clear that the COE concept has appeal well beyond IT, but if it can deliver these benefits for world governing bodies and major corporations, then it clearly has benefits for IT (Figure 2 [15-11]).

COEs enable ITOs to bring together like processes (e.g., application quality, application performance, and availability management), which helps to ensure consistency across the organization, broad use of best practices, and willingness of various groups to learn from each other across the company. Typically, ITO fragmentation and wasted effort is the result of an

The ITO center of excellence is a logically related group of processes that yields synergies (e.g., knowledge sharing) and increased efficiencies by grouping the related activities into an actual or virtual organizational structure. It may or may not require adjusting reporting structures directly, but it does require alignment of processes and potentially technology. Operational improvements are not specific to improvement activities, but attributed to the synergies of the new relationships. The determining factor in the creation of an operational improvement COE should be the volume of similar projects, groups, or functions.

Source: META Group

15-11 Figure 2. Defining an ITO COE

excessive number of people doing the same thing in different ways, driven by siloed decision making. COEs enable physical reorganization or virtual realignment of people, the processes they support, and even the technology they use, under a single cohesive structure.

This does not mean that there is a single COE for the entire enterprise—that would never work. However, this does mean that there are single COEs for single functions. (See the following for specific examples.)

Key Components of a COE

Successful COEs have several key elements defined when they are established:

- Definition: A clear identification of why the group exists, its key functions, what their boundaries are (e.g., single business unit, enterprisewide), and what the business should expect as a result of this group's existence.
- Goals: What goals should this group strive to accomplish? Improved availability? Better customer service? This element encompasses identification of what the group should set its sights on and the mission they are aiming toward, and provides direction to the COE leaders on how to optimize the group's direction.
- Measurements: This is identification of how the goals will be measured. These measurements are often referred to as key performance indicators (KPIs). Some items may be in place already (e.g., availability, application quality), while others may still need to emerge (e.g., securability). It is critical that these measures closely align with the business goals laid out in the COE definition. KPIs will exist at multiple levels (e.g., business, IT, business partners), but they must be coordinated and be agreed upon with each interested party.
- Process linkages: Identification of how to link to processes that are owned by another COE or other groups. Some linked processes are tightly integrated. For others, a COE must simply be aware of the process's existence, but not be involved. COEs need clear lines of

distinction between them. As companies mature toward being proactive and adaptive, definition of process linkages is the critical component. Without COEs working in concert, the results of COE efforts are just new silos. Total optimization of an organization will be realized when COEs are not only working well, but also are working well together.

- Incentives: Defines for group members how they will be rewarded for success.
- Key processes: An outline of the key processes the COE is responsible for executing. This is critical, since the scope of the COE is contained in the processes it owns. It is also important to outline who owns a process. Process ownership is the key to a successful process.
- Process definitions: Detailed definitions of processes (see Figure 5. [Editor's note: Figure 5 does not appear in the original article.]), including the steps, flows, and ties to other processes.
- Skills: What are the necessary skills the COE requires, and what people in the organization map to those skills?
- Tools/technology: What are the preferred or selected tools that a COE uses?

Clear identification of the key processes, their definitions, and their linkages can be diagrammed. Figure 3 [15-12] provides an example of a process diagram that can be created for a COE. It includes a listing of the processes (in order of importance to that COE) and the level of involvement expected in all of them (owned and non-owned processes).

Organizational Impact

The changes a COE brings to organizational structure must be carefully considered. Many organizations will choose to fully reorganize staff around

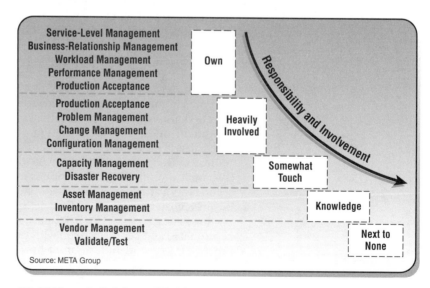

15-12 Figure 3. Defining an ITO COE

a COE structure. Others will instead create "virtual" organizations, using a matrix organizational structure. For a critical COE (e.g., availability/command center COE), META Group recommends that it must exist as a true organizational group. However, COEs that may not require full-time attention or do not provide daily critical functions (e.g., asset COE) may be virtual as long as the roles and responsibilities are clearly defined.

Regardless of which option is selected (full reorganization or virtual structure), every COE must share process definitions and, in most cases, technology.

Technology Impact

Although much attention is given to organizational issues within a COE, the technology impact cannot be overlooked. Sharing technology within a COE not only fosters communication, as discussed earlier, but it also assists in saving money (by tying to the earlier business goals).

Currently, individuals working on the same tasks but using different technologies to communicate can easily come to different conclusions. Tools work differently and different terms are used, which foster differences in processes. There have been many instances of two individuals looking at the same situation, but from different data-based perspectives, and coming to different conclusions. This is unlikely to occur in a COE structure.

There is education involved in using tools. From understanding the scripting mechanisms through detailed configuration, this knowledge becomes a key part of shared intellectual property expected within a center of excellence. Increasing individual productivity through COE structures relies on sharing technology.

Does this mean throwing everything out and starting over? It does not; rather, organizations should seek to select a lead vendor from the current toolsets they use, identifying key "areas" or "groupings" of tools (e.g., server monitoring, load testing, and change workflow) and then selecting the vendor to be lead for that grouping. This may result in several vendors being involved within a single COE. That is not a problem, as long as clear integration points among those vendors' tools are identified in advance. This opportunity should be leveraged to determine what is best in current use and then to turn increased use into a better price from a vendor. Savings are also gained by having fewer vendors to engage and integrate.

The Value of a Center of Excellence

ITOs should seek various values through use of a COE structure, including the following.

Gains in Efficiencies and Flexibility

Currently, ITOs are inflexible, often due to cumbersome internal politics, a major complaint of business leadership. One goal of a COE is to break down some of these barriers by having a wide range of people involved in working toward a singular goal and communicating with each other in the process. This communication occurs on multiple levels, including shared nomenclature for a process through the sharing of information from tools and technology (since frequently various people involved will be using the same tools). This enables individuals to be more efficient in doing their jobs—they do not have to figure out everything on their own and they can leverage the experience of others. In addition, the enhanced communication will make it easier for organizations to make changes.

Since a COE has well-documented processes (discussed below), there is a single place to go to impact a broad process organization wide. This is the polar opposite of the current structure of seeking out pockets of teams, learning how they operate, and then attempting to influence change. Now when a business change is demanded, there is one spot to go and begin to see its impact.

Consolidation

A critical efficiency gain is in consolidation of technology and processes. A COE will be more efficient if all the members are using the same underlying technology. This will promote data sharing, streamlining of processes, and shared decision making. This blends well with efforts META Group sees in vendor consolidation. Many organizations have targeted vendor consolidation as a key cost-cutting effort. A logical manner for identifying key vendors is aligning product use along the lines of a COE. It is also possible to consolidate staff. If efficiencies are increased, fewer people may be required for a single area and some individuals can be reassigned.

Increased Knowledge Sharing and Collaboration

The information sharing previously discussed results in better collaboration. Currently, we see organizations that desire collaboration, but they are lost because the various groups do not understand one another. Each group has its own way of operating, its own data, its own interpretation, etc. It takes considerable time just to establish a baseline for a discussion, and this occurs each time a discussion is necessary.

In a COE structure, with well-documented processes, flows, and technology sharing, collaboration becomes easier. People no longer look at the same IT environment and make different decisions. There are also institutionalized manners of sharing information, instead of the random sharing that currently occurs. Collaboration and knowledge sharing within a COE result in a smarter staff, faster responses, and cost savings on the necessary technology (not just via volume deals, but because the groups communicating can identify overlap and waste).

Business Alignment

COEs should be driven based on business goals. The mission, definition criteria, and even COE-level goals should all tie directly to the goals of the business consumers of these services. Through use of the COE construct, it is easier to achieve these goals. Instead of having to drive numerous disconnected groups toward singular user goals (e.g., the goals of a specific business unit), those needs are better centralized and easier to manage.

Businesses want ITOs to respond faster, so a COE aligned with a specific goal will produce a more responsive organization. As previously discussed, with increased collaboration, technical silos being broken down, and fewer political barriers, an ITO can respond to requests and change faster when leveraging the COE structure.

Reduction of Costs

Saving money is always a key driver for the business. Therefore, any plan that contains savings usually gets fast business backing. Cost savings come from more efficient use of IT capital, human and technology. The staff will experience an increase in productivity, operate at a more efficient state, have fewer overlapping tasks, and encounter fewer political barriers to overcome. Using well-established, coordinated processes enables people to be more productive today (e.g., more servers per admin, more tests per analyst). In addition, as processes become well understood, they are then candidates for automation, which further drives up productivity and drives down costs. Once COEs are established, seeking processes that are candidates for automation is the next step.

Technology-wise, cost is reduced through leveraging fewer vendors and having less integration to build and maintain. Vendors often give price breaks to larger customers through volume agreements. The hidden costs of maintaining knowledge of multiple overlapping tools as well as maintaining multiple relationships will be further reduced.

COE Examples

META Group has outlined a number of possible COEs an organization may create (Figure 4 [15-13]). The list is not exhaustive. While there is almost no limit to the number of COEs an organization can leverage, no organization will be successful in attacking all COEs at once, or even doing each one enterprisewide. It is critical to take steps and learn, as opposed to doing it all in one fell swoop.

Command Center/Business Availability COE

The command center or business availability COE is focused on real-time monitoring of the end-to-end business process and the real-time business impact. Users consume technologies through executing business

- Application COE
- Asset management COE
- Availability/command center COE
- Customer advocacy COE
- Database support COE
- Governance COE

- Media management COE
- Outsourcing support COE
- Security COE
- Server support COE
- Storage support COE
- Quality/testing COE

Source: META Group

15-13 Figure 4. Examples of COEs

processes that touch many different technologies to accomplish tasks. Therefore, a COE is required to manage the breadth of technology used for any business process. This is where organizations will do initial diagnostics of performance bottlenecks and other user-impacting issues. They then direct (or escalate) the issue to the appropriate group. This may mean passing the problem-resolution tasks to an operational team (e.g., network COE) or even passing them back to the development group.

The command center/business availability COE will deliver:

- True end-to-end availability and performance monitoring by application by users.
- Real-time, business perspective interfaces to visualize performance and availability metrics.
- The foundation of service-level management (SLM), including quantification of downtime, assessment of the business impact of performance and availability issues, and directing resources to fix the issues that have the biggest impact on the business.
- Integrated applications for system availability management, SLM, customer impact, end-user management, and analytics.
- Proactive measurement of availability and performance.
- Awareness of business impact as a guide to prioritize resolution activities.

Performance COE

While the command center/business availability COE focuses on the status of the environment, the performance COE focuses on how to optimize the application and infrastructure. It is a central point of performance analysis, testing, and improvement. It is used not only to prevent issues (e.g., by being proactive), but also to ensure that organizations are getting the most out of the current resource investments. The goal of the performance COE is to attain an end-to-end view of the organization to ensure that an application or business process is optimized and that it achieves full use of all the resources it requires. A key goal is to prevent adding on additional capacity, instead ensuring that what is currently in place is being fully leveraged. This COE is also used to find bottlenecks internal to the applications that slow its processing.

A performance COE will deliver:

- Performance testing (e.g., tests the scalability and performance of the application).
- End-to-end view of business process performance—not just availability.
- Diagnostics for inspecting internal components of applications to identify slowdowns.
- Capacity planning, including simulation of "what if" scenarios.
- Assessment of current environment use and strategies for improvement.

Quality COE

A quality COE is responsible for operating and facilitating the application testing process. It is troubling today that various groups deliver technology in different states to production, which can directly impact a company's bottom line (not to mention the perception of the ITO). As a result, the performance COEs and business availability COEs attain no consistency in the quality of product they are then asked to support. To eliminate those variances, the quality delivery functions within a COE should be consolidated. This will coordinate activities such as requirements management, planning, scheduling, test automation, issue management, and project status analysis.

A quality COE will deliver:

- A consistent, reusable, and proven testing process.
- A testing environment.
- Centralized reporting (via portals or dashboards) on the status of current projects, upcoming projects, and outcomes of previous activities.
- A delivery process for placing technology into production.
- Testing automation technology and expertise in leveraging that technology.
- Overall acceleration of delivery, improvement in production-level quality, and reduced overall cost of quality assurance.

Governance COE

The effective governance of IT has become a significant issue. IT governance includes operating the business of IT, better understanding how IT investments are being used, and being aware of the business value being delivered, and tracking programs and projects to ensure they are on time and on budget. Unfortunately, this is currently taking place primarily via disconnected individuals using spreadsheets and then poorly communicating the data to the business audience. The business needs strategic management of its application portfolio, its projects, and its programs. Therefore, these tasks should be brought together under a governance COE.

A governance COE will deliver:

- Centralized processes for assessing project health and success on an ongoing basis.
- Ongoing strategic analysis of the organization's application portfolio mix and assessment of business value and impact.
- Improved and consolidated business communication of status and rationale of investments (e.g., via portals or dashboards), enabling more educated and faster decision making.
- A central point of contact to identify available resources, status of investments, and trouble points in need of action.

Bottom Line

There is no question that companies are seeking to achieve better alignment of the IT organization with the business. This alignment includes bringing additional capability at a reduced cost, which is a tall order. ITOs should explore leveraging COEs as a way of delivering against these requirements. Centers of excellence can produce savings and increased efficiency—simply through taking a business perspective. META Group believes that the COE structure is one that companies must learn to exploit.

About META Group

META Group is a leading provider of information technology research, advisory services, and strategic consulting. Delivering objective and action-able guidance, META Group's experienced analysts and consultants are trusted advisors to IT and business executives around the world. Our unique collaborative models and dedicated customer service help clients be more efficient, effective, and timely in their use of IT to achieve their business goals. Visit *metagroup.com* for more details on our high-value approach.

References

[1]*Disruptive Change*, Gilbert, Clark and Joseph Bower. *Harvard Business Review* May 2002.

[2]Value = Worth in usefulness or importance to the possessor. Source: *www.dictionary.com.*

[3]*www.coe.faa.gov*—COE meeting proceedings.

[4]*www.4women.gove/coe.*

[5]*http://www.hhs.gov/news/press/2003pres/20031003.html.*

[6]*http://www.hynet.info/ecactiv/docs/Mapping_Centers_of_Excellence.pdf.*

Project Closing

Chapter 16 Contents

Chapter Overview

When one considers the time and effort associated with project planning, execution, and control, project closeout seems anticlimactic. The work is finished, the software system is implemented, and business focus is shifting toward the next assignment. Thus, project closeout is often treated as an afterthought. In many instances, project closeout is not even conducted and the project management world believes that it is no worse for the wear as a result of this omission. Yet, there are benefits associated with completing all project activities and bringing the project to a formal close.

The most immediate benefits realized from project close are to confirm the following:

- The project is completed in an acceptable manner.
- All project documentation is archived.
- Formal release of project resources is completed.
- Initial assessment of return on investment is evaluated and documented.
- Information is captured to apply learned lessons to future projects.
- The project team members celebrate their hard work and success.

Completion criteria for project closing formally marks the milestone when all paperwork is completed and archived, all parties are notified that the project is finished, learned lessons are captured, and appropriate acknowledgements and rewards are disseminated. The most important processes associated in project closing are as follows:

- Announce the end of the project.
- Review and complete project paperwork and closeout activities.
- Capture learned lessons.
- Acknowledge and reward.

Announce the End of the Project

Formal announcement of the end of the project is conducted when all project requirements have been satisfied and the customer approves all project deliverables. An alternative event associated with project end can occur when management has decided to terminate the project based on business reasons. Regardless of which of these events occur, all team members and organizations involved must be made aware that the project is finished. This includes support organizations, partners, subcontractors, and vendors. Notification of the end of the project is particularly important when a project is terminated prematurely. Any delay in terminating ongoing work adds to the sunk cost of the project.

Complete Paperwork and Closeout Activities

At project closing, there is follow-up to ensure all closeout activities have been completed. There are any number of business reasons for closeout activities, and principal among them are to accomplish the following:

- Return or appropriately store confidential information.
- Return borrowed equipment and recover loaned equipment.
- Conduct the formal or informal post-implementation review.
- Obtain final project sign off.
- Close out all contracts.
- Identify and turnover the project deliverables to the groups responsible for maintenance.
- Archive project documentation including:
  - Project plan, schedule, and budget.
  - Business and technical requirements for audit compliance.
  - Test requirement and test results for audit compliance.
  - Change log that reflects change management decisions.

Capture Learned Lessons

Project management and the overall business benefits from a post-implementation review. Generally, as many team members as possible are included in the closeout review.

The purpose of the review is to minimize problems in the future, not to point fingers at individuals or assign blame for project difficulties. Learned lessons can be identified through a formal or informal review to capture explicit and subtle actions that were taking place during project execution. The review should not be used as a club, but rather to enhance project management processes. If managers use the review results as a source of information for discipline, negative project attributes will not be reported. When conducted constructively, learned lessons can provide new, effective procedures or documentation. Among the topics that can be the focus of this meeting are the following:

- Review performance against the project success criteria.
- Discuss what went right and what went wrong.
- Discuss how major successes can be shared with other projects.
- Discuss how things can be improved on future projects.
- Solicit ideas for improvements to processes.
- Share key information that will be useful when planning future projects.

Learned lessons should be formally documented and archived for future use. In reality, learned lessons represent a project evaluation, which allows the project team to ascertain how well its project plan worked. The actual number of issues seen, any post-implementation issues that remain unresolved, and a look back on what worked versus what did not work should be the focus.

The project evaluation contains a comparison of the project plan against the project actuals, including an evaluation of what went well and recommended improvements accompanied by an action plan. Successes and problems are identified to promote best practices and to improve inadequate practices. Evaluation of deviations from the original estimates is included with explanations of why the deviations occurred. There are generally four major sections within the project evaluation, and each is briefly described below:

OVERVIEW

This section is a brief review of the project objectives and scope as well as the overall schedule. In the overview, there is often an actual versus defined plan comparison in which a discussion of how the actual project execution and process varied from that defined in the baselined plan. A useful component of the overview is a summary of significant delays. This information describes any significant delays or deviations from the original schedule, their causes, and their ultimate impact to the project.

AREAS OF SUCCESS

This section consists of areas that went well and need no further comment. Areas to be considered may include, but are not limited to, communication (inter- and intra-team), processes (for example, execution of, relevancy of), scheduling and estimation, project management, tools/automation usage/needs, environment and other technical support, and general stability of products delivered by the project.

AREAS FOR IMPROVEMENT

This section consists of the areas identified as significant issues. Based upon the evaluation, an issue might be tagged as an action item in the improvement plan.

IMPROVEMENT ACTION LIST

This section is a list and discussion of specific actions that will be taken to address items from the areas for improvements section. There should be valid economic justification for recommended actions. Where possible, identify individuals responsible for formulating an implementation plan and target dates.

Acknowledge and Reward

Acknowledge and reward is a simple, but often overlooked, process. In order to acknowledge team contributions, project closing should offer formal recognition for the hard work accomplished by the team. Identify who performed extra effort and made special achievements contributing to the project success. Then, provide rewards for these efforts in the form of public acknowledgement, gifts, or bonuses. Rewards do not have to be large, and recognition can be a token gift to all team members. The point is somewhat obvious. When acknowledging special achievements, project closing identifies the positive consequences the project team contributed to the project's success. So, acknowledge and reward is a celebration of project success, not a reward for the most hours worked without results. The recognition could be a formal gathering planned by the organization or something less formally organized by the project manager and core team. Because project team members will probably work with the some of the team members again in the future, some form of celebration is a nice way to wrap things up in a relaxed atmosphere.

Readings

The single reading for this section, "Closing the Project," is contributed by the Department of Premier and Cabinet, Tasmania. Although not a place that one would anticipate being a source of contemporary methodology, this organization has done a very credible job of defining, documenting, and publishing their procedures. The article presented here is an adaptation of their closing process. The reader is pointed to the Web site to review the remainder of their methodology.

Closing the Project

Editor's Note: We are grateful for the willingness of the Department of Premier and Cabinet, Tasmania to share their Project Closure materials and allow this adaptation. It would be very worthwhile to browse their Web site for more details on their project management methodology [see www.projectmanagement.tas. gov.au]. Most of the structure and content shown here is adapted from their PM035 Project Closure Report documentation, dated October 2003. All changes made to the original document are the responsibility of the editors.

The *PMBOK® Guide* defines goals for the closeout of a project and requires that all projects formally execute such a process. For multi-phase projects there would be a formal close for each phase, and for projects that are terminated early the same approach would apply. Also, the close process applies to all process groups and their related knowledge area activities.

The enterprise is expected to establish formal procedures for project closure. Basically, the goal of this activity is to verify project deliverables, formally accept the deliverables in coordination with the appropriate stakeholders, describe any unfinished issues related to the project, describe lessons learned, and investigate and document any reasons for early termination.

Uses of the Project Closing Data

Data collected during this activity is used to:
- Determine if the appropriate project management framework has been selected and appropriately applied, enabling any deficiencies to be remedied.
- Provide validation of a decision to 'stop' the project.
- Make an informed decision about closing the project and capturing the lessons learned.
- Record historical results from the project and formally closing the project.
- Provide validation of a decision to proceed to the next phase of the project.
- Provide decision information to a Project Sponsor and/or Steering Committee to 'tidy up' any loose ends and formally close the project.

There are two basic organizational procedures involved with the closing activity:
  a. Administrative closure procedure.
  b. Contract closure procedure.

The administrative closure is a step-by-step process to define stakeholder approval processes, actions to confirm that the project has met all required deliverables, and actions necessary to satisfy exit criteria for the project. These activities involve steps such as collecting appropriate project records, analyzing project status, gathering lessons learned, and archiving project records for future use.

The contract closure process is tightly linked to the procurement knowledge area processes and involves actions needed to settle and close all contractual agreements in place for the project. This activity includes verifying contractual delivery status and supporting records archiving from the administrative process. In some cases, contracts require a formal statement of closure and this would be executed during this activity. Also, a general status of the contract would be produced describing delivery, budget, resource, or quality issues.

The documentation of project closing is reflected in a formal document titled Project Closure Report.

Why Would You Develop a Project Closure Report?

A Project Closure Report is developed to:
- Detail activities undertaken to close the project.
- Outline outstanding issues, risks, operational matters, and recommendations.

The document lists the closure activities, any outstanding matters, and recommends how they should be addressed.

When Would You Develop a Project Closure Report?

The Project Closure Report is usually developed once the project is completed and all the project outputs have been delivered to the Business Owner(s), or it has been decided to close the project for some other reason. An early closure may be the result of a recommendation from a review of the project where the findings are negative or may be the result of changed priorities within the enterprise. An end stage project review should have been completed prior to the development of a Project Closure Report.

PREREQUISITE EVENTS

- Agreement to proceed with the development of the Project Closure Report from the Project Sponsor and/or Steering Committee.
- Completion of the end stage review process.
- Creation of a lessons learned document to be included in the final report.
- A copy of specified project documentation, for example, the Project Business Plan, Project Status Reports, Project Risk Register, Project Issues Register, contract documentation, etc.
- Knowledge and understanding of the enterprise standard process for this activity (usually specified in the development methodology).

OPTIONAL ITEMS

- Original Project Proposal or Business Case.
- Corporate/Business Plan for the Department/Business Unit.

ROLE OF THE FINISHED PROJECT CLOSURE REPORT DOCUMENT

A completed Project Closure Report should aid the Project Sponsor and Project Steering Committee to decide whether the project should be closed and to provide recommendations for dealing with any outstanding issues, risks, or operational matters.

The Project Closure Report Content

The structure and general content of the closure report should be standardized across the enterprise to enhance usability by other project teams. The key information in this document relates to the historical performance data for the project, lessons learned, project archives, and contract documentation.

The Project Closure Report is a managed document. Version control is important and each page should contain a release number and a page number. Changes will only be issued as a complete replacement document. Recipients should remove superseded versions from circulation. This document is authorized for formal release once all appropriate management signatures have been obtained.

A sample three-part Table of Contents is shown below:

TABLE OF CONTENTS

1.0 Executive Summary
1.1 Background
1.2 Reason for closing the project
1.3 Summary of recommendations
2.0 Closure Activities
2.1 Project staff
2.2 Issues management
2.3 Risk management
2.4 Financial management
2.5 Asset management
2.6 Records management
2.7 Post project responsibilities
2.8 Recommendations
3.0 Appendices

Basic contents for each section are outlined below:

1.0 Executive Summary
    Briefly describe the historical background of the project.

1.2 Reason for Closing the Project
    State the reason why this project is being closed. This may be because the outputs have been delivered, the outcomes have been achieved, the closing date has been reached, and/or the budget has been expended. In some cases, a project may be closed for other reasons, for example a change in policy or agency priorities, or funding has been fully expended.

1.3 Summary of Recommendations
    List the recommendations that appear in this Report. One of the recommendations should be for the Project Steering Committee to agree that the project can be deemed closed. The project has fulfilled

all of the requirements as documented in the relevant Project Business Plan, or the Steering Committee is satisfied that all outstanding items have been satisfactorily addressed, or there is some other reason to close the project (e.g. no more resources). For ease of reference, each recommendation should be uniquely numbered and a reference provided to the relevant section within this Report.

2.0 Closure Activities

This subsection covers the various activities required to close the project.

2.1 Project Staff

Describe what steps are being taken to manage the movement of project staff from the project to other roles, including the timing of their move, the capture of their project knowledge, and handover of that knowledge to the Business Owners.

2.2 Issues Management

Identify any outstanding issues and who will responsible for dealing with the item and by what time frame.

2.3 Risk Management

Identify any risks which will transfer to an operational area and who has responsibility for monitoring them.

2.4 Financial Management

Identify any outstanding financial issues, such as budget overruns or excess funds, and how they will be handled.

2.5 Asset Management

Describe any assets which were acquired for the project, and who will take ownership of them upon completion of the project.

2.6 Records Management

Identify what arrangements have been put in place for the storage, security, and backup of hard copy and soft copy (electronic) records and project documents. Identify who is responsible for these activities.

2.7 Post Project Responsibilities

List any matters that are outstanding, what actions are required to address them, and who is responsible. This should include things that are outstanding or have not been formally agreed upon prior to this stage, such as outcomes yet to be achieved, outputs not yet delivered, maintenance of the outputs, or other operational matters such as meeting future training requirements.

2.8 Recommendations

List any recommendations that arise from this section of the Closure Report. This includes such things as the transfer of responsibility for the outcomes to the Business Owner, how outstanding outputs and issues should be addressed, and any recommendations for the continued operation by the Business Owner.

3.0 Appendices

Appendices can be attached to provide any relevant supporting information, such as:

- A copy of the signed declaration of acceptance by the relevant Business Owner(s) for each of the outputs (deliverables).

■ A copy of any project reviews undertaken (e.g., Project Review and Evaluation Report or Post Implementation Review).

Summary

The project closing activity is often ignored as part of the project management process, but it has strategic value to the enterprise as well as representing an orderly way to be sure that the project is terminated in an orderly fashion. Organizations cannot improve unless they evaluate the successes and failures of past efforts. Lessons learned are a key part of a continuous improvement mentality.

Project Management Contemporary Topics

PART THREE Contents

Part Overview

Many concepts and processes in the IT project management domain have not yet reached full sophistication and maturity. Part III covers concepts and processes whose implementation in many organizations can be characterized as being important but not fully developed. Based on this assessment, the reader should look at all writings in this section as works-in-progress.

Part I described topics that represent what we currently understand regarding basic project management theory—that is, what a project is, why it generally fails, and some of the other environmental topics that surround the project. Part II described the general model of the *PMBOK® Guide*, which has a reasonable level of stability in its structure regarding the high-level processes and the nine knowledge areas that need to be explored as part of the management activity. The contemporary topics that could be included in Part III could be quite extensive, but space constraints necessitated that only the most mature of the set be presented. The topics selected were those considered by leaders in the field to be valid areas of concern, and each topic was being used or actively explored by the more mature project management organizations. Those criteria led to the following list:

- **Professional Responsibility and Ethics (Part III, Chapter 17)**—Recent headlines have pointed out the catastrophic effects that improper employee behavior can have on the enterprise. In addition, PMI is including this subject in its accreditation.
- **Third-Party Sourcing (Part III, Chapter 18)**—Allocating IT work to third-party providers has been on the rise for several years. This trend jumped into high gear with the maturity of Indian and other inexpensive technical service providers. Sourcing is now a fast-moving area of IT, but one that is not well understood by many organizations. The lure of cheap labor often clouds the complexity of the venture.
- **Project Management Office (PMO) (Part III, Chapter 19)**—Implementation of a PMO is likely the hottest current IT organizational topic, and it is closely related to the concept that supports a formal portfolio management initiative. The PMO is viewed as a central clearing function for global project decision-making. Some organizations are beginning to look at the PMO structure for both IT and non-IT projects.
- **Project Portfolio Management (Part III, Chapter 20)**—There is a fundamental axiom that you cannot manage what you cannot define. Not surprisingly, IT has learned that you must define what is included in the IT asset base and make decisions using that base. Portfolio management follows that theme and also builds a planning environment for the dynamic portfolio.
- **IT Governance (Part III, Chapter 21)**—This subject has been recognized by project managers for some time under the terms of authority and control. However, the new view is that the new term, *governance*, encapsulates one integrated decision environment with senior management being the driving force.

Each of these contemporary topics is a high-potential candidate for changing the future project management landscape.

Two of the topics in this section are actually spillovers from the *PMBOK® Guide* discussion in Section II. First, ethics questions have been added to the PMP certification exam in response to current concerns regarding that topic in the financial and IT environments. More structure and rigor surrounding this subject will evolve as corresponding government regulations are implemented. Second, the topic of procurement was discussed in Section II. However, it was mentioned during that discussion that human outsourcing would be moved to a separate section based on the current global popularity of third-party outsourcing. [Third-party outsourcing] is having a significant impact on the U.S. workforce and will also affect the manner in which projects are managed. So, it is procurement but a different scope than we have seen in the past.

Sections 19 and 20 are dedicated to the concept that projects should be managed at an enterprise level. The Project Management Office (PMO) is a central group with responsibilities for managing the various activities related to the enterprise project slate. Roles for the PMO remain quite varied across organizations, and there is still controversy regarding how much actual control to give this organization. Indeed, some would argue that it does not have sufficient value to exist. Nevertheless, the concept of some central control process seems necessary if we are to gain more control over the organizational projects. All evidence suggests that this is a mandatory activity from the standpoint of the senior executive. A support requirement for centralized oversight is the need for a defined project portfolio consisting of existing production applications, operational infrastructure components, and all project activities related to the evolution of these assets. *Portfolio Management* is the term associated with this activity.

The final contemporary section of the text is titled IT Governance (III.21). This is the newest topic in this list and the one that has the least public recognition. Our view regarding the topic is that there must be some formalized process in place to manage project-related activity external to the project team. This process must function as a global decision-making and oversight function if project expenditures are to achieve their planned results.

When we look at these topics from a philosophical view, the concept of ethics might be paraphrased as "do the right thing; be honest." However, the other four topics take on a different philosophical flavor. For these we were tempted to title the section "Silver Bullets." In each of the four cases, the topic is often viewed as being a savior for the organization. Outsourcing is going to save significant resources. PMO and Portfolio Management are keys to saving significant dollars by focusing on the right targets. IT governance is likewise going to save the organization by putting senior decision makers into a proper role for project activities. In the past, we have found that silver bullets seldom achieve their promise; that will probably remain true with these four topics. Nevertheless, each of the topics clearly occupies a gap in the current project management macro process. For that reason we see a strategic focus on these four areas. If government interest in internal financial control continues with regulations such as Sarbanes-Oxley, then the general topic of ethics/honesty could also transcend into a long-term management focus as well.

For all these reasons, we feel that this slate of topics is appropriate to conclude the text. We hope that the provided exposure will supply a broader conceptual perspective by recognizing that future projects will have to be created and survive in these new environments.

Professional Responsibility and Ethics

Chapter 17 Contents

Chapter Overview

The positive value of ethical behavior has been increasingly recognized in recent years. Improper actions by middle and upper management can destroy promising careers and even the organizations for which they work, and have far-ranging negative impacts on others' interests as well. In all such cases, a poor choice of decisions lays at the root of the failure. We place these under the category of Professional Responsibility and Ethics. Project managers are frequently faced with opportunities to obtain additional rewards for themselves or their organizations if they are willing to take a professionally or ethically inappropriate action, such as conducting one fewer safety study than they know they should, "looking the other way" when faced with clear evidence of others' wrongdoing, etc. Unfortunately, such actions can have far-reaching negative impacts, as well as ruin the manager's career if the acts are discovered. Some such actions might be ones that might not seem clearly unethical to the project manager on their face, but would be deemed violations of an organization's ethics policy. Even the simple act of accepting a meal or a baseball ticket is judged unethical in some organizations. It is important to know what each organization defines as their ethics and behave according to those rules. Some situations can be a veritable minefield if a project manager does not clearly understand which actions constitute inappropriate professional and ethically irresponsible behavior. An understanding of more general principles and lessons based on other actions can also provide a valuable guide to managers. That is the role played by this section. We encourage project managers to understand their organization's own policies and use the lessons presented here as an additional guide.

Professional Responsibility and Ethics Summary

It is essential that project managers not only be good employees of the organization for which they work, but also follow a number of more global professional responsibility and ethical principles. These external influences reflect the various needs and interests of those groups with the greatest stake in a project. A general set of behavioral principles that project managers need to follow include:

- Ensuring individual integrity.
- Contributing to the base of project management knowledge.
- Enhancing individual performance.
- Balancing stakeholders' interests.
- Interacting with the project team and stakeholders in a professional and cooperative manner.

Ensuring one's individual integrity requires taking a number of actions. Generally speaking, the project manager must do what is right. Specifically, written and oral communications with project stakeholders and governmental authorities must be truthful. The project manager must also adhere to the approved processes for project management activities. Lastly, any violations of applicable laws and ethical standards must be immediately reported to the appropriate authorities.

To contribute to the project management knowledge base, a project manager must do a number of things. First, he must share any lessons learned from his personal project experiences with others who would profit from that knowledge. Following this principle also requires that the project manager contribute to the education of and mentoring to less-experienced project managers. In addition, the project manager needs to engage in research to determine the best practices and share the findings of this research. Finally, he should strive to find techniques for improved measurement of project performance and continuously work to improve those outcomes.

In order to improve individual competence, the project manager must take a number of steps. Initially, it is important to appraise and understand personal strengths and weaknesses. Next, the project manager needs to take advantage of learning opportunities to address these weaknesses. Furthermore, there should be a personal development plan. Finally, the individual must continue to improve knowledge related to relevant professional topics. This entails seeking out new information about project management and the industry.

Balancing stakeholders' interests requires that a project manager consider the interests of all players in the project. Initially, the project manager needs to examine the interests and needs of these individuals and groups, seeking to understand the ways in which they can conflict. Following this, he must also work to resolve them with the understanding that the customer's needs must usually take precedence over the other groups. To minimize future conflict of interest it is vital to obtain the clearest and most complete requirements possible before the initiation of the project. Using this as a base, the project manager needs to address scope issues and other problems when they arise, rather than waiting until time has passed and they have become more serious.

Interacting with the project team and stakeholders in a professional and cooperative manner requires a number of actions. Cultural differences can impact the smooth functioning of a project. The project manager needs to understand these and take them into account in his dealings with the various stakeholders. In addition, he must uncover any differences in communications preferences, work ethics, and work practices among these groups. All future dealings with stakeholders should respect these differences. Cultural differences across country boundaries are particularly critical. When projects contain multinational stakeholders, the project manager needs to follow local practices and customs so long as doing so does not violate laws.

Significant differences in interests can also occur within a single country environment. These include customers, government agencies, other business functions involved in the project, sponsors providing financial resources for the project, the internal project team, parties from inside or outside the organization, end users of the project's product, members of society who will be affected by the project, and others. Clearly, this diversity of interest requires that project managers give adequate attention to numerous potential problem areas during the course of a project. These dealings will almost assuredly create ethical concerns in regard to information handling and project decision-making. It is only by giving this area proper attention that the manager can ensure that he effectively and properly discharges his ethical responsibilities to these stakeholders.

Readings

The readings present thought-provoking material that offers both abstract and concrete guidance to project managers on how to conduct themselves in an ethical and professionally responsible manner. Two of the readings present general principles that can guide these professionals. There are also lessons to be learned when managers make the wrong choices and face the very public repercussions of their actions. Recent corporate scandals, for example, WorldCom, are cases in point. This chapter does not neglect the lessons that stem from such cases either. No matter their format, the readings assembled here provide valuable advice about ethical and responsible professional conduct that managers should live by throughout their careers.

First, Professor Timothy McMahon provides simple but powerful advice to managers, based upon the misdeeds of the executive leadership of Enron Corporation, in his reading, "Enron's Leaders Still Don't Get It: The Issue is Ethics and They Showed None." For McMahon, the danger presented by managers such as these stems from the fact that they tried to achieve their ends at any cost, believing that their way was the right way and not being open to arguments to the contrary. Of course, what they did was not right, an evaluation affirmed overwhelmingly by American citizens.

The second reading, "The Ethics of Software Project Management," by Simon Rogerson and Don Gotterbarn, examines the key aspects of what constitutes professionally and ethically responsible behavior for project managers. The most basic aspect of this requires that managers truthfully report their actions and those of others. In addition, project managers must take actions to maintain their competence and those of others, and do what is necessary to respect the diverse interests of those affected by these projects. We conclude by providing a series of rules of thumb for responsible and ethical behavior to which managers should turn again and again as they examine their options for responding to ethically challenging situations. Though we cannot prepare project managers for every possible professional responsibility and ethics contingency they may face, reading this chapter should make them better able than ever before to face such challenges successfully.

Professional Responsibility and Ethics Rules of Thumb

Clearly, maintaining professionally responsible and ethical conduct requires that a project manager understand and respect a complicated web of interests and ethical principles. We offer a number of basic rules of thumb to supplement the presented advice and guide managers in their efforts to respect these interests. Following these rules does not guarantee appropriate behavior but should help managers to conduct themselves in an ethical and professionally responsible manner. In dealing with stakeholders a project manager should:

- Not misuse access to or control over financial resources that stakeholders have given them for legitimate use in the project, for example, engage in theft.
- Not mislead stakeholders about the status of the project by providing them with inaccurate information or failing to provide them with information relevant to the project.
- Inform the proper authorities of legal or professional violations by other stakeholders taking place in the context of the project.
- Not reveal trade secrets that stakeholders have given them in confidence, unless keeping such information in confidence would violate a law or professional responsibility/ethical rule.
- Not use information obtained in the context of the project for the purpose of gaining an unfair advantage over the stakeholder (that would be harmful to the stakeholder, if revealed).

Reference

Mulcahy, Rita. *PMP Exam Prep: A Course in a Book*, 2002. RMC Publications, Inc.

Enron's Leaders Still Don't Get It: The Issue is Ethics and They Showed None

J. TIMOTHY MCMAHON

Houston Chronicle, February 3, 2002. Reprinted here with the author's approval.

J. Timothy McMahon is professor of management at the Bauer College of Business at the University of Houston. He can be e-mailed at tmcmahon@uh.edu.

We are drowning in the details of the Enron debacle: SEC, FASB, EBITDA, AICPA, SPVs, market-to-market accounting, off-balance sheet financing, an impotent internal audit committee, a board of directors that is missing in action, national energy policy, accepted auditing principles, fox-in-the-henhouse accounting operations, tax havens, document shredding, political favors, executive privilege, corporate governance, 401(k) regulations, aggressive accounting, misguided analysts, hedging operations, details of deregulation, corporate citizenship, and more. The upcoming congressional hearings will surely generate a blizzard of additional details.

Are these details important? Of course! Will they help us understand what happened? Yes. Will the eventual consequences guarantee no Enrons in the future? Of course not.

Enron leaders often chided the uninitiated that they didn't get "it"—unconstrained deregulation and the Enron method of operation. Well, obviously, Ken Lay, Jeffrey Skilling, Andrew Fastow, et al. are the ones who didn't get the most important "it" (Figure 1 [17-1]).

What happened, and its causes, really is quite simple, in spite of the swirling details. Much of what was done was "wrong." A CBS poll of average citizens denounced Enron's actions 20 to one. But some legal eagles, aggressive accountants, finance wizards, and other business experts continue to tell us that, well, you know, many of the "wrong" actions are technically OK because they are not illegal. There is no legal statute, government regulation, or agency rule that tells us we should return a lost wallet when we happen upon it. Does that mean it is right to keep it? Of course not! Despite all the complexities, this is how simple the Enron fiasco is. The behaviors were wrong. It has to do with ethics.

Why do some companies do what's right while others do what's wrong? Why did BP decide and announce, much to the chagrin of many politicians and businesses, that it would, contrary to the conventional wisdom, be able to meet the clean air standards in Texas? Why did 3M pull Scotchguard, with $500 million in annual sales, from the shelves? Why does Ben & Jerry's donate 7.5 percent of pretax profit and have social good as part of their mission statement? Why is Johnson & Johnson still the standard for corporate conduct for the way the Tylenol murders crisis was handled?

17-1 Figure 1.

There are many more examples. The answer is the real "it"—leadership, values, and organization culture.

Although no one has owned up to it, responsibility for the Enron tragedy rests at the feet of the leadership—top management and the board of directors. This fact is inescapable. What was done was wrong and technical loopholes carry no weight here. It is really that clear. Leadership, and its reflection in organization culture and processes, is the cause of the disaster. Yet again we are reminded that the "soft stuff" really is the hard core. And it will be this soft stuff that will be the strongest deterrent to future Enrons.

While the leadership issues here are multifaceted, the most predominant is the very real danger of narcissistic leaders. The arrogance of Enron's top leaders is well known and well documented—Lay, Skilling, and Fastow easily fit in the narcissistic category. Amazingly, I have yet to read or hear disagreement with this observation.

Narcissistic leaders, driven to attain power and recognition, are, according to noted anthropologist and psychoanalyst Michael Maccoby, characterized by both very good and very bad attributes. On the positive side, these leaders often have great vision resulting in important transformations. Their vision is realized because these leaders have the skills to accumulate significant numbers of highly motivated and committed followers. These "productive narcissists" differ from "unproductive narcissists" who, lacking self-awareness and any restraints, have illusions of grandeur and attribute failures to external factors, never to themselves.

These out-of-control narcissistic leaders are poor listeners and often overreact to what they perceive as criticism. Warnings of questionable practices were repeatedly ignored by Enron leadership and several stock analysts experienced the rash reactions of Skilling to their simple request for information.

Narcissistic leaders also are not very good learners, as they much prefer to convert others to their way of thinking. *The Economist* documented an occasion when Lay was singing the praises of Drexel Burnham Lambert and its star Michael Milken who, he claimed, was simply "innovative and aggressive." But the arrogant Drexel collapsed and Milken ended up in jail. It appears that an important lesson was missed here.

Narcissistic leaders are ruthless competitors. Winning, in terms of stated earnings and stock price, was really the only goal for Enron. Its "take no prisoners" attitude is well known; and winning big and fast was at the core of Enron's culture. Reward systems encouraged this short-term view. Progressively better quarterly earnings and higher stock prices would be attained—obviously, in any way possible (Figure 2 [17-2]).

This ruthless, relentless, competitive philosophy and behavior is reflected in the culture of organizations led by narcissistic leaders. These organizations are characterized by arrogance and intense internal

17-2 Figure 2.

competition, much of which is dysfunctional. These are also well-known attributes of Enron.

Finally, these narcissistic leaders lack empathy. They rarely have any regrets and can easily direct down-sizing, layoffs, destructive cost-cutting, and other related initiatives—actions which are gut-wrenching for other leaders. I have heard precious little regret from either Skilling or Fastow—few or no signs of empathy for employees who lost their jobs and retirement funds or for others who experienced staggering financial losses.

"Unproductive" narcissistic leaders, who have low self-awareness and are left unchecked (by the board of directors in this case), can lead to the self-destruction of the organization. When one or two narcissistic leaders cause an entire organization the size of Enron to self-destruct, the message is frightening: a similar fate potentially exists for other companies.

The flip side of this depressing information is found in a recent *Harvard Business Review* article about great corporate leaders. Jim Collins' five-year study identified four characteristics of exemplary, role-model corporate leaders:

1. They have an intense desire to build an outstanding company that benefits all stakeholders.
2. They are humble and modest.
3. They shine the light on others, not themselves, when the company is successful.
4. They shine the light on themselves when things go badly and they accept responsibility for it.

The good news here is that leaders can learn to get their egos under control. It is possible for all leaders to learn to be better listeners, better learners, and more empathetic; in short, it is possible to develop more emotional intelligence, the stuff of true success.

The implications here are not only relevant but should have a sense of urgency for all leaders. Honest and fearless self-assessments are in order. Leaders with narcissistic tendencies should have highly trusted colleagues who can supply honest feedback and keep them grounded. Were Enron's escapades in water, broadband, Dabhol, paper and pulp, and metals sound business ventures? Or were they simply grand schemes and illusions?

Some leaders may learn that it is time to embark on career counseling or a serious personal development program. If you are a leader, no matter what your organization level, consider this information. If you know a leader who needs this information, see that they receive it in a caring and professional manner. If appropriate, the time to act is now—it may be more important than all of us can imagine.

The Ethics of Software Project Management

S. ROGERSON AND D. GOTTERBARN

Centre for Computing and Social Responsibility, De Montfort University, UK

Abstract

Software project management is the collection of techniques used to develop and deliver various types of software products. This developing discipline traditionally includes technical issues such as: the choice of software development methodology, how to estimate project size and schedule, how to ensure safety, what resources to reuse, and which programming environment to use for the development. The discipline also includes management issues such as: when to train personnel, what are the risks to the project success, and how to keep the project on schedule. These choices are then embodied in a software project management plan.

None of the traditional software project management materials address the ethical issues that arise because of the choices made during software development. Consequently, these materials do not provide any insights as to how to address these issues. In this paper, we identify several critical ethical issues that arise in most software projects and provide a proactive way of addressing these issues which is consistent with most professional software development standards.

Introduction

Software project management is the collection of techniques used to develop and deliver various types of software products. This developing discipline traditionally includes technical issues such as: the choice of software development methodology, how to estimate project size and schedule, how to ensure safety, what resources to reuse, and which programming development environment to use. The discipline also includes management issues such as: when to train personnel, what are the risks to the project success, and how to keep the project on schedule. These choices are then embodied in a software project management plan. Software project management addresses both the process of software development and the desired functional characteristics of the final software product. A complete software project management plan is the design, implementation, control, and test strategy for a software development process.

Developing software is frequently complicated, involving many people from different areas and with different skills, experiences, and social attitudes. There are many operational decisions to be taken during this extended activity. There are many different approaches to control the complexity of this activity, which can be viewed at two levels. There are those approaches which are concerned with high level decisions and

382

processes such as the Capability Maturity Model and the ISO 9000 series, and there are methods which deal with the details of the day to day activities of the project managers and software development teams. These latter methods include COCOMO, PRINCE, and Function Point Analysis.

All of these methods have as a major function the attempt to anticipate and avoid all possibilities which may negatively impact a software project. The negative possibilities are those which would delay the delivery of the software that performs the desired functions in a timely and cost effective manner. An additional function is to avoid late changes to the system because the later the change, the more expensive it becomes. However, none of these methods consider the ethical issues that need to be identified and addressed during the planning stages and reconsidered throughout the development process.

Effective software project management is a vital ingredient in achieving a successful outcome. The objectives for the project need to be agreed upon at the outset. In deciding the objectives, their implications need to be considered, in terms of the actual outputs and the impact these outputs will have. There is also a need to consider the impact of the development process itself. The project team should be well briefed on these issues and have the opportunity to debate them fully to establish its own conclusions. The team should consider all the implications of the plan, including ethical ones. It may need to call on additional resources from inside and outside the organisation. To confine the discussions within close boundaries (in an attempt to save money and time) is misguided. Broader issues will inevitably arise during the course of the project. If the team members are unprepared, they will lack direction and perform poorly. The sponsor of the project therefore needs the vision and the authority to ensure that the project team is supported and coached to consider both technical and ethical issues.

The purpose of this paper is to consider how software project management might embrace ethical sensitivity, ensure ethical issues are considered throughout the development process, and provide timely feedback of possible negative and positive social impacts of a piece of software. [Rogerson and Bynum, 1996] suggest that a comprehensive set of ethical tools and techniques needs to be identified and developed that will promote responsible practice in software development. One such item in this set is the Social Impact Statement, which can be effectively used to focus attention on the ethical issues associated with each stage of the software development process [Shneiderman, 1990, Huff and Jawer, 1994].

Applying Ethics

Relevant ethical principles must be established in order to identify the ethical issues associated with software project management. Ethics comprises both practice and reflection [van Luijk, 1994]. It is sufficient to consider only ethics practice in this paper because software project management is concerned primarily with action that guides others towards some common goal rather than conceptual reflection of the role and value of project management.

An interesting list of generic questions was devised by John McLeod in [Parker et al, 1990 pp 207–209] to help determine the ethical nature of actions within IT. These are relevant to software project management because they address many of the project management tasks, with the exception of full consideration of the supplier-customer relationship. The software project is concerned with the delivery of an output by a supplier (the project team) to a customer under some agreement. It is irrelevant whether this is an in-house arrangement or whether it is between two independent organisations or whether it is a combination of both. According to [Velasquez, 1992], such an agreement is concerned with output quality and moral liability. Velasquez argues that the principles of due care and social cost must take effect in these situations so that suppliers accept their obligations to customers and the wider community to provide goods and services that are adequate and beyond moral reproach.

By combining and building upon the ideas of McLeod and Velasquez, a set of ethical principles can be derived, as shown in Figure 1 [17-3] [Rogerson, 1997]. The principle of honour is to ensure that actions are beyond reproach, which in turn demands honesty from the professional. The principle of bias focuses on ensuring decisions and actions avoid the possibility of conflicts of interest and eliminate bias in judgements. Professional adequacy is concerned with the ability of individuals to undertake allocated tasks. The principle of due care is linked with the concept of software quality assurance. Fairness focuses on ensuring all affected parties are considered in project deliberations. Following these principles adds a social

Honour	Is the action considered beyond reproach?
Honesty	Will the action violate any explicit or implicit agreement or trust?
Bias	Are there any external considerations that may bias the action to be taken?
Professional adequacy	Is the action within the limits of capability?
Due care	Is the action to be exposed to the best possible quality assurance standards?
Fairness	Are all stakeholder's views considered with regard to the action?
Consideration of social cost	Is the appropriate accountability and responsibility accepted with respect to this action?
Effective and efficient action	Is the action suitable, given the objectives set, and is it to be completed using the least expenditure of resources?

17-3 Figure 1. Eight Ethical Principles

cost which recognises that it is not possible to abdicate from professional responsibility and accountability. Finally, the principle of effective and efficient action is concerned with completing tasks and realising goals with the least possible expenditure of resources.

These principles can be used to analyse, inform, and colour practice within computing, and software project management in particular. Within software development there are numerous activities and decisions to be made and many of these will have an ethical dimension. It is impractical to consider each minute issue in great detail and still hope to achieve the overall project goal. By considering which of the principles apply it is possible to ascertain which activities and decision-making points are the most ethically charged. The focus of attention must be on these ethical hotspots because they are likely to influence the success of the particular software project and promote ethical sensitivity in a broader context. [Rogerson and Bynum, 1995] define these ethical hotspots as points where activities and decision making are likely to include a relatively high ethical dimension.

Generic Software Project Management

Whilst it is recognised that the development of a piece of software might have its own special set of problems and challenges that have to [be] managed, [because] there are many similarities in all software projects, that means it is worth considering a generic approach which will lay down foundations for the management of all software projects. In his book, *How to Run Successful Projects*, in the British Computer Society Practitioner Series, [O'Connell, 1994] provides details of the Structured Project Management (SPM) approach. He explains that SPM is a practical methodology that, as [De Marco and Lister, 1987] state, is a "basic approach one takes to getting a job done." This appears to be a generic approach which is practical rather than conceptual and provides practitioners with realistic guidance in undertaking the complex activity of project management.

SPM comprises ten steps, as shown in Figure 2 [17-4]. The first five steps are concerned with planning and the remaining five deal with implementing the plan and achieving the goal. O'Connell states that most projects succeed or fail because of decisions made during the planning stage, thereby justifying the fact that half of the effort expended in the SPM approach is on preparation.

It is this planning element of project management which lays down the foundations on which the project ethos is built. Here the scope of consideration is established, albeit implicitly or explicitly, which in turn locates the horizon beyond which issues and people are deemed not to influence the project or be influenced by it. How the project is conducted will depend heavily upon the perceived goal. The visualisation of this goal takes place in Step 1. It is here that the scope of consideration is established, which should lead to effective discussion by all parties (stakeholders) on all issues resulting in the defining of the project goal(s). Often limited time is spent on this crucial first step. This is because the project manager is under pressure to deliver and so the tendency is to reduce the horizon and establish an artificial boundary around the project with only the obvious issues in close proximity to the project being considered. Steps 2 to 5 are concerned

Step	Description
1	Visualize what the goal is.
2	Make a list of the jobs that need to be done.
3	Ensure there is one leader.
4	Assign people to jobs.
5	Manage expectations, allow a margin of error, and have a fallback position.
6	Use an appropriate leadership style.
7	Know what is going on.
8	Tell people what is going on.
9	Repeat Step 1 through 8 until Step 10 can be achieved.
10	Realize the project goal.

17-4 Figure 2. The Ten Steps of Structured Project Management

with adding detail and refinements, thus arriving at a workable and acceptable plan. Steps 6 to 8 are concerned with implementing the plan, monitoring performance, and keeping those associated with the project informed of progress. Step 9 defines the control feedback loops which ensure that the plan remains focused, current, and realistic. Finally, Step 10 is the delivery of the project output to the customer and an opportunity to reflect upon what has and has not been achieved.

Ethical Management

The eight ethical principles can be used to provide an insight to how ethical management might be achieved. The activities within each of the ten steps of SPM have been analysed in order to identify the dominant ethical issues of each step [Rogerson, 1997]. The results of this analysis are shown in Figure 3 [17-5]. It is recognised that most of the eight ethical principles will have some impact on each step, but it is important to identify those which will have a significant impact on each particular step. The mapping in Figure 3 shows those relationships which are considered significant. Those with the highest ethical significance, indicated by the number of ethical principles that prevail are, at this level, the ethical hotspots of a generic approach to software project management.

This analysis suggests that Step 1, which is involved with defining the project goal, Step 5, which assigns people to tasks, and Step 8, which communicates project progress to all concerned, are the most significant ethical areas. The first area defines a project that is ethically, as well as, technically and economically acceptable. The second area concerns the sensitive alignment of people's skills and aspirations with the project tasks. The third area concerns progress reporting to stakeholders and provides ongoing checks

Principle	Step 1	Step 2	Step 3	Step 4	Step 5	Step 6	Step 7	Step 8	Step 9	Step 10
1. Honour	X			X		X		X		X
2. Honesty	X			X	X			X		
3. Bias	X	X	X	X				X		X
4. Adequacy			X	X		X				
5. Due care	X		X		X			X	X	
6. Fairness	X				X			X		
7. Social cost	X				X	X				X
8. Action		X	X	X		X	X		X	X
	6	2	4	5	4	4	1	5	2	4

17-5 Figure 3. The dominant ethical principles in the steps of SPM

and balances throughout the life of the project. [...] Step 1 will now be used to illustrate the difficulty in achieving ethical sensitivity and showing how this sensitivity might be achieved in practice.

Scope of Consideration

STAKEHOLDERS

As mentioned previously, establishing the right scope of consideration is essential in defining acceptable project goals. The scope of consideration is influenced by the identification and involvement of stakeholders. In traditional software project management, the stated needs of the customer are the primary item of concern in stating the project objectives. Recently, there has been some recognition that in defining how software will address those needs the customer is also presented with a predefined set of constraints which limit the customer's freedom of expression [McCarthy, 1996]. There is a mutual incompatibility between some customer needs, for example, the amount of code required to make a system easy to use makes a system difficult to modify. The balancing of these items is an ethical dimension in the development of a software product. But such considerations are limited in scope to the customer. Investigating 16 organisational IS-related projects led [Farbey, Land and Targett, 1993] to conclude that regarding evaluation of IT investment, "... the perception of what needed to be considered was disappointingly narrow, whether it concerned the possible scope and level of use of the system, [or] the range of people who could or should have been involved...." They discovered, with the exception of vendors, all stakeholders involved in evaluation were internal to the organisations. The reason for this restricted involvement is that these are the only stakeholders originally identified in the traditional project goals. However, we do not limit our consideration of stakeholders to those who are financing the project or politically influential, but broaden it to be consistent with models of ethical analysis. By stakeholder we mean individuals or groups who may be directly or indirectly affected by the project and thus have a stake in the development activities. Those stakeholders who are negatively affected are particularly important regarding ethical sensitivity because they are often the ones overlooked.

Negative effects include both overt harm and the denial or reduction of goods. So obviously the development of a medical software package which delivered erroneous dosages of medicine that killed patients would have a negative effect; but we would also include as having a negative effect software which limited people's freedom of expression. Limitations on positive ethical values and rights are negative effects. It can also be argued that the failure to promote positive ethical values is also a negative effect.

Therefore, we extend the traditional software project stakeholder list from customers and corporations or shareholders to include all those who will be affected by the software and by its production. This includes: users of the software, families of the users, social institutions which may be radically altered by the introduction of the software, the natural environment, social communities, software professionals, employees of the development organisation, and the development organisation itself. Given such a range of stakeholders, how is one ever to identify the relevant and significant stakeholders?

Stakeholder Identification

[Gert, 1988, Green, 1994] use a rights model to help identify relevant stakeholders. Once the stakeholders are identified one can itemise the specific obligations owed by the software developers to each of these stakeholders. Gert gives 10 basic moral rules. Although this is a deontological theory, it has been argued elsewhere that these rules are consistent with a Rawlsian approach to moral standards for software professionals [Gotterbarn, 1991]. Gert's rules include: Don't kill, Don't cause pain, Don't disable, Don't deprive of freedom, Don't deprive of pleasure, Don't deceive, Don't cheat, Keep your promises, Obey the law, and Do your duty. These rules carry with them a corresponding set of rights such as the right to liberty, physical security, personal liberty, free speech, and property. A preliminary identification of software project stakeholders is accomplished by listing each of these rules and rights, and examining the system plan and goals to see who is affected and how they may be affected. For example, according to rule 2 we should ask if the system changes the level of pain felt by anyone. Some of the rights and obligations identified when following this method may be in conflict and it will become necessary to prioritise how these rights are addressed and which of them can, within the bounds of the eight principles above, be addressed. One of the ways to help prioritise the ethical obligations within a project is to determine what actions are necessary to satisfy the perceived obligation and evaluate those actions in terms of whether they are morally required, morally wrong, or are merely morally permissible. This approach to evaluating potential actions is a variation on Green's decision tree for assessing obligations [Green, 1994].

In determining the rights and obligations of the developers of a software product, one can use one of the professional codes of ethics. A code such as the Software Engineering Code of Ethics [Gotterbarn et al, 1997] defines the rights of the developer and others related to the software process and the final software product. The imperatives of the ACM Code of Ethics (Appendix A) can be used to guide the stakeholder search. The process of identifying stakeholders also identifies their rights and the developers' obligations to them.

Involvement

Once the stakeholders have been identified, it is necessary to seek their involvement in the development process in order to meet their rights in the most effective way. As indicated above, in traditional project development there is a very narrow range of stakeholder involvement. Such restricted stakeholder involvement reduces the likelihood that any relevant ethical issues are properly considered. The evidence from Farbey substantiates our claim that no current method of software project management considers ethical issues.

Appropriate people from the whole range of stakeholder groups should be consulted. Participation by owners and employees is obvious but it may be desirable for other groups to take part in particular situations. For example, if a manufacturing company wishes to improve links with suppliers and customers, then it would make sense to involve representatives from both groups. Similarly, if an organisation wished to form a strategic alliance with a competitor in an attempt to increase market share through synergy, then participation by that competitor would be essential. Finally, the drive for efficiency gains through applying IT by a large local employer could mean a reduction in the workforce or employing a different workforce group. In such circumstances the involvement of unions and relevant community groups is probably desirable.

The widespread use of and dependence upon software within organisations and society affects the lives of most individuals. The project management process must consider, from the start, the views and concerns of all affected parties and do so using the principles of due care, fairness, and social cost. Concerns over, for example, deskilling of jobs, redundancy, and the breakup of social groupings can be then aired at the earliest opportunity. Fears can be allayed and project goals adjusted if necessary.

Generic Software Development Impact Statement

One way of addressing the need to modify project goals in a formal way is to use a modification of a social impact statement. A social impact statement is modelled on an environmental impact statement, which is required before major construction is undertaken. The environmental impact statement is supposed to specify the potential negative impacts on the environment of the proposed construction and specify what actions will be taken to minimise those impacts. Proposed social impact statements have been described for identifying the impact of information systems on direct and indirect system users [Shneiderman and Rose, 1995], whereas our Software Development Impact Statement (SoDIS) is intended to reflect the software development process as well as the more general ethical obligations to various stakeholders.

There are two types of SoDIS. The first is a Generic SoDIS which has as its primary function the identification of stakeholders and related ethical issues. In the light of the identified issues a preliminary project management plan is developed. A second more detailed SoDIS is then employed. This is the Specific SoDIS. There will be a number of Specific SoDIS within a particular methodology. Each SoDIS is tied to a particular development methodology and to each step in that methodology. Even though each Specific SoDIS is tied to a development methodology, they all include the means of revisiting and reevaluating ethical issues in the light of the unfolding development process. This organic nature of the SoDIS is very different for the environmental impact statement model.

Any SoDIS requires a set of instructions which include information about what data to gather, how to gather it, and how to document the entire process. The set of instructions should also include information about monitoring the SoDIS development process for accuracy, completeness, objectivity, and enforcement of the results. This paper will not deal with the monitoring and the enforcement issues. These fall within the communications and reporting ethical hotspot mentioned previously and indeed must wait until the SoDIS process becomes a part of typical development methodologies. A SoDIS should have a standardised physical structure which will help its users to organise the issues and the information.

ELEMENTS IN THE GENERIC SODIS FORM

The elements included in a Generic SoDIS (see Appendix B) are directly related to the software project management process. In SPM these elements were described at a high level of abstraction as Step 1: Visualise what the goal is. Step 2: Make a list of the jobs that need to be done. These two steps are reflected less abstractly in individual software development methodologies and indeed further detailed in SPM itself. For example, Figure 4 [17-6] shows the outline for the IEEE standard model for a software project management plan [Fairley, 1995].

All software project management plans will include similar elements to those included in this model. This plan starts with a project overview which generally states the functions desired, called the requirements, for the software by the customer and constraints on the development process such as time, budget, and resources. These are stated from the customer's point of view. The preliminary material in a plan also includes a list of those things which will be delivered to the customer at the end of the project. This constitutes the developer's contract with the customer. What we propose with a SoDIS is to broaden the developer's contract to include a commitment to develop a product which is ethically sensitive. The Generic SoDIS would be part of the deliverables section of the software project management plan.

IEEE Model for a Software Project Management Plan

Introductory material Title Page
Revision Sheet
Preface
Table of Contents
List of Figures
List of Tables

1.0   Introduction
1.1   Project Overview
1.2   Project Deliverables
1.3   Evolution of the SPMP
1.4   Reference Materials
1.5   Definitions and Acronyms

2.0   Project Organization
2.1   Process Model
2.2   Organizational Structure
2.3   Organizational Interfaces
2.4   Project Responsibilities

3.0   Managerial Process
3.1   Management Objectives and Priorities
3.2   Assumptions, Dependencies, and Constraints
3.3   Risk Management
3.4   Monitoring and Controlling Mechanisms
3.5   Staffing Plan

4.0   Technical Process
4.1   Methods, Tools, and Techniques
4.2   Software Documentation
4.3   Project Support Functions

5.0   Work Elements, Schedule, and Budget
5.1   Work Packages
5.2   Dependencies
5.3   Resource Requirements
5.4   Budget and Resource Allocation
5.5   Schedule

17-6 Figure 4. The IEEE model for a software project management plan

Section 1.3 of the IEEE model recognises that software development is a very organic process and that all eventualities can not be fully anticipated at the beginning of the project, so it is necessary for the plan to be flexible. The way in which a plan may change and what is needed to approve such changes are included in section 1.3. The ethical impact of a software product will change as the product changes, so a Generic SoDIS must also include a section describing its change mechanism. Several large companies now employ ethics officers. If the software development company has an ethics officer, then s/he should be involved in the change process.

The change process requires the same care as was taken in the original development of the SoDIS. If the impact on particular stakeholders changes in a negative way, then the ethical obligations to those stakeholders, as stated in the original SoDIS, must be reevaluated. If necessary, new action plans need to be developed to meet the new obligations and these plans need to be integrated into the software development process.

IDENTIFY THE STAKEHOLDERS

Primary stakeholder issues

The development of a piece of software involves many stakeholders, each having various rights and obligations, and a method is needed to sort out these issues. The process we propose is an iterative one which starts from a consideration of the software requirements and asks of the two obvious stakeholders, the developer and the customer, how those functions will impact upon their rights. One method of completing this analysis is to use Gert's moral rules. Each of these moral rules can be expressed as a right of an individual or group or as an obligation to someone. For example, the rule against killing can be expressed as a right to life, or the rule against depriving of freedom can be expressed as a right to liberty. The list of Gert's ten moral rules/rights can be used as the rows of a matrix. For example, one row could be "Does this requirement affect the level of pain?" This method will identify both the ethical negatives (increased pain) and the ethical positives (decreased pain) of a system. The columns in the initial matrix represent the developer and the customer. For each requirement in the software requirements statement, visit each cell in the matrix and make a note if satisfying that requirement violates that right of the stakeholder. Since rights have matching obligations, this process can be used to develop an obligation list. For each right that is violated, someone has an obligation to prevent that violation. An obligation list should state the ethical concern and clearly assign the obligation to address this concern. Later this obligation list will be used in developing the list of jobs that need to be done to complete the software development process. In this stage, the list will also be used to determine the initial feasibility of the project as stated in the requirements. Because the analysis as described is organised by particular software requirements, it will be easy to identify those requirements which generate a high level of ethical concern. Thus, the list will also be used to determine if particular requirements have to be modified to avoid significant ethical problems.

This method focuses on the individual requirements, but it can be used at this stage to give a composite picture of the ethical impact of the entire project from the point of view of these two stakeholders.

BROADER STAKEHOLDER ANALYSIS

This process is now used to both identify additional stakeholders and to determine their rights. The previous analysis should have identified some areas of broader ethical concern and some additional stakeholders. The primary stakeholder analysis is repeated for these newly identified stakeholders. Even if there were no new stakeholders identified, at a minimum the analysis should use software users, related cultural groups, and society as potential stakeholders.

HIGHER MORAL OBLIGATIONS

Each of these processes should be repeated using professional ethical codes to identify ethical issues. Using the imperatives of the ACM Code of Ethics helps the SoDIS team to ask questions which have been of concern to practising computer professionals.

Specific Software Development Impact Statement

WORK BREAKDOWN STRUCTURE

Most software project management models proceed by decomposing each task into smaller, more manageable tasks. These smaller tasks are then carefully described in terms of resource needs, costs, and expected time to complete. Once a project is decomposed in this way, the costs of the individual tasks are added together to estimate the total project cost. These individual task descriptions are elaborated and included in the software project management plan. This set of task descriptions, sometimes called the Work Breakdown Structure (WBS), is used in the reviewing and monitoring of the completion of tasks. The entire software development process is organised in terms of an ordered hierarchy of tasks, the WBS. Each WBS task is dependent on the completion of other WBS tasks. Each WBS task includes a description of the other WBS task on which it depends.

Like the project as a whole, each WBS task can have a significant ethical impact which may not have been anticipated by the generic SoDIS. The particular way in which the WBS is designed may endanger the software user or have significant social consequences. The specific SoDIS is used to address this problem. It is included as an integral part of a WBS task document, as shown in Appendix C. A standard WBS task document only addresses technical issues relating to software and hardware, but the modified WBS task document, which includes a specific SoDIS, addresses the potential ethical issues generated by that WBS task and the ways to address or avoid those potential issues. A WBS task document also specifies the criteria the WBS task must satisfy to be considered complete. The SoDIS version of a WBS task document also includes a discussion of the ethical criteria which have to be satisfied by this task. The techniques used in the development of the generic SoDIS are used in the development of the specific SoDIS.

Once the SoDIS WBS task documents are completed, their implementation must be monitored. This monitoring process is another ethical hotspot which will be discussed later in this series of papers.

Conclusion

Just as producing software of high quality should be second nature to the software engineer so should producing software that is ethically sensitive. Indeed there is clearly an overlap in these two requirements. The project management process for software development must accommodate an ethical perspective. The major criticism of current practice is that any ethical consideration tends to be implicit rather than explicit, which has a tendency to devalue the importance of the ethical dimension. By using ethical principles, identifying of ethical hotspots, and using SoDIS, it is possible to ensure that the key ethical issues are properly addressed as an integral part of the software development process. Quite simply, project management should be guided by a sense of justice, a sense of equal distributions of benefits and burdens, and a sense of equal opportunity. In this way software development project management will become ethically aligned.

References

Collins, W. R., K. W. Miller, B. J. Spielman, and P. Wherry (1994). *How Good is Good Enough*, Communications of the ACM, Vol 37 No 1, January, pp 81–91.

De Marco, T. and T. Lister (1987). *Peopleware*, Dorset House Publishing.

Fairley, R. (1995). IEEE Software Project Management Plan Standard, revised, IEEE.

Farbey, B., F. Land, and D. Targett (1993). *How to assess your IT investment*, Butterworth Heinemann.

Gert, B. (1988). *Morality*, Oxford University Press.

Gotterbarn, D. (1991). *Computer Ethics: Responsibility Regained*, National Forum, The Phi Kappa Phi Journal, Vol 71 No 3.

Gotterbarn, D., K. Miller, and S. Rogerson (1997). Software Engineering Code of Ethics, SIGCAS Newsletter, July.

Green, R. M. (1994). *The Ethical Manager*, Macmillan Publishing.

Huff, C. and B. Jawer (1994). *Towards a design ethic for Computing Professionals*, in Huff, C. and Finholt, T. (eds) Social Issues in Computing, McGraw Hill.

McCarthy, J. (1996). *Dynamics of Software Development*, Microsoft Press.

O'Connell, F. (1994). *How to run successful projects*, Prentice-Hall.

Parker, D. B., S. Swope, and B. N. Baker (1990). "Ethical Conflicts in Information and Computer Science, Technology, and Business." QED Information Sciences.

Rogerson, S. (1997). "Software Project Management Ethics," in Myers, C., T. Hall, and D. Pitt (eds) *The Responsible Software Engineer*, Springer-Verlag, pp 100–106.

Rogerson, S. and T. W. Bynum (1995). "Identifying the ethical dimension of decision making in the complex domain of IS/IT," ETHICOMP95, Leicester, UK, April.

Rogerson, S. and T. W. Bynum (1996). "Information ethics: the second generation, The future of information systems," UK Academy for Information Systems Conference.

Shneiderman, B. (1990). "Human Values and the Future of Technology: A Declaration of Empowerment, Computers and Society," Vol 20 No 3, October, pp 1–6.

Shneiderman, B. and A. Rose (1995). "Social Impact Statements: Engaging Public Participation in Information Technology Design, Technical Report of the Human Computer Interaction Laboratory," September, pp 1–13.

van Luijk, H. (1994). "Business ethics: the field and its importance," in Harvey, B. (ed) *Business Ethics: A European Approach*, Prentice-Hall.

Velasquez, M. G. (1992). *Business ethics—concepts and cases*, 3rd Edition, Prentice-Hall.

Appendix A—ACM Code of Ethics Imperatives

1.1 Contribute to society and human well being.

1.2 Avoid harm to others.

1.3 Be honest and trustworthy.

1.4 Be fair and take action not to discriminate.

1.5 Honour property rights including copyrights and patents.

1.6 Give proper credit for intellectual property.

1.7 Respect the privacy of others.

1.8 Honour confidentiality.

2.1 Strive to achieve the highest quality, effectiveness, and dignity in both the process and products of professional work.

2.2 Acquire and maintain professional competence.

2.3 Know and respect existing laws pertaining to professional work.

2.4 Accept and provide appropriate professional review.

2.5 Give comprehensive and thorough evaluations of computer systems and their impacts, including analysis of possible risks.

2.6 Honour contracts, agreements, and assigned responsibilities.

2.7 Improve public understanding of computing and its consequences

2.8 Access computing and communication resources only when authorised to do so.

3.1 Articulate social responsibilities of members of an organisational unit and encourage full acceptance of those responsibilities.

3.2 Manage personnel and resources to design and build information systems that enhance the quality of working life.

3.3 Acknowledge and support proper and authorised uses of an organisation's computing and communication resources.

3.4 Ensure that users and those who will be affected by a system have their needs clearly articulated during the assessment and design of requirements; later the system must be validated to meet requirements.

3.5 Articulate and support policies that protect the dignity of users and others affected by a computing system.

3.6 Create opportunities for members of the organisation to learn the principles and limitations of computer systems

Appendix B—Generic SoDIS

The generic SoDIS is part of the deliverables section of a software project management plan and it is revised according to the revision schedule contained in the software project management plan.

1. Software Requirements:
   Could be included by reference to other project documents.
   The requirements should be numbered for easy reference in the SoDIS development process.

2. Change Process
   Frequency of review
   Review team members
   Approval process

Who is on the review team?

How open is it to public stakeholders?

3. Primary Stakeholder Analysis

Obligations list

Right violated _____ by _____ causes _____ obligation to _____.

Requirements with a high level of ethical concern.

Requirements review in the light of this analysis.

Review of analysis process in the light of professional code of conduct.

4. Extended Stakeholder Analysis

Identify potential stakeholders.

5. Prioritised obligations list divided into actions which are morally wrong, permissible, and required.

Appendix C—Specific SoDIS

Typical Work Breakdown Structure task document with SoDIS modification

Name: Name and numeric identifier of the task

Description: Technical function of the task

Dependencies: What technical and SoDIS tasks must be complete before this task can be started?

Project Members: People who will work on this

Duration: Estimated time to complete this task

Resources: Technical and other resources needed to complete this task

Product: Product description

Completion criteria: What are the technical and ethical marks of task completion?

Acceptance criteria: Who has the authority to certify that this WBS task is complete in terms of its technical and social requirements?

Risks: Potential risks to timely successful WBS task completion

Risk Resolution: Plan to address these risks should they arise

Specific SoDIS Risks: Stakeholder analysis and risk identification

SoDIS Risk: Resolution

Third Party Sourcing

Chapter 18 Contents

Chapter Overview

Procuring services provided by professionals in other organizations has become an increasingly popular option among companies seeking to reduce costs. Much of this procurement has come from off-shore service providers in nations such as India, Malaysia, and Ireland. This section highlights critical aspects of this topic, human sourcing (also frequently and confusingly referred to as off-shoring or simply outsourcing). This section complements Section II.11 and its discussion of material procurement. The aim is to make clear that this practice, done well, can provide benefits to organizations in addition to cost savings. However, obtaining these benefits requires understanding and making decisions that account for the greater complexity and additional challenges for procurement relative to simple materials procurement.

Organizations considering human sourcing are revising their understanding of the nature of procurement and the capabilities offered by service providers. A growing number of these providers call upon considerable pools of expertise to meet sourcing requirements, separating themselves from providers that can only offer cost advantages. So, the range of benefits potentially available to organizations that utilize human sourcing is growing. Unfortunately, many organizations that employ this practice fail to realize even a small fraction of its possible benefits. These failures may stem from a lack of understanding of the complexities of human sourcing. Organizations seeking to employ this practice must understand it sufficiently to be able to navigate successfully through its complexities, avoiding the mistakes of unsuccessful outsourcers.

The complexities of human sourcing build upon the issues that make materials procurement a challenging activity. Much of this complexity stems from dealing with an organization headquartered in a foreign nation. An organization that is considering a potential foreign service provider must understand the extent to which foreign laws may impact its relationship with such a company and how conflicts over relevant domestic and foreign laws will be decided. In addition, a human sourcing arrangement carries the potential for violations of an organization's intellectual property rights. If these rights are meant to protect a key source of competitive advantage, the risks and benefits must be carefully weighed before partnering with a human services provider with access to sensitive information. Clearly, human sourcing is fraught with complicated issues that can prevent an organization from obtaining its potential benefits. The following articles build upon this brief introduction with the intent of making managers better able to help their organizations deal successfully with human sourcing challenges.

Readings

The readings in this chapter provide managers with an understanding of how to deal effectively with the challenges of third party sourcing, while reminding them of the need to be open to different perspectives. First, in "The Building Blocks of Global Competitiveness," C.K. Prahalad and M.S. Krishnan provide a detailed perspective on the challenges and opportunities provided by human sourcing through overseas providers. A key benefit that these authors highlight is the potential ability of companies that outsource to respond more quickly and cost-effectively to changing conditions in the markets in which they compete.

In the second reading, "Bush Lays Off Congress," Jay Slupesky reminds managers who are considering human sourcing of the need to keep a perspective as well as their sense of humor when dealing with human sourcing scope. Given the many organizations rushing to outsource more and more of their business processes, this reading presents what may be a far-out vision of the ultimate outcome. We leave you with a final thought: "Is there life after outsourcing?"

The Building Blocks of Global Competitiveness

C.K. PRAHALAD AND M.S. KRISHNAN

Information Week, September 2004, Issue 22.

Innovation and growth in a global market require a focus on quality and results, not just cost. Outsourcing is just one piece of the complex puzzle.

Talk about the global IT market almost invariably focuses myopically on outsourcing and, in turn, the job-loss debate. We believe it's time to broaden the discussion to illuminate a more strategic and advantageous approach for U.S. businesses: innovation and optimization of global resources in a competitive landscape.

There's no doubt that the loss of well-paying jobs in the United States creates a climate of animosity and fear. However, in considering total business strategy in a global economy, outsourcing is but a small fragment of the shifting dynamics of innovation and competitiveness. We suggest that capitalizing on global resources is a critical element in the process of innovation in a global market. The latest challenge for business-technology managers is coming to terms with a new competitive reality: how to achieve lower costs, high quality, rapid innovation, and change, as well as manage complexity while offering customers personalized experiences. These challenges will drive the value-creation process. Global competition will force companies, large and small, to compete differently, and the search for ways to manage in this environment calls for new capabilities—ones embedded primarily in managerial processes, decision analytics, and behaviors.

The search for new skills can't be confined to one country or a region. Leveraging offshore resources won't be a one-way street in the flow of investments or jobs. Though China, India, the Philippines, Thailand, and other countries endowed with an abundance of talent at low cost are currently prominent, the focus may shift in the future to some other, as yet unknown, region. For the time being, India is the hotbed: Bharati Televentures in India has signed a $750 million IT-outsourcing deal with IBM; Infosys Technologies and Wipro Technologies plan to expand their U.S. subsidiaries and consulting operations and hire more than 1,000 new consultants. Separately, non-U.S. companies' investments for setting up U.S. subsidiaries doubled in 2003, to $82 billion.

Though outsourcing is rarely considered a path to business innovation, we believe that companies that optimize global resources will emerge as winners. IT infrastructure for remote delivery is becoming commonplace, so the search for new resources—in the form of cost, motivation, talent, and teamwork—has never been more intense. The perspective on outsourcing must shift from a focus on cost arbitrage to one encompassing a global search for resources and methodologies for leveraging resources. That's the new basis for innovation. We've just started scratching the surface of the business benefits of managing global resources; companies that focus on building a core competence in managing remote delivery—that is, managing for innovation, influencing without ownership, and learning to work in intercultural teams across time zones—will have a clear advantage.

Three Stages of Business

The principal reason for this is the evolving nature of global companies. In the past, companies were firmly rooted in the traditional "make and sell" paradigm. They focused on internal efficiencies of design, development, and manufacturing (make), and persuading consumers to buy what they offered (sell). The business model has been shifting to "sense and respond;" companies sense what consumers want and respond rapidly. This approach requires companies to develop business-technology systems for an active and systematic understanding of evolving customer needs and market opportunities. It includes both customer-facing technologies that provide the knowledge of what customers need and internal development and logistics systems to deliver on those needs. In turn, the entire management process must become responsive. Sense-and-respond companies often are models of best practices.

Now, businesses are migrating to an even more advantageous position— "anticipate and lead"—requiring yet another overhaul of internal management processes and systems. Anticipate-and-lead businesses focus on innovative, or next, practices. As companies move from a make-and-sell to an anticipate-and-lead model, their pace and rhythm change. The new model puts pressure on traditional systems and processes. For example, in the make-and-sell world, managers focus on products; in a sense-and-respond environment, they increasingly have to deliver a solution that may require the support of multiple companies and a global supply chain. No single business has the full range of world-class capabilities to deliver the entire solution. As we move to the next phase, the real source of competitive advantage will be in creating unique experiences for consumers, one at a time, by leveraging global resources.

To believe that the basic impetus for this rapid shift to outsourcing is cost arbitrage and corporate greed is naive. As Figure 1 [18-1] shows, cost arbitrage is an ongoing advantage and likely will be a long-term phenomenon. (New research indicates that the cost advantage actually is diminishing. See *India's Dwindling IT Labor Advantage*.) But other advantages are emerging that make offshoring a smart choice for innovative businesses— specifically quality and speed.

India has the largest concentration of high-quality, software-development centers in the world, as measured by the Software Engineering Institute's capability maturity model (CMM), a framework that facilitates definition and measurement of the software-development process. Levels 4 and 5 are the highest process-maturity levels, with optimized processes for cost and quality outcomes. There are more than 50 software facilities in India rated at CMM level 4 or level 5. Further, as software-development work has evolved,

18-1 Figure 1.

Indian companies have learned to make process improvements to develop software on an off-site/on-site basis. A recent study by the University of Michigan, using data collected from a CMM level 5 company in India, shows that quality-adjusted prices in offshore custom-software projects decreased by roughly 14% annually from 1999 to 2002. This was due to internal-process improvements within the company and not labor-cost differences between India and the United States.

While price reductions and quality improvements can be achieved in the United States, a few of the leading Indian vendors have mastered process improvements, too. We believe that the need for documentation of their work, as well as decentralized implementation and delivery of software, prompted these vendors to innovate their software-development process and achieve these results. Indian software developers started in the early 1970s by improving repetitive tasks such as testing and porting of software systems for their foreign clients. Today Indian custom-software providers take full responsibility for the design and development of large-scale, critical systems. Increasingly, it's common to see Indian software vendors and leading U.S. solutions providers jointly bidding for global systems projects, as in the case of a recent announcement by Wipro and IBM Global Services.

Remote-service delivery vendors from India and other locations such as Ireland and the Philippines offer a variety of services. While some service providers deliver only a cost arbitrage, others provide new forms of remote delivery of analytics, such as complete back-end support for investment banking or total IT services. For example, even within the call-center industry, there are service providers that simply serve incoming customer calls based on predefined scripts, while other call centers offer market research, insights based on analytics using a customer-support problem database, and outgoing call services such as cross selling and up selling.

What are the drivers of this new competition and value creation? There's a growing demand for real-time management—accelerating the speed of reaction in the organization. It's obvious that a company can't use inventories to disconnect the demand and supply infrastructures, as it did in the make-and-sell model. Rather, fulfilling consumer experiences in the anticipate-and-lead world requires organizational capabilities for seamlessly connecting the demand and supply infrastructures with no latency. The demand for unique consumer solutions and experience fulfillment suggests that companies have to cope with more complexity. Consumers will no longer accept poor quality or unnecessary costs. They want to be involved and manage their own experience. This is one of the reasons that self-service has become an important phenomenon.

Financial-services company E-loan fits this new model. E-loan decided not only to fully disclose its decision to leverage its global resources by outsourcing, but also to offer customers a choice in whether to have their loan applications served from an offshore location, enabling two days' faster processing at lower cost. More than 85% of E-loan's customers opted for the offshore service.

What are the implications of a company's desire to anticipate and lead, and consumers' desire to create their own experiences? Both put new demands on how large companies are managed. The demands are very clear:

- A comprehensive total-cost advantage, lowering the cost of ownership.
- Increased commitment to the quality of the experience, not only the products.
- Real-time reaction to the evolving demands on the company.
- An ability to cope with more complex alliances, multiple suppliers, and relationships with multiple consumers and consumer groups; in other words, the emerging importance of stakeholders of all kinds.
- An information infrastructure to facilitate global analytics and contextual insights from business processes that integrate customers and multiple partners across the globe.
- Innovations in how companies serve consumers with personalized experiences, not only product innovations.

These demands are increasingly forcing businesses to examine and change their management processes to cope with the new competitive realities.

Innovation or Outsourcing?

Outsourcing may have started with companies recognizing the opportunity for cost arbitrage, but to believe it's only cost that's sustaining the pressure to outsource is a narrow view of the phenomenon. That kind of outlook is often found at companies in the make-and-sell stage or just at the beginning of the sense-and-respond stage. Consider what some more-sophisticated companies have done to date in outsourcing:

- Creative unbundling of core business processes. The digitization of business processes and global connectivity and access have created the ability to easily disaggregate business processes for virtual, remote delivery of services. For example, the entire customer-relations-management process can be divided into modules, such as sales transactions or call centers, that can then be outsourced. All large companies are breaking down complex processes into bite-size pieces and reaggregating them. This suggests that companies are focusing on efficiency in some parts of the core process, and flexibility and innovation in other parts. The granularity with which it's done is the real surprise. For example, a sales team may write up a sales presentation (the unique value) and have it converted into PowerPoint slides in India overnight (efficiency). A similar approach can be used for, say, researching patents. Developing a patentable product or process (the unique value) is different from writing the patent application and doing the research (efficiency), which can be sent offshore.
- Outsourcing and performance agreements can't work without an explicit understanding of the underlying processes. Companies have had to document and make explicit the decision processes within their service-level agreements (SLA). In tandem with requirements of the Sarbanes-Oxley Act, outsourcing may give companies an excuse to make their implicit processes and system interdependencies explicit. A new level of decision-process transparency is essential to accommodate rapid change, but it's difficult to change what isn't explicit. The cost of opportunistically outsourcing based on asymmetrical wage rates without preparing the internal processes for the new level of transparency can be significantly higher.

A leading U.S. auto supplier, for example, learned that the cost of last-minute changes in its design processes can be much higher when components are manufactured overseas because parts may already be in the delivery phase of the supply chain before the changes are known to the supplier. On the other hand, a leading logistics company that has outsourced its customer support to an offshore location can remotely monitor the performance of every customer agent at the end of each shift because this company installed an information infrastructure that provides this kind of visibility.

- The speed of reaction of companies that deliver remotely can be staggering. For example, Evalueserve, an Indian company that provides analytical work, such as market research, can respond to queries within two hours. So can two other Indian companies, OfficeTiger, for investment-research analytics, and 24/7 Customer, for market research or customer-problem resolution. This suggests that remote doesn't mean time delays. On the contrary: The entire global request/response system is fine-tuned to eliminate any latency. We may be seeing for the first time the building blocks for real-time management systems that transcend routine transactions. These systems are focused on abstract management questions. While this can be done in the United States, we argue that offshoring may open access to a larger base of talent, benefits in quality, and flexibility at significantly lower cost for companies that can execute global-resource leverage in the right way.

- Capacity to scale up or down selectively. Most offshore vendors can recruit and train staff rapidly. For example, Infosys in India receives 1 million job applications annually and recruits 12,000 people with only 30 human-resources professionals. The company can train 4,000 people simultaneously in its new training facility. So, Infosys can scale up rapidly for its outsourcing clients. On the other hand, the company can scale down for any one client since no client represents more than 5% of the total work. Employees can be reassigned to other projects.
- The large, well-established outsourcing vendors in India offer world-class skills. Gaining access to those skills is critical for a large U.S. company intent on competing effectively through managerial innovations (see *Indian Market Booms, But Changes Loom*).

It's obvious that outsourcing isn't just about cutting costs; building processes and capabilities for global-resource leverage will emerge as a fundamental managerial innovation. To focus on the cost issue to the exclusion of the managerial innovation potential offshoring provides is a risk no company should take.

C.K. Prahalad, a frequent contributor to *Optimize*, and M.S. Krishnan are professors at the University of Michigan Business School. Please send comments on this article to *optimizeletters@cmp.com*.

3Qs with Jim Hilton

OUTSOURCING BY THE NUMBERS

With more than 1,100 brokers in 25 countries handling $300 billion and more than a million trades annually, The Prebon Yamane Group of Companies has its IT work cut out for it. Jim Hilton, head of business planning and product management, told Optimize *associate editor Anne Donker why the brokerage, based in Jersey City, N.J., outsources some of its critical applications.*

Q: *What projects are you outsourcing?*

A: *In our business, it all comes down to connecting to our customers, and technology plays a central role in that. Currently, 15% of our technology work is outsourced to a third party to bring faster processing to our customers. That means we need to automate all post-transaction activities. To that end, we've outsourced development of a mission-critical application to Exigen Group's Latvian office, which will develop a new order-management service application. Our customers connect to us primarily by phone, so we decided to develop applications that can automate the complete transaction process as much as possible. We want to speed up transactions by capturing, distributing, and managing all information electronically. Our partner has a team of 15 experienced developers working full-time on this. It will save us a lot of time and effort. By 2006, we want at least 60% of all our transactions to use this application.*

Q: *How can businesses control intellectual property when they're outsourcing?*

A: *First, make sure you know which part of the intellectual property is important to you, and which part isn't. It's not always to your economic advantage to insist on hanging onto the ownership of intellectual property. If the product is intrinsic to your business because it gives you a distinct competitive advantage, of course you'd consider keeping ownership of the intellectual property. Otherwise,* *we actually encourage our outsourcing partner to make the application available to others. That way, they can maintain it for us, but we're not 100% responsible for the costs.*

Q: ***What are some of the pitfalls of offshore outsourcing?***

A: *There's a lot of hype surrounding outsourcing. The first thing is to take a step back and ask why you want to go that route. The No. 1 goal should be to get your product to market as quickly as possible, in a time frame that suits your budget. Accomplishing this may involve outsourcing, but outsourcing in itself shouldn't be the mandate.*

Second, never outsource your mission-critical projects without a tryout project first. Establishing a good working relationship and confidence in the people you'll be dealing with is critical.

Third, find a partner familiar with your business. This will save time, which translates into cost savings.

Fourth, be prepared to actively manage the relationship. Allocate staff to keep an eye on the project and its progress. Many businesses that outsource expect to get something delivered back to them exactly as they intended, without being actively involved. I believe one of the critical ingredients in outsourcing successfully is being proactive about managing the relationship.

Bush Lays Off Congress; Will Outsource Lawmaking to India?

JAY SLUPESKY

The Baked Beaver

Washington—Citing the growing cost of running the Federal government and the need to cut costs in order to reduce the budget deficit, President Bush announced today that he was laying off all 535 members of Congress and transferring lawmaking operations to a legislative support center in Bangalore, India. "Hey, outsourcing is the way to go these days," said Bush at an impromptu news conference where he announced the decision, adding, "the American people want to see less government waste. Since every one of those ex-Congressmen had a salary of $150,000, this move will cut our costs by over $80 million per year, and that's not even counting what we'll save on health insurance and retirement plans." Sources indicate that the Indian replacements will be paid approximately $250 per month.

The outcry from the newly laid-off Senators and Representatives was swift. Ex-California Senator Diane Feinstein said, "This is absolutely outrageous. How can a bunch of replacements over in India run Congress? What do they know about filibusters and committee hearings?" As she was being escorted out of the Hart Senate Office Building by U.S. Capitol Police officers, Feinstein complained that the newly-terminated lawmakers were only given ten minutes to clean out their desks and leave the building. "I think it's a great idea," said Vice President Dick Cheney, speaking from a secure, undisclosed location. "The American people were fed up with that expensive do-nothing Congress which didn't always give the President everything he asked for. Our new Indian replacements will be much more cooperative to the President, which is what we all want." Asked whether the outsourcing may be unconstitutional, Cheney noted, "That's up to the Supreme Court to decide, but as you know, they usually see things our way."

The new members of Congress seem thrilled with the attention they are receiving. Speaking from the offices of All-India Legislative Support Centre Ltd. in Bangalore, new Mississippi Senator Ramchandra Shektar Gupta told reporters, "The Indian people are very hard working and we will do our best as U.S. Congressmen and Congresswomen. And we are going to have some fun too. Just think: we have $2 trillion of the American taxpayers' money to spend!"

Project Management Office (PMO)

Chapter 19 Contents

Chapter Overview

The early roots of a centralized project process came from the U.S. Army in the 1980s. Since that time, the concept has been widely accepted across much of the IT industry. Depending upon the survey source, approximately one-half of all U.S. organizations have some form of a centralized project management function in place. The term has now been recognized by the *PMBOK® Guide* and, at this point, it shows all signs of becoming a strategic organizational project management component for most organizations. Some of the organizational drivers that supported this increased popularity were the growing size, complexity, and identified failure rate of IT projects during the 1990s. The typical initial high-level goals for a PMO are:

- Improve project efficiency.
- Cut overall IT costs.
- Improve project delivery (for example, time and cost).

The primary issue in attempting to improve a broad organizational process is how to do it. Installing any control-oriented activity in an organization is often resisted by the operational levels, and the PMO function has that potential. Conversely, simply enumerating the goals and passing them on to the various project teams is not a feasible approach either. Thus, the character of the PMO has to be somewhat centralized in nature. The organizational design issue becomes one of how much centralization is feasible and what tasks are assigned to this group. Unfortunately, the term "PMO" does not have a singular definition across organizations. Beyond the political ramifications of placing a control type function over the various project teams, there are also issues of the related functional breadth and scope that limit how quickly one could install a full-function PMO. It is important to recognize that a PMO-type function creates stress on existing processes in an organization and, for that reason, will generally require an incremental implementation strategy.

PMO Functions

As previously written, there is not a standard definition of PMO functions in an organization. However, there is a family of functions that fit PMO theory. Only time will tell if these actually are embraced in broad segments of organizations. A list of potential PMO design and operational functions follows:

1. Standardized processes and methods for project development.
2. A formal archiving system to capture lessons learned.
3. Administrative support for project teams.
4. Assistance or management activities in staffing projects.
5. Training programs for project teams.
6. Consulting and mentoring of teams.
7. Evaluating and managing the resource capacity issues related to a project.
8. Tracking and communicating project status to appropriate stakeholders.
9. Aiding or managing the alignment of IT and business goals.
10. Performing project quality reviews.
11. Performing post-implementation reviews.
12. Managing technical resource capacity for project efforts.
13. Managing the current and work-in-progress IT portfolio.

A review of this potential list of PMO responsibilities reveals the depth and complexity of the full function. If we distill these broad work activities into a brief set of objectives, then three general attributes surface:

1. Doing things the same way across the organization.
2. Defining a process to better identify appropriate projects.
3. Being more analytic in project control.

So, a general operational goal for a PMO is pretty clear. What is not so clear is the local meaning of this term when used in a specific organization.

Maturation Process

If an organization decided to implement the full complement of PMO functions it would require years of work. The normal implementation strategy is to pick out the most pressing need for the organization and initially focus the PMO on that target. As time goes on and the concept proves positive, more functions are added in priority order resulting in a maturation process. Similar to other maturity models, the PMO maturity model can be translated into a similar maturity scale. Hill describes the various potential functions of a PMO, and they can be categorized as follows: [Hill, 2003]

Stage 1—Project Office (oversight)
Stage 2—Basic PMO (project control)
Stage 3—Standard PMO (process support)
Stage 4—Advanced PMO (process improvement)
Stage 5—Center of Excellence (strategic alignment)

The five stages summarized above imply increasing involvement of the PMO function in the overall operational project environment. Another implication of the maturation scale is the increasing level of control over project selection and internal process. Finally, the list points out the variability in the use of this term. We need to recognize that the term PMO could mean any of the five stages with a highly variable underlying definition.

It is interesting to note that one of the readings in this section, *PMOs: Projects in Harmony*, outlines yet a different maturity scale view. This point again highlights the fact that there is no universal definition of maturity steps. The key concept of PMO maturity is that the lowerscale levels focus on critical, broad enterprise project problems, while higher levels move the organization toward achieving the more broad aspects of formal alignment with business goals. At the top maturity level, the organization would be fully integrated in its business and IT views. At this level project slates would be mapped to the business goals in such a manner as to optimize their value to the enterprise and project teams would be developing their products in a standardized manner. At this upper point the organization would be fully optimized with all of the positive results outlined in this text. One obviously does not move from stage one maturity to the top scale quickly. Organizations should anticipate at least a three-to-five year effort to grow an efficient PMO that deals with all project activities. Even then, the effort will require dedicated resources and significant support from senior management.

Do PMOs Add Value?

Control and standardization strategies often sound like great ideas, but somewhere along the implementation trail, the villains of bureaucratic communication and flexibility sabotage the goal. Wells, Dai, and Kwak at George Washington University undertook a research effort to deal with the question of whether the PMO concept was achieving its goals. The survey results are both interesting and somewhat controversial. Some of the key highlights from this study are summarized below: [Wells]

1. The use of PMOs is on the rise since 1995.
2. There was a low correlation in the existence of a PMO and project success.
3. There was a relatively high correlation between the use of an organization-wide, standard project management methodology and project success.
4. There was a low correlation between the use of a formal project archive and project success.
5. The range of services provided by PMOs varied widely.

The most disturbing finding in this study was the low correlation between the existence of a PMO and project success. If we analyze this finding, one possible conclusion would be that a PMO adds unnecessary expense and bureaucracy to an already complex environment. An alternative interpretation is that the maturation process is longer than first thought, meaning that it takes time for the organization to measure the positive results. One other potential factor that might surface could be the required role of senior management in achieving success. For example, the PMO will produce more proficient project tracking, but someone besides the PMO will have to act on the data presented. However, it is clear that more needs to be understood about the factors surrounding this organizational entity.

Placing extra non-value-added requirements on the project team could result in a negative benefit for a central function. We did see this effect in the 1980s with cumbersome standardized methodologies forced on the project team. Regardless of the strategy, there must be care taken to ensure that it results in positive contributions to the goal set. Regardless of the method, the requirement for the needed attributes will most likely evolve to a PMO-like structure for most organizations. The challenge is how to keep it from being excessive overhead.

Conclusion

PMOs are destined to be a significant part of the future enterprise landscape. They are now perceived to be the operational keystone to move an organization forward along the lines outlined here. Also, there are signs that many organizations are impressed by early PMO results and are looking at ways to expand the approach to other parts of the organizational project environment (that is, construction, training, etc.).

It is recognized that the PMO activity is tightly intertwined with several other macro processes that have to be tuned and incorporated into an integrated global management process. This implies that PMOs will be dealing with issues such as portfolio management, IT governance, value analysis (ROI concepts), progress tracking metrics/benchmarks, status report systems, development methodologies, technical resource capacity management (including outsourcing), and basic project management. Whether they do this with some authority, or more as a staff function, is yet to be seen.

Readings

The first reading in this section, "Putting the *P* in PMO," by Jim Harris, outlines the basic goals and structure of a PMO. In the second reading, Shawn Bohner lays out a maturity view of PMO in "PMOs: Projects in Harmony." The third reading in this set is titled "So Where Do I Start? Building the Effective PMO," by Mark Mullaly. This reading is the most detailed of the set and takes the reader through the full life cycle of a PMO evolution. The fourth and final reading in this section is authored by Tim Jaques and is titled "Imaginary Obstacles: Getting Over PMO Myths." The reading's implication is that there are segments of the organization that are resisting the implementation of a PMO, and these myths are the most-often-heard reasons given for why it is not a good idea.

References

DeMontmollin, Vincent. "The Schlumberger IT Project Office Experience." 2003, Published by Pacific Edge Software, Inc., Reference *www.pacificedge.com*.

Hill, Gerard. *The Complete Project Management Handbook*, Auerback, 2003.

Ludwig, Charles. "Making a Goal of Best Practices." October 8, 2003, Reference *www.gantthead.com*.

Well, William, G. Jr. and Christin Dai. "Project Management Offices." July 2001. reference *www.esi-intl.com*.

Viali, Walter. Principal in PMOToGo, An interview. Houston, TX, September 1, 2004.

Putting the *P* in PMO

JIM HARRIS

December 26, 2001. Copyright © 2005 *gantthead.com*. All rights reserved. The URL for this article is: *http://www.gantthead.com/article.cfm?ID=72185*.

Jim Harris has more than 30 years of managerial and technical experience in IT system planning, implementation, and operations in both government and commercial sectors. He has extensive experience in the areas of life cycle project implementation, cost and revenue accountability, and client satisfaction. He is presently the director for the planning and program development of IT enhancements for a major U.S. airline. Jim holds a BSBA degree from the University of Arkansas and a MBA from New York Institute of Technology.

Recently, I was asked what my profession is. I replied that I am a program manager. "Oh, you develop software!" "No, I am a program manager that . . . ," I started, but then paused and said, "I am a project manager." The individual understood and went on to ask what type of projects. I felt I was in a time warp.

So, what is the P in PM, and for that matter, PMO? What is really being managed: project, program, or portfolio? Has the PM function and its growth been typecast to yesteryear and rendered immobile? This article will explore the murky environment and a possible new direction for the PMO of the 21st century.

Evolution of the Project Office

The genesis of the PM profession started with individual projects, but project management has come a long way since the early 1980s.

In a Gartner Group strategic analysis report on Project Office (August, 2000), Matt Light states that "more than 40 percent of client organizations have implemented some form of project office to 'professionalize' project management for applications development, infrastructure change, and large-scale systems migrations (e.g., year 2000)." He continues: "Their goal is a base level improvement in project completion against schedule and budget estimates, while delivering the expected functionality with satisfactory quality. World-class organizations complete nearly 90 percent of their projects within 10 percent of budget and time estimates." It is understandable why more and more organizations are establishing some type of central office to manage the delivery of their product and services. But this is not a new or revolutionary concept.

The U.S. Army initiated the concept of a central program office when it started designating senior military officers and government officials as program executive officers back in the mid-1980s. Each major program (e.g., Switched Systems, Battlefield Intelligence, etc.) was assigned to a program executive office (PEO). The PEO managed the overall program and supporting projects from need identification through contract development, source selection, and final implementation. The PEO was a forerunner of today's program management office. The value of the PEO can best be summarized by its longevity as a cost-effective mechanism for the military to implement programs and projects.

In comparison, the PMO can have the same effect on a commercial enterprise. Almost 20 years later, the concept and organizational placement of the PMO are still being discussed within the commercial arena.

The evolution of project management from an ad hoc approach to the acknowledgement of the PMO as a shared enterprise resource led me to examine the role of the PMO, its logical mission, and where this shared enterprise resource should be in the organizational structure.

Role

If we accept the PMO as an enterprise resource and the synergy point for project management, then we must also recognize it as the natural point to manage the portfolio of programs and acknowledge its core mission of managing the delivery process. Expanding the mission statement of the PMO to include portfolio management requires the participation of the PMO in the corporate planning process and the resulting development of the corporate and departmental road maps. The historical absence of the PMO function from this process has resulted in PMOs being isolated and unaware of the corporate significance of the projects being implemented.

Establishing this planning linkage permits the PMO to manage business units, complete program portfolios and present a total view of all the programs, i.e., the state of the entire portfolio, to senior management in a single voice. With this mission, the PMO becomes the center point of a robust and fully coordinated structure for program planning and execution.

Mission

The PMO mission includes:
- Facilitation of the strategic planning process
- Program/project management
- Governance for the management
- Implementation of the program portfolio and projects

The PMO is the business unit's nerve center for the planning, programming development, and execution of programs to meet long-range goals and objectives set by executive management.

This expanded mission can only become reality with the removal of long-standing perceptions by various levels of management that the PMO is only a mid-management coordination office for individual projects, rather than a value-added enterprise resource dedicated to the corporate process of planning, program development, and execution.

Organizational Placement

The PMO's expanded mission removes it from what can only be considered a "nowhere else to put it" direct reporting scheme to a recognized asset for both senior management and business units, thus giving it the same recognition and voice as other major departments.

Central management of the program portfolio by the PMO provides a clear understanding of the portfolio's relationship to corporate long-range plans and the interaction and dependency of other business-approved programs. This visible linkage also permits early identification and coordination to minimize risk to completion of programs and meeting corporate goals.

The PMO Structure Model

The PMO manager has two primary missions, corporate portfolio manager and program manager, through three functional departments:

1. Strategic Planning and Program Development would facilitate the strategic long-range planning and road map development process. In addition, it would assist functional departments to build the business case for the program, including cost estimates and the establishment of measurable goals and objectives.
2. Program Management would tactically implement approved programs. Depending on the size of the program, either a single PM or a team would be assigned to the functional department through final delivery and post-project activities.
3. Standards and Training would manage the governance of the enterprise PMO. It would establish PM corporate standards for the execution of the delivery management process from the development of the project plan to the project close-out process. Governance is also applied to both internal and external training. Internal training would include the corporate strategic planning and program development process and continued professional development of the PMO staff. This department would establish standards for the preparation and delivery of training to clients, either for stand-alone training sessions or user training for the product being delivered.

The establishment of a PMO as a shared enterprise asset fits snuggly into a firm whose corporate focus is the delivery of a single product or aligned products. It is not uncommon for large enterprises to have identifiable business units that deliver a unique product or service. In this instance, I propose that a PMO be established within each business unit. This provides the value-added resource focused on a unique final product.

Executive Corporate Planning and Development

Multiple PMOs provide a new but manageable dimension in the planning, program development, and execution process. A proposed model begins at the executive management level with a steering committee composed of the executive managers from each major business unit and chaired by the corporate planning and development manager. This executive leadership team develops a multi-year plan detailing corporate direction, goals, and objectives. These mission statements are the basis for the development of the business unit's portfolio, consisting of major program initiatives.

The corporate portfolio is managed by the corporate development/planner in terms of budget constraints, priority/criticality to meet a specific business objective, and support to or dependence on other external programs. This committee may include the corporate portfolio manager, who:

- Issues charters for inter-departmental programs (includes designation of lead PMO).
- Issues guidelines to be adhered to by Departmental PMO, such as communications or lessons learned/process improvement procedures.
- Assembles data summary information provided from departmental data warehouse.
- Provides topic of status reports, format and frequency of reports.
- Chairs executive steering committee for approval of programs submitted by functional departments.

The next lower tier would be a functional planning committee having representatives from the business unit's PMO. Here, the broad vision statements and objectives in the corporate plan are distilled to specific major programs/projects for the various business units. Corporate priorities and interaction(s) of each program with others are identified. The functional tier is chaired by the designated lead PMO. The output of this committee is the corporate road map that shows a clear, logical path of program implementation to achieve corporate objectives. In addition, the road map identifies the linkage of departmental programs to the overall corporate goal.

The third level of the model is the business unit PMO. The PMO in this model is structured as discussed above, with planning and program development focused on department-wide initiatives and the assigned portion of the corporate road map identified in the functional planning session. The PMO planning and program development function would continue to identify items that would be submitted as part of the corporate call for departmental program initiatives.

In this model, if a department's product or service crosses over to other business units, the business unit PMO would also provide a horizontal orientation that reaches across to other departments, thus providing assistance to establish program initiatives requiring its product or service. This internal client channel permits the departmental PMO to establish a business partner relationship with other business units. (A good example is the use of IT services by other business services. The IT/PMO would identify individuals knowledgeable in product-specific business units. The IT/PMO representative would then provide assistance to his assigned business unit during its IT planning and program development process to meet desired goals.)

Summary

In the last 20 years, project management has experienced tremendous growing pains as it has moved from the sink-or-swim proposition of the past to today's structured process orientation. But nothing has been more painful than achieving recognition as a value-added enterprise asset.

The time has come to place the PMO function in its proper organizational alignment, i.e., as a major department combining the corporate planning process with effective delivery of products and services. In addition, the PMO can provide external clients with traditional client services for the enterprise as a whole or for respective enterprise business units.

PMOs: Projects in Harmony

SHAWN BOHNER

Increasingly, IT executives face initiatives like e-business, customer relationship management (CRM), and supply chain integration that demand close tracking of resources, dependencies, and risks across the plethora of projects spawned by IT groups and lines of business (LOBs). While PMOs waned in the mid-1980's, Y2K efforts have sparked a renewed interest at the highest corporate levels. The effectiveness of these PMOs has varied widely, but a pattern of maturity has emerged that gives IT executives insight into exploitation strategies.

Shawn A. Bohner, Vice President of META Group's IT Performance Engineering and Measurement Strategies (PEMS) Service, is internationally recognized for his work in software metrics, impact analysis, maintenance, modernization, and reengineering. Dr. Bohner is a regularly invited speaker at Software and Information Technology events. He is a Vice Chair for the IEEE Technical Council on Software Engineering, member of the Journal on Software Maintenance *Editorial Board, and is past-Chair of the ACM Professional Development Committee in Washington, D.C.*

Our research shows that over 55% of IT organizations have plans to transition their Y2K PMOs into permanent PMOs for supporting their mounting mega-projects. While many organizations are targeting an enterprise-wide PMO, fewer than 5% of IT organizations have actually deployed resources to do so. Our research also shows that the range of effectiveness (as measured by on-time, on-budget, on-quality products) for PMOs varies as much as 15 to 1. Over 30% of projects are cancelled, while fewer than 20% are successful as defined by schedule, cost, and quality parameters.

During 2000–2002, as IT organizations realize increasing value from key program management practices, PMOs will advance in maturity. We believe that over 45% will be stymied at the lowest level (defined by low project management capability and high variance) by not getting corporate commitment to invest in key practices. Over 20% will attempt to over-invest trying to do the entire journey to the higher levels in less than 2 years (most failing to advance beyond level 2). About 15% of the PMOs will advance to higher levels (Level 4 and 5) in 2 to 3 years, but it will be accomplished as a journey through the lower levels first.

Project Management Maturity

Less mature PMOs are simply a corral around the project managers so that basic reporting becomes consistent. At the other end of the spectrum are mature PMOs where traditional project issues (resource management, project prioritization, planning and tracking, project risk management, and the like) are coordinated to generate better economies of scale along with vendor, training, procurement, outsourcing, and risk management at the corporate level. Management moves from managing in-the-small projects to managing in-the-large initiatives and business portfolios.

While a few instances of capability maturity models for project management exist, none are complete or relevant enough to be accepted by the project management community at large. For practices, the Project Management Body of Knowledge (PMBOK) has provided a reasonably well-accepted framework for project managers. However, IT executives must be able to characterize the capabilities and practices for project management performance from the corporate perspective.

The PMO CMM

The Program Management Office Capability Maturity Model (PMO-CMM) (Figure 2 [19-1]) provides a maturity framework from which to systematically advance an organization's program management capabilities. The practices outlined in the key process area concentrations represent those observed in various Program Management Offices at different levels of effectiveness. Patterns emerged from our study of these organizations indicating that there is more emphasis of the practices at strategic inflection points in their development. The more mature PMOs had a broader span of influence for managing projects and programs.

While concept of this model is based loosely on the Software Engineering Institute's Capability Maturity Model, there are details that do not conform. The PMO-CMM has not been reviewed or confirmed by the Software Engineering Institute.

LEVEL 1 PMO—INITIAL

As with process maturity (espoused effectively by the Software Engineering Institute's IDEAL model), the initial level reflects a high dependence on project management heroes, the individual PMs that when they are on the project, the likelihood of success is considerably higher. Unfortunately, there is significant diversity in PM practice resulting in project performance variability that often leads to low confidence among LOBs. The PMO is more a label applied to the group of PMs that are available to the myriad initiatives tasked to the IT organization. A typical key process area is acquiring PMs to replace those drawn away by the competition or promoted into other areas of the organization.

LEVEL 2 PMO—STABLE

Since the PMO is all about management, the transition to Level 2 is a strategic inflection point since it indicates stability. The basics of project management are in place so that the project performance becomes more predictable and worrisome variability is under control. At Level 2, the PMO is effective primarily at the single project level. While they will invariably face multiple project issues, their zone of project performance will be best on single, albeit large, projects. As multiple projects persist, coordination issues will dominate the problems list.

LEVEL 3 PMO—DEFINED

At Level 2, project performance was not improved greatly; rather, it was stabilized. At Level 3, macro-level practices are defined to boost project performance. It is no longer sufficient to be stable; instead, the objective is to establish common best practices that will lead to overall organizational project performance. Local optimums of an individual project (e.g., favorite

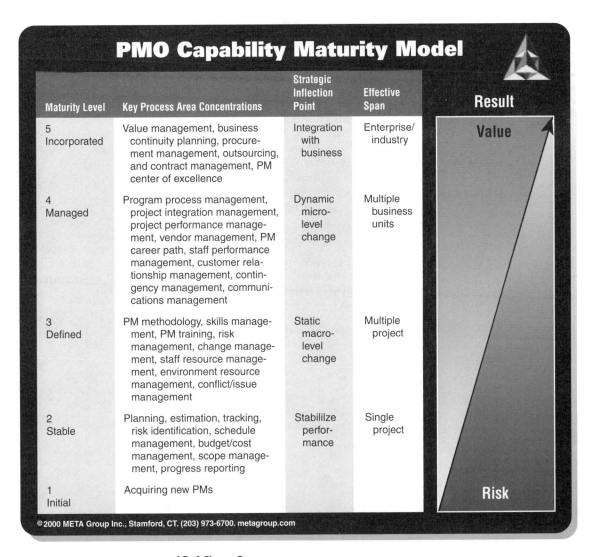

19-1 Figure 2.

project management reporting style or project estimation tool) are discouraged in favor of common approaches to attain economies of scale.

LEVEL 4 PMO—MANAGED

Level 4 is the level where a Project Management Office moves to a Program Management Office. With key PM practices in place, PM activities move from static improvements to dynamic change reflecting the LOB's perspective. The key practices at Level 4 move the bar up for PMs to be handled as portfolios of initiatives, ultimately tuning the program of projects to the business needs.

LEVEL 5 PMO—INCORPORATED

Once a PMO is adept at dynamic management of LOB initiatives, it is prepared to integrate into and support other corporate-wide capabilities such as Procurement, contracts, and value management. These represent areas necessary to manage the portfolio of corporate initiatives and manage business continuity risks. At Level 5, Program Management becomes a corporate competency bringing value through risk entrepreneuralism.

While Y2K catalyzed many PMOs, many of them are readily characterized as a Level 1. Advancing to upper maturity levels reduces the business risks and increases visibility into increasingly valuable decisions. More mature project management offices will enable enterprises to better assess business risk and to improve IT project rates.

Bottom Line

Since all PMOs are not created equal, IT organizations must assess their maturity to determine appropriate performance levels and plan for their improvement overtime. Otherwise, key IT initiatives will risk failure and lost value from ineffective program and project management.

So Where Do I Start? Building The Effective PMO

MARK E. MULLALY, PMP

Mark Mullaly is president of Interthink Consulting Incorporated, an organizational development and change firm specializing in the creation of effective organizational project management solutions. Since 1990, it has worked with companies throughout North America to develop, enhance, and implement effective project management tools, processes, structures, and capabilities. Mark is also the author of Interthink's Project Management Process Model (PM2), a maturity model that has been used to assess over 550 companies worldwide.

As I have assumed responsibility for gantthead's Program Management Office department, I have tried to raise some of the fundamental challenges and issues that the typical PMO faces in an organizational context. While admittedly theoretical in some regards, the first few columns have endeavoured to lay the groundwork for a more involved discussion of developing PMOs. This column begins a multi-part series that addresses the practical steps and considerations in setting up a PMO in today's organizations.

One of the greatest challenges that we face as we are tapped to develop a PMO capability is the not-so-rhetorical question, "Where do I start?" As some of my earlier columns have discussed, there are as many different interpretations of the purpose and role of the PMO as there are companies—and arguably, probably a few more. While the stock consulting answer "It depends" is tempting here, it doesn't necessarily provide a whole lot of value.

The best advice that I can give anyone as they undertake the development of a PMO is this: treat it as you would any other project. It is, in fact, one of the more complex projects that any of us will manage. The PMO brings the dimensions of process, structure, organization, tools, and business transformation into one highly visible, strategically important initiative. Because of this complexity, it is easy to get bogged down in myriad details, spending so much time analyzing the problem and its causes that we forget to implement solutions that can help work toward their resolution.

As with any project, the first place we need to start is with an understanding of what has happened in the past to bring us to today. What were the drivers that led up to a PMO being seen as a good idea? While there may be one single factor that finally triggered the initiative, this is typically the proverbial straw that broke the camel's back. It provides the rationale and the reason, but not necessarily the full explanation. There may well be a number of reasons—from failed projects to consultant recommendations to scathing audit reports—that collectively bring the organization to the realization that this whole PMO idea might have some merit.

The more we understand the background leading up to today, the better positioned we are to answer the next question: Just what will define success? And "It depends" is not a viable answer. The development of a PMO is, in most companies, an expensive investment that is not without risk.

Any organization that undertakes such a comprehensive initiative expects to see a return that goes well beyond feeling better about how its projects are managed. But what is this return? How will it be measured? How will we know when we have attained it?

For many, the success of the PMO is similar to what defines great art: we may not be able to describe it, but we know it when we see it. Success measures must be objective and quantifiable. It may be defined in terms of a reduction in overruns, delays, or support costs of the projects. Success may be reflected in an increased maturity of the organization. We may define it based upon the percentage cost of managing the project relative to its cost of delivery. Or we may evaluate the satisfaction of our customers, sponsors, and even our project managers in delivering the project. Whatever the means, the measures must be objective, defined, and tied back to the fundamental rationale for the PMO's development.

With success criteria defined, and clear means of measuring them identified, we can begin to take steps toward their attainment. Critical for success is that these steps be tangible, visible, and discrete. They must produce results quickly, and they must make a visible impact—even on a pilot basis, for a single project or a handful of initiatives. It is tempting to define a complete strategy and proceed single-mindedly toward its attainment, but it is a temptation that is to be resisted. As with any organizational change effort, people need to perceive value and feel ownership. Change cannot happen in a vacuum. This evolution must take place in the real world, and the successes and failures that are encountered need to influence future progress. By committing to incrementally delivering value, our constituents not only are able to provide feedback, but they are provided with tangible evidence that the focus of the improvement effort is upon helping them.

Finally, as we proceed with development, it is critical that we evaluate success—objectively and often. It is a product of human nature that incremental change is typically not viewed objectively. Once we realize the compelling logic and value of a particular approach, it becomes difficult for us to remember a time when we didn't do it that way. As the idea of a project plan takes root, we can't imagine not writing one—it just makes too much sense. To measure how far we have come, we need to know where we were when we set out. A journey of a thousand miles begins with a single step. Repeat as necessary.

Imaginary Obstacles: Getting Over PMO Myths

TIM JAQUES

Tim Jaques is a consultant with Canal Bridge Consulting, a leader in strategy implementation. His work focuses on performance management within the project environment.

Tips for PMO Implementation:

Create a repository
The PMO would be an instant hit if every project in the company were cataloged and maintained in a repository.

Use inexpensive technology and resident knowledge
Intranets, databases, networks, and templates—these critical technologies can be readily implemented in most organizations.

Become self-service
Let the users feed and water the PMO. Drive the ownership of the PMO down to the project staff, the folks who will make or break the PMO.

Focus on everyday transactions
Nobody gets away clean. Make every transaction a way to increase the knowledge and support the strategy.

With so many companies adopting the project-based approach to completing work, it is no wonder that the concept of the project management office, or PMO, is gaining popularity. The concept is not new, but recent incarnations of the PMO have proven effective in marshaling resources and focusing communications across the organization. While the PMO concept suggests a strategic and tactical center of operations that delivers value across projects, many companies are reluctant to implement a PMO because of perceived barriers to implementation. Three myths have kept companies from exploring the benefits of the PMO:

- The PMO is cost-prohibitive.
- The PMO has a limited ability to operate across a wide range of projects.
- The PMO is just another layer of bureaucracy, adding little value to the organization.

However, establishing a scalable PMO—one that expands vertically into the organization and horizontally across functional areas—is a measured approach that will increase the likelihood of successfully implementing projects.

So, what is a project management office really? One recent article in the *Project Management Journal* described the PMO as a "combination of managerial, administrative, training, consulting, and technical services for projects within an organization and for upper management." [Wells, April 2000] At its heart, the PMO is an organizational entity that supports project-based work with communications, training, and leadership capabilities to effect lower costs, reduced risks, and successful outcomes. A public-sector PMO was recently chartered to "develop, document, and publish a statewide project management methodology, standards, tools, templates, processes, and procedures," and also "operate the Project Management Mentoring Program (PMMP)." [New York State—Office of Technology Planning Web site] The trend has been toward utilizing the PMO as a link between the project objectives and the organization's strategy. The December 2000 issue of *PMNetwork* highlighted the role of the "Strategic Program Management Office" [Eidsmoe], as an interface providing essential project management capabilities that map to the organization's strategic plan.

Given this trend of strategically oriented PMOs, implementing a scaled project office that is initially limited in scope, technology, and service offerings can minimize the pitfalls embedded within each of the PMO myths.

Myth #1: Implementing a PMO Is Cost Prohibitive

Planning and implementing a PMO is not an inherently expensive proposition. PMO capabilities can range from providing templates, training, and communications via a self-service Web site, to operating a real-time project office that manages resources, tracks schedules, and maintains budgets. Regardless of size, many organizations have the essential components of a PMO within their current makeup. Consider the technology required to implement the PMO. Most organizations have word processing, spreadsheet, and presentation applications from which communication and deliverable tracking templates can be developed and posted to a Web site or server for use by the project teams. Project management software forms the cornerstone in the fledgling PMO as an interface for reporting progress both within and across projects. Using existing technologies like Web sites and document templates, the PMO can rapidly provide benefits to the project teams via self-service collection and distribution of information.

Planning a PMO entails developing the processes, policies, and content that will drive the delivery of the PMO products and services. Using the knowledge and skills already in the company can dramatically decrease the costs and ensure that the services provided are reasonable and practical. PMO design should focus on those critical areas where a PMO can add the most value to its customer base. For instance, maintaining a repository of project plans directly supports critical project dependencies and can be implemented with minimal expense. In this case, templates can be used to gather critical project data at regular intervals—an effective and low-cost method that can be employed almost immediately. Additional cost savings can be achieved through strategic staffing or part-time resource allocation where each role is defined with accountabilities and deliverables prior to reallocating the resources to the PMO project.

Table 1 [19-2] describes the key roles in developing and implementing a PMO.

Whatever the budget may be for the PMO, many companies can maximize the expertise and existing technologies to offer a core set of services that can be of great value to the organization.

Myth #2: Projects in the Organization Are Too Varied to Implement a PMO

What do a network expansion project, HR training program, performance measurement project, and business reengineering project all have in common? For starters, these seemingly disparate projects have common elements that can be managed together in the PMO. Through the implementation of a project management methodology, the PMO can promote efficiencies across projects in the areas of cost, resources, and scheduling. A methodology standardizes the structure of managing projects and

Staff	Planning Role	Implementation Role
Executive sponsor	Secure funding Make go/no go decisions Link strategy with PMO objectives	Integration across other organizational strategic initiatives Advocate the PMO to other executives
PMO project manager	Oversee content development Specify technology, staffing, and rollout requirements Oversee PM methodology development	Run the day-to-day operation Be responsible for all PMO deliverables Champion PM methodology implementation Implement continuous improvement process changes
PMO staff	Develop content (e.g., templates, forms) Document methodology Solicit and document customer requirements	Maintain project deliverables, implement upgrades, solve problems Maintain all project documentation files
Company project managers	Provide subject matter expertise and guidance on methodology and PMO operation Agree to PMO concept and operation	Access and use the PMO as agreed upon Implement PM methodology Implement PM training via the PMO
Customer	Provide project management support requirements	Provide critical feedback on PMO product and services Support PMO continuous improvement proces

19-2 Table 1. PMO Staffing

sequences the project phases so that there is predictability and more efficient utilization of resources. A PM methodology also reduces the risk of cost and schedule overruns by promoting a deliverable-based program for every project. The project management office focuses project deliverables into discrete, measurable data that can be used by a variety of stakeholders throughout the organization. In this fashion, the project office can effectively service many projects across a wide range of disciplines. With a little research, many off-the-shelf methodologies can be readily implemented, like PMI's OPM3 (Organizational Project Management Maturity Model), or the PMBOK.

Managers who are contemplating a PMO should consider implementing a PM methodology in one functional area of the company—like IT or production, for example. This "pilot" strategy provides a venue to test and refine the methodology for a given set of project deliverables, while offering an excellent training opportunity for the managers. Managers would do well to choose an area that they know with authority and adopt a well-known methodological approach that can be tailored to meet the specifics of the environment. After a success, the methodology and the PMO can then move in concert to another functional area of the organization and modify the approach yet again. This course of action complements the low-cost, scalable approach, as described in Myth #1.

Myth #3: The PMO Is Just Another Layer of Bureaucracy, Adding Little Value to the Organization

Successful project offices adhere to two basic principles: provide value for the customer in every transaction, and support every phase of the project life cycle. Without these guiding tenants in place, the PMO will suffer from lack of use. Project managers are customers of the PMO, so it has to be easy for them to access the services and share information. As well, every transaction should provide value to the user, such as automatic notifications and reminders. These types of interactions need to be identified in the development stages and implemented over time. The PMO must also address every phase of the project life cycle to claim success. Why? Well, imagine having to choose which phases to incorporate and which to leave out of the PMO. There is value beyond the deliverables that a PMO serves, and this value is derived from supporting the projects in a comprehensive, timely manner. Within the scaled approach to implementation, a prioritized list of services should be offered. Many of these offerings overlap from phase to phase, so that a resource usage template, for instance, can add value from project scoping to closeout.

Cutting across the phases of the projects, three basic "value areas" should be explored to determine what value the PMO will bring to the organization. These value areas—communication, leadership, and training—address the benefits that are derived through operating a PMO. Activities in each of these areas should reveal the line of sight between the strategy and the project outcomes, and ultimately effect lower costs and smoother implementations. Communication activities include dissemination of project results to stakeholders, maintaining project plans, conducting roundtables, and gathering and disseminating project skill requirements. Leadership activities include prioritizing tasks, making decisions across projects, advocating on behalf of the projects and providing guidance to project managers. Training activities should address project management skill development and can be shared between the individual projects and the PMO. Table 2 [19-3] illustrates the value of communication, leadership, and training to the organization, the project manager, and the project itself.

Implementing a PMO does not require vast resources or technical expertise. A small, part-time staff can quickly open shop with a series of

Value Area	To the Organization...	To the Project Managers...	To the Project...
Project communication	• Channeled communications • Common project language in organization • Resource issues quickly identified	• Increased inter-project resource utilization • Concerns raised to executives in a timely manner	• Risk identification and mitigation • A common, consistent method of communications delivery
Project leadership	• Clarity of outcomes and objectives • Reduced risks	• Line of sight between project and organizational strategy	• Increased likelihood of project success • Advocacy for a given project
Project training	• Reduced costs • Increased likelihood of success	• Professional development • Networking	• Objectives met • Consistent application of methodology

19-3 Table 2. The Value Added PMO

templates, and a methodological approach to completing the work. Scalability is an essential component in developing the PMO, because many organizations phase in an office over several years, increasing the capabilities to match the organizational needs.

Project Portfolio Management

Chapter 20 Contents

Chapter Overview

This section contains material that is a continuation of the topic introduced as Business Alignment in Section I.4. The earlier section contained basic material designed to prepare the reader for the *PMBOK® Guide* discussions that were developed in Section II. Here, the topic is given more emphasis on how to pursue it in the enterprise, along with the more important management components.

Historically, IT projects have been spawned from a variety of sources, usually at middle levels in the organization and focused on their local needs. The net result was frequently an array of disjointed efforts that did not necessarily mesh with the overall enterprise goals. During the 1980s, it became increasingly obvious that IT expenditures needed to be viewed in much the same way as other capital-forming activities. In 1981, a classical article by Warren McFarland in the Harvard Business Review, titled "Portfolio Approach to Information Systems," outlined this concept to the business and IT community. This article postulated that IT investments should be viewed as a cohesive collection of initiatives focused on business objectives and managed similarly. The reasonableness of this concept was obvious and generally accepted, however, executing the related process was found to be difficult for a number of reasons. Early efforts to implement the underlying operational mechanics were stymied by the lack of available computer power and related software needed to process the data related to the process. In many cases, the internal operational processes did not even collect data that could be used in the analysis. Rectifying the measurement issue remains a challenge for most organizations.

Conceptually, the Portfolio Management process is needed by a PMO organization in order to have decision support information related to their business alignment activities. Dye and Pennypacker provide a working definition of project portfolio management:

"Project Portfolio Management is … the art and science of applying a set of knowledge, skills, tools, and techniques to a collection of projects in order to meet or exceed the needs and expectations of an organization's investment strategy." [Dye]

PPM also interacts with two more traditional processes in the IT environment. First, the existing legacy IT asset inventory defines a current system's operational cost and capability for the organization. The legacy base is continually under pressure to change as a result of technology and business dynamics. When a new initiative is approved, it is moved into a project management structure for execution and eventual migration to the asset base. So, project and portfolio management are cooperating to support the evolution of technology processes within the enterprise. This complex process manages the evolution of hardware, software, and networks to a different capability level (size, scope, and functionality). The primary link between these two functions is an enterprise planning and strategy process. It filters proposals to change the legacy state and moves the selected items into the work queue while attempting to optimize their collective value. This analysis process takes into account the initiative benefits, costs, and risks. At the core of the allocation process is the concept of diversification. Diversification helps spread investments between alternatives that contain varying tactical, strategic, and risk characteristics. The role in the PPM allocation process is to balance costs to undertake the project, the risks involved in the project, and the potential returns on the investment.

Several vendors have entered this market space with consulting skills and tools designed to jump-start the portfolio management process. One high-level exacerbating dilemma that seems to be common for IT organizations today is the continual tactical budget squeeze. A short-term focus on investment flows runs counter to the portfolio management goal of seeking long-term optimization of investment value. The financial analogy would be to invest as little as you can today and hope to achieve maximum long-term portfolio value. These goals run counter to one another. PacificEdge, one of the vendors in this area, labels these short- and long-term strategies as Run the Business (RTB) versus Grow and Transform the Business (GTB and TTB). The latter two goals would be strategic in nature and require current investment with longer-term payback, plus, most likely, increased risk.

Paul Harder offers us a comedic—a' la Jeff Foxworthy—list of ways you can tell if you might need PPM. His test list follows:

- If your organization's idea of the earned value of a project is the number of free T-shirts given by vendors at the end of the year, you might need PPM.
- If you ask how your new project meets the organization's strategic objectives, and you are told, "Well, this one won't lose money," you might need PPM.
- If you call a meeting to kick off a new project, only to find the room chock-full of senior managers all seeking credit and oversight, you might need PPM.

- If your organization thinks that resource management means seeing who is not asleep at their desk and assigning those people more work because they must have "free time," you might need PPM.
- If project schedules are kept on whiteboards around the office with big "DO NOT ERASE" signs on them, you might need PPM.
- If risk management in your organization means keeping a fire extinguisher close by during testing, you might need PPM.
- If your project ends and your organization considers a post-project review to be a keg party out back, you might need PPM.
- If a new project requires resources and your organization responds by seeing who's been surfing to "those" Web sites and putting them on YOUR project, you might need PPM.
- And finally, if approving a new project to update the corporate Web site requires approval from the president, CEO, CFO, CIO, board of directors, and 13 random people standing outside the building during a smoke break, you might need PPM. [Harder]

Although the listing above is a little facetious, the points made do highlight some Dilbert-like analogies for many organizations.

A more serious survey designed to define organizational readiness for portfolio management adds further insight into implementation constraints for this concept: [PacificEdge]

- 84% of the companies either do not do business cases for their IT projects at all, or just do them on a select few key projects.
- 83% of the companies are unable to adjust and align their budgets with business needs more than once or twice a year.
- More than 67% of IT organizations are not "market-ready"—benchmarking is done less frequently than once a year.
- 89% of companies are flying blind—virtually no metrics except for finance (measuring funds flow).
- 57% of companies perceive they are balancing the pressures of cost-cutting and IT effectiveness.

In order for IT organizations to prepare themselves for properly moving into a managed PPM domain, they pass through several transformation steps. PacificEdge summarizes these steps as follows: [PacificEdge]

- Restructure IT to a value-based organization, rather than a cost center.
- Structure IT as a business focused on producing products and services.
- Align IT with business strategies.
- Adopt an IT budgeting model that considers all projects as a portfolio of business investments.
- Involve key executives in the decision-making process.
- Define the key drivers for IT performance today and tomorrow.
- Use a disciplined assessment process based on metrics and benchmarking.

In order to begin the evolution through these transformation steps, it is necessary for IT to adopt a measurement attitude toward their work products and keep those measures visible in real-time for decision makers to deal with. Another attribute of this process is that the slate of project initiatives should balance between tactical, risk, and strategic goals. The PacificEdge report states that one company was able to produce a savings of $8.7 million in 18 months through more disciplined project investments. Savings of this magnitude will get senior management attention and help sell the concepts discussed here.

Readings

The first reading in this section is authored by Paul Harder and is titled "PPM and CMM: Kindred Spirits?" The reading maps parallels between these two concepts and shows the type of activities that an organization encounters as it moves through the levels of increasing maturity which support PPM. The second reading, by Cameron McGaughy, "Gartner Shines the Light on PPM," outlines impressions collected from a 2004 Gartner conference on this topic. The important idea reflected is that these impressions come from professionals who are struggling with PPM in their organizations. In this reading, we see the role of IT governance recognized as a key part of PPM. More on IT governance can be found in Chapter 21. Also, many of the topics discussed in this text weave in and out of each other. Various readings describe the interlinking between such areas as PPM, project management, PMO, and governance.

The final two-part reading by Lee Merkhofer, titled "Choosing the Wrong Portfolio of Projects," describes the project selection process from the standpoint of risk assessment and the optimum portfolio. Dr. Merkhofer's full discourse on this topic can be found on the referenced Web site.

There is strong evidence in the literature that PPM will represent a major IT industry initiative over the next several years, but we should expect the journey to be a difficult one given the breadth and scope of the underlying process. Terms such as PMO, alignment, governance, benchmarking and risk management will be companions to this activity. Thoughts on portfolio management are evolving rapidly now, and there are numerous excellent Web sources such as *www.portfoliomgt.org* that capture articles on this topic from many other sources and thereby simplify the search process.

References

Dye, Lowell D. and James S. Pennypacker (ed.). Project Portfolio Management, Center for Business Practices, West Chester, PA., 1999.

Harder, Paul. "What is Project Portfolio Management?" May 7, 2002, *www.gantthead.com*, Article 114344.

"IT Investment Management: Portfolio Management Lessons Learned," Meta Group, *www.metagroup.com*, 2002.

PacificEdge, "Project Portfolio Management." A presentation by PacificEdge, *www.pacificedge.com*, 2004.

PPM and CMM: Kindred Spirits?

PAUL HARDER

When considering advances in IT management in the last 30 years, several concepts come to mind. Rapid development opened the doors to faster development cycles. Global development organizations allowed for software and hardware to be created at any time in any location. Flat management structures and smaller teams allowed organizations to be more flexible and adaptive as the market changed.

Two concepts that have also changed the way organizations manage IT projects came into being during this time. Both grew out of different arenas but both have a complementary goal—that of improving IT organizations. Taken separately, project portfolio management (PPM) and the Capability Maturity Model (CMM) provide frameworks for evaluating different aspects of a company's IT projects. Together, however, the two form a unique alliance for maximizing returns on a company's investments.

Growing Up In Different Ways

No two ideas could come from such different origins than PPM and CMM. Project Portfolio Management arose from the research of Dr. Harry Markowitz and the application of financial portfolio management. Twenty years ago in the *Harvard Business Review* article, "A Portfolio Approach to Information Technology Projects," Dr. F. Warren McFarland proposed the treatment of projects as financial investments, and thus should be measured by the company as investments used to achieve an overall investment goal. How closely an investment will achieve the goal, the levels of return, and the amount of risk will determine whether the project remains within the portfolio.

PPM focuses on the creation of project portfolios and the management of project risks and success in groups instead of individually. PPM relies on providing IT portfolio managers with sufficient data to evaluate the risks, returns, and likelihood for success for each project. Without sufficient information, a portfolio manager cannot evaluate whether a project represents too much risk for a portfolio, will not generate the expected returns, or will not meet the strategic goals of the company.

CMM, on the other hand, was born by software engineers at the Software Engineering Institute of Carnegie-Mellon University. CMM provides a framework for evaluating the processes used by organizations to create software. The idea is that if a particular project or organization creates high-quality software following a certain process, and the organization demonstrates that this process is reused elsewhere, then there is a high likelihood that the other projects will also generate high-quality software products.

CMM measures organization by one of five levels, with Level 5 indicating organization-wide activities characteristic of the best IT organizations. Such items that are measured include collection and use of project metrics, organizational focus on development and strategy, and high-level engagement in process improvement. CMM measures the organization's ability to repeat the successful processes as documented. This is done through the documenting of processes and through the collection of metrics. Metrics indicate that an organization receives information about projects, learns from this information, and applies this knowledge to the next set of projects.

When Methodologies Come Together

So PPM and CMM provide different ways to achieve project success. But can they co-exist? Can an organization attempting to implement CMM-compliant processes also use PPM to manage their portfolios? In fact, PPM may help organizations achieve higher levels of CMM.

The first place this starts is in the organization's focus on projects. Many measures are required for CMM, including risk management, project management, quality assurance, and training. The organization, at higher levels, must demonstrate that they are aware of the overall goals of the organization, and the individual areas of measurement are addressed. This is where PPM can help.

By creating portfolios, organizations can demonstrate that these measurements are gathered to support the activities of the portfolio. Thus, risk management activities may be tailored to meet the specific needs of the portfolio. Processes can be modified for a portfolio of hardware manufacturing that will be different from that of software development. By forming portfolios, oversight of the projects is consolidated for easier management.

The second place where PPM helps CMM is in the gathering of metrics. Many metrics are required for PPM in order for portfolio managers to understand the value of their portfolio. However, each portfolio will have different measures that are unique to their needs. Under CMM, each project would have to be evaluated based on certain measurements and waivers granted on a project-by-project basis.

Using PPM, the portfolio managers can craft their metrics needs and can modify data collection to support their decision-making. As long as this process is documented, efforts to collect unnecessary data are avoided while CMM processes for metrics gathering is preserved.

The third key area where PPM assists organizations with CMM is in the effort to reuse lessons learned from past projects. CMM requires organizations to improve processes by learning from past efforts to feed improvements. Using PPM, these improvements can be further focused to support the differing needs of the portfolios. For example, process improvements to increase hardware component production are not necessarily valuable to the operating system group. Using PPM, such process changes are targeted by the portfolio manager to support the lessons learned within the portfolio. This leads to faster improvement without jeopardizing the activities of the other portfolios.

PPM in the CMM Levels

The CMM methodology specifies areas of performance that organizations must demonstrate in order to be ranked at a certain level. These levels, ranging from Level 1 for the most basic to Level 5, are achieved through demonstrated performance of certain project and organization activities. PPM can help organizations achieve CMM at the following levels:

LEVEL 1

At Level 1, organizations are run by "heroes" who do the work without process or procedures. Each time a new project comes along, lessons are learned all over again. PPM can bring organizations out of Level 1 by bringing together the same "heroes" under a single management structure, forcing random activities to become institutional processes.

LEVEL 2

At Level 2, organizations have project processes that are reused. These processes apply to the project management efforts. PPM enforces this by keeping similar projects together. Processes specific to these projects can then be tailored at the portfolio level rather than on a project-by-project basis.

LEVEL 3

At Level 3, process management and improvement rise to the organizational level. Here is where PPM really makes a mark. By having a portfolio management approach in place, organizations can collect metrics about projects and activities within the individual portfolios, then aggregate the information across the organization. Process improvements can be made at an organizational and portfolio level, then filter down to the projects.

LEVELS 4 AND 5

At Levels 4 and 5, organizations focus activities based on specific strategies. Activities are measured against strategic objectives. Portfolio management requires the alignment of projects to corporate strategies. Portfolios help organize metrics to analyze and measure achievement of corporate strategies. The organization measures activities and uses the information to improve processes. Portfolio managers streamline the collection of information to senior management, providing faster analysis and improvement.

Conclusion

Independently, PPM and CMM represent models organizations can use to improve the way projects are executed. Together, using PPM can help organizations achieve higher levels of Capability Maturity Model validation. PPM and CMM present the opportunity for organizations to respond rapidly to changing strategies and potential improvements by tailoring processes for each portfolio.

Gartner Shines the Light on PPM

CAMERON MCGAUGHY

When Derry Simmel arrived at Gartner's Project Portfolio Management 2004 conference in San Diego last month, it was perfect timing.

"We're about a year old, and more than anything we're trying to bring project management and portfolio management into the culture of the company," says Simmel, the director of the Project Management Office for Synovus Financial Corp. in Columbus, Georgia. "We don't have a lot of methodologies, we don't have a lot of consistency. We're trying to work that in such a way as to not be onerous, which is our real trick. We want to make sure it's very enabling as opposed to overwhelming."

The company just got a charter to start portfolio management, and Simmel came to the conference mostly to hear how people have created the same system and find out what has been the most valuable, as well as look at different vendors.

"Our CEO is probably sending out the memo this week, and everything about getting the people together, using a prioritized weighted system—all of those things are going to be brand new when we get everybody together," he says, adding his budgeting process is going to start in September. His hope is to get into it with a prioritized list of projects. "Now, how well they're used in that process, or whether they're ignored ... I suspect they might be ignored. We need to try to make that information available, bring it up during budgeting, ask questions about it during budgeting so that we can make some further progress in that area. And then in the following year, my hope is that that will actually turn out to drive the budgeting process."

And there were many other attendees trying to get a grasp on exactly how to use portfolio management—and how to justify it to skeptics, proving that while the concept has grown and matured in the last decade, conferences such as Gartner's are still crucial in aiding the cause. Matt Hotle, Gartner's general vice president of infrastructure and development, notes that he has seen the evolution of project management and project portfolio management the process—as opposed to project and portfolio management in terms of tools and vendors. He noted that 1995 (when he started at Gartner) was market by "Microsoft Project, desktop stuff, critical path ... that was the differentiator for tools in the market in 1995."

Then the difference moved to workflow, "in other words, notifying people when a process or task was completed, and then also resource management. So from 1997 to 1999, you started to look at this whole idea of workflow and resource management in addition to all of the other stuff. Project management 2001 through now is really focused on managing portfolios of stuff, so the tools out there have certainly evolved and the market has evolved over the nine years I have been at Gartner."

Hotle pointed out that PPM is a five-step process for prioritizing and managing initiatives: define initiatives, evaluate them, prioritize and balance them, match your resources, and manage the portfolio. But given the evolution of the process, Hotle insists that one thing has been very stable.

"This is not a tools game—this is a people and process game," he says. "You absolutely need technology, but this is foremost about people and process. This is not rocket science, this is not brand new stuff that somebody's dreamed up. This is stuff that we know, it's stuff that has worked in other industries. So what we really talk about is changing the behaviors of people in your organization."

Portfolio management is most organizations, he notes, is about a behavioral and cultural change issue.

"People forget that project portfolio management is an ongoing process that you should go through on a regular basis: quarterly, monthly ... it's a regular process," he says. "The term was kind of unknown in 1995. Now, the vast majority of organizations I have talked to have one of two things in place. They either have a written project portfolio management process in place—or a very experienced one—or they have the desire to move toward one."

Hotle notes that the benefits are vast: "If you are an experienced organization with project portfolio management and resource management, your gains will be roughly automation-focused, and you should plan your return on investment along automation lines. If you are not doing this stuff right now, your benefits will be much larger and they will include doing things more effectively ... the process is not sequential. You don't come to an end at any point. If you've got a robust project portfolio management process, it begins whenever you begin it, and it ends whenever your company goes bye bye."

Gartner research and interviews uncovered six critical success factors for PPM:

- Making a portfolio management process work requires strong governance and holding participants accountable.
- Portfolio management is such a major undertaking that it needs to be treated as a project itself to succeed. It needs a process owner and a qualified support team.
- Having a disciplined process means that all proposals go through the same screening. The process is ongoing and approved initiatives are reviewed when conditions change.
- The objective prioritization framework should include investment categories and risk-adjusted evaluation criteria.
- Communication and education programs are needed to develop stakeholder buy-in and support for the project portfolio management process.
- To facilitate the use of PPM, provide tools that make compliance easier. Tools ensure consistency and support group decision making.

The four key phases of PPM are **charter,** involving how an IS organization receives work requests and manages them; **prioritize,** where projects are funded and approved; **execute,** where they are scheduled, balanced, and delivered; and closure, which provides the chance to learn from the work done via project reviews and metric analysis.

During his insight session, "Project Portfolio Management: Within Reach?" Matt Light noted that the keys to getting a grip on PPM are establishing a process for it by blending prioritization techniques and getting good data for solid analysis; by using the established process (or losing it) by having few pet projects, a formal and stringent assessment, and planning and staffing; and by monitoring external projects as part of the portfolio (more so with large projects).

Blending multiple prioritization techniques is crucial to yield more profitable project portfolios. Those techniques include risk analysis, payback (like internal rate of return), comparative, scoring (by few weighted criteria), using portfolio matrices (like bubble diagrams), optimization (multifactor sensitivity), cost estimates (total cost of ownership), and project repository that supports estimation.

"We borrowed this term from the financial industries, and one of the first lessons we learned about managing a portfolio of investments is that it's diversified," says Light, Gartner's research director for application development. "There are a lot of different kinds of investments that can be made. And you prioritize them not against each other in a mishmash, but in their different categories. It's like you would identify what is an optimal level of risk you would be willing to take with stocks. You may be willing to take a risk in order to hopefully realize some higher levels of return, and maybe we can compare that to some of our IT projects, as opposed to bonds, where the interest is a slow. It's a steady performer, maybe that's the Legacy systems of your application portfolio."

That point stood out to Wendy Macfarland, director of IT Program Management and Information Technology at Scottsdale Insurance Company in Arizona.

"There's a new group that's been formed within our IT area that I'm directing now, so I'm trying to learn more about project portfolio management and how I can use that and what that means in my new role, what some of the best practices are, how I can take what we've got today in our present world and try to forge something for tomorrow that looks more like a portfolio management type of an organization," she said. "The role of strategic planning and the budgeting process with project portfolio management, and how that can work together with the PMO, and also the prioritization process and how to prioritize within categories as opposed to across categories . . . those are two things that jumped out at me."

Light noted a study from last year by the Kellogg School of Management and Diamond Cluster survey of 130 Fortune 1,000 companies, "IT Portfolio Management: Challenges and Best Practices," showed that most enterprises surveyed lacked a formal process to access project ROI, and that most PPM processes are manual, showing a significant opportunity for improved efficiency and effectiveness.

"There have been a couple of trends that have the potential to make some of those metrics worse. There are some countertrends, like the tendency to slice up major projects into lots of minor increments," Light says. "I think conceptually it's very good, and we've been trying to shy away from big projects that suffer from analysis paralysis and take a long time to deliver functionality and be validated. This is what the business users needed, so we're trying to shy away from that kind of scenario."

But sometimes when moving toward smaller, more agile projects, Light notes that companies can throw out the baby with the bathwater.

"Very often we see the smaller projects being downsized to avoid a budgeting process, to avoid a requirements process, to try and roll things out one thing at a time, to try and avoid any kind of planning and tracking—really to avoid a budgeting process and get in through the back door," he says. "Many organizations will have a threshold of a couple hundred thousand, or a $500,000 project that becomes subject to scrutiny and review is tracked carefully. So people, being smart, say, 'Okay, what I'll do is instead of having one project of $300,000, we'll have three projects of $100,000, that way we can avoid this whole process and not have to do all this justification.'"

And that's what scares Light.

"For the right reasons we shift our project definition and delivery load, but the unintended consequences of that is actually a deterioration of what professionalism we have brought to project portfolio management in the past few years," he says. "Things like the numbers on that study, like two-thirds said they didn't track benefits and 58 percent said they didn't define success . . . that could get worse before it gets better."

Light notes that a big roadblock is the confusion about governance. The coordination of and cooperation between a governance board and a project office should be established, he noted, so an enterprise can more easily make rapid adjustments to the project portfolio. While Light says it is certainly important to have good IT investment planning and control, control is not governance.

"Yes, you want to have an IT environment where you can provide control both of your projects and your application maintenance and enhancement and your service levels, and you want to have procedures and tools in place to help provide that control, support planning through good execution," he says. "That's all very good, but it's not really governance."

Governance, he says, has more to do with your decision-making structures. So before you get to project management and even project portfolio management, you need to understand what the different domains of IT are, such as business applications, IT infrastructure, and some of the legacy applications.

"But then, who has the decision-making authority in those domains, and who has input rights? Your IT folks, your IS management, may very well have significant input into the decision about which business applications are selected, but you might determine for your enterprise that the business unit executives are going to have the final decision. You've got input rights to find, you've got decision rights to find."

"And similarly for the infrastructure, you might say that it's important to be heard from maybe the user community, but ultimately it's the IT folks that are going to make the decision about infrastructure. So that's governance, and certainly governance does get involved in issues about control. Hopefully your PMO, your IT managers are going to take care of controlling the execution around issues of hardware assets and network assets and application portfolio and projects, but sometimes there will be issues that need to be escalated, control issues that need senior level decision making, so you might get involved with governance."

The governance board could meet monthly or quarterly. "That's a governance type of decision that gets drawn into the by your ordinary control processes, but there is that distinction between investment planning control and IT governance, and above and beyond that we get into corporate governance, but again, that's a confusion that I think could be a real stumbling block for a lot of organizations."

Light says there is learning going on around the roll of project portfolio management in working with externally sourced projects. In one of his presentations at the conference, Light alluded to a trend in organizations in the past year.

"There's been a feeling of, 'Oh, I outsourced this. So we're paying for it, we've got service levels and stuff, it should be fine,' to now understanding better that just because you outsourced the execution aspect doesn't mean that you're not still involved with that project intimately," Light says. "I think there's been a partial understanding of that, to kind of a tendency to take the execution for granted. But in recent years, some of the failed outsourced projects, some of the low satisfaction with it I think prompted organizations to say, 'Okay, we've got to be more engaged at front-end analysis, making sure we confirm that the contractor knows what we want, how we want it, and that we are engaged with them on a day-to-day, week-to-week basis.' Looking at their progress, looking at their quality procedures, and trying to manage that relationship a little more proactively—I think that's a good realization that's becoming more prevalent."

Light notes that he sees a few trends convergence-wise—tools that have been focused on application portfolio management, tools that have been focused on portfolio prioritization, analysis of the different categories of the IT portfolio—that have attracted a lot of user and vendor interest.

"So there have been interfaces, integrations, acquisitions—a couple of interesting acquisitions the last couple of years: Mercury acquiring Kintana, Compuware acquiring Changepoint. It kind of brings project portfolio management together with application portfolio management in a convergence that [Gartner Research Vice President] Jim Duggan and I predicted in some research last year, and also some interesting integrations between some of the portfolio prioritization analysis tools like ProSight and United Management Technologies, interface integrations with them and some of the tools that provide more powerful functionality in the area of resource allocation, project multi-project scheduling, resource loading resource leveling, understanding the project portfolio in more detail that way."

Light says that those acquisitions and integrations have other vendors looking at that kind of activity and building homegrown functionality in the direction of application portfolio management, focused on tracking the cost of service requests, and projects you wouldn't necessarily plan and schedule but that are important to the application portfolio.

"They're building that into some of the portfolio management applications—building in some portfolio analysis and prioritization functionality when you're not necessarily integrating or interfacing two other tools, but trying to develop functionality in those directions," he says. "So there's some interesting stuff going on there."

READING 3

Choosing the Wrong Portfolio of Projects—
Part 5: Attending to Risk

LEE MERKHOFER, PH.D.

Risk management is receiving greater attention since September 11 and the stock market losses that occurred shortly thereafter. Yet, while nearly all organizations are focusing more on security, assurance, and liquidity, when it comes to selecting projects many still don't adequately address risk. Inattention to risk is the fourth reason organizations choose the wrong projects.

There are important reasons that more attention to project risk is needed. The increasingly competitive economic environment is putting tremendous pressure on managers to produce results quickly. Meanwhile, projects are becoming more complex due, for example, to new technologies, more regulatory requirements, increased product liability, and the greater interdependency organizations have with external business partners.

Organizations are being held to higher standards by shareholders, customers, regulators, and the public. Executives are much less tolerant of budget overruns and inferior project outcomes. A serious project mishap can seriously damage the reputation and profitability of the organization. Coming in on time, on budget, and to project specifications is no longer good enough.

What is risk?

The first step toward better addressing project risk is to understand it. Risk, according to Webster, is "a possibility of loss." Risks arise from uncertainty, our inability to foresee the future. If an uncertainty creates the potential for loss, we refer to it as a risk. The opportunity to quantify risk is provided by the language of probability. A probability distribution (sometimes called a risk profile) characterizes a risk by describing the range of possible consequences and their probabilities of occurrence, as shown in Figure 5 [20-1].

Types of Risk

There are many different kinds of risks of concern to projects. For example:

- Governance risk relates to board and management performance with regard to ethics, community stewardship, and company reputation.
- Strategic risks result from errors in strategy, such as choosing a technology that can't be made to work.
- Operational risk includes risks from poor implementation and process problems such as production and distribution.
- Market risks include competition, foreign exchange, commodity markets, and interest rate risk, as well as liquidity and credit risks.

438

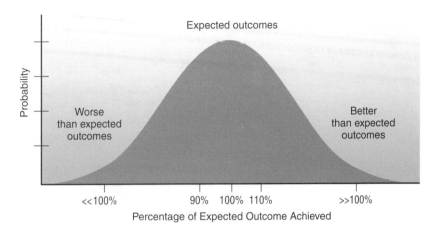

20-1 Figure 5. Risk Probability versus Percentage of Expected Outcome

■ Legal risks arise from legal and regulatory obligations, including contract risks and litigation brought against the organization.

As indicated by these examples, project risks include both internal risks associated with successfully completing each stage of the project, plus risks that are beyond the control of the project team. These latter types include external risks that arise from outside the organization but affect the ultimate value to be derived from the project. In all cases, the seriousness of the risk depends on the nature and magnitude of the possible end consequences and their probabilities.

Project Risk Management

Project risk management, as defined by Max Wideman, is "an organized assessment and control of project risks." The level of risk management that is required obviously depends on the level of risk. Riskier projects, such as new product launches, global initiatives, projects involving new technology, major regulatory-driven projects, and so forth, tend to have complex interacting elements and involve high stakes. A poor track record on similar projects is an indicator or risk. While risk management is most needed for the most risky projects, some level of project risk management should be provided in all cases.

An organization can practice risk management in several different contexts. Projects are proposed throughout the organization in response to perceived needs and opportunities. Sometimes, the identified need is reducing a risk. For example, an organization operating a hazardous facility may invest in projects to reduce health, safety, and environmental risks. In such cases, the project is itself an investment in risk management. Regardless of the need or opportunity the project is intended to address, there are three main contexts for project risk management. As shown in Figure 6 [20-2], these are project planning, project selection, and project execution.

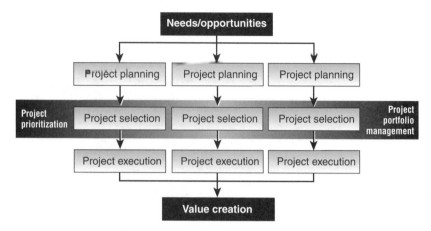

20-2 Figure 6. Opportunities for Risk Management

Although many organizations have instituted risk management processes within project planning and project execution, risk management in project selection is often little more than a yes/no answer to "Should we accept the project risk?" This limited view, coupled with project-by-project decision making, creates problems for risk management.

The Need for Project Selection Risk Management

Important types of project risk are best addressed by project selection because they are outside the scope of project managers. A paper by the accounting firm Ernst & Young provides this example [1]:

> A company conducted a project to install new equipment to increase capacity. However, the project planning team failed to evaluate whether the market could absorb the increased supply made available by the added capacity. Narrowly defined, the project was a success because the new equipment was installed successfully, on time and on budget. However, because there was insufficient demand, the company could not sell its extra output at its prevailing price. It ultimately had to shut down some of its production lines.

As illustrated, risk management within project planning and project execution often fails to address external project risks. Project portfolio management provides an opportunity to account for external risks and to get senior executives to take some ownership of project risks before the project commences.

Risky Projects May Be Good Projects

For many organizations, project risk is simply something to be avoided. But, as Alan Greenspan has stated, "Risk-taking is indeed a necessary condition for the creation of wealth" [2]. Successful organizations deliberately take risks when it is to their advantage. According to Suzanne Labarge, Vice Chairman of the Royal Bank of Canada, "Risk in itself is not bad. What is bad is risk that is mismanaged, misunderstood, mispriced, or unintended" [3].

Failure to recognize, understand, and accept risk often leads to project portfolios skewed toward low-risk projects with little upside potential. It can also lead to an occasional, unrecognized, high-risk project that endangers the enterprise.

Treating Risk as an "Intangible"

When evaluating projects to support project selection decisions, many organizations view risk as an "intangible." To describe risk, they use qualitative terms such as "likely" versus "unlikely" and "significant" versus "insignificant." Such words are insufficiently precise and mean different things to different people. For example, a lower-level manager might have a very different notion of what qualifies as a significant risk compared to that of the CEO.

The fact that most organizations do not have a clear policy on risk-taking is a major reason project portfolios tend to be biased toward low-risk projects. Unless risk is measured, it is difficult to use it as a consideration for project selection.

Hurdle Rates

Most organizations that account for risks when selecting projects do so using hurdle rates. The hurdle rate is a risk-adjusted cost of capital used to discount future project costs and benefits. Increased hurdle rates are applied to projects considered to be risky.

Using hurdle rates is preferable to ignoring risk or treating it as an intangible. However, hurdle rates have limitations. For one thing, organizations are frequently unclear about what hurdle rate should be applied. Studies have shown that the rates used by firms vary considerably. According to finance theory, the "correct" hurdle rate is the "opportunity cost" of the investment, which is the return available from investing in securities equivalent to the risk of the project being evaluated. Most companies don't adjust the hurdle rate for risk nearly enough.

A more fundamental problem is reflected in research on real options showing that the discount rate needs to vary with the project management strategy (e.g., an irreversible project investment would call for a higher hurdle rate), as well as with time (the discount rate is not a constant, but changes depending on when the future discounted outcomes are expected to occur), and with project outcomes and other changing information. Using a constant hurdle rate for a project implicitly assumes that uncertainty increases over time in a specific way (geometrically). Hurdle rates tend to create a bias toward short-term, quick-payoff projects because they severely penalize project benefits that occur in the longer term.

Characterizing Risks with Probabilities

The best way to understand project risk is to characterize it by describing the range of possible outcomes, estimating when they could occur (risk timing), and assigning probabilities. If relevant data are available (e.g., as might be the case for system failure probabilities for evaluating reliability maintenance projects), probabilities for characterizing risks can be derived using statistical analysis. In the absence of such data, probabilities must still be assigned, and it makes sense to do so directly based on expert judgment.

Although quantifying risks requires more inputs to describe proposed projects, note that the additional inputs need not be very complex. If some aspect of a project's performance is uncertain, instead of obtaining only a middle-value, point estimate, get a range of possible values (e.g., a 90% confidence interval) as well as a mean or most-likely value. (As I described in Part 1, techniques should be used to guard against overly narrow ranges caused by overconfidence.) With practice, it takes no more time to specify a range than it does to generate a single point estimate. The necessary probabilities can be roughly estimated from the range and a mean or most-likely value.

Once probabilities have been assigned to important risks, those probabilities can be propagated through the value model (described previously) to derive the uncertainty over the various benefits and total value of the project. This can be done using Monte Carlo analysis or event trees. The probabilities can be displayed graphically to show how uncertainty evolves over time (as in Figure 7 [20-3]). The amount of uncertainty caused by project risks and the specific project benefits that are impacted may be used to better estimate what hurdle rates should be used and the types of benefits to which they should be applied.

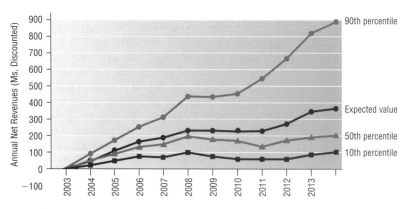

20-3 Figure 7. Evolution of Risk Values Over Time

Project Managers Benefit from Characterizing Project Risks

Although project managers may initially feel uncomfortable with probabilities, my experience is that this group can benefit significantly from moving away from using artificial point estimates. The following is a summary of an example devised by Mark Durrenberger of Oak Associates making this point [4].

Imagine that a project manager is asked to complete a project in 3 weeks. Suppose the project manager feels that this estimate is unrealistically optimistic; that everything would have to go just right to make the deadline. The project manager may feel apprehensive about going to the project sponsor to address the problem. It may not be easy to explain why an optimistic, aggressive project schedule isn't a good one.

Suppose, instead, that the project manager estimates as a range the time required to complete each project step. Those ranges can be combined (by adding the means and variances) to determine the probability of completing the effort within any specified time. Rather than feeling "at the mercy" of the sponsor, the project manager can now say, "I understand your desire to complete the project within three weeks. However, my calculations suggest that we have less than a 5% chance of meeting that deadline."

The sponsor will want to know more, including how the probability estimate was obtained. This gives the project manager the opportunity to discuss the realities of the job and to negotiate tradeoffs. Such tradeoffs might include reducing project scope or deliverables so as to increase the likelihood of meeting the desired schedule.

Note that specifying ranges is not a license for the project manager to make baseless claims. Over time, performance can be compared with range estimates. A project manager whose performance routinely beats the means of his specified uncertainty ranges, for example, will be exposed as one who pads estimates.

Risks of the Project Portfolio

Another important reason to consider quantifying project risks is it that the overall risk of the project portfolio can then be determined. Conducting a portfolio of projects reduces risks through risk diversification (hedging) in the same way that an individual can reduce financial investment risks by investing in a portfolio of diversified stocks. In a stock portfolio there is a limit to how much diversification can reduce risk. This limit is determined by the degree to which stock prices tend to move together; that is, the degree to which the prices of the stocks in the portfolio are statistically correlated with overall market movements. To understand the risks of a stock portfolio, it is necessary to measure these correlations (this is typically done using the correlation statistic called "beta").

In a project portfolio there are risks that impact multiple projects simultaneously. So, in exactly the same way as with stocks, a project portfolio is not as effective at reducing correlated risks. The only way to estimate accurately the risks of alternative project portfolios, and thereby choose projects that collectively produce maximum value at minimum risk, is to quantify these project risks, including distinguishing risks that impact single projects from those that impact multiple projects.

Fully characterizing project risks shows whether the assumptions required for using hurdle rates are satisfied and supports the selection of project-specific hurdle rates. It also allows the use of another approach involving the concept of risk tolerance.

Risk Tolerance

An individual's or company's aversion to risk taking can be quantified and measured. The concept works as follows. If decision makers did not care about risk, they would want to "go with the odds;" that is, they would want to make decisions so as to maximize expected value. The expected value is defined as the probability-weighted sum of the distribution of possible uncertain outcomes. Decision makers unconcerned about risk would want to maximize expected value because the expected value is the amount that they would obtain on average each time the uncertainty is faced. As an example, the expected value of a coin flip that pays $1 on "heads" and zero on "tails" is 50 cents. If you participated in a thousand such coin flips, your winnings would be very close to $500, so that the value of each flip would be 50 cents.

For substantial risks, organizations as well as individuals tend to be risk averse, meaning that they value uncertainties at less than their expected values. The "certain equivalent" is defined as the amount of money for which a decision maker would be indifferent between receiving that amount for certain and receiving the distribution of uncertain payoffs represented by the gamble. For example, a risk-averse decision maker might assign a certain equivalent of $500,000 to a risky project with equal chances of yielding $0 and $2,000,000, even though the expected value for this alternative is $1,000,000. The goal of a risk averse decision maker is to maximize the certain equivalent.

For risks with complex payoff distributions, it is generally difficult to determine the certain equivalent. However, the certain equivalent can be estimated for a simple gamble and the results used to infer the certain equivalents of more complicated risks. The approach involves constructing a "utility function" that represents the degree of aversion to taking risks.

Figure 8 [20-4] illustrates the form (exponential) often chosen for the utility function. The horizontal axis shows possible values or certain equivalents. The vertical axis shows the corresponding "utility," where utility is a numerical rating assigned to every possible value.

The shape of the utility function determines the degree of aversion to taking risks. The more the plot curves or bends over, the more risk aversion is represented. With the exponential utility function, the degree of curvature is determined by the parameter R, known as the risk tolerance. Thus, risk tolerance is an indicator of a decision maker's or organization's willingness to accept risk. Risk tolerance, as defined here, is not the maximum amount that the decision maker can afford to lose, although decision makers and organizations with greater wealth generally have larger risk tolerances.

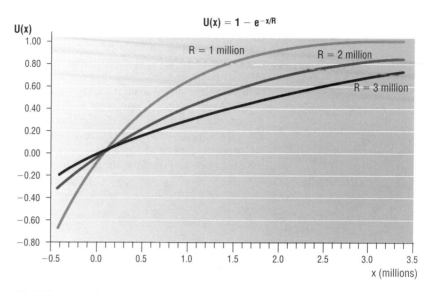

20-4 Figure 8. The Exponential Utility Function Is Often Used to Model Risk Aversion

Once the risk tolerance is set, the utility function may be used to compute a certain equivalent as follows. First, locate each possible payoff x on the horizontal axis and determine the corresponding utility U(x) on the vertical axis. For example, if risk tolerance is $1 million and the risk is 50% chance of $0 or $2 million, the corresponding utilities (from Figure 8 [20-4]) are 0 and approximately 0.8. Second, compute the expected utility by multiplying each utility by its probability and summing the products. For the example, the expected utility is roughly $0.5 \times 0 + 0.5 \times 0.8 = 0.4$. Third, locate the expected utility on the vertical axis and determine the corresponding certain equivalent on the horizontal axis. The result for the example is approximately $500,000.

There are several ways to determine the risk tolerance for an organization. One is to ask senior decision makers, ideally the CEO, to answer the following hypothetical question. Suppose you have an opportunity to make a risky, but potentially profitable investment. The required investment is an amount R that, for the moment, is unspecified. The investment has a 50–50 chance of success. If it succeeds, it will generate the full amount invested, including the cost of capital, plus that amount again. In other words, the return will be R if the investment is successful. If the investment fails, half the investment will be lost, so the return is minus R/2. Figure 9 [20-5]) illustrates the possible outcomes of the opportunity. As indicated, the expected value of the investment is R/4.

If R were very low, most CEOs would want to make the investment. If R were very large, perhaps close to the market value of the enterprise, most CEOs would not take the investment. The risk tolerance is the amount R for which decision makers would just be indifferent between making and not making the investment. In other words, the risk tolerance is the value of R for which the certain equivalent of the investment is zero.

Various studies have been conducted to measure organizational risk tolerances. The results show that risk tolerances obtained from different executives within the same organization vary tremendously. Generally, those lower in the organization have lower risk tolerances. As a rough rule of thumb for publicly traded firms, typical risk tolerances at the CEO or Board level are equal to about 20% of the organization's market value.

Once risk tolerance has been established, the certain equivalent for any risky project or project portfolio can be obtained via the utility function. The effect, as illustrated in Figure 10 [20-6], is to subtract a risk adjustment factor from the expected value. The risk adjustment factor depends on the risk tolerance and the amount of project risk. If the projects are independent

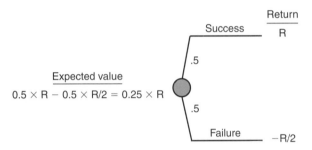

20-5 Figure 9. What is the Maximum Amount (R) You Would Accept in This Gamble?

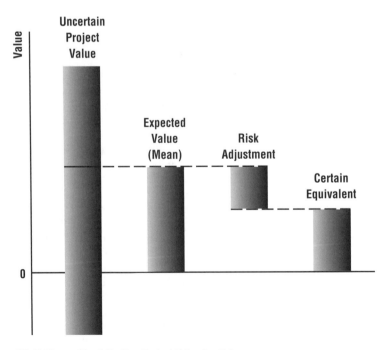

20-6 Figure 10. Adjusting Project Value for Risk

(i.e., their risks are uncorrelated), then the certain equivalent of the project portfolio will be the sum of the certain equivalents of the individual projects. If project risks are correlated, the certain equivalent for the portfolio can be obtained once the distribution of payoffs for the portfolio are computed (accounting for correlations as described above).

The major advantage of this approach is that a single risk tolerance can be established for the organization. Use of the common risk tolerance ensures that risks are treated consistently, thus avoiding the common bias in which greater levels of risk aversion tend to be applied by lower-level managers.

Part 6

The sixth part of this paper describes the final reason organizations choose the wrong projects—inability to find the efficient frontier.

References

[1] "Project Risk Mitigation: A Holistic Approach to Project Risk Management," Assurance & Advisory Business Services, Ernst & Young, 2002.

[2] L. Kahaner and A. Greenspan, *The Quotations of Chairman Greenspan*, Adams Media Corporation, 2000.

[3] S. Labarge, "Valuing the Risk Management Function," Presentation at the Risk Management Association's Capital Management Conference, Washington DC. April 10, 2003.

[4] M. R. Durrenberger, "True Estimates Reduce Project Risk," Oak Associates, Inc., 1999.

Choosing the Wrong Portfolio of Projects— Part 6: Get on the Effective Frontier

LEE MERKHOFER, PH.D.

The goal for selecting projects is to pick project portfolios that create the greatest possible risk-adjusted value without exceeding the applicable constraint on available resources. Economists call the set of investments that create the greatest possible value at the least possible cost the "efficient frontier." Most organizations fail to find the best project portfolios and, therefore, do not create maximum value. Inability to find the efficient frontier is the fifth reason organizations choose the wrong projects.

If the problems discussed in the previous parts of this paper are addressed, value-maximizing project portfolios can be found. Specifically, if the organization has the right metrics and models in place, including the ability to value risk, and it has taken steps to minimize errors and biases in inputs provided to those models, the capability exists to estimate the value that would be added by doing any proposed project portfolio. It is a relatively easy last step, then, to find the best combination of projects. The concept of the efficient frontier is highly useful in this regard.

Definition of the Efficient Frontier

Suppose that an organization is currently conducting a set of projects represented by the point labeled Portfolio A in the graphic shown in Figure 11 [20-7]. Economists would describe Portfolio A as inefficient because there is another project portfolio, Portfolio B, that produces more value for the same cost. Similarly, there is also a Portfolio C that produces the same value for less cost. Furthermore, there is a Portfolio D with a combination of these two characteristics.

Now suppose we consider all of the alternative portfolios that can be constructed from a set of project proposals. Typically there are many, and Figure 12 shows a real example. In this case, the organization had 30 project proposals under consideration in one budget cycle. Four of those projects were considered mandatory (3 process fixes and a new initiative required by regulators) leaving 26 discretionary projects. In general, if there are N potential projects, there are 2N possible project portfolios because there are a total of 2N subsets within a set of N items. (For more explanation, see the paper "Mathematics: Methods for Solving the Capital Allocation Problem," available on my Web site). Thus, this application required evaluating 226 or approximately 67 million portfolios, far more than shown in Figure 12 [20-8]! The best portfolios define the efficient frontier.

Notice how the efficient frontier is curved, not straight. This is because the efficient frontier is made up of the best possible projects in the

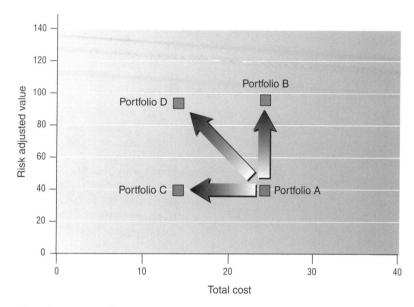

20-7 Figure 11. Different Project Portfolios Have Different Costs and Values

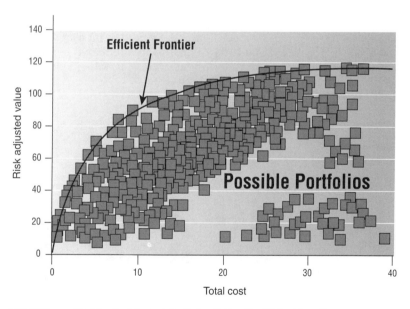

20-8 Figure 12. The Best Project Portfolios Define the Efficient Frontier

least-cost portfolios, that is, those portfolios that show up first on the left side of the curve. Such portfolios create the greatest "bang-for-the-buck." As the cost constraint is relaxed and more projects can be added, the new projects are not quite as good as those included earlier. The slope of the curve encompassing these projects is flatter because their bang-for-the-buck is not quite as high. Thus, there is a declining return in the value obtained with each additional increment of cost. This is what causes the curve to bend as shown in Figure 12 [20-8].

Finding the Frontier

It is relatively easy for a computer, with an efficient optimization engine, to try various combinations and locate the efficient frontier, provided the right algorithms are in place. These algorithms must be set for determining how the costs and benefits of individual projects combine to determine the costs and benefits of the project portfolio as a whole. In simple situations where projects are independent and risks are either independent or do not matter, the costs and value of the project portfolio are basically just sums of the costs and values of the individual projects. However, if there are interdependencies or a need to adjust for risks, more sophisticated models are required.

Evidence that Finding the Efficient Frontier Adds Considerable Value

If we locate the efficient frontier, then for any specified total cost we can pick the specific portfolio that produces the greatest possible value. Figure 13 [20-9], derived from an actual application, shows that an alternative portfolio was found that increased value by over 30% without increasing costs. Similarly, an alternative portfolio was found that reduced costs by 40% without decreasing value. This result is typical. Application of the

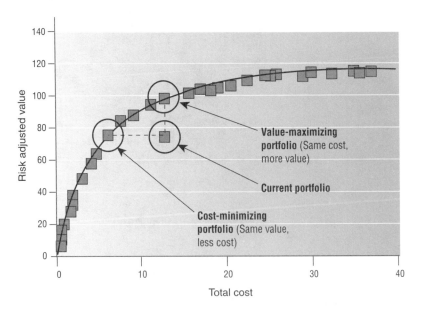

20-9 Figure 13. Project Portfolio Enhanced by Applying the Efficient Frontier

efficient frontier approach shows that current project portfolios are often well below their potential.

The Efficient Frontier Moves Over Time

It should be noted that the efficient frontier is not static. Organizations face the challenge of finding project alternatives that advance the frontier. As project managers better understand the link between their project designs and the value derived by the organization, they create better project proposals. Also, better technology creates new opportunities that create more value for less cost. This causes the efficient frontier to move up over time. The fundamental goal, though, remains the same—Create as much value as possible using as little capital as possible. To do this, you must find the efficient frontier.

Part 7

The final part of this paper provides a summary and recommendations for what organizations should to do if they are to better manage their project portfolios. It also describes the two pitfalls that must be overcome if effective tools for portfolio management are to be successfully introduced into the organization.

CHAPTER 21

Governance

Chapter 21 Contents

Chapter Overview

The term "governance" is well recognized in the English language, but the term's application to IT is still expanding. Certainly, the implication is that someone is trying to control IT processes. What are the targets? A starting point dictionary definition of the term is provided by Princeton's Worldnet Dictionary: [WorldNet]

1. Administration, governing body, establishment, brass, organization; the persons, committees, or departments who make up a body for the purpose of administering something;
2. Government, governing, government activity; the act of governing; exercising authority.

Another definition offers "the persons (or committees or departments, etc.) who make up a body for the purpose of administering something." [Dictionary] Note that this one adds the concept of committees or departments as associated with business administration.

The concept of governance is being driven in various ways today. One of the most visible of these is the increased degree of governmental regulation. In the IT community, the most notable is Sarbanes-Oxley. However, there are numerous sources of control objectives that impact the IT area. These new classes of regulation decree more rigorous process controls and require that top executives and Boards of Directors be more closely involved in IT activities, well beyond what most have been historically. IT processes impacted include project management, risk management, business alignment with IT, security controls, data integrity, and others. Collectively, governmental actions will put increasing pressure on IT organizations to improve their internal management processes along the lines outlined in this text. Inside the IT function, there is now a recognized fiduciary responsibility to execute the required processes and communicate results to the senior leadership. The key governance concepts are timely delivery of planned business value from IT investments and mitigation of risk as a result of that activity.

Searching for an IT Governance Definition

Within the IT environment, the governance definition becomes more focused and two well-known industry experts provide clarity. Dr. Howard Rubin defines the term as "a framework for measuring the value of IT." [META Group] Second, MIT's Peter Weill says that "an effective IT governance structure is the single most important predictor of getting value from IT." [Weill] As we look at various IT sources for further insight into the definition of governance, certain functions and processes emerge. A sample of these follows:

- Board of directors review of IT practices
- Ensuring use of best practices in the organization
- Competent decision-making practices in place
- Adequate internal controls
- Defined managerial responsibility and accountability
- Proper evaulation of enterprise technology risks

As the view of IT governance evolves away from the traditional cost control focus, it moves to a higher view that involves such factors as the optimal value delivery of technology and risk management within that process. Now the requirement is to both define and deliver it within stakeholder expectations. It is interesting to note that even the 2004 edition of the *PMBOK® Guide* does not include governance in its glossary of definitions. Nevertheless, the concept of enterprise IT management governance is consistent with the *PMBOK® Guide* philosophy and is fundamental to other aspects of IT management discussed therein.

The above functions and processes provide a tidbit definition of a scope or process attribute. This definition may help you understand what governance means in an operational sense. Realize that the items are a composite of multiple views, not a singular absolute. However, one general observation seems consistent. The intent of a formal governance process is to ensure that IT is being run in a manner defined by senior management across many organizations. To some extent, governance is locally defined.

Within the IT organization, there are four underlying responsibilities involved in IT governance, as follows:

- Alignment of IT with the enterprise and realization of the promised benefits
- Use of IT to enable the enterprise by exploiting opportunities and maximizing benefits
- Responsible use of IT resources
- Appropriate management process applied to IT-related tasks

These responsibilities imply that IT management should strive to accomplish the attributes described. More importantly, IT has the obligation to produce visible evidence to this fact. The broad framework of the governance process includes four key steps:

- Understanding the basic goal structure of the enterprise
- Forming a slate of IT activities that supports the business goals

- Measuring and comparing results in a timely manner
- Providing IT direction with the key decisions that optimize output value

PlanView, a consulting organization with expertise in portfolio management, is pioneering some of the definitional and procedural aspects of enterprise governance. Figure 1 [21-1] offers a high-level overview of their model and the key steps in the process. [PlanView] More on this approach can be obtained from the PlanView corporate Web site at *www.planview.com*. The steps shown in this model are consistent with the previous discussion.

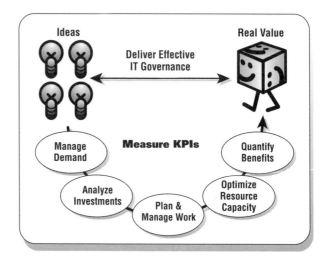

21-1 Figure 1. PlanView Governance Model

Project View of Governance

An additional step in the governance process occurs at the working level. The project manager has the responsibility to ensure that proper governance procedures are followed. Those procedures would be formulated from the principles outlined in the various sections of this text. It is common for a project to be externally guided by a higher level structure formally defined for it. In this view, an aspect of external control is clearly imposed on the project level.

PROJECT BOARD

One common strategy associated with IT governance is to appoint a project board for local project oversight. The board is normally constituted by middle-level management representatives from various segments of the business, usually those areas most affected by the project. This group is often delegated certain management authority and responsibility in regard to the project. As an example, they may be able to approve scope changes up to a defined limit and generally deal with tactical decision making for the project. In some cases, the board will manage the contingency funds for allocation based on their approval. This group will be intimately involved in the schedule, budget, and functional aspects of the project effort and will be senior management's "eyes on the ground."

The list below outlines responsibilities of the project board in an actual large organization. In this case, the project board was delegated an approved budget limit from the charter approval and from that point handled all aspects of the external management decision process so long as the project stayed within defined boundaries. For this example, the responsibility list follows:

- Authorize project initiation.
- Appoint/approve project manager and define/approve his/her responsibilities and objectives.
- Appoint/approve other project team roles.
- Review and approve project plans.
- Review and approve next stage plans.
- Assign project resources.
- Provide overall guidance and direction to the project.
- Review an action Exception Plan.
- Monitor and control technical exception situations (quality, schedule, budget, and functionality).
- Conduct mid-stage and end-stage assessments.
- Ensure project is conducted using the approved Project Management process.
- Ensure project is conducted using the agreed-to Work Breakdown Structure.
- Ensure that agreed-to deliverables are completed.

Future Considerations

The concept of IT governance is destined to continue to be a complex topic in organizations because it invades many time-honored customs and places more structure on the project activities than has existed in the past. Also, as organizations increase their level of third-party outsourcing, this subject will evolve to yet a more complex state. The general decision-making requirements will remain as outlined, but control over the internal process will evaporate in the third-party model. Oversight requirements will be more complex, and still more control will be required in this business model. Internal activities will continue to require more attention to the value definition and risk aspects. Along the way, the IT group must pay more attention to their internal process. Proper execution of the governance process may well be the key to the IT organization's survival because it will force outsiders to be more involved. As a result, the participants will come to understand the IT environment better, which is both a key to project success and understanding how the other half lives—both positive aspects.

Reading

There is only one reading presented in this section. This reading, titled "The Challenge of Change," is authored by John Thorp, a well-recognized visionary in the field of IT governance. Dr. Thorp previously wrote a groundbreaking book, *The Information Paradox*, on this topic area, which made a great impression on organizational views related to IT governance. The view presented here is a strategic one. We believe that is appropriate given the current immature state of development in organizations. The interested reader should also review materials created by the IT Governance Institute (*www.isaca.org*). This reference source contains items that are more conceptual in nature than found in most sources. Also, be aware that a great deal of new literature and thinking continue to be refined in this area. Actual organizational techniques to implement operational governance will be the next major wave of material. Organizational structures and responsibilities for entities such as a project board will be popular topics. Meanwhile, PMI and other such organizations will continue to evolve their singular project management models into an enterprise framework and increasingly recognize the role of portfolio management and the PMO as part of the governance process.

References

Dictionary.com, *http://dictionary.reference.com/search?q=governance&r=67*.

META Group, *www.metagroup.com*.

PlanView, *http://www.planview.com/solutions_prisms.asp*.

Weill, Peter, "IT Governance Models Linked to Business Objectives." Presented at *CIO Magazine* Retreat, Palm Springs, CA, January 26, 2004.

Weill, Peter, "Business Value Targets, Investment Benchmarks and Evidence for Pay Off." Presented at *CIO Magazine* Retreat, Palm Springs, CA, January 26, 2004.

WorldNet Dictionary, *http://wordnet.princeton.edu/*.

The Challenge of Change

JOHN THORP, PH.D.

(10/1/2003) CFO Project Volume 2

The strategic governance framework offers an approach that continually manages the alignment of strategy, business change programs, projects, and the enterprise architecture.

High-profile scandals involving companies such as Enron, Tyco, and WorldCom, and resulting legislation including the Sarbanes-Oxley Act, have brought renewed focus on corporate governance and new demands on the CFO. Even before this, however, corporate governance was in need of major surgery.

The failure of many, if not most, organizations to deliver demonstrable value from major change initiatives, including mergers and acquisitions, business process re-engineering, and major information technology investments is a symptom of the failure of corporate governance to evolve to meet the needs of a complex and rapidly changing business environment.

Current governance processes are woefully inadequate to manage what is, in most cases, an uncertain journey to an uncertain destination. We need a continuous and dynamic governance process that manages the full investment cycle from concept to cash, one that senses and responds to changes in the internal and external environment, our understanding of what is working and not working as expected, and our assumptions. Without such a process, the risk of ending up in the wrong place, with the associated undesirable business consequences, is significantly increased.

To be effective in delivering value, the governance process must ensure that organizations:

- Understand their desired business outcomes, understand their sources of value, and develop value-focused strategies.
- Take a structured approach to developing comprehensive, value-based business change programs to execute business strategies.
- Manage the realization of value using program-based portfolio management and a comprehensive and dynamic governance process.

Strategic Governance

In the revised edition of *The Information Paradox* (2003), we introduced the strategic governance framework (Figure 1 [21-2]), which defines an approach that continually manages the alignment between business strategy, the portfolio of business change programs, individual programs, the projects (including business, process, people, technology, and organizational change projects) that make up the individual programs, and the enterprise architecture.

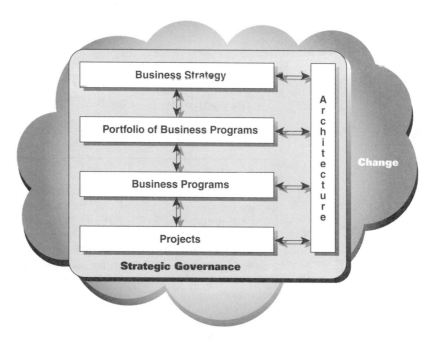

21-2 Figure 1. The Strategic Governance Framework

The total focus of strategic governance is on optimizing business value through effectively managing change in a constantly changing business environment.

The Challenge of Value

Value is complex, context-specific, and dynamic. Value and strategy are tightly related, in that value results from the successful execution of well-chosen and focused strategies. The key word here is focus. No one can do it all.

The underlying cause of the difficulty in realizing business value lies in the increasing rapidity and complexity of change and in the changing sources of value creation. Organizations today are increasingly generating value from intangible assets, like brand, knowledge, improved governance processes, and re-engineered organizational structures.

The challenge is in understanding and managing a value-creation process that is dynamic and complex and is dominated by these kinds of intangible assets. The value-creation process must be anchored to an explicit, clear, and focused business strategy. Without a clearly articulated and understood strategy, it is difficult to align investment decisions with strategic direction, to select the right things to do, and to decide what you will not do.

Rethinking the Strategy Process

Traditional strategic planning, the way we have done it in the past, doesn't cut it. We cannot, however, just stop doing it. Strategy is even more important in today's fast-moving and uncertain business environment. Strategy today must be value-driven and asset-based. Business value results from the successful execution of business strategies, which configure and manage all the assets of the organization to deliver the greatest possible value in line with business objectives. Our understanding of assets must evolve to include all those capabilities or resources, tangible or intangible, internal or external to an organization, that the organization can influence, and how they interact with each other to impact the bottom line.

Strategy is of no value if it is not successfully executed. Unfortunately, one of the few areas that rivals the poor track record of IT projects (or more accurately, IT-enabled change) is that of strategy implementation. In a *CIO Insight* magazine article, David Norton, co-author of *The Balanced Scorecard*, cites research conducted by CIO Insight and the Balanced Scorecard Collaborative that found that barely half of the companies adequately communicate goals to employees, only a quarter of employees have even a general understanding of the strategy, and fewer than 30 percent of executives believe that their budgets are strongly linked to strategy.

Most strategies are both too wide in scope and too shallow in detail. The statements are often unarguable, but unimplementable. If the process of strategy is to be more effective, we must approach strategic planning and strategy execution very differently. What's required is a strategy process that recognizes the complexities of managing that uncertain journey to an uncertain destination.

Recognizing, Understanding, and Managing Complexity

A major cause of the failure to successfully execute strategy is that many leaders make overly simplistic statements of strategy and do not want to be bothered with drilling down to the complexities of implementation. In his book *Execution: The Discipline of Getting Things Done*, co-authored with Ram Charan, Larry Bossidy writes, "Lots of business leaders like to think that the top dog is exempt from the details of actually running things. It's a pleasant way to view leadership: You stand on the mountaintop, thinking strategically and attempting to inspire your people with visions, while managers do the grunt work." I refer to this as the Star Trek school of management. All that the leader has to do is say "Make it so!" and wait for it to happen. Unfortunately, in most cases, no one understands what "it" is, or worse, they all have a different idea of what "it" is. The result is a lot of activity, but little if any value.

We cannot wish complexity away by denying that it exists. Organizations cannot continue to respond to the continuing speed and scope of change and increasing complexity with simplistic solutions. Only when complexity is understood and managed can simplification occur. While they may wish to hand off the complexity of execution, it is incumbent on leaders to understand the complexity of strategy execution and to ensure that those executing the strategy both understand and are managing the complexity. As Bossidy goes on to write, "Execution requires a comprehensive understanding of a business, its people, and its environment. The leader is the only person in a position to achieve that understanding.

Recognizing, accepting, and managing this complexity is today's leadership challenge." To do any less is an abdication of leadership responsibility.

The Role of Portfolio Management

One approach that organizations are adopting to increase value from their assets and investments is portfolio management. Portfolio management has been around for some time in the financial world, as well as in new-product development. Portfolio management related to IT assets and investments is now getting a lot of press and attention. Unfortunately, much of the writing and talking about portfolio management as it relates to IT is missing the point. The primary objective is cost reduction, and the focus is on the technology project. While portfolio management is indeed useful in understanding and managing costs, the real prize in portfolio management is in driving increased value.

If organizations are to seriously tackle the question of value with a portfolio management approach, they must recognize that the challenge is managing change. They must shift their focus beyond activities to the desired outcome. This involves:

- Defining comprehensive programs of business change—programs that include all the business, process, people, technology, and organizational change projects that are both necessary and sufficient to deliver the desired business outcome.
- Developing complete and comparable business cases.
- Selecting investments based on the overall value to an enterprise, not to individual silos, either functional or geographic.
- Recognizing that the decision to select and proceed with an investment is only the beginning of an ongoing governance process, with clear accountability and relevant measurements of realized value.

Putting Teeth in the Process

Every business change program should have a complete and comparable business case that will be evaluated throughout the portfolio-management process. Few organizations have comprehensive, rigorous, or consistently applied business-case processes. In a recent Web poll of more than 200 organizations, only 20 percent felt that they had an effective process, while 60 percent felt that their process was inadequate or very inadequate.

Where business cases are created, there is usually far more rigor applied to the cost side than to the benefits side and they are seldom looked at after the decision to proceed. If they are looked at, it is usually some form of post-implementation review, an event akin to an autopsy.

Business cases must apply the same level of rigor to business benefits as to costs, and they must look at the total lifetime cost and value of investments. They need to look beyond ROI to include alignment with business objectives and the risk of not realizing the anticipated benefits. They must be used, not as a one-time "go, no-go" document, but as an ongoing operational tool to both select high potential investments and to manage the realization of value. They must be updated as we learn more and as circumstances change, and must be continually reviewed as part of the governance process.

Enterprise Architecture

Another root cause of many execution problems today is the lack of robust and flexible enterprise architectures. Enterprise architecture is not limited to technology nor technical architecture. It is broad and comprehensive. It is about how the whole enterprise is structured. It includes every value-creating component of the enterprise and the relationships between them. Enterprise architecture components include business units, business processes, information, applications, and technology, as well as knowledge, relationships, etc.

The enterprise architecture view enables organizations to properly structure programs of business change, ensuring that all the necessary components of change are considered, and that individual programs of change are not moving in conflicting directions. Failure to take such a view may result in unintended consequences, including long-term structural problems that may be showstoppers to future change.

Putting It All Together

Most organizations have elements of strategic governance. While their effectiveness may vary, strategy and project management are well-established disciplines. Many organizations have an individual, a group, or multiple groups responsible for strategy, although this is often still seen as more of an annual ritual than a process. Most organizations have some focus on project management, often through a project management office. Many organizations also have an architecture role, although usually within the IT function. The focus is often on the technology aspects of architecture and on the definition of those aspects rather than the ongoing management and implementation of the architecture, and integration with the overall enterprise architecture. An increasing number of organizations have established program management offices, although in some cases these view programs as a number of related technology projects, rather than business change programs incorporating all the aspects of business, process, people, technology, and organizational change. A few organizations are implementing some form of value management office to support the value aspects of portfolio management. But rarely do these five critical components come together, even in an annual review, let alone as part of an ongoing governance process.

There are critical relationships between these functions. The integration of these functions, managed well, will provide tremendous competitive advantage to organizations.

Conclusion

If they are to survive, let alone prosper, organizations must continue to demonstrate that they understand how to create value, have strategies capable of delivering value both quickly and over the long term, and must have a track record of successfully executing those strategies. They must stop going for the big bang and structure change into doable chunks that deliver real and measurable value in 60- to 90-day increments. In the private sector, how well this is done plays an increasingly significant role in determining market valuation. In the public sector, the mandate, public perception, and viability of the organization may well hinge on the clarity with which its actions and investments can be tied to value.

Adopting and implementing this new governance approach will not be easy. The CFO has both an opportunity and a responsibility to take a leadership role in making this change. It will require vision, discipline, and the courage to stay the course. It represents a fundamental change in how we think, manage, and act. Without such change, however, we will continue to dismally underperform. There will, as always, be a few bright stars, but most results will be mediocre at best and appalling at worse. Organizations, the people they serve, the people who work in them, and society as a whole deserve better. Investors and analysts will demand that we do better.

We can and must do better.

Other Web Resources

Note: The editors wish to thank Tenstep.com and George Pasieka for allowing inclusion of their Web reference listings here. Readers should review *www.tenstep.com* as a good source for other project management materials, including a full development methodology.

The Web sources listed here are good places to search for more material in this topic area. There are obviously many more sources that could be listed, but this should provide a good starting point for most topics. Specific topics can be found by using a search engine such as *Google.com* or *Yahoo.com*.

Organization	Web Site Link	Description
Advanced Project Management Certification	*www.allpm.com*	This is a collaborative community for project managers. It provides forums for project management questions and answers, and for discussion of tools, training, special interest groups, and others. The site contains some information on project management products, services, best practices, and templates.
American Society for the Advancement of Project Managemet	*http://www.asapm.org/*	ASAPM is a not-for-profit professional society dedicated to advancing the project management discipline. Site material is designed to provide professional growth for project practitioners and the project management community. ASAPM material is defined to be at the forefront of the project management discipline for best practices, procedures, and techniques.
Arras	*www.arraspeople.co.uk*	Arras specializes in three focus areas: 1. Arras People provides project management recruitment with the additional focus on the specialist area of program and project support personnel. 2. Arras Services works with SMEs to provide support and delivery capability within programs and projects, including training. 3. Arras Consult delivers consulting services to help organizations understand, define, and transition to a program-centric methodology aligning business strategy and the delivery of operational plans.
Atlas Business Software	*atlasbusinesssoftware.com*	Leaders in low-cost project management and time management software.

(continued)

Organization	Web Site Link	Description
Baseline	*http://www.baselinemag.com/*	This site is labeled as the on line project management center. It includes articles focused on how projects work. The general topics relate to projects, tools, and industry news items. Some download items require payment.
Boston University Interactive	*www.bu.edu/interactive*	Boston University Interactive offers courses through a variety of technologies, including live satellite broadcasts, videotape, and online programs via the Internet. Programs offered at a distance come from a number of colleges and departments at Boston University. They represent the University's commitment to high-quality programming for distance learners.
Business Process Management (BPM) Solution	*business-process-management-solution.com*	Online business process management, BPM, software with electronic forms for process and workflow automation—available as a hosted or ASP solution.
Business Process Management Initiative	*http://www.bpmi.org/*	This site is dedicated to reporting the industry activities related to the area of business process management. This includes the industry standards that are currently evolving. This is the owner organization for an industry standard titled Business Process Modeling Language.
Celoxis	*project-management-software.celoxis.com*	Comprehensive, integrated PM (Gantt, dependencies, client collaboration), Workflow, Time & Expense (online approval, rate, and audit history), Collaboration (calendar, contacts, meetings, forums, documents).
Center for Business Practices	*http://www.cbponline.com/*	The CBP is a knowledge center that captures, organizes, and transfers business practice knowledge to project stakeholders to help them excel in today's rapidly changing business world. The CBP domain includes project management knowledge and expertise and integrates it into a variety of products to deliver fact-based and timely information through publications, research, and benchmarking forums.
CFO Project	*http://www.cfoproject.com/*	A site focused on the financial aspects of IT and project management.
CPM Solutions, Inc.	*http://www.cpm-solutions.com/*	A project management site dedicated to senior management's point of view. This includes tips, training, and other industry-related topics.
Crosstalk	*http://www.stsc.hill.af.mil/crosstalk*	*Crosstalk* is the Journal of Defense Software Engineering. This repository includes articles dedicated to software quality improvement and best practices.

Organization	Web Site Link	Description
Cutter Consortium	www.cutter.com	Cutter Consortium helps companies leverage IT for competitive advantage and business success through its comprehensive range of consulting, training, and technical articles.
DM Review	http://www.dmreview.com/	DM Review is an on line repository containing material in the business intelligence, data warehouse, integration, and analytics domain.
Gantthead	www.gantthead.com	Gantthead.com is a premier community for Information Technology (IT) project managers. Developed by project managers for project managers, Gantthead serves as an online destination for IT managers to ensure the success of their projects by offering resources, subject matter experts, deliverables, access to the Gantthead process library, and connections to other project managers. With over 50,000 members and growing, Gantthead is the largest community of IT project managers on the Web.
Harris Kern Consulting	www.harriskern.com	A site labeled as "Solutions for IT Professionals." Articles included here are typically contemporary in nature and some have been used in preparation of the text material. An excellent technical resource.
iManage	workknowledge.imanage.com	iManage provides knowledge management systems and knowledge management software for business growth and communication.
Information Systems Audit and Control Association	http://www.isaca.org/	This site has become recognized as a pace-setting global organization for material related to information governance, control, security, and audit professionals. Its IS auditing and IS control standards are followed by practitioners worldwide.
InterPlan Systems Inc.	interplansystems.com	Offers free tutorials covering industrial plant (oil refinery, petrochemical plant, etc.) maintenance, shutdown/turnaround project planning, scheduling, tracking, and management, based on over 25 years of industry experience.
Max Wideman	http://www.maxwideman.com/	This site is the personal Web site of Max Wideman. It is an excellent repository of book references, papers, personal project management advice from various authors, and other related project-oriented items.
Method 123	www.method123.com	Method 123 specializes in providing document templates for Project Managers, for example business cases, project plans, change and risk management processes, and forms.

(continued)

Organization	Web Site Link	Description
Ovitz Taylor Gates	*ovitztaylorgates.com*	IT Management resources for information technology projects, offering how-to workbooks, project plans, and information technology planning guides, tools, templates, and checklists. A valuable IT Management resource.
PM Boulevard	*www.pmblvd.com*	PM Boulevard contains information that will help you be successful on your project, including updated columns, news, links, and templates. Much of the information is available for free to registered subscribers. Other content, such as on line classes, is available on a fee basis. Additional services and content, such as access to a template library and expert advice, are available through a personalized corporate membership.
PM Toolbox	*http://pm.ittoolbox.com/*	A broad IT knowledge base resource site dedicated to various IT- and PM-related topics, including job information.
Portfolio Management Forum	*http://www.portfoliomgt.org/*	A site dedicated to the topic area of portfolio management and its related disciplines.
Prince	*http://www.ogc.gov.uk/prince*	A United Kingdom-sponsored methodology that has become popular in the European commercial environment. Prince2 is a process-oriented planning and development methodology.
Project Management Forum at Tek	*www.tek-tips.com*	Provides tips through a Project Management technical support forum and mutual help system for computer professionals. Selling and recruiting is strictly forbidden.
Project Management Institute	*www.PMI.org*	With over 60,000 members worldwide, PMI™ is the leading nonprofit professional association in the area of Project Management. PMI establishes Project Management standards, provides seminars, educational programs, and professional certification that more and more organizations desire for their project leaders.
Project Perfect	*Projectperfect.com.au*	Provides PM consulting, training, and software as well as white papers. Their software helps manage risks, issues, scope, actions, benefits, budgets, QA, reviews, timesheets, documents, glossaries, checklists, and diary notes and integrates with Microsoft Project for planning and scheduling.
Root Systems	*www.rootsystems.com*	SPS provides an integrated, complete, yet extensible software solution for your CRM, BPM, SFA, project management, software change management, help desk, and other collaboration needs.

Organization	Web Site Link	Description
TechRepublic	*www.TechRepublic.com*	TechRepublic.com has garnered international attention as an information resource for IT professionals of all ranks, from support staff to executives. The site targets IT executives, managers, consultants, strategists, network administrators, and other computer-related support staff. TechRepublic is organized into five "Republics," organized by job category. In addition to the Republics, the site also hosts TechProGuild, a premium online service, featuring in-depth technical content and the ERP resource site.
Tenstep	*http://www.tenstep.com/*	An excellent source for development methodology documentation and examples. Much of the site can be downloaded for free; however, there are some subscription items that require payment.
Workflow Management Coalition	*http://www.wfmc.org/*	The Workflow Management Coalition is dedicated to promoting and developing uses of workflow through establishment of standards for various architectural components.
ZDNet	*www.zdnet.com*	A source for articles and research related to a wide range of IT topics.
Ziff Davis	*www.ziffdavis.com*	Ziff Davis is a leading publisher of IT-related journals and associated on line articles repositories.

Part I: Introduction to Project Management Concepts

CHAPTER 1

p. 1, Reading 1. Maria Schafer, "People Powered: The New Millennium IT Organization," *Softwaremag.com* (April 2001). Available at *http://www.softwaremag.com/l.cfm?doc=archive/2001apr/PeoplePowered.html*. Used by permission of the publisher.

p. 9, Reading 2. Paul Glen, "Competing Visions of Corporate IT's Future," *IT Professionalism Newsletter*. Available at *http://www.c2-consulting.com/pages/Article_24.htm*. Used by permission of Paul Glen of C2 Consulting.

CHAPTER 2

p. 17, Reading 1. Research Center for Business Practices, "Value of Project Management in IT Organizations" (Publication date not available). Available at *http://www.pmsolutions.com/articles/pdfs/value/valueofpm_it.pdf*. Used by permission of Center for Business Practices.

p. 21, Reading 2. Comprehensive Consulting Solutions, Inc., "Project Management in an Information Technology (IT) World" (March 2001). Available at *http://www.comp-soln.com/whitepapers*. Used by permission of Comprehensive Consulting Solutions, Inc.

p. 26, Reading 3. Neville Turbit, "Vision, Business Problem, Outcome, Objectives and all that stuff…" *Project Perfect Pty Ltd*, Project Management Software, Consulting and White Papers. Available at *http://www.projectperfect.com.au*. Used by permission of Neville Turbit.

p. 32, Reading 4. Barry Flicker, "The Five Myths of Project Breakdown (and What You Can Do About It)," *PM Boulevard* (March 14, 2004). Available at *http://www.pmboulevard.com*. Used by permission of Barry Flicker.

p. 37, Reading 5. "The Face of Project Management: An Interview with Jim Highsmith," Cutter Corsortium (October 2000). Available at *http://www.cutter.com/index.shtml*. Used by permission of Jim Highsmith.

CHAPTER 3

p. 46, Reading 1. Michael Poli and Aaron J. Shenhar, "Project Strategy: The Key to Project Success," Proceedings of the 2003 PICMET Conference (2003). Available at *http://www.picmet.org*. Used by permission of Portland State University.

CHAPTER 4

p. 59, Reading 1. Robert Kaplan and David Norton, "Plotting Success with 'Strategy Maps,'" *Optimize* (February 2004). Used by permission of the publisher.

p. 66, Reading 2. Lee Merkhofer, "Choosing the Wrong Portfolio of Projects and What Your Organization Can Do About It. Part III—Finding the Right Metrics" (December 2003). Available at *http://www.maxwideman.com/guests/portfolio/abstract.htm*. Used by permission of Lee Merkhofer.

Part II: Exploring the *PMBOK*® Guide

CHAPTER 5

p. 81, **Reading 1.** David Liss, "Gimme a P!" (October 2001), Gantthead. Available at *http://gantthead.com*. Used by permission of Erin DeCaprio.

CHAPTER 6

p. 90, **Reading 1.** Department of the Air Force Software Technology Center, "System Integration," *CrossTalk: The Journal of Defense Software Engineering*, U.S. Air Force Software Technology Support Center (2003). Available at *http://www.stsc.hill.af.mil/resources/tech%5docs/gsam4.html*. Used by permission of Tracy Stauder.

CHAPTER 7

p. 100, **Reading 1.** Elizabeth Larson and Richard Larson, "How to Create a Clear Project Plan in Six Easy Steps" (August 2004). Available at *http://www.darwinmag.com/read/080104/project.html*. Used by permission of Richard G. Larson.

p. 103, **Reading 2.** Douglas M. Arnstein, "Gaining Visibility and Commitment on Technology Projects" (2004). Available at *http://www.projectmagazine.com/v5i1/v5i1arnstein1.html*. Used by permission of Douglas M. Arnstein.

CHAPTER 8

p. 119, **Reading 1.** Rich Schiesser, "Change Management—Part I" (2002). *IT Systems Management,* Prentice Hall, 2002. Available at *http://www.informit.com/guides/content.asp?g=it_management&seqNum=26*. Used by permission Pearson PrenticeHall.

p. 125, **Reading 2.** Rich Schiesser, "Change Management—Part II" (2002). *IT Systems Management,* Prentice Hall, 2002. Available at *http://www.informit.com/guides/printerfriendly.asp?g=it_management&seqNum=27*. Used by permission Pearson Prentice Hall.

p. 132, **Reading 3.** James R. Chapman, "Work Breakdown Structure (WBS)" (November 2004). Available at *http://www.hyperthot.com/pm_wbs.htm*. Used by permission of James R. Chapman.

CHAPTER 9

p. 141, **Reading 1.** Tom Gilb, "The 10 Most Powerful Principles for Quality in Software and Software Organizations," *CrossTalk: The Journal of Defense Software Engineering* (November 2002). Available at *http://www.stsc.hillaf.mil*. Used by permission of Tom Gilb.

p. 152, **Reading 2.** Suzanne Robertson, "An Early Start to Testing: How to Test Requirements" (December 2–6, 1996). *The Atlantic Systems Guild, Inc.* Paper presented at EuroStar '96, Amsterdam. Used by permission of Suzanne Robertson.

CHAPTER 10

p. 166, **Reading 1.** Rex Lovelady and Andrew Anderson, "Psst—Want To Take A Risk?" (April 2004). Available at *http://www.pmboulevard.com/Default.aspx?page=View%20Content&CID=663&parent=Search&search=pssst&ContentType=&Category=&SubCategory=*. Used with permission of Rex Lovelady.

p. 172, **Reading 2.** Lt. Col. Steven Glazewski, "Risk Management (Is Not) For Dummies" (23 February 2005). *CrossTalk: The Journal of Defense Software Engineering,* U.S. Air Force Software Technology Support Center. Available at *http://www.stsc.hill.af.mil/resources/tech%5docs/gsam4.html*. Used by permission of Lt. Col. Steven Glazewski.

p. 179, **Reading 3.** Frank Martens and Lucy Nottingham, "Enterprise Risk Management: A Framework for Success," *Executive Perspectives,* Copyright © 2003 by PricewaterhouseCoopers LLP. Available at *http://www.pwcglobal.com/extWeb/service.nsf/8b9d788097dff3c9852565e00073c0ba/f45c1d8b50537aa685256dcf007dda4e/$FILE/COSORiskFramework.pdf*. Used by permission of Jane Butterfield.

CHAPTER 11

p. 188, Reading 1. Department of Energy, "Contracting and Procurement," from Project Management Practices (Publication date not available). Department of Energy Archives. Available at *http://www.science.doe.gov/SC-80/sc-81/PDF/pract15.pdf*. Used by permission of Department of Energy.

p. 199, Reading 2. Richard Laub, Rob Woodstock, and Martin Sjög, "Procurement Transformation: A Holistic Approach to Best Practice Procurement," *Accenture* (16 May 2001). Available at *http://www.ascet.com/documents.asp?grID=147&d_ID=1088*. Used by permission of Accenture.

CHAPTER 12

p. 210, Reading 1. Jan Warko, "Curiosity: The Prerequisite for Good Estimates," Gantthead (5 February 2001). Available at *http://.gantthead.com*. Used by permission of the publisher.

p. 213, Reading 2. Capers Jones, "Software Project Estimation in 2002," *CrossTalk: The Journal of Defense Software Engineering* (June 2002). Available at *http://www.stsc.hillaf.mil*. Used by permission of Capers Jones.

p. 225, Reading 3. Kathleen Peters, "Software Project Estimation." Adapted from a three-part series that originally appeared in *Project Management Journal* (March 1999). Available at *http://www.spc.ca*. Used by permission of the Software Productivity Centre.

p. 242, Reading 4. "Fundamentals of Function Point Analysis," Introduction to Function Points, Longstreet Consulting (2005). Available at *http://www.SoftwareMetrics.com*. Used by permission of David Longstreet.

p. 252, Reading 5. Eberhard Rudolph, "Tool-based Estimating Tutorial" (2002). Available at *http://www.cit.gu.edu.au/teaching/2182CIT/estimate-case.pdf*. Used by permission of Eberhard Rudolph.

p. 262, Reading 6. Mark Kelly, "PERT Tutorial" (October 2001). Available at *http://www.mckinnonsc.vic.edu.au/la/it/ipmnotes/ganttpert/pert-tute/perttute.htm*. Used by permission of Mark Kelly.

CHAPTER 13

p. 272, Reading 1. Tammo Wilkens, "Earned Value, Clear and Simple" (April 1999). Available at *http://www.acq.osd.mil/pm/old/paperpres/wilkins_art.pdf*. Used by permission of Tammo Wilkens.

p. 283, Reading 2. U.S. Air Force Software Technology Support Center, "Cost Management," *CrossTalk: The Journal of Defense Software Engineering,* U.S. Air Force Software Technology Support Center (February 2003). Available at *http://www.stsc.hillaf.mil*. Used by permission of Tracy Stauder.

CHAPTER 14

p. 296, Reading 1. Patricia Davis-Muffett, "Communications as a Strategic PM Function, Part I," Readings in Information Technology Project, (2004), Intronet/Robbins-Gioia. Available at *http://www.pmboulevard.net/Default.aspx?page=View%20Content&cid=1710&parent=Content%20Map&pageNum=3*. Used by permission of Patricia Davis-Muffett.

p. 302, Reading 2. Patricia Davis-Muffett, "Communications as a Strategic PM Function, Part II," Readings in Information Technology Project, (May 2004), Intronet/Robbins-Gioia. Available at *http://www.stsc.hill.af.mil/resources/tech_docs/*. Used by permission of Patricia Davis-Muffett.

p. 306, Reading 3. Jamie Barber, "The Numbers Game: Nine Steps to Making the Most of Your HR Metrics" (2004). IntroNet. Used by permission of Jamie Barber.

p. 311, Reading 4. Brad M. Jackson, "The Post-Internet Organization: The Real Virtual Organization" (June 2004). Available at *http://www.cordin8.com/cOrdin8WebSite/Post-Internet%20Organization.pdf*. Used by permission of Brad M. Jackson.

CHAPTER 15

p. 322, Reading 1. A. Andrew Anderson, "Project Managers as Politician: A Shift in Roles," *Project World* (5 September 2005). Available at *http://www.PMBoulevard.com*.Used by permission of A. Andrew Anderson.

p. 325, Reading 2. Johanna Rothman, "Successful Software Management: 14 Lessons Learned," *CrossTalk: The Journal of Defense Software Engineering* (December 2003). Available at *http://www.stsc.hill.af.mil/resources/tech%5docs/gsam4.html*. Used by permission of Johanna Rothman.

p. 333, Reading 3. Doug Putnam, "Team Size Can Be the Key to a Successful Project," *QSM* (Spring 1997). Used by permission of Doug Putnam.

p. 338, Reading 4. Bill Curtis and William E. Hefley, "Experiences Applying the People Capability Maturity Model," *CrossTalk: The Journal of Defense Software Engineering* (April 2003). Available at *http://www.stsc.hill.af.mil/resources/tech%5docs/gsam4.html*. Used by permission of Bill Curtis.

p. 349, Reading 5. META Group, "Maturing to Centers of Excellence: The Next Step in IT Organizations" (February 2004), Meta Group, Inc. Available at *http://www.metagroup.com*. Used by permission of Stephen H. Cummings.

CHAPTER 16

p. 365, Reading 1. Tasmania Department of Premier and Cabinet, "Closing the Project" (Publication date not available). Used by permission of Tasmania Department of Premier and Cabinet.

Part III: Project Management Contemporary Topics

CHAPTER 17

p. 378, Reading 1. J. Timothy McMahon, "Enron's Leaders Still Don't Get It," *Houston Chronicle* (3 February 2002). Used by permission of J. Timothy McMahon.

p. 382, Reading 2. Simon Rogerson and Donald Gotterbarn, "The Ethics of Software Project Management" (1998). In G. Collste (editor), *Ethics and Information Technology*, Delhi, India:New Academic Publishers, 1998, pp. 137–154. Available at *http://www.ccsr.cse.dmu.ac.uk/staff/Srog/teaching/sweden.htm*. Used by permission of Donald Gotterbarn.

CHAPTER 18

p. 399, Reading 1. C.K. Prahalad and M.S. Krishnan, "Building Blocks of Global Competitiveness," *InformationWeek* (September 2004). Used with permission of CMP Media LLC.

p. 406, Reading 2. Jay Slupesky, "Bush Lays Off Congress; Will Outsource Lawmaking to India?" *The Baked Beaver* (2003). Used with permission from Jay Slupesky.

CHAPTER 19

p. 411, Reading 1. Jim Harris, "Putting the P in PMO," Gantthead (16 December 2001). Available at *http://gantthead.com*. Used with permission of Gantthead.

p. 415, Reading 2. Shawn Bohner, "PMOs: Projects in Harmony," Gantthead (2000). Available at *http://gantthead.com*. Used with permission of Gantthead.

p. 419, Reading 3. Mark E. Mullaly, "Where Do I Start Building the Effective PMO," Gantthead (28 May 2002). Available at *http://gantthead.com*. Used with permission from Gantthead.

p. 421, Reading 4. Tim Jaques, "Imaginary Obstacles: Getting Over PMO," Gantthead (5 March 2001). Available at *http://gantthead.com*. Used with permission of Gantthead.

CHAPTER 20

p. 430, Reading 1. Paul Harder, "PPM and CMM: Kindred Spirits?" Gantthead (25 November 2002). Available at *http://gantthead.com*. Used with permission of Gantthead.

p. 433, Reading 2. Cameron McGaughy, "Gartner Shines the Light on PPM," Gantthead (10 August 2004). Available at *http://gantthead.com*. Used with permission of Gantthead.

p. 438, Reading 3. Lee Merkhofer, "Choosing the Wrong Portfolio of Projects, Part 5: Attending to Risk," *The Measured, PMI Metrics SIG Newsletter* (March, June, and September 2004). Used with permission of Lee Merkhofer.

p. 448, Reading 4. Lee Merkhofer, "Choosing the Wrong Portfolio of Projects, Part 6: Get on the Effective Frontier," *The Measured, PMI Metrics SIG Newsletter* (March, June, and September 2004). Used with permission of Lee Merkhofer.

CHAPTER 21

p. 457, Reading 1. John Thorp, "The Challenge of Change," *The CFO Project* (1 October 2003), MRI Montgomery Research. Used with permission of John Thorp.